LUNKERMETRICS
THE SCIENCE AND ANALYTICS OF BIG BASS FISHING

FRANK GRIFFIN

Copyright © Frankie M. Griffin 2023
All Rights Reserved.
ISBN: 13:

Table of Contents

0	**Dear Reader**	
1	**Introduction to LunkerMetrics**	1
	Methods Used in This Book	5
	The Big Picture	6
	A Note about Lake Fork and TPWD	13
2	**Big Bass Are Different**	22
	Special	22
	Rare	23
	Defining "Largemouth Bass"	25
	Lunker Bass are Nationwide	30
	Lunkers Prefer Reservoirs	31
	Lunkers and the 30th Parallel	36
	Lunker Genetics	39
	Lunker Sex	44
	Reactive Thinkers	46
	Loners?	54
	Landing Lunkers	56
3	**Study 1: Best Month to Catch a Lunker**	60
	Previous Research	61
	My ShareLunker Database Research	62
4	**The Spawn**	74
	Pre-spawn	76
	Nest Excavation and Courting	78
	Mating	82
	Post-spawn	87
	Overview/Summary	90

	Question Box:	
	Distinguishing the sexes	93
	Analytics of the Spawn	93
	Question Box:	
	Is it okay to fish for bedding bass?	99
5	**Study 2: Moon Phases and Big Bass**	100
	Generalities and Prior Research	101
	The Eight Moon Phases	106
	My ShareLunker Database Research	107
	Individual Angler Results by Moon Phase	120
	Conclusion	121
6	**Home Ranges & Personalities**	124
	Single Home Range Bass	
	(i.e., "Homebodies")	127
	Bass with Multiple Home Ranges	
	(i.e., "Snowbirds")	130
	Bass with No Home Range	
	(i.e., "Nomads")	131
	Conclusion	132
7	**Water Temperature: The Master Factor**	135
	Metabolic Processes	138
	Physiologic Processes	142
	Developmental Processes	145
	Water Temperature Adaptations	
	and Limitations	147
8	**Study 3: Barometric Pressure and Big Bass**	152
	Previous Research	153
	What is Barometric Pressure?	154
	Direct Effects of Barometric Pressure	156
	Barometric Pressure and the Weather	158
	My ShareLunker Database Research	159
	Individual Angler Results	
	by Barometric Pressure	171
	Conclusion	172

9	**Feeding Mechanisms and the Senses**	176
	The "Large Mouth" Feeding Mechanics	176
	Hunting and Schooling Behavior	181
	Inactive Bass and Feeding	184
	Vision	187
	Hearing	194
	Lateral Line	196
	Smell	199
	Taste	202
	Electroreception?	204
10	**Prey**	206
	Crayfish	207
	Shad	213
	Bluegill Sunfish (*Lepomis macrochirus*)	226
	Worms	231
	Other Prey	232
11	**Study 4: Time of Day**	234
	Solunar Tables and the Moon	235
	Dawn and Dusk	239
	Night Bite	241
	My Online Database Research	242
	Individual Angler Results by Time of Day	254
	Conclusion	256
12	**Seasonal Patterns**	258
	Generalities	258
	Winter (Water Temperature <45 to 50°F)	261
	Spring (Water Temperature 55 to 75°F)	271
	Summer (Water Temperature >80°F)	283
	Fall (Water Temperature 75°F to 55°F)	295
13	**Last Cast**	299

Preface

I am a surgeon and a lawyer writing a book on bass fishing. Yes, I know that's weird. But I was a bass fisherman long before I became a surgeon or a lawyer. I grew up in rural Arkansas on a farm and spent my free time driving the dirt backroads to fish farm ponds for largemouth bass. While working on the farm, I studied Bassmaster magazine in the farm trucks and tractors whenever we stopped for a break.

College, medical school, and orthopedic surgery residency training took me away from those country roads, but bass fishing stayed near to my heart. Dad would often meet me halfway between home and medical school towing the boat so we could go fishing together. Fishing and time with Dad helped keep me sane and anchored during the difficulties of medical school, which helped me finish second in my medical school class. After Dad died, I found a fishing buddy in an older friend who had lost his orthopedic surgeon son, and we fished his carefully nurtured private lake whenever I could sneak away from my practice. But my medical practice took up most of my time, so bass fishing took a back seat for too many years of my life.

Cancer sent me back to bass fishing by ending my career as a practicing orthopedic surgeon. The cancer in my leg bone (femur) left me with some complications that make it hard for me to stand up for more than 15 to 20 minutes at a time. I traded a bass boat for a wide, stable aluminum boat that required no steps up to accommodate my new physical limitations. After years of working hard on the farm and as an orthopedic surgeon, I needed additional intellectual stimulation, so I got a doctorate in law between fishing trips. The time alone on the water helped me think clearly and finish in the top 5 of my law school class in my early 50's while spending most of my time on more important activities like my kids' athletics, family time, and fishing. After law school, I spent a few years teaching health care and disability law and working a couple of legal jobs.

I love to write, so I published scientific studies during my medical career and published law review articles during my legal career and have published over 60 articles scattered between medical and legal publications. My papers have been published in journals ranging from medical publications like *Clinical Orthopedics and Related Research* and the *Journal of Arthroplasty* to legal publications like the *Journal of Health and Biomedical Law*, the *Rutgers University Law Review*, the *DePaul Journal of Health Care Law*, and the *Minnesota Journal of Law, Science, and Technology*. I've written book chapters on topics ranging from total knee replacement to the legal ramifications of artificial intelligence in health care.

Nowadays, in my late 50s, I mostly fish and chase lunker bass, but I still like to write. Much of the current bass fishing literature is based upon personal experience, anecdotal evidence, and strong opinions without any references to allow the reader to check reliability of the information. Due to my background in medical and legal research, I often find writings on bass fishing lacking the scientific support and reliability that I am looking for in my increasing passion to chase lunker bass. So, I wrote this book to (1) answer some of my questions about lunker bass fishing, (2) apply a similar level of scrutiny to lunker bass fishing research when possible as I have applied to scientific information throughout my medical career, and (3) report only reliable and relevant information similar to legal writing with references from reliable sources in footnotes.

Truthfully, I wrote the book mostly for myself because the writing process helps solidify my knowledge and confidence, but I share the book in hopes that other bass fishermen find it helpful. The book is meant for serious lunker bass anglers who are willing to wade through the deep weeds to learn the science behind bass fishing. Sometimes the science and math get dense as I show each step in reaching a conclusion, so I *highlight the key conclusions in italics* in sections where the reading, math, or science get deeper into the weeds. I also add a summary or conclusion section to some of the chapters.

I use pictures from my own fishing trips to give the book some color and because I enjoy playing with pictures and videos of the awesome world around me during fishing trips. I have a deep Christian faith that is continually reaffirmed by the incredible Design I see in the world around me while bass fishing, just as it was reaffirmed as I studied the intricacies of the human body in medical school.

I hope you enjoy the book and find something useful inside!

Tight lines and happy trails,
Frank

1

Introduction to LunkerMetrics

The line suddenly stopped coming toward me as my Zebco 33 reel locked up. Dang. My crankbait was hung on a log. Wait. The log started to move. My rod bent . . . A LOT . . . more than it had ever bent. My 12-year-old heart raced when I realized it was not a log . . . it was a fish . . . a GIANT fish! The battle was on. My knees buckled when the lunker's monstrous head cleared the surface as it tried to shake my crankbait. It was the biggest bass I had ever seen in person! I had seen them in magazines maybe, but never in person. I waded into the muddy farm pond and kept reeling. It jumped again, and my heart missed a couple of beats. Finally, the huge bass made one last run as I got it close to the bank. The rod strained, the reel drag gave more line than I thought it should, and the line was so taut that it made a musical sound in the wind—something was going to have to give . . . either my line would break, the reel would fail, my rod would break, or the fish would finally give up. The seconds felt like minutes, but finally . . . the fish gave, and I landed my first lunker bass—a five-pound skinny farm pond bass on a hot August day. Two casts later, I landed another big bass . . . a 3.5 pounder! What a great day! I was hooked forever.

Almost fifty years later, I'm still hooked on catching big bass. My heart still races, and my knees still get weak when I hook a lunker. Those two farm pond bass are in the Polaroid below with the weights written by my mother—frozen solid for the mounting process that would put them on my childhood bedroom wall.

I am addicted to chasing lunker bass. I love the time on the lake alone, the focus on each cast, and the intellectual challenge of trying to figure out the way to catch a lunker in the new day. Do I need to switch baits? Go to a different spot? Get up early or stay late? I know it is not luck when I catch a big bass, at least not completely, but by how much? Luck definitely plays a role. Some days, I get skunked and don't catch a single bass. Some days I just catch little bass. But some days, I catch lunker bass! Those days are awesome!

I look for patterns, often when there seem to be none. One day, I will catch several big bass with a certain technique and at a certain location under certain conditions. I leave thinking I have got it all figured out. Then, the very next day, under the same conditions, I will not be able to get a bite using the same technique in the same and similar locations under the same conditions, and I am reminded that I really do not have it figured out. So, I stay on the water longer and look harder fighting self-control and moderation, searching for that next big bite, and compulsively casting at every spot that I can find that looks like it could hold the next lunker bass.

I buy too many fishing rods—rods to use in every circumstance. I buy too many lures—lures for every condition, every water color, every weather pattern, every depth, and every situation. And then I buy more. Big baits, small baits, in-between baits. I have them all.

My appetite for chasing lunker bass is voracious. Twenty-five miles-per-hour winds in 35-degree weather do not stop me. I fish in pouring rain and in any weather that is warm enough that my reels and rod eyelets don't freeze solid. The hot July sun is not a barrier; I read up on heat exhaustion and heat stroke, use shade and water to stay safe, and cut the day short if necessary to avoid signs of either.

As I look at my electronics and think about the topo map of the lake searching for the next lunker, I get into a trance-like state that is pure fun. I will search endlessly for that next lunker, and then once I find it, I start searching for another one. I want to find more of them and catch them more often. I crave predictability in bass fishing as I struggle to figure out patterns behind my lunker bass catches. My search is relentless.

Magazine articles and books often confuse me because fishermen contradict each other, and one fisherman says to try the exact opposite thing that another one recommends. Recommendations are made in strong statements with no referencing and no data to back up the opinion. Often these strong statements conflict with my own experiences. I wanted one source with as much valid scientific data, as many opinions from respected fisheries biologists and other experts, and my own experiences in one place. I like to write. So . . . that's why I decided to research and write LunkerMetrics!

I got the idea for LunkerMetrics while watching professional football games. Professional football has "analytics" where football coaches use data-driven analytical strategies to make in-game decisions; consequently, more teams are "going for it" on fourth down, and announcers are using analytical terms like "win probability" and "expected points added" when analyzing these decisions.[1] Coaches and assistants pour over data and use computer statistical models to quantitate the "value of a play" and the probabilities of various outcomes based upon decisions made in running that play.[2]

LunkerMetrics is about finding ways to improve the predictability and probability of catching lunker bass by studying the science and the analytics of bass behavior and fishing outcomes. Fishermen do not have armies of coaches and assistants pouring over game film and sending data to statisticians to build computer models to predict the "value of a cast," so we cannot usually precisely quantitate the "value of a cast" on every fishery or the "value of a move" from one type of spot to another. However, we do have fisheries biologists and other scientists writing papers and studying the behavior of largemouth bass. We also have large databases documenting lunker catches just waiting to be analyzed in depth. Here, I hope to organize that research in one book and to conduct some original research to answer important bass fishing questions quantitatively and in ways that help the average bass fishing reader increase his or her odds of catching a lunker bass.

In addition to being an avid bass fisherman, I'm an orthopedic surgeon and a lawyer. I intend to combine my background in medicine and law to write a book on bass fishing that is accessible to the layperson but holds to the principles of scientific and legal writing. I've published numerous articles in scientific journals and intend to use the same type of scientific research and writing methods to report findings here with a scrutinizing eye on all data reported. In the scientific traditions, data will be reported, scrutinized, and weaknesses acknowledged. I'm also a lawyer and have published numerous law review articles and written many legal documents. I intend to use the same types of standards of evidence to report only relevant and reliable information here. Therefore, almost every assertion in this book will have a footnote, so that you can look up my sources for making that assertion. I have focused on resources that are publicly available and should be assessable to most readers with

---

[1] Liam Fox, *How the NFL uses analytics, according to the lead analyst of a Super Bowl champion*, FORBES, August 12, 2021, available at https://www.forbes.com/sites/liamfox/2021/08/12/how-the-nfl-uses-analytics-according-to-the-lead-analyst-of-a-super-bowl-champion/?sh=189013c5424e.
[2] Id.

internet access. Further, personal opinions and anecdotal evidence will be reported as such.

Methods Used in This Book

Reliable, quality scientific studies and reports from researchers, biologists, and other scientists were sought out and used extensively in this book. Sources include at least ten tracking studies of around 300 largemouth bass surgically implanted with tracking devices and monitored for months in fisheries ranging in size from small ponds to a 180,000-acre lake. Information is included from approximately 50 scientific research papers published in scientific journals like *Nature*, *Journal of Fish Biology*, *Journal of the Southeast Association of Fish and Wildlife Agencies*, *Ecology of Freshwater Fish*, *Fisheries Management and Ecology*, *Comparative Biochemistry and Physiology*, *Transactions of the American Fisheries Society*, *Frontiers in Genetics*, *Journal of Neurophysiology*, *Canadian Journal of Zoology*, and *Ecology of Freshwater Fish*—just to name a few. In addition, over 100 articles in fishing publications (e.g., *In-Fisherman*, *Bassmaster*, etc.), government reports (e.g., Texas Parks & Wildlife Department, National Oceanic and Atmospheric Administration, U.S. Geological Survey), and other publications featuring opinions of respected fisheries' biologists are referenced. I have done my best to find reliable and scientifically valid sources for the information included.

Four original studies of my own are also included. I used publicly available data from Texas' ShareLunker program to conduct three original studies of lunker bass catches to determine the best months to catch lunkers, the effects of barometric pressure on lunker catches, and the effects of the moon on lunker catches. My findings may surprise you in some instances. In addition, I use publicly available data from a Texas big bass tournament to do another original study to see what time of day is best for lunkers.

Finally, I report information that I learned during my own bass fishing education at something I call "Lake Fork University." I am big into education and have doctorates in both law and medicine, so I naturally wanted to get a doctorate in bass fishing. However, I could not find a campus to obtain any such degree. So, "Lake Fork University" was my self-made education system where I hired 5 different well-respected fishing guides as my "professors" on the world renown fishing campus at Lake Fork, Texas over around 8 years during all the different seasons to get an education in high level big bass fishing. Overall, I spent around 120 hours with those 5 guides in total. The guides ranged in age from their 20s to their 60s with some guides being into modern electronics and others having fished the lake since it opened using many different fishing techniques. The Lake Fork guide community is well educated in big bass fishing as they chase big bass with clients from all over the world year-round. And I chose five of the best. I also started taking my own boat to Lake Fork and fished it on my own over the past few years. See the note about Lake Fork and the Texas Parks and Wildlife Department at the end of this chapter.

In addition to all of the resources above, I have spent and continue to spend a lot of time fishing several different Arkansas lakes . . . usually about two full days per week over the past 5 years or so. I have also spent a full day from dawn to dusk with a well-known big bass guide at O.H. Ivie Reservoir in Texas, as well as a few days at O.H. Ivie in my own boat. So, while I'm not a professional fisherman, I have an excellent education in big bass fishing.

The Big Picture

No matter how you approach bass fishing, luck will always play a role in catching lunker bass because lunkers by definition are rare and hard to catch—but knowledge and skill can increase your odds dramatically. The average angler catches one average bass approximately every 4 hours spent fishing (i.e., 0.25 bass per hour).[3]

At Lake Fork, a world class fishery, bass over 7 pounds made up 1.1% (1730/155,587) of the bass counted in the 2021 Texas Parks and Wildlife Department (TPWD) survey. Anglers in 2021 spent 502,943 hours chasing 1730 lunkers over seven pounds at Lake Fork; in other words, around 291 hours were spent fishing for each bass over seven pounds reported.[4] Since it only takes 4 hours to catch an

---

[3] Steve Quinn, *The effects of Solunar forces on bass fishing*, IN-FISHERMAN, July 13, 2021, available at https://www.in-fisherman.com/editorial/solunar-forces-on-bass-fishing/377272 (also noting that in some highly rated lakes in the southeastern United states, the average is around one bass every 2.5 hours (i.e., 0.40 bass per hour)).

[4] Jacob Norman, et al., *Lake Fork: 2021 Fisheries Management Survey Report*, TEXAS PARKS AND WILDLIFE DEPARTMENT, available at

average bass, anglers must spend over 70 times (i.e., 291/4) as many hours to catch one seven pounder at Lake Fork as it takes them to catch an average bass. 291 hours is around 36 full eight-hour days of fishing per 7+ pound bass caught. That works out to a 0.34% chance of catching a 7+ pound bass for each hour fished at Lake Fork in 2021.

Using the same study and logic to analyze bass over 10 pounds at Lake Fork in 2021, bass over 10 pounds accounted for only 0.07% (i.e., 105/155,587) of the catches.[5] Anglers spent 4,790 hours fishing for each double-digit bass reported. That is almost 1,200 times as long as it took to catch an average-sized bass. That's 19.7 months of full eight-hour fishing days per double digit bass reported at Lake Fork in 2021. It works out to a 0.02% chance of catching a double-digit bass per hour. So, if you fished one eight-hour day at Lake Fork in 2021 and were an average angler, you had a 0.16% chance of catching a double-digit bass at that world class fishery. Your odds were actually lower because many of the double-digit bass reported were caught by guides' clients and other experts who were certainly not "average" anglers.

Let's go one step farther with the math. Football coaches get the "value of a play" from analytics. Can we calculate the "value of a cast" at Lake Fork in 2021? First, how many casts did it take to catch a lunker at Lake Fork in 2021? Again, anglers spent 502,943 hours fishing. Based upon my experience as an angler and observations while fishing with guides, I would guess that average anglers spend around 75% of their time on the water casting with the rest of the time spent moving from spot to spot, eating, talking, and generally enjoying the lake. So, that works out to 377,207.25 hours purely casting in 2021. Depending upon what bait you are using, the average cast lasts from 30 to 90 seconds for many commonly used baits (yes, I know you can work some baits much slower and some much faster, but I'm just trying to get a ballpark average)—so an average is likely around 60 seconds between casts. That means that an average angler probably makes around 60 casts per hour—with some casting much more and some much less. So, at a rate of 60 casts per hour over 377,207.25 hours in 2021, a total of 22,632,435 casts were made at

---

https://tpwd.texas.gov/publications/pwdpubs/media/lake_survey/pwd_rp_t3200_1293_2021.pdf.
[5] Id.

Lake Fork in 2021. Out of those over 22 million casts, a total of 1730 bass over 7 pounds were landed, which means it took an average of 13,082 casts per 7+ pound lunker caught over seven pounds. Since there were only 105 lunkers over 10 pounds landed, anglers made approximately 215,547 casts per double digit bass in 2021 at Lake Fork. That means each cast at Lake Fork in 2021 gave you approximately a 1/13,000 chance at a lunker over seven pounds and an 1/215,000 chance at a double-digit bass. That's my best guess of the "value of a cast" at Lake Fork in 2021 if you are an average angler. Hopefully, after reading this book, your odds will be much higher than that because you will no longer be an average angler!

My Lake Fork University education showed me that you can dramatically improve those odds by understanding bass behavior and being in sync with your fishery. I spent around 120 hours fishing at Lake Fork with 5 different guides over approximately 15 different days. During that time, I caught two double digit bass! That works out to one double digit bass for every 60 hours spent on the water with knowledgeable Lake Fork guides, which is WAY better than the almost 4,800 hours spent per double digit bass by average anglers.[6] So, you can obviously greatly improve your chances with knowledge. Specifically, for me, in 60 hours on the water with guides at Lake Fork, I likely spent 45 hours per double digit bass casting (assuming 25% of the time was spent moving between fishing spots, eating lunch, etc.) at a rate of around 60 casts per hour. This works out to around one double digit bass for every 2,700 casts; in other words, my "value of a cast" with good guides at Lake Fork was 1/2700 per cast chance of catching a 10+ pounder. That is MUCH better than the 1/215,000 cast value I calculated for the average Lake Fork fisherman. So, the "value of a cast" can change dramatically with knowledge of lunker behavior and an understanding of your fishery! Part of the guide's advantage is the fact that he is on the water every day, and he is communicating with other guides to keep track of exactly what the fish are doing on a daily basis. In other words, he is dialed in on exactly what the fish are doing on his fishery every day. I learned a lot from my Lake Fork guides and hope to transfer some of that knowledge along here.

The best thing that you can do to increase the likelihood of catching a lunker bass is to be in a location with lunker bass present

---

[6] Id.

when they are active and looking to feed—in other words, *be in the right place at the right time*. In one study, the movements of 49 largemouth bass with surgically implanted GPS tracking devices were tracked simultaneously with five tournament anglers wearing GPS tracking devices during weekly tournaments over four months.[7] Researchers found that, unsurprisingly, "bass that [were] encountered by anglers" were more likely to be caught and that catchability is higher when angler/bass location overlap is higher.[8] In other words, fishermen caught more of the bass when they were near them.[9] The researchers found that the catchability of largemouth bass "depends on the ability of anglers to successfully locate areas where fish are present" and to "selectively target areas where fish reside."[10] Notably, the anglers in the study were often in the wrong place at the wrong time as they failed to understand the movements of the bass in the fishery studied.[11]

Similarly, conventional bass fishing wisdom may lead you to fish in the wrong place at the wrong time. For example, in a tracking study of bass with implanted tracking devices at Toledo Bend, biologists broke down lake habitat into the following six types: points, drops, drains, flats, creek channels, and channel swings.[12] Take a second and rank those six types of habitat in the order that you would fish them based upon the things that you have read and heard about bass fishing. The biologists are finding (the study is still underway) that *bass in Toledo Bend find nondescript "flats" to be the most desirable habitat* where they have been found 41% of the times tracked. The bass (including a nine-pound lunker) were scattered randomly over these flats 50 to 100 yards from any sharp breaks like

---

[7] Andrea Sylvia, et al., *Influence of largemouth bass behaviors, angler behaviors, and environmental conditions on fishing tournament capture success*, TRANSACTIONS OF THE AMERICAN FISHERIES SOCIETY, November 19, 2019, available at https://afspubs.onlinelibrary.wiley.com/doi/10.1002/tafs.10216.
[8] Id.
[9] Id.
[10] Id.
[11] Id. (In this particular study, the tournament anglers catch rates fell when they appeared to concentrate their efforts too deep too early in the season, causing a "potential mismatch in overlap with bass later in the season.").
[12] Ken Smith Fishing YouTube Channel, *Toledo Bend Telemetry Tracking Study Update Todd Driscoll TP&W Biologist Feb 2022 Part 5*, available at https://www.youtube.com/watch?v=f1sL9FZnS4g&list=PLLzhji805wVzkLnAA97I8VmdZpR8arB_Q&index=5.

ledges or humps.[13] The worst two structure classifications to find the bass being tracked in this study were channel swings (worst) and points (second worst).[14] Yet, at one lake where I fish regularly, some days it is hard to find a point unoccupied by a bass fisherman, while the open flat areas remain largely unoccupied by fishermen.

Bass fishing is about being in the right place at the right time, which is a statistical gamble based upon factors like season of the year, time of day, water temperature, weather factors, and moon phase. Understanding the biological behavioral patterns of bass based on available science should help increase your chances of being in the right location during a particular season of bass fishing. In addition, bass are affected by many factors. Some factors were quantifiable and accessible to me in public databases, such as barometric pressure, time of day, percentage moon illumination, and month of the year for many lunker catches. Other factors affecting bass were not available in those databases like individual fishing effort/expertise, lure chosen, water clarity, turbidity, dissolved oxygen, wind speed and direction, water temperature, water quality and water color (including FDOM and chlorophyll).[15] So, I quantified and reported the ones that I could in this book.

One of the reasons that lunker bass fishing is fun is because it is not simple; you can't simply say on this type of day and in this type of circumstance throw this bait at this depth, and, BOOM, you have an eight pounder on the deck. Nope.

Lunker bass fishing is a combination of application of knowledge to be in the right place at the right time, skillful execution of lure presentation, persistence, and luck. But, sometimes, luck takes the day. For example, one cold February day as I pulled away from the launch ramp my boat was sinking because water was leaking around my frozen plug. I stopped in the middle of the lake to bail water and get another plug in place from inside the boat to keep from sinking. When I finished, the wind had blown me near a point. I was drenched and cold and needed a few minutes to recover from the ordeal, so I picked up a rod with a big glide bait on it and started casting near the point to which the wind had randomly blown me. On

---

[13] Id.
[14] Id.
[15] Sanibel-Captiva Conservation Foundation, *Fishing: Where should I fish today?*, available at https://recon.sccf.org/sport-fishing.

the first cast, a 7.18-pound lunker T-boned the bait about 20 feet from the boat in a bite I saw in the clear water and will never forget. After landing that fish, I caught a 6.5 pounder and a 5 pounder on the next two casts. Those catches were mostly luck. I did have the glide bait tied on and planned to use it that day and did know how to retrieve it, but the serendipity of a sinking boat and a west wind blowing me into the right place at the right time had much more to do with me catching those lunkers than any knowledge or skill. I did not catch another fish that day. Here is a picture of the 7+ pounder:

Don't let those lucky days throw you off the path to catching more and bigger fish on a consistent basis. This book is about using the knowledge of science and analytics to increase your statistical chances of consistently being near big bass. It is not about "one day wonders." My tackle box is full of lures and specific colors that excelled on one day when I caught a lot of fish or caught big fish using that specific lure or color, so I stocked up—only to never catch another fish on that bait or color. One summer day, I was sure that I had the late summer big bass bite "figured out" on a lake that I fish a lot. I knew some of my buddies were catching smaller bass on squarebills and small chatterbaits. But the bigger bass I was trying to catch were about 27 feet deep, and I could not get a crankbait to them and small chatterbaits would not stay down there very well. The fish would not touch a jig or a worm on bottom. So, I ordered some heavy chatterbaits with a football-shaped head and anxiously headed out to the lake full of confidence when I got them in the mail. On that first day, I threw the heavy chatterbait out into 35 feet deep water and then reeled it just fast enough to move the blade for a few cranks up to 5 or 10 feet off the bottom and then drop it to the bottom and then repeat. I caught 5 bass between five and seven pounds that day using that technique. I was pumped! I knew that I was going to have the greatest summer ever catching 5-7 pounders daily the rest of the summer, so I ordered several more of those giant chatterbaits including a few different colors. Guess what? I have never caught another bass on one of those chatterbaits—even though I went back to that lake the next few days under the same weather, moon, and other conditions. I try the technique again every once in a while on that lake and others, but so far, that was a one day bite. But my tackle box is ready, if that bite ever takes off again. I have a lot of specific color worms in my arsenal as well that were "one day wonders" that I stocked up after a good day.

  Those are some fun and awesome days, but this book is more about consistency. Knowledge helped me find those fish 27 feet deep which put me in position to find that special bait for that particular day. More times than not, the application of knowledge to your bass fishing days will increase your odds of catching lunker bass. I have caught at least fifty times more lunkers in the past five years than my prior 45 years combined since I got serious about catching big bass. The goal of this book is to increase your knowledge of bass and lunker behavior to increase your chances of catching lunker bass by making more casts and spending more time fishing in the right place at the right time.

  Hopefully, the knowledge I pass along in this book will increase your odds. If you are going to put in the time, you should do it full of knowledge and potential analytics information. So, let's get started!

A Note About Lake Fork and Texas Parks and Wildlife Department

  The campus for much of my bass fishing education over the past few years at Lake Fork University has been the world class fishery at Lake Fork and the community that surrounds it. I love the whole area because it is all about bass fishing. I see new and innovative fishing gear in stores and talk to fishermen from all over the country with different and unique takes on the sport. It is a fun place to visit as an avid bass fisherman. The 154 launch ramp is exactly 4 hours from my house, and on several occasions, I have left my home at 4 am to launch at 8 am, fish all day, leave at 5 pm, and arrive back home before 10 pm. So, in case you can't tell, I love Lake Fork and will mention it throughout this book at relevant times.

  Lake Fork is a 27,264 acre nationally-recognized trophy largemouth bass fishery that opened in 1980 under the watchful eye of the Texas Parks and Wildlife Department (TPWD).[16] Luckily, the head of TPWD at the time recognized an opportunity to turn it into an unrivaled trophy bass fishery.[17] TPWD imported Florida bass and

---

[16] Kevin Storey and Aaron Jubar, *The Lake Fork trophy largemouth bass survey: Benefits and limitations of using volunteer data to assess the performance of a trophy fishery*, J. OF THE SOUTHEASTERN ASSOCIATION OF FISH AND WILDLIFE AGENCIES 5:10-16, 2018; Hal Schramm, *Lake Fork: anatomy of a trophy fishery*, IN-FISHERMAN, January 29, 2018, available at https://www.in-fisherman.com/editorial/lake-fork-anatomy-of-a-trophy-fishery/154619.

[17] Hal Schramm, *supra* note 16.

stocked farm and brood ponds with adult Florida bass in the area that would become Lake Fork long before the lake was flooded in the early 80s.[18] One of the Lake Fork guides that I have fished with numerous times remembers the location of many of those ponds, so I've fished a few of those long ago flooded spots over the past few years.[19] TPWD has used continued stocking, slot limits, and harvest control to produce a world class big bass environment.[20]

    The TPWD ShareLunker program started on November 26, 1986, under the name Operation Share a Lone Star Lunker when Mark Stevenson, a Lake Fork guide fishing with clients, landed a 17.67 pound and 27.5 inch long giant largemouth bass from Lake Fork for a new state record.[21] The fish was named "Ethel" and became a celebrity. One of the misconceptions at the time was that really big bass could not be kept alive for very long in captivity after being caught, so Operation Share a Lone Star Lunker program was surrounded with great skepticism.[22] Doubters also insisted that fishermen would not be willing to hand over their monster bass to TPWD.[23] Stevenson and his clients took Ethel to a local bait shop to weigh her and left her in the store's minnow tank for the afternoon for TPWD to collect her and certify her as a new state record while they went back out on Lake Fork for the afternoon to finish their fishing trip.[24]

    News of Ethel got out quickly and by the time Stevenson returned to the shop, the parking lot was full of onlookers there to see the fish, which was one of the first signs to TPWD of Texans' great interest in giant bass.[25] TPWD took Ethel to their hatchery in Tyler that afternoon.[26] Ethel was a very popular attraction at the hatchery with 10,000 people signing the guest book in her room at the hatchery during her six months there.[27]

---

[18] Id.
[19] Id.
[20] Id.
[21] Larry Hodge, *A fish called Ethel: How a 17-pound largemouth bass chanced the world*, TEXAS PARKS & WILDLIFE MAGAZINE, April 2008, available at https://tpwmagazine.com/archive/2008/apr/ed_4/.
[22] Id.
[23] Id.
[24] Id.
[25] Id.
[26] Larry Hodge, *A fish called Ethel*, *supra* note 21.
[27] Id.

Ethel's popularity attracted the attention of Bass Pro Shop's Johnny Morris, and Stevenson agreed to give Ethel to Morris for display at Bass Pro Shops; Morris built her an aquarium at the Springfield, Missouri store.[28] Stevenson transported Ethel from Tyler, Texas to Springfield, Missouri in a galvanized livestock watering tank, i.e., a cattle trough, in the back of his Suburban.[29] Johnny Morris described her as "the best thing that ever happened to Bass Pro Shops as far as getting people in there."[30] Ethel was visited by thousands of fishermen at her aquarium at Bass Pro Shops in Springfield, Missouri—including a teenage me![31] Ethel lived at the Springfield Bass Pro Shop aquarium until 1994 when she died at 19 years of age.[32] One thousand five hundred people attended her memorial service on August 25, 1994, including Johnny Morris and over 35 outdoor writers.[33]

Ethel helped bass conservation and management greatly in several ways.[34] First, she showed that really large fish could in fact live for years after being caught proving that "stewardship of wildlife and management can actually work better than if you just let nature take its course."[35] Second, she showed that the ShareLunker program was possible because a giant bass could survive and spawn in captivity.[36] Third, she showed that the management at Lake Fork was working.[37] Ethel was between 9 and 10 years old when she was caught in 1986 just six and a half years after Lake Fork was impounded in 1980.[38] This meant that she was likely one of the Florida bass stocked in the brood ponds before the lake was impounded.[39] These ponds later became part of the lake as it naturally filled with water.[40] Finally, Ethel helped solidify what would eventually become the ShareLunker program by showing the

---

[28] Id.
[29] Id.
[30] Id.
[31] Hal Schramm, *supra* note 16.
[32] Larry Hodge, *A fish called Ethel*, *supra* note 21.
[33] Id.
[34] Id.
[35] Id.
[36] Id.
[37] Larry Hodge, *A fish called Ethel*, *supra* note 21.
[38] Id.
[39] Id.
[40] Id.

worth of giant bass and by helping secure funding to take the program further. After Ethel, the legislature appropriated $8 million for Texas fish hatcheries.[41]

Today, TPWD's ShareLunker program is setting the standard for state agencies trying to develop lunker bass populations. TPWD has the only state program that is breeding fish to increase the odds that their offspring will grow big.[42] Florida largemouth bass were introduced in Texas in 1972.[43] By 1986, as a result of TPWD's efforts in introducing Florida bass genetics to the state and especially the development of Lake Fork, the Texas state record largemouth bass increased from 13.5 lbs. to 18.18 lbs.[44] The previous state record of 13.5 had stood for 37 years until Florida bass were introduced.[45]

In 1986, with the ShareLunker program, TPWD began using a selective breeding program to produce a "new and better strain of largemouth bass for Texas anglers" based upon the idea that "fish of trophy size had a better chance of producing offspring that might also grow unusually large."[46] The director of the program described it as being similar to breeding horses to win the Kentucky Derby.[47] Under the program, anglers lend fish weighing more than 13 pounds to TPWD for spawning.[48] Any Texas angler who catches a 13+ pound bass in January, February or March can loan the bass to TPWD.[49] These months are when big female bass are full of eggs. Biologists from TPWD travel to wherever the fish is caught, give the fish top-notch medical care, and take it to their special facility in Athens, TX for controlled breeding.[50] Once in Athens, the ShareLunkers are

---

[41] Id.
[42] Kyle Roberts, *The Texas wildlife program working to ensure the future of big bass fishing in the state*, WFAA8 ABC, May 19, 2021, available at https://www.wfaa.com/article/features/originals/texas-sharelunker-program-works-future-big-bass/287-580dacd0-cfbc-48c4-b45a-56fbd4bc14fc.
[43] Larry Hodge, *ShareLunker Science: Bass DNA is slowly revealing its secrets through TPWD research*, TEXAS PARKS & WILDLIFE MAGAZINE, March 2013, available at https://tpwmagazine.com/archive/2013/mar/scout2_sharelunker/.
[44] Id.
[45] Id.
[46] Kyle Roberts, *supra* note 42; Larry Hodge, *ShareLunker Science*, *supra* note 43.
[47] Kyle Roberts, *supra* note 42.
[48] Larry Hodge, *ShareLunker Science*, *supra* note 43.
[49] Kyle Roberts, *supra* note 42.
[50] Id.

paired with male offspring of previous ShareLunkers so that "you get a ShareLunker spawning with a ShareLunker."[51]

Breeding of fish with big fish genetics with other fish with big fish genetics increases the odds that their offspring will also be big, like their parents.[52] The big ShareLunker bass can "lay anywhere from 20,000 to 100,000 eggs," and in the controlled environment in Athens, more of these eggs survive and hatch than in the wild.[53] Once the hatchlings grow enough, "they are transferred to outdoor ponds at the fisheries center, where they continue to grow until they are big enough to be put into the lake their mom was caught from–or into other lakes across Texas," with hopes that they will eventually grow into ShareLunkers.[54]

The program is paid for by sponsors, currently Toyota. DNA testing has been developed using ShareLunker sponsorship funding.[55] TPWD collects tissue samples (a small piece of a fin or a scale) from every fish entered into the ShareLunker program.[56] Today, the TPWD geneticists can tell if a current ShareLunker is a descendant of a ShareLunker donated to TPWD years ago.[57]

TPWD hired geneticists in 2009 when Gulf States Toyota became the key ShareLunker sponsor providing the money to fund genetic research on the samples that TPWD had been collecting from Sharelunkers.[58] First, they analyzed the purity of Florida strain largemouths among the ShareLunkers and found that "the odds of getting a true lunker were higher with a pure Florida bass than it was with a bass that only had a percentage of Florida genes."[59] Next, they started trying to define the gene sequences fueling the 13 pound bass, which they compared to searching for a needle in a haystack.[60] "DNA fingerprints" are used to trace ShareLunkers back through the program.[61] Biologists compare it to a pedigree system for fish,

---

[51] Id.
[52] Id.
[53] Id.
[54] Id.
[55] Larry Hodge, *ShareLunker Science*, *supra* note 43
[56] Id.
[57] Id.
[58] Craig Lamb, *ShareLunker goes to next level*, BASSMASTER, May 5, 2019, available at https://www.bassmaster.com/news/sharelunker-goes-to-next-level/.
[59] Id.
[60] Id.
[61] Id.

instead of dogs, and can "identify direct offspring from ShareLunker parents."[62] Researchers have proven that ShareLunker Florida largemouth bass "get heavier and longer than what you see in a native bass population."[63] Eventually, all of TPWD's brood stock at their hatchery will be ShareLunker offspring, which have already been proven to outperform the current Florida bass in their hatchery system and also to outperform pure Florida bass.[64] The expectation is that these bass will "grow bigger, faster, and the more we stock the sooner they will reach trophy size."[65]

By 2013, more than 1 million of those fishes' offspring had been stocked into Texas lakes.[66] Based upon DNA testing, the program has been successful. For example, in 1988 a 16 pound bass from Gibbons Creek Reservoir was turned over to TPWD as the ninth ShareLunker in the program.[67] Thirty-two years later, in 2020, a fish from Lake Nacodoches that was over 15 pounds and the new lake record was proven to be the great-, great-, great-granddaughter of the fish caught in 1988![68] More evidence of success is apparent by simply looking at 2021.[69] Twenty-three ShareLunkers were entered in 2021 with one from O.H. Ivie Reservoir weighting 16 pounds, making it the sixteenth biggest bass ever caught in Texas.[70]

In 2022, TPWD's ShareLunker program had a banner year.[71] A total of 24 bass weighing over 13 pounds (Legacy Class ShareLunkers) were caught and donated to the program between January and March, which is the most since 1995.[72] All of those fish survived at Texas Freshwater Fisheries Center (TFFC) in Athens, Texas, and all 24 were "returned back alive to the lake she was caught in for somebody else to go and have the best day of their life," said

---

[62] Id.
[63] Craig Lamb, *supra* note 58.
[64] Id.
[65] Id.
[66] Larry Hodge, *ShareLunker Science*, *supra* note 43
[67] Kyle Roberts, *supra* note 42.
[68] Id.
[69] Id.
[70] Id.
[71] Brett Anthony, *Hooked on east Texas: 2022 ShareLunker season one for the record books*, CBS19, May 20, 2022, available at https://www.cbs19.tv/article/tech/science/hooked-on-east-texas-takes-you-in-depth-to-the-best-sharelunker-season/501-1f7ed357-42f0-4c30-bb84-8c12ddc99f08.
[72] Id.

Tom Lang, TFFC director.[73] This is amazing considering that those giant bass are the "senior citizens of the fish world."[74]

    Genetic analysis of the fish shows that the ShareLunker program is paying off.[75] For example, one of 2022's ShareLunkers caught in Lake Austin was the offspring of a 2008 ShareLunker caught 14 years earlier in 2008 from Richard Chambers Reservoir.[76] In another example, a 2022 O.H. Ivie Sharelunker is the daughter of an O.H. Ivie Sharelunker caught in 2012 and also related to another O.H. Ivie Sharelunker caught in 2021.[77] Lang notes that "it's that partnership between the anglers, the industry, Toyota, our sponsor and our biologists…all working together for 36 years to create fish like that all across the state."[78] In 2022, five of the ShareLunkers were over 15 pounds and one O.H. Ivie giant was over 17 pounds and the biggest fish caught in Texas in 30 years.[79] The 17 pounder was the 7th largest bass verified in Texas.[80] Four of the 2022 ShareLunkers made the top 50 biggest largemouth of all time in Texas. The 24 fish came from 9 different bodies of water.[81] After the 2022 season, a total of 75 different public Texas lakes have produced ShareLunkers over 13 pounds.[82] TPWD is taking the program further by pairing male ShareLunker offspring with female ShareLunker offspring to grow a new bass they have dubbed the "Lone Star Bass."[83]

    In 2018, TPWD started the ShareLunker program year-round.[84] The catch date and other information on these bass is available to the public on the TPWD ShareLunker website and is the basis for several of my "studies" that make up chapters in this book. The 2023 ShareLunker numbers are likely to rival or beat those of

---

[73] Id.
[74] Id.
[75] Id.
[76] Brett Anthony, *supra* note 71.
[77] Id.
[78] Id.
[79] Id.
[80] Id.
[81] Brett Anthony, *supra* note 71.
[82] Id.
[83] Id.
[84] TPWD News, *Toyota ShareLunker Program to begin new year-round season Jan. 1*, September 29, 2017, available at https://tpwd.texas.gov/newsmedia/releases/?req=20170929a.

2022 because many 13+ pound bass have already been recorded by late spring, including another 17+ pounder from O.H. Ivie.

In 2018, Lake Fork was the "source of almost half of the 565 thirteen pound and larger bass entered into the ShareLunker Program" over the years since it started and 13 of the top 20 fish ever caught in Texas.[85] Over the past few years, Lake Fork has been surpassed by O.H. Ivie in production of ShareLunkers, but remains a big bass mecca.[86] Fork is unique because it was "built on fertile ground and has a good forage base of gizzard and threadfin shad as well as crappies, bluegill, yellow bass, and white bass" that are of good size to feed big bass.[87] The good genetics of Fork's bass population also is a big factor.[88] According to the 2021 Lake Fork creel survey, the percentage of Florida bass alleles ranged from 48 to 57% since 2006.[89] Fork was stocked with 13.7 million fingerling Florida bass from 1995 to 2016, averaging 621,000 per year.[90] More recently since 2006, Fork has been stocked with an average of 10,500 ShareLunker offspring per year.[91] This combination has allowed Fork to continue to put out trophy bass.[92] The slot limit requires anglers to release all bass from 16 to 24 inches immediately—including no exceptions for tournaments—which has contributed to Lake Fork's success.[93] The other thing that helps Fork is habitat.[94] When Fork was filled, most of the timber was left in place leaving a lot of deep water wood.[95] Lake Fork, in 2018, had an annual total economic impact of around 38 million dollars.[96]

Lake Fork is a special place! If you love bass fishing, it should be on your bucket list in my opinion.

Texas plans to go even further in the future with the 16,641 acre Bois d'Arc Lake in North Texas outside of Bonham in Fannin County by the North Texas Municipal Water District (NTMWD) to

---

[85] Hal Schramm, *supra* note 16.
[86] Id.
[87] Id.
[88] Id.
[89] Jacob Norman, *supra* note 4
[90] Hal Schramm, *supra* note 16.
[91] Id.
[92] Id.
[93] Id.
[94] Id.
[95] Hal Schramm, *supra* note 16.
[96] Id.

serve as a water supply for northern suburbs of Dallas-Fort Worth, which is being created as a "nursery of sorts for giant bass," and the "first major reservoir built in the State of Texas in 30 years."[97] Thousands of 1 to 2 year old ShareLunker offspring are already being stocked into the creeks and ponds that will eventually become the lake to give the lake a head start—similar to the strategy used at Lake Fork.[98] In addition, 30,000 to 40,000 fingerlings (offspring less than 1 year old) are already scheduled to be stocked as well.[99] NTMWD has also left standing timber, natural vegetation, as well as "areas of pipes, concrete, and piles of brush scattered about the area," so that once the lake fills, these underwater areas will become "reefs or structure" 10 to 20 feet deep to provide habitat for the bass to help them remain healthy and reach their full growth potential.[100]

---

[97] Kyle Roberts, *supra* note 42.
[98] Id.
[99] Id.
[100] Id.

2

Lunker Bass are Different

Special

    Lunker bass are special because they create lasting memories that stick with fishermen for a lifetime. For me, a lunker is a memorable bass that is significantly bigger than usual for the places that I fish. Lunker bass can make grown men cry tears of joy or sadness. Some lunker bass elicit tears of sadness as they live as almost mythical creatures in fishermen's minds as "the one that got away." I will never forget one giant that jumped with my favorite glide bait in its mouth before bending out the hooks. I can still see it today as the glide bait flew from its mouth with the giant bass in mid-air. It may have been the biggest bass I've ever hooked in my home state of Arkansas. Lunker bass can also bring tears of joy and emotional outbursts from even the quietest and most reserved fishermen. I've seen videos of grown mean squealing like little girls upon landing a giant bass, and I might have done the same on occasion but won't admit it here. Here's a picture of a lunker I have remembered for 45 years:

I caught the 6-pound "giant" on a grape-colored Mann's Jellyworm in a farm pond in July 1978. During the battle, the fish ran into a giant bush and hung me up in the middle of the pond on a small, flooded island. My 13-year-old buddy waded out into the pond to free the bass from the bush, and I landed it. My heart was racing, and I was out of breath as I finally got the lunker in my hands. The picture was taken outside of the only grocery store in the area where we took the bass to get a weight. This lunker bass hung on my wall as my personal best for most of my teen years.

    For me, a lunker bass is a five pounder because they are rare in the places that I fish in Arkansas and because they put up such a great fight that they are always memorable to land on the gear that I usually use.

Rare

    What about a more scientific definition of a "lunker"? A "lunker" is a fish that is unusual or relatively rare, but not mythically rare. One way to define a lunker would be by rarity in a particular location or body of water.

Let's look at Lake Fork because data is readily available. During the 2021 survey at Lake Fork, Texas Parks and Wildlife Department estimated that around 1% of the bass caught by anglers were between 7 and 10 pounds.[101] That means that for every 100 bass caught, only 1 weighed between 7 and 10 pounds.[102] For me, scientifically, that is a good definition of a "lunker." So, for Lake Fork, a seven pounder or bigger might be considered a "lunker" by some, if you only want to count the top 1% of bass in a fishery. In my home state of Arkansas, I bet a 5 pounder would be considered a lunker in most fisheries using the same definition of the top 1%.

In contrast, TPWD reported that only 0.07% of bass caught in Lake Fork in 2021 were over 10 pounds.[103] That's about 1 out of every 1,667 bass caught. That's a little too close to mythical for me—so I would define "lunker" a little more loosely.

On the other end of the spectrum, around 10% of Lake Fork bass caught were between 4 and 7 pounds, so that is 1 of every 10, which may be too common for some to consider a 4-pound Lake Fork bass "lunker" status. But honestly, to me a 5 pounder is still a lunker no matter where I catch it! Here is a pie chart with the Lake Fork 2021 survey results (note that the >10-pound category is too small of a slice of pie to see in the chart):

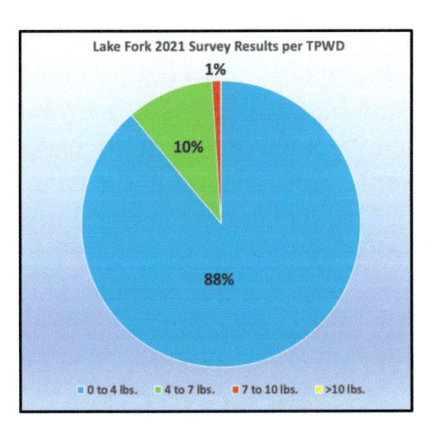

---

[101] Jacob Norman, et al., *Lake Fork: 2021 Fisheries Management Survey Report*, Texas Parks and Wildlife Department, available at https://tpwd.texas.gov/publications/pwdpubs/media/lake_survey/pwd_rp_t3200_1293_2021.pdf.
[102] Id.
[103] Id.

For purposes of the studies in this book, I will use 8 pounds as the cutoff point for lunker status in Texas because Texas Parks and Wildlife Department (TPWD) defines an 8 pounder as a "lunker" in its ShareLunker program and reports data on bass in this category which I can use to conduct some statistical studies of my own. In the ShareLunker program, TPWD designates bass between 8 and 10 pounds as "lunker" status, bass from 10 to 13 pounds as "elite" status, and bass 13 pounds or over as either "legend" (released) or "legacy" (taken to the hatchery to spawn) status.

For purposes of this book, the term "lunker" means whatever you decide it means for you in your location. I just hope this book helps you find more bass that meet your definition.

Defining "Largemouth Bass"

Before we dig too deeply into the special characteristics of a lunker, I want to make it clear that this book is about largemouth bass—which I will define here. The largemouth bass is a top predator carnivore in the lakes and rivers in North America.[104] They can reach lengths of over two feet and weights of over 20 pounds.[105] Their pound-for-pound fighting power, voracious appetites, and relative ease of catch helped largemouth bass emerge as one of the "quintessential sportfishes" in America as early as the 1800s.[106]

Today, bass fishing is among the top five participant sports in the United States with over 30 million anglers (nearly 10% of the population) spending around $60 billion per year.[107] More of America's freshwater anglers (43%) fish for bass than for any other

---

[104] Jeff Schmerker, *Among largemouth bass, wild and hatchery populations fight for genetic dominance*, Integrated DNA Technologies In The News, November 30, 2020, available at https://www.idtdna.com/pages/community/blog/post/among-largemouth-bass-wild-and-hatchery-populations-fight-for-genetic-dominance.
[105] Id.
[106] Daemin Kim, et al., *Phylogenomics and species delimitation of the economically important Black Basses (Micropterus)*, NATURE: SCIENTIFIC REPORTS 12: 9113 (2022), https://www.nature.com/articles/s41598-022-11743-2 (stating, "Because of their popularity, species of Micropterus have been stocked throughout the world since the early 1800s.").
[107] Florida Museum of Natural History, *Discover Fishes: Micropterus salmoides*, available at https://www.floridamuseum.ufl.edu/discover-fish/species-profiles/micropterus-salmoides/.

type of freshwater fish.[108] In 2020, recreational anglers generated $1.7 billion for conservation through excise taxes ($650 million), fishing licenses ($752 million), and private donations ($283 million) leading to cleaner water and preservation of habitat for fisheries throughout the country.[109] Bass fishing is such an industry that bass boats often cost more than luxury cars.[110] Bass fishing is celebrated with festivals, songs, television shows, and huge tournaments.[111]

Over time, largemouth bass became so popular that they were stocked in at least 57 countries and are now among the "top ten most common aquatic species on every continent except Antarctica."[112] They are present in "Cuba, Guatemala, Honduras, Puerto Rico, Columbia, Brazil, South Africa, Zimbabwe, Kenya, Portugal, Spain, France, Germany, Italy, Hungry, Croatia, Serbia, Lebanon, Japan, Philippines, Russia, China, South Korea, Fiji and New Zealand."[113]

Largemouth bass are a type of black bass (*Micropterus*).[114] Black basses are native to North American rivers and lakes east of the Rocky Mountains from northern Mexico to southern Canada.[115] In all, there are at least 19 species of black bass including the largemouth bass, Florida bass, smallmouth bass, and spotted bass, among others.[116] This book is about the largemouth bass alone, although the other species of black bass may bear significant resemblance in behavior in some instances.

Just to be complete with the scientific classification information: Black bass (*Micropterus*) belong to the Division *Teleosts* (boney fishes) and the Order *Perciformes* (perch-like fish). They are in the sunfish Family *Centrarchidae*, along with bluegill sunfish and crappie, and the Subfamily *Lepominae* (bass, sunfish).

---

[108] Id.
[109] American Sportfishing Association, Sportfishing in America: A reliable economic force, 2020, available at https://asafishing.org/wp-content/uploads/2021/03/Sportfishing-in-America-economics-report.pdf.
[110] Jeff Schmerker, *supra* note 104.
[111] Id.
[112] Daemin Kim, *supra* note 106.
[113] Steven Bardin, *Fish Biology: Largemouth bass: A comprehensive species guide*, Wired2Fish, January 28, 2023, available at https://www.wired2fish.com/fish-biology/largemouth-bass-a-comprehensive-species-guide/.
[114] Daemin Kim, *supra* note 106.
[115] Id.
[116] Id.

Black bass have been around for a long time; the oldest bass fossil was discovered in Texas and dated back to 23 million years ago.[117]

Largemouth bass were first formally described by the French naturalist Bernard Germain de Lacepede in 1802.[118] The Largemouth bass (a.k.a., "Northern Largemouth Bass") has been officially known as *Micropterus salmoides* since 1884.[119] Florida bass (*Micropterus floridanus*) were first described by biologists in 1822 and were first officially recognized as a species in 2002.[120]

Until very recently, scientists considered the Northern largemouth bass and the Florida bass to be closely related subspecies and referred to both simply as largemouth bass commonly.[121] For 75 years, scientists believed that largemouth bass diverged evolutionarily during geological changes at northern and southern latitudes into two generally recognized subspecies: (1) the Florida largemouth bass (*Micropterus floridanus*) and (2) the Northern largemouth bass (*Micropterus salmoides*).[122] The American Fisheries Society still considered Florida bass to be a subspecies of Largemouth bass in 2018.[123] However, some debate persisted over whether Northerns and Floridas are "separate species or simply closely related subspecies."[124]

More recent research has resulted in some controversy among ichthyologists and fisheries biologists over the proper classification of largemouth bass and Florida bass. Genetic analysis of DNA from

---

[117] Steven Bardin, *Fish Biology*, *supra* note 113.
[118] Id.
[119] Id.
[120] Steven Bardin, *How to identify all 9 species of black bass*, Wired2Fish, October 23, 2018, https://www.wired2fish.com/fish-biology/how-to-identify-all-9-species-of-black-bass/#slide_1.
[121] Daemin Kim, *supra* note 106.
[122] Dan Wang, et al., *Global diversity and genetic landscape of natural populations and hatchery stocks of largemouth bass Micropterus salmoides across American and Asian regions*, SCIENTIFIC REPORTS 9:16697, (2019), available at https://www.nature.com/articles/s41598-019-53026-3; Jinxing Du, et al., *Genetic diversity analysis and development of molecular markers for the identification of largemouth bass based on whole-genome re-sequencing*, FRONTIERS IN GENETICS Vol. 13, August 29, 2022, available at https://www.frontiersin.org/articles/10.3389/fgene.2022.936610/full; Daemin Kim, *supra* note 106.
[123] Steven Bardin, *How to identify all 9 species ...*, *supra* note 120.
[124] Wes Neal, *Unraveling the bass genetic code for pondmeisters*, Bass Resource, July 21, 2016, available at https://www.bassresource.com/fish_biology/bass-genetic-code.html.

hundreds of bass specimens by Yale and Auburn ichthyologists in 2022 revealed that the accurate scientific name for Florida bass is *Micropterus salmoides* while the Northern largemouth bass "should be reclassified as *Micropterus nigricans*, the oldest available scientific name for largemouth bass."[125].

Regardless of the scientific debate, throughout this book, when I use the term "largemouth bass," I am including largemouth bass (a.k.a., Northern largemouth bass) AND Florida bass. I will rarely, if ever, mention their scientific names—so I'm not going to spend any more time on these naming controversies.

Largemouth bass have 23 chromosomes, unlike most Perciformes which have 24, with 1 chromosome apparently resulting from fusion of two into 1.[126] Largemouth bass are closely related phylogenetically to European seabass and spotted seabass and are believed to have evolved (diverged) from those two seabass species 64.1 million years ago.[127] Some genetic adaptations for salinity tolerance allow largemouth bass to live in both fresh and brackish water.[128] Bass in brackish water tend to grow slower and reach smaller maximum size than their inland sisters because salinity increases the metabolic energy required by bass for survival.[129]

Appearance: Largemouth bass are olive green to greenish gray in color with cream coloring on their bellies with black blotches

---

[125] Mike Cummings, *Revelations of genetic diversity of bass species can enhance conservation*, Yale News, June 6, 2022, available at https://news.yale.edu/2022/06/06/revelations-genetic-diversity-bass-species-can-enhance-conservation; Daemin Kim, *supra* note 106 (noting that their studies "reveal that the scientific names *Micropterus salmoides* and *Micropterus floridanus* have been incorrectly applied to the Largemouth Bass and Florida Bass over the past 75 years"); Steven Bardin, *Fish Biology*, *supra* note 113.

[126] Chengfei Sun, et al., *Chromosome-level genome assembly for the largemouth bass Micropterus salmoides provides insights into adaptation to fresh and brackish water*, MOLECULAR ECOLOGY RESOURCES 21(1): 301-315, January 2021, available at https://onlinelibrary.wiley.com/doi/10.1111/1755-0998.13256.

[127] Id.

[128] Id.

[129] D.C. Glover, et al., *Effects of temperature, salinity and body size on routine metabolism of coastal largemouth bass Micropterus salmoides*, J. OF FISH BIOLOGY 81(5): 1463-1478, October, 2012, available at https://onlinelibrary.wiley.com/doi/10.1111/j.1095-8649.2012.03385.x.

along a line on the side of their bodies.[130] The black blotches on the fishes' sides can come together to create a lateral stripe in individual bass.[131] Water color, water clarity, season, depth, and water temperature can all affect coloration of individual bass, so considerable variation in coloring is common.[132]

    The main distinguishing feature of a largemouth bass from many other species of black bass is that its upper jaw extends back past the rear margin of the eye when the bass's mouth is closed as shown by the red line in the picture below of a 10-pound largemouth bass from Lake O.H. Ivie in Texas.[133]

    Additional distinguishing features of largemouth bass are (1) a spiny anterior dorsal fin and a soft-rayed posterior dorsal fin that is joined with a deep notch between them, (2) a stripe formed from dark blotches along its side from snout to caudal fin—although this varies with water turbidity, (3) a dorsal fin with 9 anterior spines (and 12-14 soft rays on the posterior dorsal fin) and an anal fin with 3 spines (and 11-12 soft rays), and (4) 59-72 scales on the lateral line.[134] Note that

---

[130] Indiana Department of Natural Resources, *Largemouth bass fishing*, available at https://www.in.gov/dnr/fish-and-wildlife/fishing/largemouth-bass/ ; Steven Bardin, *Fish Biology*, *supra* note 113; Jeff Schmerker, *supra* note 104.
[131] Steven Bardin, *Fish Biology*, *supra* note 113.
[132] Id.
[133] Id.
[134] Steven Bardin, *How to identify all 9 species …*, *supra* note 120; Id.

the presence or absence of a tooth patch on the tongue is not considered reliable to identify largemouth bass.[135]

Florida bass generally have the same characteristics listed above for Northern largemouth bass (a.k.a., Largemouth bass). Some scientists report that Florida bass tend to have smaller scales than pure Northern largemouth bass, so the scale count along the lateral line can be used to "indicate the presence of Florida genetics" because Florida bass may have 69-73 lateral line scales whereas Northern largemouth bass more typically may have 59 to 65.[136]

No matter what your buddy or your local expert says, Florida bass and Northern largemouth bass are virtually impossible to distinguish without advanced genetic testing.[137] In this book, the term "largemouth bass" will include Northern largemouth bass and Florida bass, but not other black bass species.

Lunker Bass Are Nationwide

If you live in the United States, lunker bass likely live near you because largemouth bass are "established in every state in the continental U.S. and Hawaii."[138] So, depending upon how you define a lunker, you can catch one almost anywhere where you can catch largemouth bass. You even have a shot at a giant bass almost no matter where you live in the United States because the state record is over 10 pounds in all but 8 states and is over 7 pounds in every state except Alaska. To help illustrate this point, here is a list of the approximate record largemouth bass by state (these records vary a little by source, so look to your state agency for an accurate up-to-date weight if you catch a potential record!):[139]

---

[135] Steven Bardin, *Fish Biology*, supra note 113.
[136] Id.
[137] Jason Kinner, *Creating trophy fishing opportunities in Kentucky with F1 largemouth bass*, Eastern Outdoors Media, December 16, 2021, https://www.easternoutdoorsmedia.com/creating-trophy-fishing-opportunities-in-kentucky-with-f1-largemouth-bass/; Steven Bardin, *Fish Biology*, supra note 113 (noting, "Largemouth bass, Florida bass and their sub-crosses are extremely difficult to delineate from each other"); Steven Bardin, *How to identify all 9 species …*, supra note 120.
[138] Steven Bardin, *Fish Biology*, supra note 113.
[139] Bass Fishing Facts, *Record holding largemouth bass from all 50 states*, January 2022, available at https://bassfishingfacts.com/record-holding-largemouth-bass-from-all-50-states/.

Alaska	0.5 lbs.	Alabama	16 lbs. 8 oz.
Arizona	16 lbs. 7 oz.	Arkansas	16 lbs. 8 oz.
California	21 lbs. 12 oz.	Colorado	11 lbs. 6 oz.
Connecticut	12 lbs. 14 oz.	Delaware	11 lbs. 1 oz.
Florida	17 lbs. 4 oz.	Georgia	22 lbs. 4 oz.
Hawaii	9 lbs. 9 oz.	Idaho	10 lbs. 15 oz.
Illinois	13 lbs. 1 oz.	Indiana	14 lbs. 12 oz.
Iowa	10 lbs. 12 oz.	Kansas	11 lbs. 13 oz.
Kentucky	14 lbs. 9 oz.	Louisiana	16 lbs.
Maine	11 lbs. 10 oz.	Maryland	11 lbs. 6 oz.
Massachusetts	15 lbs. 8 oz.	Michigan	11 lbs. 15 oz.
Minnesota	8 lbs. 15 oz.	Mississippi	18 lbs. 2 oz.
Missouri	13 lbs. 14 oz.	Montana	9 lbs. 9 oz.
Nebraska	10 lbs. 11 oz.	Nevada	12 lbs.
New Hampshire	10 lbs. 8 oz.	New Jersey	10 lbs. 14 oz.
New Mexico	15 lbs. 13 oz.	New York	11 lbs. 4 oz.
North Carolina	15 lbs. 14 oz.	North Dakota	8 lbs. 8 oz.
Ohio	13 lbs. 2 oz.	Oklahoma	14 lbs. 14 oz.
Oregon	12 lbs. 2 oz.	Pennsylvania	11 lbs. 13 oz.
Rhode Island	10 lbs. 6 oz.	South Carolina	16 lbs. 2 oz.
South Dakota	9 lbs. 5 oz.	Tennessee	15 lbs. 3 oz.
Texas	18 lbs. 3 oz.	Utah	10 lbs. 2 oz.
Vermont	10 lbs. 4 oz.	Virginia	16 lbs. 4 oz.
Washington	12 lbs. 8 oz.	West Virginia	12 lbs. 4 oz.
Wisconsin	11 lbs. 3 oz.	Wyoming	7 lbs. 14 oz.

Although lunker bass live in most states, statistically, your odds of catching a 10-pound bass or a 7-pound bass are much different depending upon where and when you are fishing—as you will see in this book. Largemouth bass growth rates are related to climate, genetics, habitat, sex, and other factors.

Lunkers Prefer Reservoirs

Some fisheries produce bigger bass than others—even when they may outwardly appear similar. Genetics, forage species, forage abundance, climate, latitude, type of fishery, habitat, and water quality are all important factors determining size of bass in a fishery.[140] Florida genetics play a role, and Florida bass have a northern

---

[140] Robert Montgomery, *Big Old Bass*, BASSMASTER, September 28, 2011, available at https://www.bassmaster.com/news/big-old-bass/.

boundary as discussed below. You have better chances of catching a lunker if more lunkers live where you are fishing.

Reservoirs are generally better for lunker bass fishing than smaller bodies of water like ponds or power plant lakes. Several states have top-notch stocking programs to increase Florida bass genetics and to provide forage fish in reservoirs, so this is not surprising. In his 18-year study, Manns found that he and his partners caught more lunker bass from reservoirs than ponds or power plant lakes with ponds being the least productive for lunkers.[141] However, if you are looking for numbers of bass, ponds produced the most catches in the least time, and power plant lakes finished second for numbers.[142]

Bass in rivers and coastal waters generally do not grow as fast or as large as bass in reservoirs.[143] In rivers, flowing water means more difficulties catching prey and more energy expended fighting current.[144] Coastal waters' salinity and diet make bass smaller.[145]

Reservoirs fluctuate in lunker potential. For example, in 2011, Lake Chickamauga in Tennessee was producing many double-digit lunkers and yielded a new state record 15.2-pound giant in 2015.[146] Fisheries biologists working for Tennessee Wildlife Resources Agency helped by improving habitat and introducing Florida bass genetics.[147] Similarly, Lake O.H. Ivie in Texas produced 12 lunkers over 13 pounds in 33 days in February 2021 and has continued to yield giants since then.[148] I have added a few bass to my top 15 in 2023 by fishing at O.H. Ivie, including bass weighing 11.14, 10.05, 9.32, and 8.09 pounds, plus another one that was 25.5 inches and likely over 8 pounds but my scale was not working in the extreme heat. Below is a picture of one O.H. Ivie sunrise I experienced:

---

[141] Ralph Manns, *Moon Magic Largemouth Bass*, IN-FISHERMAN, June 23, 2023, available at https://www.in-fisherman.com/editorial/moon-magic-largemouth-bass/154779.
[142] Id.
[143] Robert Montgomery, *Big Old Bass*, supra note 140.
[144] Id.
[145] Id.
[146] Victor Papaiz and Hal Schramm, *Bucket list bassin': Beating the crowd to the best bass fisheries*, IN-FISHERMAN BASS GUIDE 2022.
[147] Id.
[148] Id.

In contrast, Lake Fork has been relatively stingy with double digit bass in recent years and has produced very few over 13 pounds. In my own experience, my favorite power plant lake has gotten stingier as well; in the past, that power plant lake produced 65 bass over 5 pounds for me in 2021, but only 32 the next year in 2022, and has only produced 1 (an 8.45 pounder) for me over 6 months in 2023. So, part of catching lunkers is finding a fishery where they are available.

Bass need forage of the right size at each stage of their lives to become lunkers.[149] Shad have higher bioenergetic value than bluegill, so a shad diet (especially threadfin shad) improves growth rate.[150] In contrast, "crawfish aren't nearly as nutritious" because "their weight is mostly indigestible shells."[151] Trout are even better than shad.[152] Trout "have high levels of lipids and protein when compared to more traditional prey."[153] Bass eating a primarily trout-based diet grow faster and larger than others because of the high lipid and protein content of trout; "Dottie" was a trout-eater that reached over 25

---

[149] Robert Montgomery, *Big Old Bass*, *supra* note 140.
[150] Id.
[151] Id.
[152] Id.
[153] Id.

pounds in California, for example.[154] Trout are not generally present in southern reservoirs, so lunker bass rely on other prey species. For example, in the 2021 survey, Lake Fork had abundant threadfin shad and moderate availability of gizzard shad and bluegill.[155]

The energy required to catch forage also matters because if it takes more energy, then the bass will not grow as much.[156] Chasing shad in open water requires more energy, which leads to less growth potential.[157] When plants get too abundant, bass have a harder time catching prey, so growth rates can drop as well.[158] However, fewer plants are sometimes associated with less forage, so it is about balance.[159] Off color water can impede visual feeders like bass decreasing the size potential of a fishery.[160]

Habitat can be more important than age in some instances, even though big bass are usually old. Exceptional habitat can lead to exceptional growth rates. For example, scientists found that one 10-pound largemouth bass was only 4 years old.[161] In cooler northern climates, largemouth bass tend to live longer (but grow smaller than southern bass) averaging 15 years with a maximum of 23-24 years compared to warmer southern climates where the average is closer to 10 years and a maximum of 16 years.[162] In Montana a 3.5 pound bass was found to be 19 years old based on a tag it carried for 14 years.[163] So, "a 4 pound bass in Minnesota or Montana might not be impressive in terms of weight, but it could be a real trophy if age is given equal consideration."[164] Otolith rings (a.k.a., ear bones) were used to determine that the longest living largemouth bass was caught in 1992 at the age of 23 to 24 years at Mariaville Lake in New York; it weighed 6.78 pounds.[165] In the Texas ShareLunker program, the

---

[154] Robert Montgomery, *Big Old Bass*, *supra* note 140.
[155] Jacob Norman, *supra* note 101.
[156] Robert Montgomery, *Big Old Bass*, *supra* note 140.
[157] Id.
[158] Id.
[159] Id.
[160] Id.
[161] Robert Montgomery, *Big Old Bass*, *supra* note 140.
[162] Id.
[163] Id.
[164] Id.
[165] Steven Bardin, *Fish Biology*, *supra* note 113; Robert Montgomery, *Big Old Bass*, *supra* note 140.

oldest fish of 500 tested by 2011 was a 12-year-old six-pound male.[166] However, the biggest bass are usually older females, as will be discussed shortly.

Fisheries biologists can sometimes predict when a fishery is about to become a haven for lunker bass. According to biologists, the best opportunity to find a reservoir with surging lunker bass populations tends to be in "new or recently renovated reservoirs," reservoirs with "rising water levels" to produce "strong year-classes in fluctuating reservoirs," reservoirs with good habitat, and reservoirs with "well-planned Florida bass stocking efforts."[167] Specifically, "look for reservoirs where water levels are rising after a protracted low-water period" because they function basically like a new or recently renovated reservoir and likely have some strong class year bass up and coming.[168] Reservoirs with "stable or expanding—but not excessive—aquatic vegetation" are best with biologists recommending avoiding "lakes where vegetation has been greatly reduced."[169]

Online research can be used to help figure out places to go lunker bass fishing including state agency information, tournament results, and fishing publications. First, state agencies can be a good source of information. Florida's Trophy Catch program (www.trophycatchflorida.com) provides lunker data on date and place where lunker bass are being caught in Florida. Texas Parks and Wildlife Department's ShareLunker database is public and is used for several studies in this book.[170] The TPWD ShareLunker website also gives you current lunker counts from the top fisheries in the state in the "Hot Lakes" section, so it is easy to see which lakes are producing the most lunkers at any time.[171]

Second, tournament results can be helpful in your search for lunker bass. Tournament results in many states are also often available online and on social media sites. I follow several local bass

---

[166] Robert Montgomery, *Big Old Bass*, *supra* note 140.
[167] Victor Papaiz and Hal Schramm, *supra* note 146.
[168] Id.
[169] Id.
[170] TEXAS PARKS AND WILDLIFE DEPARTMENT, *Texas ShareLunker Archives*, available at https://texassharelunker.com/archives/.
[171] TEXAS PARKS AND WILDLIFE DEPARTMENT, Toyota ShareLunker Program Texas Parks and Wildlife, available at https://texassharelunker.com.

clubs in Arkansas and can check tournament weights to see if nearby fisheries are perking up.

Finally, fishing publications often produce useful reports. In-Fisherman magazine in 2022 compiled data from major bass tournaments to see which lakes produce the "best catches and the biggest fish."[172] They used the "complete catch records from 2011 to 2021 for B.A.S.S., FLW, and MLF professional-level events" including 173 tournaments on 31 different fisheries.[173] They "calculated the average size of fish caught . . . and the biggest fish caught during the entire tournament."[174]

Here is the top ten ranking for average largemouth bass size according to In-Fisherman in 2022 (eliminating tournaments where smallmouth bass were weighed in): (1) Lake Fork, TX (3.24 lbs.), (2) Guntersville, AL (3.11 lbs.), (3) Kentucky Lake, TN (2.91 lbs.), (4) Grand Lake O' the Cherokees, OK (2.78 lbs.), (5) Toledo Bend (2.69 lbs.), (6) Eufaula, AL (2.69 lbs.), (7) Chickamauga, TN (2.62 lbs.), (8) St. Johns River, FL (2.54 lbs.), (9) Okeechobee, FL (2.54 lbs.), and (10) Potomac River, MD (2.51 lbs.).[175]

Here is the top ten ranking for the biggest largemouth bass caught in the tournaments evaluated according to In-Fisherman in 2022: (1) Lake Fork, TX (10.38 lbs.), (2) St. Johns River, FL (10.30 lbs.), (3) Toledo Bend, LA (9.46 lbs.), (4) Okeechobee, FL (9.28 lbs.), (5) Sam Rayburn, TX (9.28 lbs.), (6) Chickamauga, TN (9.19 lbs.), (7) Pickwick, AL (9.13 lbs.), (8) Harris Chain, FL (8.91 lbs.), (9) Kentucky Lake, TN (7.80 lbs.), and (10) Eufaula, AL (7.78 lbs.).[176]

So, if you are looking for a good place to go to catch that bass of a lifetime over 8 to 10 pounds, then those are some excellent candidates for lunker bass fishing trips!

Lunkers and the 30th Parallel

Climate and water temperature help determine the size of bass in a fishery. Largemouth bass "grow continuously throughout their lives" with good food and habitat.[177] Adult largemouth bass grow

---

[172] Victor Papaiz and Hal Schramm, *supra* note 146.
[173] Id.
[174] Id.
[175] Id.
[176] Id.
[177] Steven Bardin, *Fish Biology*, *supra* note 113.

optimally at water temperatures from 75-86°F (24-30°C), and juveniles grow better on the upper end of this range from approximately 80-86°F (27-30°C).[178] When the water temperature is below or above those temperatures, their growth rate diminishes.[179] In reservoirs in the southern United States, the water temperature is in these optimum ranges for a greater portion of the year, so bass generally grow bigger the farther south in the U.S. that you go.[180] In bodies of water that do not reach optimal temperature ranges or only remain in the optimal temperature ranges for short periods of time, the bass will be smaller and less healthy.[181] In other words, bass have a longer growing season in the southern U.S. than the northern U.S., so they are more likely to reach lunker sizes.

The length of the growing season for largemouth bass "determines maximum possible size."[182] In the United States east of the Rockies, the biggest bass tend to live between the 25th and 35th latitudinal parallel north because the growing season for largemouth bass is ideal in this range.[183] For reference, the 35th parallel runs through Oklahoma, Arkansas, Tennessee, and North Carolina and represents the northern boundary of this range. The 25th parallel runs through Key Largo, Florida, Durango, Mexico, and Hawaii and marks the southern boundary of this range. The biggest bass tend to be caught nearer the 30th parallel with state records generally decreasing farther away from the 30th parallel.[184] The world record bass from Georgia was caught at Lake Montgomery, which is between the 31st

---

[178] Tyler Peat et al., *Comparative thermal biology and depth distribution of largemouth bass and northern pike in an urban harbour of the Laurentian Great Lakes*, CANADIAN J. ZOOLOGY 94: 767–776 (2016); Fernando Diaz, et al., *Temperature preference and oxygen consumption of the largemouth bass acclimated to different temperatures*, AQUACULTURE RESEARCH 38 (13): 1387-1394 (2007); Texas State University, San Marcos, Department of Biology, *Fishes of Texas: Micropterus salmoides*, available at http://txstate.fishesoftexas.org/micropterus%20salmoides.htm.

[179] Wes Neal, *supra* note 124 (noting that fish have optimum temperatures for growth); Tyler Peat, *supra* note 178.

[180] Steven Bardin, *Fish Biology*, *supra* note 113; Wes Neal, *supra* note 124.

[181] Tyler Peat, *supra* note 178.

[182] Mississippi State University Extension, *Trophy Bass Management Basics*, available at http://extension.msstate.edu/content/trophy-bass-management-basics.

[183] Id.

[184] Pond Boss Magazine, *Is it Too Hot for Bass?*, available at https://www.pondboss.com/news/inside-pond-boss/is-it-too-hot-for-bass.

and 32nd parallels. Lake Fork is between the 32nd and 33rd parallels and O.H. Ivie Reservoir is between the 31st and 32nd parallel. Lake Okeechobee is around the 27th parallel.[185] Falcon International Reservoir is near the 27th parallel. California has a unique climate associated with ocean-related factors, so fisheries in California may not follow this rule; same with Japan.[186]

The bass tend to get bigger as you travel from northern to southern states along a longitudinal line. To illustrate this point, look at the map below and notice that the size of the state record fish in each state increases as you go from north to south along a longitudinal line going from North Dakota to Texas. Progressing from north to south, the records go from 8.50 lbs. (North Dakota) to its southern neighbor at 9.19 lbs. in South Dakota to the next southern neighbor of Nebraska with 10.69 lbs. to the next state south of Kansas with 11.08 lbs. to the next state of Oklahoma with 14.86 lbs. and finally to Texas with 18.18 lbs. Note that the record jumps by seven pounds from Kansas to Texas, and factors other than climate (like genetics discussed below) factor into these larger jumps. This trend generally holds across the United States, with a few exceptions (e.g., Louisiana's record is smaller than Arkansas's, Florida's record is smaller than Georgia's, Indiana and Massachusetts' records are bigger than other states in their latitude).

---

[185] Id.
[186] Id.

Lunker Genetics

Florida bass genes increase the size of largemouth bass. Largemouth bass have 23 chromosomes, and the genes on those chromosomes determine growth characteristics with Florida bass having different genes than Northern largemouth bass.[187] Florida bass have "heritable characteristics that allow them to achieve unusually large size" and grow larger than Northern largemouth bass.[188] Both "grow most rapidly in length for the first two years of life" and then fill out with age.[189] Florida bass can reach 14 inches in length in 2 years, are often 3 pounds after three years, and gain up to one pound per year thereafter.[190] Northern largemouth bass have a similar growth rate for the first 3 years, but grow much slower after 3 years of age.[191] Pure Northern largemouth bass rarely reach 10 pounds, whereas Florida bass can grow to over 20 pounds.[192] Therefore, most of the biggest bass have significant Florida bass genetics.[193] Because Florida bass grow faster and larger than Northern largemouth bass, their genetics have been introduced farther north than their native range, and Florida genetics are now present over much of the southern United States.[194]

Climate and water temperature help determine the distribution of Florida genetics because Florida bass are much less tolerant of cold water than Northern largemouth bass with Florida bass dying at temperatures that Northern largemouth bass easily tolerate.[195] Florida bass have a "winter temperature limitation" that limits their size and life expectancy and results in a northern boundary for their

---

[187] Id.
[188] Larry Hodge, *ShareLunker Science: Bass DNA is slowly revealing its secrets through TPWD research*, TEXAS PARKS & WILDLIFE MAGAZINE, March 2013, available at https://tpwmagazine.com/archive/2013/mar/scout2_sharelunker/.
[189] Maureen Mecozzi, Wisconsin Department of Natural Resources, Bureau of Fisheries Management, *Largemouth Bass*, August 2008, available at https://dnr.wisconsin.gov/sites/default/files/topic/Fishing/Species_lmbass.pdf.
[190] Jason Kinner, *supra* note 137.
[191] Id.
[192] Id.
[193] Wes Neal, *supra* note 124.
[194] Dan Wang, *supra* note 122.
[195] Wes Neal, *supra* note 124.

distribution.[196] Therefore, biologists don't generally stock pure Florida bass in Wisconsin, for example, where they would just die under the winter ice.[197]

The boundary for Florida bass is farther north than biologists have previously believed based on genetic research conducted by Major League Fishing in 2023.[198] Two fish from Lake of the Ozarks in Missouri had 97.82% and 85% Florida genetics.[199] These fish appear to provide a new northern latitude boundary for Florida bass as they were caught at the farthest northern latitude for documented Florida bass catches.[200]

Florida bass and Northern largemouth bass can interbreed. A first generation cross between a pure Florida and a pure Northern is called a "F1" bass.[201] F1s have 50% Florida genes and 50% Northern genes. Researchers call F1s "intergrades" or "hybrids" (depending upon currently evolving understanding of species versus sub-species issues).[202]

Genetic instructions are "stored on chromosomes, with each trait controlled by a specific gene or group of genes on the chromosome."[203] Different versions of each gene are often present on each chromosome, and these are called "alleles"—so you may hear biologists talk about Florida alleles, which is just a fancy way of talking about their genes.[204] A F1 hybrid or intergrade fish has one copy of each chromosome from each species, and one allele from

---

[196] Robert Montgomery, *Biologists refine the native range of Florida bass*, BASSMASTER, December 17, 2021, available at https://www.bassmaster.com/conservation-news/news/biologists-refine-the-native-range-of-florida-bass.
[197] Wes Neal, *supra* note 124.
[198] Steven Bardin, *Two successful years of MLF lunker DNA initiative data has been analyzed*, MAJOR LEAGUE FISHING, February 16, 2023, available at https://majorleaguefishing.com/conservation/two-successful-years-of-mlf-lunker-dna-initiative-data-has-been-analyzed/.
[199] Id.
[200] Id.
[201] Scott Smith, VIRGINIA DEPARTMENT OF WILDLIFE RESOURCES, *DWRs F1 largemouth bass stocking program FAQ*, available at https://dwr.virginia.gov/blog/dwrs-f1-largemouth-bass-stocking-program-faq/.
[202] Id.
[203] Wes Neal, *supra* note 124.
[204] Id.

each species for each gene or group of genes associated with a specific trait.[205]

When F1s interbreed, the genetics get more complicated with each generation (termed Fx generations). Fx generations have both Florida and Northern ancestry but are "not the direct offspring of pure parents."[206] Geneticists describe them based upon the percentage of genes present from each species. For example, according to the 2021 TPWD report, the percentage of Florida bass alleles at Lake Fork ranged from 48 to 57% since 2006.[207]

The world record 22 pound 4 ounce largemouth bass caught in Georgia in 1932 by George Perry was originally believed to be a Northern largemouth bass or possibly a Fx cross because Florida bass were thought to be confined to Florida, and this bass was caught at Lake Montgomery, an oxbow lake of the Ocmulgee River in Georgia.[208] However, researchers at Auburn university now believe that Perry's bass was "most likely a Florida bass" after finding that the natural range of the Florida bass is much more extensive than originally believed and includes Georgia, where Perry caught the record bass.[209] In this recent study, Florida bass were found to be dominant in coastal rivers like Ocmulgee, with Floridas making up "essentially 100%" of the bass in a similar river in Georgia.[210] These Auburn researchers found Floridas extending all the way into North Carolina coastal regions and also likely into Virginia.[211] Yale researchers have similar data that supports the Auburn researchers' claims.[212]

Fisheries biologists still have much to learn. Biologists are not sure whether the fishery itself or the genetic makeup of the bass population is more important to bass size in some instances. It is not always clear why bigger bass thrive in one fishery but not in another. For example, Florida genes are common in Lake Guntersville, but

---

[205] Scott Smith, *supra* note 201.
[206] Id.
[207] Jacob Norman, *supra* note 101.
[208] Robert Montgomery, *Biologists refine the native range of Florida bass*, *supra* note 196.
[209] Id.
[210] Id.
[211] Id.
[212] Id.

"almost nonexistent downstream in Wheeler Lake" in spite of similar stocking history and the fact that these two lakes are connected.[213]

Sometimes predominantly Northern genetics produce surprising results. In 2022, MLF tested the genetics on 45 lunker bass bigger than seven pounds from Lake Fork caught during MLF events by collecting a DNA sample on the fish before release.[214] These lunker Lake Fork bass averaged 57.42% Florida genetics with a range of 28.33 to 88.1%—so Florida genetics were clearly important.[215] However, seven of those bass had less than 50% Florida genetics; in other words, they were more Northern largemouth bass than Florida bass.[216] One 9 pound 4 ounce bass was only 28.33% Florida bass.[217] The biologists considered the data "eye-opening to the fact that Florida genetics may have an important role in advanced size growth, but that some fisheries are predisposed to grow fish to trophy size naturally."[218] The researchers were seeking more data on double digit fish to try to determine whether the fishery itself or the Florida genetics is more important for bass reaching trophy size.[219]

The results in the same MLF study at Guntersville raised similar questions. Nine Guntersville samples were collected and averaged 56.38% Florida genetics ranging from 26.09 to 75%.[220] Three of the nine were less than 50% Florida.[221] Of the two largest fish (an 8-12 and an 8-7), one was 75% and the other was only 26.09%.[222] Also, the biggest bass tested at Rayburn in 2022 by MLF was 11 lbs. 15 oz. and was more Northern than Florida with only 48% Florida genetics.[223] However, 90% (18/20) of the Rayburn bass over 7 pounds collected over two years in the MLF study were over 50% Florida genetics—so Florida genetics are clearly important.[224]

---

[213] Robert Montgomery, *Biologists refine the native range of Florida bass*, supra note 196.
[214] Steven Bardin, *Two successful years*, supra note 198.
[215] Id.
[216] Id.
[217] Id.
[218] Id.
[219] Steven Bardin, *Two successful years*, supra note 198.
[220] Id.
[221] Id.
[222] Id.
[223] Id.
[224] Steven Bardin, *Two successful years*, supra note 198.

In most southern states, "present day management practices . . . promote stocking of Florida bass . . . to promote increased growth rate or maximum sizes."[225] Instead of pure Floridas, many states stock F1 hybrids.[226] Generally it is not fruitful to grow bigger bass to stock pure Floridas in lakes that already have an intergrade population.[227] On the other hand, "if climate and habitat are conducive, putting Floridas into a lake inhabited solely by pure Northern largemouth can result in hybrid vigor from crossing of the two subspecies and bigger bass."[228] Hybridization between Floridas and Northerns can transfer good traits of both species in some climates and also improve genetic variation of offspring, which is good.[229]

F1 hybrids sometimes exhibit "hybrid vigor," which means they "tend to exhibit the benefits of both species getting the best genes from both, which can lead to good growth, cold tolerance, and relative ease of catch."[230] This has happened in Texas, Tennessee, Oklahoma, and California.[231] F1s are more aggressive and can potentially grow to larger size than native Floridas in some environments.[232] They may even grow up to three pounds per year in some settings.[233]

Lake Chickamauga is a good example of hybrid vigor. In 2000, Lake Chickamauga was chosen by Tennessee Wildlife Resources Association (TWRA) to stock Florida largemouth bass because it had adequate forage and habitat.[234] Five Florida strain fingerlings per acre were stocked in sizes similar to the fingerlings that naturally spawned in the lake.[235] After five years, genetic testing showed that Florida strain genetics was responsible for only 5% of the

---

[225] Daemin Kim, *supra* note 106.
[226] Robert Montgomery, *Biologists refine the native range of Florida bass*, *supra* note 196.
[227] Id.
[228] Id.
[229] Jinxing Du, *supra* note 122.
[230] Wes Neal, *supra* note 124.
[231] Robert Montgomery, *Biologists refine the native range of Florida bass*, *supra* note 196.
[232] Jason Kinner, *supra* note 137.
[233] Id.
[234] Id.
[235] Id.

lake's bass population.[236] In 2005, TWRA made adjustments and only stocked targeted locations with plenty of forage and habitat with larger fingerlings of 2 to 3 inches.[237] Five years later, the results were better with Florida genes accounting for 33% of the bass in Lake Chickamauga in 2010.[238] By 2011, six years after the 2005 stocking, Chickamauga began showing tournament bags of five fish weighing over 30 pounds (i.e., averaging 6 lbs. each), and in 2012, a 45 lb. bag (i.e., averaging 9 lbs. each) was weighed in.[239]

TWRA studied 48 bass from Chickamauga over 8 lbs. and found that all 48 had some degree of Florida genetics and 63% of these bass were F1 largemouth (i.e., a cross between the stocked Floridas and the native Northerns).[240] In 2015, Lake Chickamauga produced a new state record of 15.2 pounds breaking the old record that had stood for 50 years.[241] Lake Chickamauga is now a premier bass fishing destination and a regular stop on the major professional tournament trails.[242]

Lunker Sex

Lunkers are almost always females. Male and female bass have different growth potential with females growing significantly larger and faster than males. Females are typically about an inch longer (25 mm) than males by their fifth year.[243] Adult females "tend to grow disproportionately fatter and less streamlined" especially once they get over 5 pounds.[244] Males are rarely over 5 pounds.[245]

---

[236] Id.
[237] Jason Kinner, *supra* note 137.
[238] Id.
[239] Id.
[240] Id.
[241] Id.
[242] Jason Kinner, *supra* note 137.
[243] Texas State University, San Marcos, *supra* note 178.
[244] Ralph Manns, *Life of bass: Size factors*, IN-FISHERMAN, March 28, 2019, available at https://www.in-fisherman.com/editorial/life-of-bass-size-factors/358997.
[245] James Davis and Joe Lock, *Largemouth bass biology and life history*, Southern Regional Aquacultural Center SRAC Publication No. 200, August 1997.

Females may exceed 20 pounds.[246] In fact, *95% of bass 6 pounds or bigger are female.*[247]

Female bass typically live longer than males by at least 3 to 5 years.[248] Age helps determine size of bass, and bass usually get bigger the longer they live.[249] To reach 13 pounds, it takes an average of 11 years for a Florida largemouth bass.[250] Bass growth slows as they get older but does not stop.[251] Largemouth bass live in the wild around 10-15 years on average depending upon habitat and climate.[252] In one study of 822 double digit lunkers preserved by a taxidermist in Florida, the mean age was 9.7 years, ranging from 4 years to 16.5 years.[253]

Some researchers report that the lifestyle of male largemouth bass leads to higher mortality and lower body weight due to higher energy expenditures around the spawn.[254] Males do not eat much around the spawn and their duties during the spawn are extremely demanding from an energy standpoint resulting in poor body condition with some dying.[255] Female bass also have foraging advantages during springtime. Larger size means female bass can ingest larger meals and more diverse forage. In springtime, this is particularly important because bigger shad are more abundant due to a size-differential mortality over winter when smaller shad are more

---

[246] Id.
[247] Ken Smith Fishing YouTube Channel, *Toledo Bend Telemetry Tracking Study Update Todd Driscoll TP&W Biologist Feb 2022 Part 2*, available at https://www.youtube.com/watch?v=vBZBhEmkbAU&list=PLLzhji805wVzkLnAA97I8VmdZpR8arB_Q&index=2.
[248] James Davis and Joe Lock, *supra* note 245; Texas State University, San Marcos, *supra* note 178; Maureen Mecozzi, *supra* note 189.
[249] Wes Neal, *supra* note 124.
[250] Larry Hodge, *ShareLunker Science: Bass DNA*, *supra* note 188.
[251] Robert Montgomery, *Big Old Bass*, *supra* note 140.
[252] Emily Steed, Animal Diversity Web, *Micropterus salmoides: American black bass*, U. Michigan Museum of Zoology, available at https://animaldiversity.org/accounts/Micropterus_salmoides/; Steven Bardin, *Fish Biology*, *supra* note 113; Maureen Mecozzi, *supra* note 189.
[253] Robert Montgomery, *Big Old Bass*, *supra* note 140.
[254] K.C. Hanson, et al., *Intersexual variation in the seasonal behaviour and depth distribution of a freshwater temperate fish, the largemouth bass*, CANADIAN J. ZOOLOGY 86: 801-811 (2008), available at http://fishlab.nres.illinois.edu/Reprints/Hanson%20et%20al%20CJZ%202008.pdf.
[255] Id.

likely to die, which can give larger female bass access to a better and more energy-filled diet during spring.[256]

So, pay particular attention to the behavior of female bass as you read this book. Bass behave differently based on sex year-round.[257] Sex-specific differences in behavior are most apparent during the spawning period (including immediately before, during, and after each fish spawns—see chapter 4 on The Spawn), which is also when the biggest bass are usually caught.[258] In addition to spawning differences, big female bass behave differently from smaller male bass "relative to feeding, predator avoidance, aggression, migratory behavior and swimming activity."[259] Bass bigger than 5 pounds "accelerate slightly more slowly, tend to cruise more slowly, and use more energy due to bulk and greater inertia."[260] However, lunker bass can accelerate short distances faster than smaller bass. Bass swim in spurts about 2.5 times their body length per second, which is 2 mph for a small bass and 12 mph for a big bass.[261]

Reactive Thinkers

Big bass are smart. Giant bass follow my glide baits to the boat only to slowly disappear into the abyss as their evil laugh cackles through my mind while I watch helplessly as they sink out of sight chuckling at my poor attempt to trick them. However, they aren't *that* smart. After all, I've never seen a largemouth bass trained to jump in the air and do flips through hoops like orcas or dolphins at SeaWorld. If bass were super geniuses, I probably wouldn't be writing this book because they would be almost impossible to catch.

Scientists say that largemouth bass have high I.Q's, especially regarding visual perception and the ability to discern and make

---

[256] S. Marshall Adams, et al., *Energy partitioning in largemouth bass under conditions of seasonally fluctuating prey availability*, TRANSACTIONS OF THE AMERICAN FISHERIES SOCIETY 111(5): 549-558, September 1982, available at https://afspubs.onlinelibrary.wiley.com/doi/10.1577/1548-8659%281982%29111%3C549%3AEPILBU%3E2.0.CO%3B2.
[257] K.C. Hanson, et al., *Intersexual variation, supra* note 254.
[258] Id.
[259] Id.
[260] Ralph Manns, *Life of bass: Size factors, supra* note 244.
[261] James Davis and Joe Lock, *supra* note 245.

judgements.[262] Researchers describe largemouth bass as cautious predators that only need to strike an artificial lure once to learn it is not edible.[263]

Bass also learn about anglers and "learn to avoid noises, waves, and vibrations created by fishing boats, trolling motors, electronics, water-pumps, lure splashes, and even the sights and sounds associated with frequently used lures and lines."[264] Catch-and-release practices give bass opportunities to learn from mistakes by gaining experience.[265] For example, according to a TPWD biologist, an outboard motor idling in a figure-of-eight pattern over bass causes them to move 42% of the time overall, 25% of the time in water 10 feet deep and 20% of the time in water 20 feet deep.[266] And the biggest bass may spook first.[267] The biggest bass have had more time to learn—which makes it likely they are the first to react. Even if they don't move immediately after the boat idles over them, the fish may now be on alert. After idling over them, the fish that did not move initially would then move 31% of the time when an angler casted towards them five times.[268] *So, your odds of catching the biggest bass in a group are likely higher if you approach them without idling over them with an outboard motor.*

Fish have a well-documented capacity for learning to avoid predators and identifying good feeding areas/situations.[269] Fish also have a documented ability to learn to avoid recreational fishing lures and other fishing gear like nets.[270] The vulnerability of individual fish varies. The individual variabilities in other fish have been linked to

---

[262] Maureen Mecozzi, *supra* note 189.
[263] Id.
[264] Ralph Manns, *Life of bass: Size factors*, *supra* note 244.
[265] Id.
[266] Ken Smith Fishing YouTube Channel, *Toledo Bend Telemetry Tracking Study Update Todd Driscoll TP&W Biologist Feb 2022 Part 5*, available at https://www.youtube.com/watch?v=f1sL9FZnS4g&list=PLLzhji8O5wVzkLnAA97I8VmdZpR8arB_Q&index=5.
[267] Id.
[268] Id.
[269] Michael Louison, et al., *Quick learning, quick capture: largemouth bass that rapidly learn an association task are more likely to be captured by recreational anglers*, BEHAVIORAL ECOLOGY AND SOCIOBIOLOGY 73, Article 23 (2019), available at https://link.springer.com/article/10.1007/s00265-019-2634-7.
[270] Id.

things like differing genetic metabolic requirements, hormone levels, and thinking/coping style.[271]

Lunker bass may be "smart," but not in the way that you would think. Individual largemouth bass have their own personalities, coping styles and ways of thinking, which lead them to approach tasks in different ways.[272] Some bass are bold thinkers and quickly solve problems, but usually these bass are risk-takers and more prone to mistakes.[273] These bold problem-solvers might be viewed as the smarter fish in some circumstances (i.e., they are more likely to be trainable), but in the wild, these may not be the fish that become lunkers because their mistakes may limit their lifespan.

In one study, sixty largemouth bass[274] were trained to avoid a net when a light came on to warn them.[275] The overhead light would come on and the net would immediately chase the bass after a short delay.[276] A small opening into a safe area was available, and some of the bass quickly learned to get through that small opening as soon as the light came on.[277] These quick learners were called "proactive" by the researchers because they tended to respond to threats with a quick "fight or flight" response.[278]

Other bass took longer to respond to the light and were described as "reactive" by researchers because they tended to freeze or remain still in threatening situations.[279] The researchers found that bass with slower reactive strategies "may take longer to initially learn a task, but are superior at retaining that information and adapting to new information and environmental cues."[280] Faster proactive thinkers are more likely to make mistakes.[281] On average it took the bass around 16 times of the light coming on before they beat the net the first time by going through the opening; but once they figured it out once, it only took 4 more trials before they no longer failed to

---

[271] Id.
[272] Id.
[273] Id.
[274] Ranging in size from 16 to 21 cm (i.e., less than 8 inches), which limits application to lunker sized bass.
[275] Michael Louison, et al., *Quick learning, quick capture, supra* note 269.
[276] Id.
[277] Id.
[278] Id.
[279] Id.
[280] Michael Louison, et al., *Quick learning, quick capture, supra* note 269
[281] Id.

respond.[282] It is possible that proactive thinkers may make more mistakes early and not reach lunker size, whereas more cautious reactive fish are the ones that are more likely to become lunkers—but more study of lunker behavior is needed to verify this statement.

The study continued with researchers putting the fish in "naturalistic" research ponds and fishing for them using plastic worms and spinnerbaits.[283] Twenty-one of the sixty fish were caught (four times more were caught on plastic worms than spinnerbaits, but comparison of baits was not the purpose of this study).[284]

Guess which bass were more likely to be caught: the proactive thinkers or the reactive thinkers? The bass that were caught were twice as good at avoiding the net when the light came on; in other words, the more catchable bass were proactive thinkers, i.e., the bass that learned to avoid the net the fastest in the tank.[285] The bass that freeze (i.e., those deemed "reactive" thinkers by researchers) may be slower to escape the net, but they also are less likely to strike an artificial lure.[286] Striking a fishing lure may be viewed as a major mistake, which proactive fish are more likely to make.[287] So, the fast, higher risk method of processing information used by some bass may make them more vulnerable to being caught by anglers because they are more prone to make mistakes.[288] What's more, researchers have found that this way of thinking is heritable.[289]

In a study at the University of Illinois that started in 1975 and lasted over 20 years, researchers "found that vulnerability to being caught by anglers is a heritable trait in largemouth bass."[290] The study started at an experimental study lake where the fishing was tightly controlled and monitored with anglers making reservations and measuring and tagging every fish that was caught over the first four

---

[282] Id.
[283] Id.
[284] Id.
[285] Michael Louison, et al., *Quick learning, quick capture*, *supra* note 269.
[286] Id.
[287] Id.
[288] Id.
[289] Id.
[290] Science Daily, *Born to be caught: Largemouth bass vulnerability to beign caught by anglers is a heritable trait*, Science News, April 15, 2009, https://www.sciencedaily.com/releases/2009/04/090414153532.htm.

years of the study.[291] The fish were released back into the lake after being tagged.[292]

Over four years, thousands of catches were recorded; one fish was caught 16 times in one year and another was caught 3 times in two days.[293] After four years, the lake was drained and over 1700 bass were carefully collected alive.[294] Two hundred of those fish (all adults older than four years of age) had never been caught, despite being in the lake throughout the study. These 200 bass were called "Low Vulnerability" (LV) fish because they had never been caught during the entire four years, so they were not very vulnerable to being caught by anglers.[295] Males and females from the Low Vulnerability group were intermingled and bred in university research ponds to produce Low Vulnerability (LV) offspring.[296] Fish that had been caught four or more times were designated as "High Vulnerability (HV)" and similarly spawned with other HV fish in different university research ponds.[297] The LV and HV offspring were then tagged for future identification and raised in a pond together until they were big enough to be fished.[298]

Eventually, the LV and HV bass were released with fin-clips for identification into a lake for controlled fishing similar to the controlled experimental lake described above.[299] The researchers found that the vulnerability to being caught was passed along to offspring because the HV offspring were more likely to be caught than the LV offspring.[300] The experiment continued for 20 years and several generations of offspring with the selection process being repeated.[301] In fact, with each generation, the "difference between lines in angling vulnerability grew even larger."[302] This was mainly

---

[291] Id.
[292] Id.
[293] Id.
[294] Id.
[295] Science Daily, *supra* note 290.
[296] Id.
[297] Id.
[298] Id.
[299] Id.; Michael Louison, et al., *Hormonal responsiveness to stress is negatively associated with vulnerability to angling capture in fish*, J. OF EXPERIMENTAL BIOLOGY 220: 2529-2535 (2017).
[300] Science Daily, *supra* note 290.
[301] Id.
[302] Id.

because the LV fish became less and less vulnerable to angling over the generations.[303] The HV lines had a small increase in vulnerability.[304] The researchers believed this same phenomenon happens in the wild and makes bass harder to catch over time through natural selection.[305]

However, in a study of angler efficiency in catching bass at seven Illinois reservoirs from 2005 to 2015, researchers found that "angler efficiency has generally improved through time."[306] Specifically, scientists found "a greater than threefold increase in the efficiency of anglers to exploit a static population of largemouth bass" over the ten years from 2005 to 2015.[307] They attributed these improvements to "gear and technological advances."[308] The researchers expect anglers to continue to improve due to "improvements in sonar systems, satellite communications, global positioning systems, fishing gears and information-sharing technologies" which may continue to "contribute to greater catch rates per unit effort relative to fish stock abundance by increasing anglers' capacity to search, find, and exploit populations effectively."[309]

Bass's response to *stress hormones (like cortisol)* may affect their way of thinking in the two vulnerability groups above according to another study.[310] Researchers found that largemouth bass that are more vulnerable to angling have lower increases in plasma cortisol levels when stressed than bass that are harder to catch.[311] Post-stress cortisol was 48% higher in uncaptured fish.[312] Perhaps the lower increases in stress hormones makes the vulnerable bass bolder and more likely to take risks than less vulnerable bass that experience

---

[303] Id.
[304] Id.
[305] Science Daily, *supra* note 290.
[306] Thomas Detmer, *Fishing efficiency of competitive largemouth bass tournament anglers has increased since early 21st century*, FISHERIES MANAGEMENT AND ECOLOGY 27(5), July 2020, available at https://www.researchgate.net/publication/343233253_Fishing_efficiency_of_competitive_largemouth_bass_tournament_anglers_has_increased_since_early_21st_century.
[307] Id.
[308] Id.
[309] Id.
[310] Michael Louison, et al., *Hormonal responsiveness to stress*, *supra* note 299.
[311] Id.
[312] Id.

higher increases in their stress hormones with stressors making them more cautious and less likely to be risk takers.[313] The high vulnerability bass (lower stress response) have also been found to find "greater aggression and angling vulnerability while nesting" and "lower rates of prey rejection."[314]

In many animal behavior studies, "high stress responsiveness, as defined by relatively large rises in cortisol following a stressor," has been associated with the reactive type personality described above.[315] Scientists have found this type of cortisol response to be associated with a "shyer and less aggressive" behavioral personality among animals; these personality types also tend to be more flexible and have a higher learning capacity when dealing with changes in their environment.[316] Bass with this reactive personality type/higher stress hormone responses also tend to freeze or not respond aggressively when a fishing lure is nearby which makes them less vulnerable to being caught by anglers.[317] [Interestingly, during the fishing trials, the bass were more likely to be caught on a plastic worm (62% of catches) than a spinnerbait (30%) or night crawler (8%), but again, bait comparisons was not the purpose of this study.[318]]

Researchers also looked at *metabolic rates* to see if bass with higher metabolic rates (i.e., needing more food input) were more vulnerable to angling.[319] The scientists were surprised to find that higher metabolic rates in individual bass did *not* increase angler vulnerability.[320] In another study, researchers broke down the steps to a successful angling capture into "activity rates, encountering a lure, lure inspection, lure-striking, and ingestion."[321] In this study of "activity behavior, stress (cortisol) responsiveness, and food availability," the researchers found that "food deprivation decreased

---

[313] Id.
[314] Id.
[315] Michael Louison, et al., *Hormonal responsiveness to stress*, supra note 299.
[316] Id.
[317] Id.
[318] Id.
[319] Id.
[320] Michael Louison, et al., *Hormonal responsiveness to stress*, supra note 299.
[321] Toniann Keiling and Cory Suzki, *Food deprived largemouth bass are inactive and stressed, but do not show changes in lure inspections*, COMPARATIVE BIOCHEMISTRY AND PHYSIOLOGY, PART A 238: 110556 (2019).

activity rates and increased baseline cortisol concentrations of largemouth bass."[322] They also found that "fish with low baseline cortisol concentrations" (i.e., the proactive fish) "were more likely to inspect lures in both the fed and food deprived" groups.[323] These researchers found "no relationships . . . between activity, stress responsiveness, and food availability to determine lure inspections."[324] Thus, in most bass fisheries, *whether or not a bass inspects your lure will likely have more to do with its personality type than whether or not it is hungry.*

Some guides say that "really big fish are less aggressive by nature, or more wary, or a combination of the two."[325] It is possible that *lunker bass become lunkers because they have the reactive personality type and are less prone to mistakes that lead to their capture or early demise to another predator.* If so, then *lunkers may tend to freeze when uncertain and be less likely to respond aggressively toward the sudden appearance of a lure.*

Based upon my own observations and the lessons of several of my guide professors, I think *slow moving, soft plastic baits and jigs are likely to be best for lunker bass.* In a study of ShareLunkers in 2004, soft plastics and jigs were the lures most often used for catching these big fish with soft plastics accounting for 45% and jigs 23% of the ShareLunkers studied.[326] Both of these baits are typically fished as slow movers that would be less likely to cause a big bass to freeze. Faster moving baits accounted for much lower percentages of ShareLunkers with spinnerbaits catching 12% and crankbaits 9%.[327] During the spring, soft plastics accounted for an even higher percentage of ShareLunkers including 50% in March and 72% in April.[328]

One guide gives a typical account similar to my Lake Fork University professor guides when he observed that "a slow moving bait does not make a lot of noise, . . . you don't move a lot using it. . .

---

[322] Id.
[323] Id.
[324] Id.
[325] Larry Hodge, *March is big bass month*, TEXAS FISH AND GAME MAGAZINE, 2004, available at https://tpwd.texas.gov/fishboat/fish/didyouknow/inland/bassinmarch.phtml.
[326] Id.
[327] Id.
[328] Id.

. Plus a slow moving bait will penetrate that fish's zone."[329] Several of my Lake Fork University professor guides voiced similar opinions and said that this is why slow moving soft plastics or slow moving jigs are better for big bass.[330] All of this makes sense when you consider the possibility that giant bass are more likely to have higher stress responses to sudden changes and simply freeze, instead of reacting aggressively when approached by faster moving baits.

Loners?

The idea that giant bass are loners is somewhat true, but also somewhat mythical. Lunker bass tend to live a more solitary life out of necessity than smaller bass in most fisheries with "the tendency to school decreasing as fish age" mainly because lunker bass have a lack of potential partners with which to form a school.[331] Old fish are rare, and most giant bass are relatively old.[332] Older fish are usually larger than younger fish and tend to be solitary when they reach really big sizes; this is mostly because the other bass born in and around their class year have died off—leaving these larger fish with fewer contemporaries.[333] In most fisheries, the annual mortality rate for bass is around 30%, but can be as low as 15% in ideal conditions and as high as 60% in unfavorable environments.[334] Most contemporaries of 24 inch or larger bass "are dead due to accumulated mortality."[335] So, the bass that make it to lunker size are more rare with few potential "friends" and "find fewer and fewer bass of similar size with which to aggregate and feed."[336]

Smaller bass are unlikely to school for feeding purposes with bass that are big enough to eat them.[337] One of my Lake Fork University professor guides with years of experience catching giants

---

[329] Id.
[330] Larry Hodge, *March is big bass month*, *supra* note 325.
[331] Maureen Mecozzi, *supra* note 189; Ralph Manns, *Life of bass: Size factors*, *supra* note 244.
[332] Robert Montgomery, *Big Old Bass*, *supra* note 140.
[333] Maureen Mecozzi, *supra* note 189..
[334] Ralph Manns, *Life of bass: Size factors*, *supra* note 244; Ken Smith Fishing, Part 5, *supra* note 266.
[335] Ralph Manns, *Life of bass: Size factors*, *supra* note 244.
[336] Id.
[337] Id.

said that a 6-pound bass can eat a 2-pound bass, and that generally a bass can eat a smaller bass of about 1/3 of its body weight. This seems about right (see chapter 9 regarding mouth mechanics), and I have rarely caught a 2-pound bass near a group of bass in the 5- to 6-pound range—so, I think he is probably right. So, younger bass tend to hunt in schools of five to ten bass, whereas older, larger bass tend to be more solitary, making it rare to see 4+ pound bass in schools of greater than five fish at most fisheries.[338]

However, in fisheries with a lot of giant bass—like O.H. Ivie and Lake Fork—the giant bass school up just like the smaller fish, just in smaller numbers. I have seen small schools or "wolf packs" of 8- to-10-pound bass in Lake Fork and in O.H. Ivie chasing shad on sonar with up to seven bass in the school, and guides have told me stories of bigger schools. I have personally caught up to five to seven bass over five pounds from a single school on multiple occasions in Arkansas and made some of my best bass fishing memories! So big bass are not always as solitary as many of the fishing magazines might make you believe. The giants likely school and feed in a manner similar to the way they fed at younger ages and smaller sizes, *if* they can find friends of similar size with which to associate.

But in many lakes, because lunker bass are less likely to be in a large school, their hunting methods are different from smaller bass. Younger, non-lunker bass tend to feed in schools using a technique of flushing their prey working as a group and also hunting offshore.[339] This type of hunting is difficult or impossible for one or two large bass to pull off, so their hunting style changes with age in these fisheries out of necessity.[340] Lunkers are more likely to focus "on key feeding areas unique to each habitat," such as areas "where current concentrates vulnerable prey, or feeding in funnel shorelines at twilight or after dark."[341] One expert believes this means that lunkers "are more likely to be lurking under cover or in shade than younger more agile bass."[342] Lunkers will also be "suspended and cruising open-water where smaller predators are attacking schooling prey."[343]

---

[338] Maureen Mecozzi, *supra* note 189; Ken Smith Fishing, Part 5, *supra* note 266.
[339] Ralph Manns, *Life of bass: Size factors*, *supra* note 244.
[340] Id.
[341] Id.
[342] Id.
[343] Id.

Lunker bass must learn to conserve energy, or else they will die.[344] Lunkers need more food because "energy reserves and absolute metabolic rate increase with body mass," which means that lunkers "may have marked differences in energy stores and metabolic rates" when compared to smaller bass.[345] Therefore, they wait for optimal feeding conditions to avoid over expending their energy reserves.[346] Lunker bass in many fisheries need to find special habitat options "where prey are abundant enough to be caught by a lone bass using short-strike, semi-ambush tactics and low-light or nighttime feeding."[347]

Consistently Landing Lunkers Requires Special Preparation

From a practical standpoint, a lunker bass on the end of your line makes several variables under the fisherman's control much more important than for smaller fish. Many variables affect whether you or the bass will win the battle. Here are a few things that I have learned from big bass guides over the years and have applied to my own fishing trips.

First, offshore fishing leads to more opportunities to encounter lunker bass, but usually fewer numbers of bass. Big bass expert, Josh Jones, in a 2023 In-Fisherman interview said that "the biggest fish in the lake live offshore 98 percent of the year" responding best to a slow presentation in deep water.[348] My lunker bass fishing success began to increase when I moved offshore in around 2016, and almost all of my biggest bass have been caught in water deeper than 15 feet—so I agree with him.

Second, boat position is a big deal when it comes to putting a giant bass in the boat. I caught a 12+ pound bass at Lake Fork while fishing with a guide in an area that is thick with standing timber. The guide positioned the boat in a way that kept the standing timber away from the fish landing area next to the boat—*before we ever made a cast*. It was critical that our boat was positioned in a way that there was no standing timber right next to the boat when it came time to

---

[344] Ralph Manns, *Life of bass: Size factors*, supra note 244.
[345] K.C. Hanson, et al., *Intersexual variation*, supra note 254.
[346] Ralph Manns, *Life of bass: Size factors*, supra note 244.
[347] Id.
[348] Steve Ryan, *The gathering legend of Josh Jones*, IN-FISHERMAN, 2023 Bass Guide, 42-45, 2023.

land that giant bass when it made a hard run under the boat and another out away from the boat. If a tree had been nearby, the fish would have broken my line for sure. Prior to learning this important controllable variable, I lost several big fish at the boat when they got me hung up in a tree that I never should have had near my landing spot. Today, I am much more aware of boat position as I make a cast into particularly promising areas. Here is a picture of my biggest bass so far, a 12.56 pounder from Lake Fork:

Boat position is also important to avoid spooking lunker bass. Most of my biggest bass have come when I positioned my boat far away from the spot I was fishing and made a long cast into the place where the fish was hooked. The cool thing about hooking a giant at the end of a long cast is that the fight can be epic to land the monster bass because she is a long way from the boat! The 12 pound plus lunker above jumped 3 times and made several deep runs near the boat in a battle I will never forget. Below is a picture of my biggest Arkansas bass, a 9.43 pounder, that was hooked on a football jig around 100 feet from the boat and also put up a memorable fight:

Third, the right rod and reel can make a huge difference. For most of my life, I used spinning tackle and medium power rods and caught lots of bass, but rarely landed a lunker. Medium heavy and heavy rods from reputable makers and baitcasting reels have made a difference for me in landing success and hookups. Hooksets are more successful, and the battle is much shorter, which makes landing the fish much more likely in my hands—especially when fishing in areas with timber or grass and any color to the water at all. In some situations, like crystal clear open water, I might change tactics; but the vast majority of my lunker chasing occurs in waters where these bigger rods and reels (and line) work great.

Fourth, the right line in good condition is critical. Until I started checking my line regularly by running my fingers along the 3 to 5 feet of line closest to my bait, I did not realize how often my line got nicked or abraded. In the past I broke off fish regularly, but today I can't remember a single fish breaking my line over the past several years. Today, nicks or abrasions on my line lead to an immediate retie. During an average eight-hour day, I probably retie a football jig that I'm dragging on hard bottom 4 or 5 times. I also usually retie after catching a big bass, especially if the lure was down inside its mouth where its teeth could damage my line. Palomar knots have served me well, so I have never investigated other types of knots. Smaller diameter line like 12-pound fluorocarbon that I use to drag big crankbaits on bottom seems to get nicked more, so I retie much more frequently when throwing those big crankbaits on smaller line. Twenty-to-twenty-five-pound fluorocarbon is my line of choice for 90 percent of my lunker fishing. Sixty-five-pound braid works great for me when frog fishing or fishing in grass, pads, or bushes. Topwater fishing in open water leads me to use 20-to-25-pound monofilament because mono floats. All my line choices have been directly influenced by various guide experiences during my Lake Fork University education.

Finally, a big extendable net helps. Landing lunker bass is different from landing smaller bass. Being prepared to catch lunkers has made a difference for me; I hope it helps you as well.

3

Study 1: Best Month to Catch a Lunker

    Most bass fishermen believe that spring is the best time to catch lunker bass. The flowers are blooming, and the bass are spawning. One of my old fishing buddies always said that when the dogwoods are blooming in Arkansas, you need to be out fishing because the big bass are biting. Spawning coves during spring at Lake Fork look like a boat show is underway on the water because there are so many boats. However, most of us are probably not certain which month is the best and by how much.
    Several of my Lake Fork University guide professors claimed that January and February were the best months for giant bass. However, I was always a little suspicious that they were simply trying to book trips during the coldest time of year when there were less people interested in fishing. I went with a guide at Lake Fork in February, and we did not catch a fish. So, did he just set me up for a payday, or was he correct and we simply didn't get the big bite that day?

If you had to pick one month to chase giant bass, which month would it be? And how much better is that month than the next or previous month? Those are some questions I hope to answer in this chapter.

Previous Research

In 2004, Texas Fish and Game magazine published a study of 346 bass weighing over 13 pounds that were entered into the Texas Parks and Wildlife Department's ShareLunker program over the years leading up to 2004.[349] The article was entitled "March is Big Bass Month," so you can guess the results.[350] Of those 346 giant ShareLunkers, 44% were caught in March.[351] The next best month was February with 26%, and April came in third place with 13%.[352] Therefore 83% of the 13+ pound ShareLunkers were caught from the beginning of February through the end of April, and only 17% were caught in the other nine months.[353] February through April were clearly the best months to catch 13+ pound giants in Texas in that 2004 study, with March being the best.

However, there was at least one major problem with that study; the ShareLunker program at that time only took in the giant bass through March and did not become year-round until 2018. So, it is possible that other 13-pound and larger bass were being caught, but not reported to TPWD at that time. The study was also heavily biased toward Lake Fork because almost 60% of the ShareLunkers came from that one fishery,[354] which could skew the data toward unique features of Lake Fork.

In fact, another researcher found that a different month was best for lunkers. Ralph Manns, a well-published fisheries biologist, gathered data on 8,900 adult bass he and his fishing partners caught over 18 years and 2500 outings including 371 bass of five pounds or more and 40 bass from 8 to 10.8 pounds mostly in Texas (often

---

[349] Larry Hodge, *March is big bass month*, TEXAS FISH AND GAME MAGAZINE, 2004, available at https://tpwd.texas.gov/fishboat/fish/didyouknow/inland/bassinmarch.phtml.
[350] Id.
[351] Id.
[352] Id.
[353] Id.
[354] Larry Hodge, *March is big bass month*, *supra* note 349.

including Lake Fork), but also some in Louisiana and New Mexico.[355] Manns reported that the catch rate of lunkers peaked in April for him and his fishing partners.[356] From a graph in his article, it appears that in April the lunker catch rate peaked at around 0.40 bass over five pounds per outing per fisherman, which means that each angler would catch a five pound lunker once in about 2.5 outings at the peak in April.[357] For Manns, May (~0.30 bass over five pounds per outing), June (~0.27), September (~0.24), and October (~0.24) appear to have been better than March (~0.20) and February (~0.17) in his graphical depiction of his data.[358] So, for Manns, April was the best month for lunkers with May and June following close behind.

My ShareLunker Databank Research

To answer the question of which month is best for lunker bass fishing, I turned to Texas's current ShareLunker public databank.[359] I will briefly review the program again here, but refresh your memory by reviewing the end of chapter 1 if you want more background information.

Texas Parks and Wildlife Department (TPWD) has a statewide program called the ShareLunker Program to develop big bass. Although some version of the program has been around since the 1980's, TPWD started the ShareLunker program year-round in 2018.[360] Since then, "anglers who reel in any largemouth bass at least 8 pounds or 24 inches can participate simply by entering their lunker catch information,"[361] which includes the bass's weight, length, location caught, date caught, and other information. Anglers can enter the information via the TPWD app or directly on their website.

---

[355] Ralph Manns, *Moon Magic Largemouth Bass*, IN-FISHERMAN, January 19, 2012, available at https://www.in-fisherman.com/editorial/moon-magic-largemouth-bass/154779.
[356] Id.
[357] Id.
[358] Id.
[359] TEXAS PARKS AND WILDLIFE DEPARTMENT, *Texas ShareLunker Archives*, available at https://texassharelunker.com/archives/.
[360] News Release, *Toyota ShareLunker Program begins new year-round season Jan. 1*, TEXAS PARKS AND WILDLIFE DEPARTMENT, September 29, 2017, available at https://tpwd.texas.gov/newsmedia/releases/?req=20170929a.
[361] TEXAS PARKS AND WILDLIFE DEPARTMENT, Toyota ShareLunker Program Texas Parks and Wildlife, available at https://texassharelunker.com.

Fishermen are motivated to enter their fish because they receive a "Catch Kit" that includes a decal, merchandise, giveaways, and entry into drawings for larger prizes.[362] I have personally entered a couple of fish in the program, and the Catch Kit is pretty cool! Plus, fish over 13 pounds may become legacy fish with offspring hatched and released into other Texas lakes.[363]

TPWD publishes an online archive of all accepted lunkers over 8 pounds or 24 inches on their website, which is available to the public.[364] I used this public archive to collect and analyze the data to answer some questions throughout this book (the information in the archive does not include all of the information collected—like bait used and time of day caught—so I concentrated just on the information included).

Data: For the five years from 2018 through 2022, a total of 2,124 lunkers eight pounds (or 24 inches) or over were reported to TPWD through the ShareLunker program. The number of 8+ pound lunker bass caught in each month are shown in Table 1.

Table 1: Number of 8+ lb. ShareLunkers caught in each month from 2018 through 2022 (5 years).

January	156
February	234
March	508
April	282
May	186
June	196
July	133
August	98
September	101
October	83
November	69
December	78
Total	2124

---

[362] Id.
[363] Id.
[364] TEXAS PARKS AND WILDLIFE DEPARTMENT, *Texas ShareLunker Archives*, available at https://texassharelunker.com/archives/.

More 8+ pound ShareLunkers were caught in March (508) than any other month with the next closest month being April (282), then February (234). So, March was the best month by far in the data reported to TPWD during this five-year time period. Figure 1 shows the data graphically.

Figure 1: Graphical representation of the per month data for TPWD ShareLunkers from 2018 through 2022.

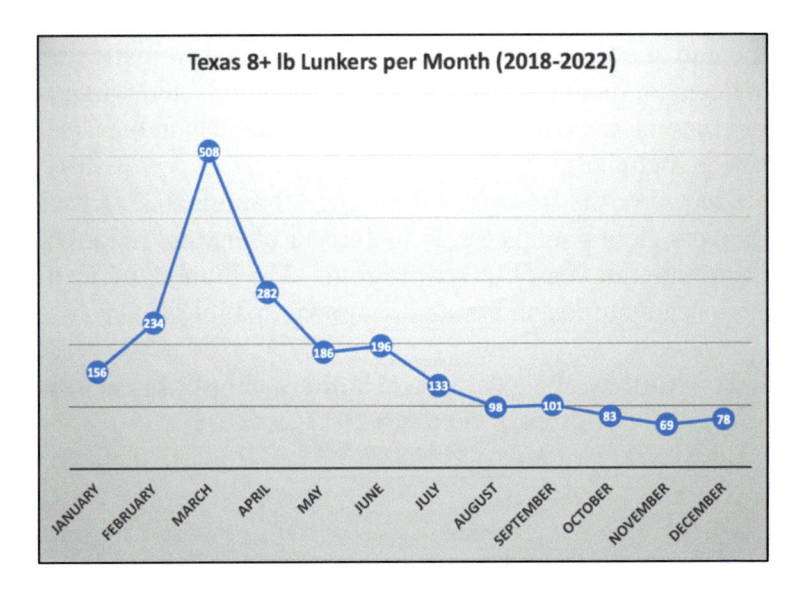

Texas 8+ lb Lunkers per Month (2018-2022)

January 156, February 234, March 508, April 282, May 186, June 196, July 133, August 98, September 101, October 83, November 69, December 78

March (508) was best, and April (282) was next. Note that the most 8+ pound lunkers were reported in March with 508 lunkers reported over the five-year period, which was more than double February (234) and more than triple January (156). April was better than February or January with a total of 282 lunker bass reported over those five years. The best months were clearly centered around the spawn in February, March, and April. *Based on these results, the best months to catch an eight-plus pound lunker bass in Texas rank in the following order: (1) March, (2) April (3) February, (4) June, (5) May, (6) January, (7) July, (8) September, (9) August, (10) October, (11) December, and (12) November.* March (the best month) was over seven times more likely to produce a lunker bass eight pounds or bigger than November (the worst month) in Texas. *February through April accounted for 1024 of the 2124 lunkers, which is 48% (almost half) of the eight-plus pound lunkers*. However, most (52%) were caught during the other nine months of the year; however, on a month-by-month basis, *March, April, and February were clearly the best months to catch an 8+ pound lunker in Texas.*

Analytics: Now, let's try to quantify the odds of catching a lunker bass for each month for comparison. I will walk you through my data and calculations step-by-step, so it is clear how I came up with the results.

Since there were 2,124 lunker bass 8 pounds (or 24 inches) or larger reported over 5 years (60 months) from 2018 through 2022, there were an average of 35.4 lunkers reported per month. Some months were better and some were worse, so we can use that average to compare each month to the theoretical average month of 35.4 per month. The total lunker numbers from the data section above (see Table 1) were simply divided by 5 months (since there were five of each month during the five year period) to come up with the number of bass reported for each month per year on average. For example, there were 508 lunkers caught during the 5 Marchs that occurred from 2018 through 2022, which means that the average March led to 101.5 lunkers being reported each year over those five years. The results on a lunkers per month (lpm) basis are shown in Table 2.

Table 2: Lunkers per month (lpm) for the five instances of each month from 2018 through 2022.

January	31.2 lpm
February	46.8 lpm
March	101.5 lpm
April	56.5 lpm
May	37.2 lpm
June	39.2 lpm
July	26.6 lpm
August	19.6 lpm
September	20.2 lpm
October	16.6 lpm
November	13.8 lpm
December	15.6 lpm

Now, remember that the theoretical average month was 35.4 lunkers per month (lpm). March had 101.5 lpm, which works out to 287% of the average month! In comparison, November had 13.8 lpm, which is only 39% of average. So, in March, anglers' odds were 2.87 times better than average. In contrast, in November they had only a fraction at 0.39 odds compared to an average month. Another way to look at this is that compared to an average month, anglers' odds were 187% higher (i.e., 287% -100% = +187%) in March than average and 61% lower (i.e., 39% - 100% = - 61%) than average in November. Table 3 shows the odds and percentage numbers for each month.

Table 3: Odds and Percentage Effect Projections for 8+ pound Lunkers for Each Month from 2018 through 2022

Month	Odds	% Effect
January	0.881	-11.9%
February	1.322	+33.2%
March	2.870	+187.0%
April	1.593	+59.3%
May	1.051	+5.1%
June	1.107	+10.7%
July	0.751	-24.9%
August	0.554	-44.6%
September	0.570	-43.0%
October	0.469	-53.1%
November	0.390	-61.0%
December	0.440	-55.9%

Figure 2 depicts the percentages graphically.

Figure 2: Percentage increase or decrease in chances of reporting a lunker 8 pounds or larger compared to an average month in Texas from 2018 through 2022

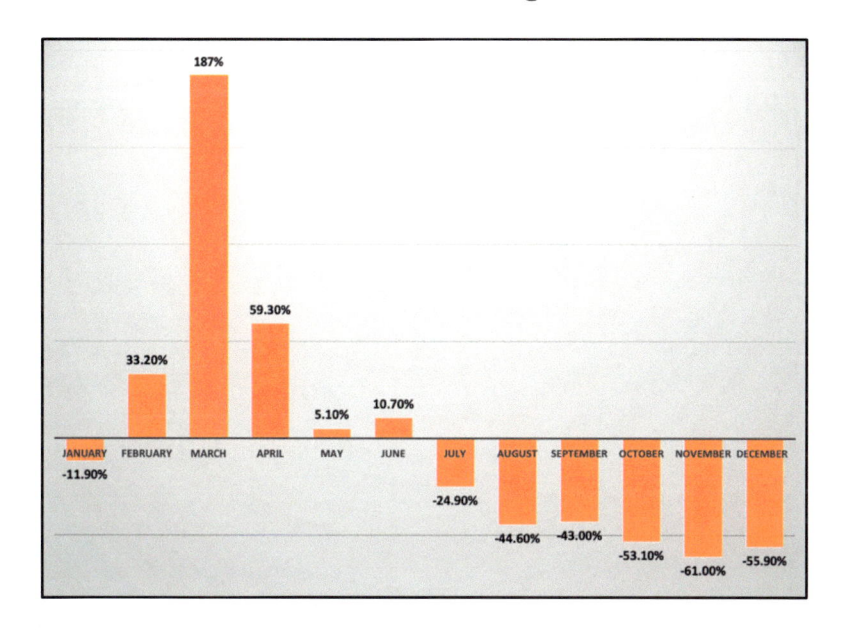

Month	Percentage
JANUARY	-11.90%
FEBRUARY	33.20%
MARCH	187%
APRIL	59.30%
MAY	5.10%
JUNE	10.70%
JULY	-24.90%
AUGUST	-44.60%
SEPTEMBER	-43.00%
OCTOBER	-53.10%
NOVEMBER	-61.00%
DECEMBER	-55.90%

The graph in Figure 5 estimates the amount the chances of reporting an 8+ pound lunker increased or decreased each month. For example, fishing in June increased the anglers' chances by 10.7% compared to an average month over the five-year period, whereas fishing in January decreased the anglers' chances by 11.9%. You can look at each month to get an idea of the effect each month had on the results.

So, based upon the data in the ShareLunker database, March was by far the most likely month to catch an 8+ pound lunker in Texas from 2018 through 2022. April was second best, and February was third best. So, maybe my Lake Fork University guide professors who pushed January and February were incorrect regarding the best month to catch an eight-plus pound Texas giant. But let's do some more digging. Maybe the guides were talking about the true giants—the *13+ pound ShareLunkers. So, let's look at the data for those.*

Eighty-seven 13+ pound ShareLunkers were entered in the program from 2018 through 2022. They were caught in each month (in order from best to worst) as follows: March 32, February 21, January 11, May 5, December 4, April 3, November 3, August 2,

September 2, October 2, June 1, and July 1. Figure 3 shows the numbers for the 13+ pound ShareLunkers graphically.

Figure 3: 13+ pound ShareLunkers reported per month from 2018 through 2022.

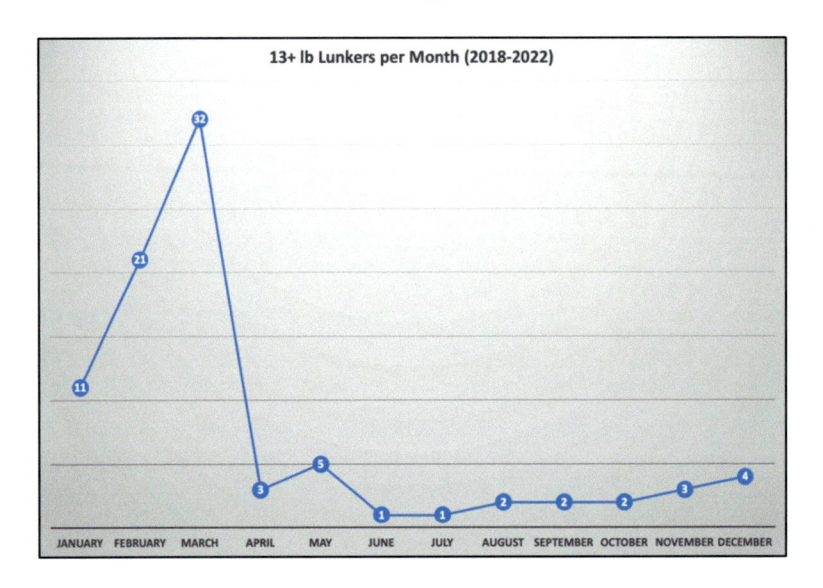

13+ lb Lunkers per Month (2018-2022)

JANUARY	FEBRUARY	MARCH	APRIL	MAY	JUNE	JULY	AUGUST	SEPTEMBER	OCTOBER	NOVEMBER	DECEMBER
11	21	32	3	5	1	1	2	2	2	3	4

Table 4 shows the odds and percentage numbers for 13+ pounders calculated in the same manner as the numbers above in Table 3.

Table 4: Odds and Percentage Effect Projections for 13+ pound Lunkers for Each Month from 2018 through 2022

Month	Odds	% Effect
January	1.517	+51.7%
February	2.897	+189.7%
March	4.414	+341.4%
April	0.414	-59.6%
May	0.690	-31.0%
June	0.138	-86.2%
July	0.138	-86.2%
August	0.276	-72.4%
September	0.276	-72.4%
October	0.276	-72.4%
November	0.414	-59.6%
December	0.552	-44.8%

Figure 4 depicts these numbers for 13+ pound ShareLunekers graphically.

Figure 4: Percentage increase or decrease in chances of reporting a lunker 13 pounds or larger compared to an average month in Texas from 2018 through 2022

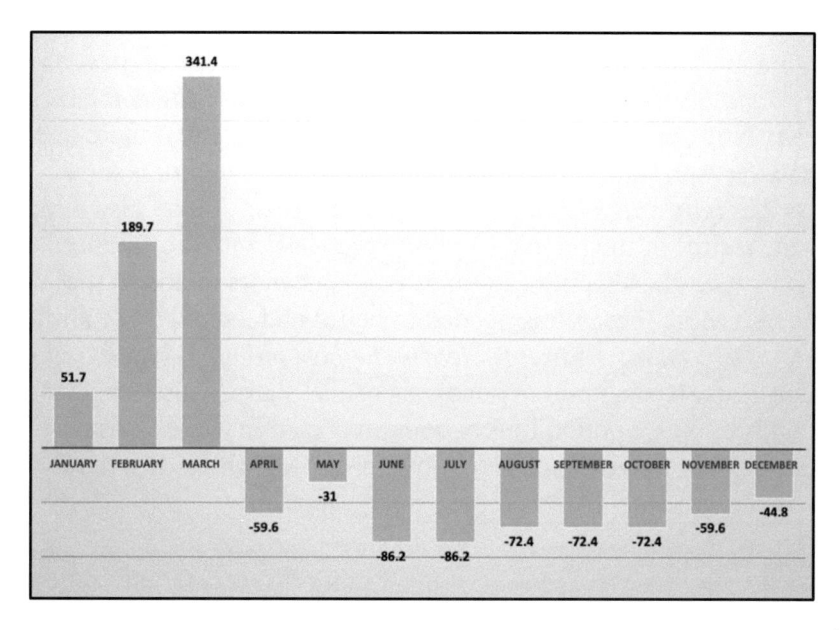

The graph in Figure 4 estimates the chances of reporting a 13+ pound lunker increased or decreased each month compared to an average month. For example, fishing in June decreased the anglers' chances by 86.2% compared to an average month over the five-year period, whereas fishing in January increased the anglers' chances by 51.7%. You can look at each month to get an idea of the effect each month had on the results.

So, based upon the data in the ShareLunker database, March was by far the most likely month to catch a thirteen plus pound lunker in Texas from 2018 through 2022. February was second best, and January was third best. So, maybe my Lake Fork University guide professors were talking more about catching a true giant bass over 13 pounds, because January through March were clearly the top months for catching these rare giants.

Compare Figure 4 to Figure 2. Remember that almost every bass over eight pounds is female. Female bass lose at least 10 percent or more of their body weight after spawning.[365] So, a 13-pound bass loses at least 1.3 pounds after spawning and becomes an 11.7 pounder at best. An 8-pound bass loses at least 0.8 pounds to become a 7.2 pounder or less. So, it's easy to see that the population of lunker bass in each of these categories drops significantly after the spawn simply because so much weight is lost during the spawn. The shape of the curves in these two graphs also suggests a couple of interesting things about the spawn. Notice the huge drop off in chances of catching a 13+ pounder after March. *This precipitous drop might suggest that 13+ pound bass are likely to spawn early and before the end of March.* Now, compare the results in Figure 2. Note that there are big drops after April and June. *This could possibly signal that some lunker bass are still spawning into June in Texas.* It may also simply indicate a shift of the bigger 13 pound plus bass into the smaller category with those being caught as post-spawners to add to the numbers. More research is needed to better understand these shifts.

Discussion: March is clearly the best month to catch a lunker bass in Texas based upon my analysis of the ShareLunker database. The odds of an 8+ pound lunker being reported in March were 7 times higher than the lowest month of November. March made even a

---

[365] James Davis and Joe Lock, *Largemouth bass biology and life history*, Southern Regional Aquacultural Center SRAC Publication No. 200, August 1997.

bigger difference for the true giant bass over 13 pounds. The odds of reporting a 13+ pound giant were 32 times higher than the lowest months of June and July.

Notice the shifts in the curves when comparing 13+ pound bass to 8+ pound bass in the database. *The three months of January through March were the best months by far for the 13+ pounders* accounting for 74% (64/87) of the 13+ pound ShareLunkers reported from 2018 through 2022. This leaves only 26% for the remaining 9 months of the year. In contrast, the curve shifts later in the year by one month and is less dramatic for 8+ pound lunkers. *The three months of February through April were the best months for 8+ pound lunkers in Texas* accounting for 48% of the total. So, there were still 52% of the 8+ pound lunkers to be reported during the remaining 9 months.

As discussed above, these data may indicate that most of the 13+ pound giants do indeed spawn earlier than their smaller counterparts with the 13+ pounders being mostly finished spawning before the end of March since a huge drop-off in reported catches occurred after March. The data may also indicate that some of these Texas lunkers, in the 8+ pound category especially, may be spawning into June since the drop-off in this category was not as dramatic after March and continued until after June. More focused research is needed to further investigate these data.

To help in translating this data to your location, *compare water temperatures in your home area.* Bass behavior is highly dependent upon water temperature (see chapter 7), which is considered the master abiotic factor. In March in Texas the water temperature is typically in the upper-50s to low-70s, and most of the bass are in the early to mid-spawn—based upon my experiences at Lake Fork over several years. The exact stage of the spawn varies somewhat each year depending upon weather and other factors. The timing likely shifts later by days to weeks to months depending upon how far north of Texas you are fishing. Regardless of where you fish, *the early to mid-spawn is likely the best time to catch a giant bass* based upon these findings. This makes sense because the biggest female bass are in the process of spawning and some of the biggest ones have not "spawned out" a lot of their weight yet.

To translate the analytics and statistics to your home state, an 8+ pound bass is probably in around the top 0.75 to 1% of bass caught in Texas—so consider the size of bass that make up 0.75 to 1% of your home bass population. In Arkansas where I live and fish most of the time, I would guess that a 6+ pound bass is likely in that same percentage range depending upon the specific body of water. So, I would guess that the analytics for 8+ pounders in Texas would likely apply to 6+ pounders in my home waters. I doubt the numbers would vary much for the 5 pounders that I consider to be lunkers in Arkansas, so I suspect the analysis would produce similar results in my home state with a slight shift toward later in the year by a couple of weeks to account for the fact that my home waters are few latitudes north of Texas so the water temperature lags behind by a couple weeks. I would guess that a 13+ pound bass in Texas is comparable in rarity to a 10+ pound bass in Arkansas, so I would make similar statements for that category.

Scientific articles should tell you potential problems with their study results, so I do that here in the scientific tradition. As with any scientific analysis, there are possible sources of errors in these calculations to be considered. First, perhaps fishermen were less likely to report their catches after March because the ShareLunker program prior to 2018 only accepted entries through March, which may have led many fishermen to fail to report fish that qualified in later months. Second, March may outperform February and January simply because more anglers are on the water in March when temperatures and weather are generally more tolerable; so more numbers may simply represent fishing effort on the water with more chances to catch a lunker bass. Third, fishermen may become hunters in the fall and abandon lakes and rivers so that again, the decreased fishing effort may result in fewer fish being caught, even though the bite may have been there if there were more fishermen on the water.

In my own personal experience, 5 of my 12 biggest bass (42%) were caught in June—even though I fish year-round. My second-best month was May, when 3 of those 12 (25%) were caught. So, for me, the pattern has not followed the ShareLunker numbers for Texas. This is probably because I spend more time fishing in Texas in June and July (and less in Arkansas) than any other time of year, so I am more likely to be fishing in waters where bigger bass are available during those months. I have favored those months generally because there are fewer fishermen on the water at Lake Fork once the heat starts setting in, and I grew up working on a hot farm—so I am tolerant of the heat. I also like to fish deep offshore, which makes my preferred fishing style more likely to be successful during June. So, your results may be different than the results of my ShareLunker study, if your fishing preferences vary from the average Texas angler as well. Perhaps you are better at finding and catching fish during certain times of the year using techniques that you like better than others. Therefore, the best time to catch a giant is generally *whenever you can go fishing*! If you have the luxury of an open schedule, then spend more time in the late winter and early spring on the water (especially in March in Texas or the equivalent month in your home state) to catch a lunker!

4

The Spawn

Love is in the air for largemouth bass when spawning season gets underway—especially for lunker bass fisherman who love catching giants. The time around the spawn is the best time of year to catch lunker bass (see chapter 3). Most bass are active and shallow making them accessible to more anglers. In addition, more lunker bass are available before and during the spawn because many females have not "spawned out" losing 10% of their body weight.[366]

The spawn begins in most locations when the water temperature stabilizes above 55-60°F (15°C) in the spring.[367] In addition to water temperature, the timing of the spawn is influenced

---

[366] James Davis and Joe Lock, *Largemouth bass biology and life history*, Southern Regional Aquacultural Center SRAC Publication No. 200, August 1997.
[367] Steven Bardin, *Fish Biology: Largemouth bass: A comprehensive species guide*, Wired2Fish, January 28, 2023, available at https://www.wired2fish.com/fish-biology/largemouth-bass-a-comprehensive-species-guide/; Id.

by the increasing length of days and by weather parameters.[368] Water temperature and length of daylight is so important to the timing of the spawn that when those factors were manipulated in one laboratory study, largemouth bass could be manipulated to spawn in atypical spawning months like December and July.[369]

The first sign of the spawn approaching is the appearance of male bass searching for nesting sites when the water temperature stabilizes at or above 55-60°F.[370] Most spawning, including egg laying, occurs between 65-75°F.[371] In more northern locations, egg laying may be more optimal at 62-65°F according to some writers.[372] The spawn generally continues until water temperatures reach 75°F (24°C).[373] Bass activity during the spawn tends to come with waves of increased activity depending upon weather conditions and possibly moon phase. The exact timing in a specific lake varies each year and may be significantly different from places farther north or south. In addition, fall or winter spawning can occur in the southern United States.[374] Further, some spawning outside the temperature parameters quoted above occasionally occurs (e.g., I have witnessed active beds on a local power plant lake during atypical water temperatures).

Spawning temperatures are reached during different months depending upon the location's latitude. So largemouth bass may be spawning from January to July (or even year-round) in the United States depending upon location; spawning season begins and ends earlier in the year in southern than northern locations. For example,

---

[368] SportsDay Staff, Sasser: *Mating largemouth bass move to shallow areas, become easier to catch*, THE DALLAS MORNING NEWS, March 1, 2014, available at https://www.dallasnews.com/news/2014/03/01/sasser-mating-largemouth-bass-move-to-shallow-areas-become-easier-to-catch/; James Davis and Joe Lock, *supra* note 366.

[369] Anthony Carlson, *Induced Spawning of Largemouth Bass*, TRANSACTIONS OF THE AMERICAN FISHERIES SOCIETY 102(2): 442-444 (1972), available at https://doi.org/10.1577/1548-8659(1973)102<442:ISOLBM>2.0.CO;2.

[370] Maureen Mecozzi, Wisconsin Department of Natural Resources, Bureau of Fisheries Management, *Largemouth Bass*, August 2008, available at https://dnr.wisconsin.gov/sites/default/files/topic/Fishing/Species_lmbass.pdf.

[371] Steven Bardin, *Fish Biology: Largemouth bass*, *supra* note 367; Id.; James Davis and Joe Lock, *supra* note 366.

[372] Maureen Mecozzi, *supra* note 370.

[373] Texas State University, San Marcos, Department of Biology, *Fishes of Texas: Micropterus salmoides*, available at http://txstate.fishesoftexas.org/micropterus%20salmoides.htm.

[374] Steven Bardin, *Fish Biology: Largemouth bass*, *supra* note 367.

in Texas, spawning season generally begins in late winter (January-February) or early spring (March-April).[375] As you go north from Texas, the spawn gets later. For example, spawning occurs from late March to mid-April on Pickwick Reservoir on the Tennessee River.[376] And even farther north in Wisconsin, largemouth bass spawn "from late April until early July; fish in the northern part of the state spawn about two weeks later than those in the south."[377] Florida is a different story altogether where water temperatures are more stable year-round with seasonal boundaries that are less rigid. So, in Florida, spawning can be triggered in some bass at random times from October through May by water temperatures 62-72°F, stable weather, low wind, and clear water.[378]

In this chapter, the shallow spring largemouth bass spawn will be discussed. The stages of the spawning period for individual bass (i.e., all bass are not in the same phase at the same time) are broken into four categories here: (1) pre-spawn, (2) nest excavation and courting, (3) mating (including aggression and shuddering), and (4) post-spawn. Throughout this discussion, if you are targeting big bass, pay particular attention to what the female bass are doing.

Pre-spawn

Bass are sexually mature when they reach around 10 inches in length, usually at 1 year of age.[379] The spawn begins with nesting behavior by male bass. When the water temperature is sustained at 57-60°F, many male largemouth bass begin cruising shallow areas near the shore to select nesting sites in water averaging around 18 inches in depth but ranging from one to four feet deep.[380] During the

---

[375] Texas State University, San Marcos, *supra* note 373; Emily Steed, Animal Diversity Web, *Micropterus salmoides: American black bass*, U. Michigan Museum of Zoology, available at https://animaldiversity.org/accounts/Micropterus_salmoides/.
[376] Texas State University, San Marcos, *supra* note 373.
[377] Maureen Mecozzi, *supra* note 370.
[378] David Brown, *The Very Odd Personality of Florida's Spawn*, Bassmaster, March 2023.
[379] Steven Bardin, *Fish Biology: Largemouth bass*, *supra* note 367.
[380] Texas State University, San Marcos, *supra* note 373; Emily Steed, *supra* note 375; Maureen Mecozzi, *supra* note 370; TEXAS PARKS AND WILDLIFE DEPARTMENT, *Largemouth bass (Micropterus salmoides)*, available at https://tpwd.texas.gov/huntwild/wild/species/lmb/.

pre-spawn the males explore nesting areas but are not yet committed to a specific site.[381] Females remain distant from the nest area and do not interact with the males.[382] The warmer water of spring also leads to increased activity in the shallows as bass cruise for food.[383]

During the pre-spawn period, bass travel to their spawning grounds. Most bass travel short distances within their home ranges, but some travel several miles from a winter home range to their spring "shallow, protected spawning sites" (see chapter 6).[384] For example, at Toledo Bend, a two-pound bass swam over 6 miles from the main lake to reach its spring spawning grounds in the back of a creek, where it stayed for a month before traversing the 6 miles back out to the main lake.[385] Similarly, a six pounder at Toledo Bend traveled 5 miles to a spawning area in the back of a creek, where it stayed 2 weeks and then traveled the 5 miles back to its home area.[386] In a different study on a different lake, one bass traveled 3.4 miles (5.5 km) to its spawning area where it spent less than a month.[387] Most bass, however, traveled much shorter distances within a more stable home area, and some bass made no migratory movement whatsoever.

During the pre-spawn period, bass transition out of stable aggregations into more unstable groupings. As the water temperature warms in the spring, the aggregations and associations of winter bass begin to become unstable and shorter term with associations with other bass "often only lasting 1 hour," whereas winter associations

---

[381] S.J. Cooke, et al., *Physical activity and behavior of a centrarchid fish during spawning*, ECOLOGY OF FRESHWATER FISH 2001: 10: 227–237 (2001), available at http://www.fecpl.ca/wp-content/uploads/2001/05/EMG-LMB-Spawn-MS.pdf.
[382] Id.
[383] C.T. Hasler, et al., *Frequency, composition and stability of associations among individual largemouth bass at diel, daily and seasonal scales*, ECOLOGY OF FRESHWATER FISH 16: 417–424 (2007).
[384] Texas State University, San Marcos, *supra* note 373.
[385] Ken Smith Fishing YouTube Channel, *Toledo Bend Telemetry Tracking Study Update Todd Driscoll TP&W Biologist Feb 2022 Part 1*, available at https://www.youtube.com/watch?v=DhCX1h6EN24&list=PLLzhji805wVzkLnAA97I8VmdZpR8arB_Q&index=1.
[386] Ken Smith Fishing YouTube Channel, *Toledo Bend Telemetry Tracking Study Update Todd Driscoll TP&W Biologist Feb 2022 Part 2*, available at https://www.youtube.com/watch?v=vBZBhEmkbAU&list=PLLzhji805wVzkLnAA97I8VmdZpR8arB_Q&index=2.
[387] Karle Woodward and Richard Noble, *Over-winter movements of adult largemouth bass in a North Carolina reservoir*, PROC. ANNU, CONF. SOUTHEAST ASSOC. FISH AND WILDL. AGENCIES 51:113-122 (1997).

often lasted up to six hours.[388] One study of bass with tracking devices showed that 80% of winter bass were in groups with multiple other bass suggesting that the bass may begin to form some relationships during winter that are relevant to the spawning season.[389] Specifically, males and females were together in pairs four times more commonly than two females, and researchers speculated that these pre-spawning associations "may be important for largemouth bass to associate with the opposite sex pre-spawn to determine pair-bonds for siring young."[390] More research is needed in this area, however, because bass do not form exclusive mating pairs (as will be discussed below).[391]

Nest Excavation and Courting

Each male bass selects a single nesting site.[392] Largemouth bass prefer "quieter, more vegetated water than other black bass" and will nest on most substrates (including submerged logs) except soft mud.[393] Male largemouth bass are very territorial, so their nests are usually separated from other nests by at least 7 feet, unless there is an underwater obstruction that keeps the bass from seeing each other.[394]

In one study of telemetered bass directly observed with cameras in a shallow water area in a research pond, one male bass spent two days searching for a satisfactory nesting site when the water temperature reached 61°F (16°C).[395] Male bass in large bodies of water or in lakes with limited nesting site options often spend much more than 2 days looking for nesting sites. This male selected a site two feet from shore in 18 inches of water depth.[396] Because this male and his mate were observed directly by scientists while recording muscle activity (using EMGi recordings), underwater videography,

---

[388] C.T. Hasler, et al., *supra* note 383.
[389] Id.
[390] Id.
[391] Id.
[392] Steven Bardin, *Fish Biology: Largemouth bass*, *supra* note 367; Texas State University, San Marcos, *supra* note 373.
[393] TEXAS PARKS AND WILDLIFE DEPARTMENT, *Largemouth bass*, *supra* note 380.
[394] Texas State University, San Marcos, *supra* note 373; Maureen Mecozzi, *supra* note 370.
[395] S.J. Cooke, et al., *supra* note 381.
[396] Id.

and additional videos, I will use this specific mating pair's behavior throughout this discussion.[397]

The nesting site is typically on a hard-packed sand, clay, marl, or gravel bottom "with a very thin layer of mud covering the material."[398] Male bass prefer to build beds in "close or direct proximity to hard structure or vegetation."[399] Nests are typically "constructed near submerged logs, brush piles, clumps of aquatic vegetation, or under overhanging limbs, usually over a firm bottom."[400] If necessary, nests can be constructed "among the roots or underground stems of submerged plants."[401] Good water circulation and oxygen content via aeration are important for egg development, so bass instinctively take those factors into consideration when selecting nesting sites.[402]

Bass have been seen spawning as deep as 20 feet in clear water, so these same types of considerations (type of bottom, nearby cover, etc.) may also affect the location of deep water nests.[403] Nest

---

[397] Id.
[398] Maureen Mecozzi, *supra* note 370.
[399] Steven Bardin, *Fish Biology: Largemouth bass*, *supra* note 367.
[400] Texas State University, San Marcos, *supra* note 373.
[401] Id.
[402] Maureen Mecozzi, *supra* note 370.
[403] James Davis and Joe Lock, *supra* note 366.

depth and location variations often occur, especially in clear bodies of water or in heavily pressured fisheries with bass spawning in deeper water or on suspended hard areas in open water.[404] I have even read about bass spawning on wide underwater branches of large trees well above the bottom of the lake. In my experience sight fishing, bigger bass tend to spawn a little deeper than average. Most lunker bass that I have personally found on beds have been 4 or 5 feet deep and difficult to see.

To construct the nest, "the male sweeps out a huge basin with his fins, sometimes as large as three feet in diameter and a foot deep."[405] The diameter of the male's nest is usually about twice his body length.[406] The male bass uses his tail to fan away silt or mud to expose the underlying gravel or hard surface in preparing the nest.[407]

When constructing the nest, the "male places his head at center of nest area and sweeps debris out in front of him by powerful undulation and lateral pushing movement of the whole body; he may repeat this process many times."[408] In the example above where the male bass was directly observed and recorded, the male bass used two tactics for digging while building the nest.[409] First, he used "slow, but powerful caudal beats of high amplitude" while propelling himself "across the nest area with [his] head elevated and mouth partially open."[410] As the motion was finished, he would "burst away, creating a large silt cloud" and disappear from the perimeter of the nest area until the silt settled and water cleared again.[411] He would then return and continue the build process.[412] Once the nest area started to take shape, the digging was less intense and "usually consisted of more gentle and controlled sweeping actions that suspended much less silt."[413] He would occasionally leave the nest for deeper water where

---

[404] Steven Bardin, *Fish Biology: Largemouth bass*, *supra* note 367.
[405] Maureen Mecozzi, *supra* note 370.
[406] James Davis and Joe Lock, *supra* note 366; Steven Bardin, *Fish Biology: Largemouth bass*, *supra* note 367.
[407] SportsDay Staff, *supra* note 368; Steven Bardin, *Fish Biology: Largemouth bass*, *supra* note 367.
[408] Texas State University, San Marcos, *supra* note 373.
[409] S.J. Cooke, et al., *supra* note 381.
[410] Id.
[411] Id.
[412] Id.
[413] Id.

a female was waiting.[414] This male bass spent one hour and 44 minutes creating the nest.[415]

During the process of building the nest, males' tails often become frayed as seen in the picture below. The bass in this picture weighed 7.01 pounds and is thought to be a male because it was on a bed at Lake Fork with a much larger bass; a 7.01-pound male is unusually large for a male.

During nest excavation, "ripe" females position themselves nearby in deeper water while the males build nests. Since most nests are built in less than two feet of water, females are typically in 3 to 6 feet water nearby.[416] For example, in the study with direct observation of the mating pair discussed above, the female remained in deeper water "somewhat near to the nest perimeter" except for a short two-minute appearance at the nest after the male had been digging for about an hour and a half.[417]

Generally, once the nest is complete, the male bass leaves the nest area to seek out a "ripe" female and lure her back to the nest by employing "courtship displays which include rapid changes in color

---

[414] S.J. Cooke, et al., *supra* note 381.
[415] Id.
[416] Id.; Emily Steed, *supra* note 375.
[417] S.J. Cooke, et al., *supra* note 381.

pattern."[418] Many females remain distant from the nest.[419] Courting initially consists of non-contact interactions between males and females including approaches and various displays.[420] The male in the direct observation study above stayed close to the nest and continued to court the nearby female.[421] "Occasional gentle nudges to the opercular area of the female" were used during courting by this male "to direct the female toward the general area of the nest."[422]

Mating

After a short courtship, the female joins the male in the nest. The male will nudge, push, and lead the female to the nest.[423] When a female approaches the nest ready to spawn, she floats "on her side, head down," otherwise the male may not allow her to enter and may nip at her and run her off.[424] Once they arrive back at the nest, the male tries to make the female stay by circling the nest and encourages her to drop her eggs by bumping into her repeatedly.[425] During this aggression phase, the male contacts the female, usually near the operculum or genital pore.[426] The male nips the female's tail and shakes the female above the nest.[427] Spawning involves the male and female tilting to the side so their vents are in proximity.[428] While spawning, the male and female stay in the nest area just above the nest on their sides with their bodies angled in a way that places their ventral areas in close proximity while the female sheds eggs and the

---

[418] Texas State University, San Marcos, *supra* note 373 (stating, "After construction of nest is complete, male leaves nest are to search for ripe females, luring them back to the nest with courtship displays which include rapid changes in color pattern."); Emily Steed, *supra* note 375 (stating, ""Once the nest is completed, the male then seeks out for a female and brings her to the nest to drop her eggs.").
[419] S.J. Cooke, et al., *supra* note 381.
[420] Id.
[421] Id.
[422] Id.
[423] Id.
[424] Maureen Mecozzi, *supra* note 370.
[425] Emily Steed, *supra* note 375.
[426] S.J. Cooke, et al., *supra* note 381.
[427] Id.
[428] James Davis and Joe Lock, *supra* note 366.

male sheds sperm ("milt") simultaneously.[429] Both "shudder" as they release eggs and sperm.[430]

Over the course of around an hour or so, the two fish float out to the nest borders and then return to the bottom intermittently, repeating the spawning act several times.[431] During mating, "the female will exhibit twisting and turning contortions alongside the male while attempting to expel her eggs" in a way that resembles the way the male fans out the nest.[432] Her motions help expel her eggs and help them mix with the male's sperm (milt).[433] These contortions and movements often leave her with a "bloody or ragged tail fin," which is why you will catch females with ragged or bloody tails—as well as males. Below are a couple of female bass with frayed tails; the top one was a 25-inch-long bass from O.H. Ivie that had clearly already spawned, and the bottom one was caught off of a bed with a smaller bass at Lake Fork and weighed 7.5 lbs.

---

[429] Steven Bardin, *Fish Biology: Largemouth bass*, *supra* note 367; Texas State University, San Marcos, *supra* note 373; Maureen Mecozzi, *supra* note 370.
[430] James Davis and Joe Lock, *supra* note 366.
[431] Maureen Mecozzi, *supra* note 370.
[432] SportsDay Staff, *supra* note 368.
[433] S.J. Cooke, et al., *supra* note 381.

In the study of the mating pair we have been following in this chapter, both the male and female bass had been implanted with EMGi telemetry transmitters that sent continuous measurements of muscular activity—especially the activity associated with gamete (egg and sperm) deposition, which the researchers termed "shuddering" including quivering and vibrations at low amplitude.[434] In that pair, the female arrived in the nest area and stayed in the nearby "deeper" water for around 44 minutes before spawning.[435] During the first 33 minutes after committing to the nest, the female bass shuddered 12 times "depositing some eggs in the process."[436] Then, the "male resumed major nest digging and egg distribution activities."[437] While he was doing this, the female moved back into deeper nearby water and waited.[438] He continued to court her intermittently while also digging for over an hour.[439] Finally, the female returned to the nest, and "the male again began to court the female even more

---

[434] Id.
[435] Id.
[436] Id.
[437] Id.
[438] Id.
[439] S.J. Cooke, et al., *supra* note 381.

aggressively, and the nest building activities ceased."[440] Spawning restarted and "lasted for 67 minutes" during which "137 acts of shuddering were observed."[441] Female muscle activity was highest during "shuddering (gamete deposition)" and peaked on the day of spawning.[442] The male remained very aggressive throughout.

Eventually, after spawning was complete, the male chased the female away into deeper water.[443] He then "immediately assumed parental care duties, including fanning the newly deposited eggs with gentle movements of the distal portion of his caudal fin and continual beats of his pectoral fins."[444] He swam in place and rotated about the nest while performing his duties.[445]

Our mating pair's spawning event took a total of 5 hours and 48 minutes from starting the nest until the male assumed parental care, which is likely of atypically short duration.[446] The female was at the nest for a total of 3 hours and 43 minutes in this case, which is a much shorter period than the "one to two days" that many articles suggest. Often, females are on the nest much longer than this example. Even so, the female is usually on the bed for only a day or two at most.[447] Females will help guard the nest with males during the time they are on the nest after spawning.

Researchers note that there are very limited field observations of mating largemouth bass because the event lasts for "no more than several hours," because it often occurs during low light conditions, because shallow water locations make fish wary and hinders observation, and because many places are too turbid to see.[448] I have not spent a lot of time sight fishing, but I have scanned a lot of shallow water for bass in spring and only witnessed the actual event once. I witnessed one pair of bass perform this spawning ritual swimming around each other at Lake Fork, and I doubt that either bass was catchable during that period because they did not seem to be distracted by anything around them except if I got my boat too close.

---

[440] Id.
[441] Id.
[442] Id.
[443] Id.
[444] S.J. Cooke, et al., *supra* note 381.
[445] Id.
[446] Id.
[447] SportsDay Staff, *supra* note 368.
[448] S.J. Cooke, et al., *supra* note 381.

I have, however, seen many pairs of bass on beds (and caught a few of the bigger ones off beds) where both appeared to be guarding the nest. During the time that the female is on the nest, she will also pick up and remove potential predators (i.e., your bait) from the nest. Usually, the smaller (likely male) bass is more aggressive and either gets caught first or is "shaken off" by the fisherman trying to catch the bigger fish. Sometimes removing the male will spook the female off the bed or make her very difficult to catch.

Male largemouth bass spawn with more than one female in their individual nests (usually at different times, but occasionally simultaneously), and females lay eggs in multiple nests (usually 2 or 3) during a single spawning season.[449] The female leaves the male behind to protect the nest after each successful spawning attempt.[450] Female bass spawn over a period up to a month (usually 7 to 10 days) in different nests.[451] Females may release around half of their eggs the first time they spawn and one fourth in a second spawning event with another male, and then later, the final fourth of their eggs in a third spawning event with a third male according to one researcher.[452] Another researcher says that female bass deposit only a fraction of their eggs each year.[453] So, the available scientific information on largemouth bass spawning can be confusing. More research is needed.

The eggs make up at least 10 percent of the female's body weight before spawning.[454] The number of eggs a female lays is proportional to her weight, with one researcher estimating 2,000 to 7,000 eggs per pound of body weight.[455] Big ShareLunker bass (13 pounds or bigger) in the Texas program lay between 20,000 and 100,000 eggs in the controlled environment of the hatchery at Athens, Texas, where more survive and hatch than in the wild.[456] In the wild,

---

[449] SportsDay Staff, *supra* note 368; Maureen Mecozzi, *supra* note 370; Emily Steed, *supra* note 375; James Davis and Joe Lock, *supra* note 366.
[450] Steven Bardin, *Fish Biology: Largemouth bass*, *supra* note 367.
[451] Ken Smith Fishing, Part 2, *supra* note 386.
[452] James Davis and Joe Lock, *supra* note 366.
[453] SportsDay Staff, *supra* note 368.
[454] James Davis and Joe Lock, *supra* note 366.
[455] Emily Steed, *supra* note 375; Steven Bardin, *Fish Biology: Largemouth bass*, *supra* note 367.
[456] Kyle Roberts, *The Texas wildlife program working to ensure the future of big bass fishing in the state*, WFFA8, May 19, 2021, available at

female bass deposit only a fraction of their eggs each year, and some females don't spawn every year.[457] One researcher estimated that the average female produces 4,000 offspring during each spawning season.[458] Bass continue mating until they are around 12 years old.[459]

Once spawning is complete, a nest contains between 5,000 and 43,000 eggs.[460] The fertilized eggs are adhesive and demersal (i.e., they stick to and stay on the bottom of the body of water).[461] Once ripe and water-hardened, the eggs are from 1.4 to 1.8 mm in diameter and are yellow to orange in color.[462] Egg size typically corresponds to the body size of the female, so the bigger eggs are usually from bigger females.[463]

Post-spawn

Once the eggs are in the nest, the male stays behind to fan the eggs with his fins, to guard the nest as the eggs hatch, and to guard the new fry until they are mature enough to survive on their own.[464] The male fans the eggs around the clock with his fins and tail.[465] Eggs usually hatch in 2 to 4 days in southern states, but hatch timing ranges from 1 to 10 days depending upon water temperature with them hatching earlier in warmer water that colder water.[466] For example, largemouth bass eggs hatch in 4 days at 60°F (15.6°C), but hatch in just 3 days at 67°F (19.6°C).[467]

The male typically guards the six foot area around a nest by actively rotating its body inside the nest and chasing off potential

---

https://www.wfaa.com/article/features/originals/texas-sharelunker-program-works-future-big-bass/287-580dacd0-cfbc-48c4-b45a-56fbd4bc14fc.
[457] SportsDay Staff, *supra* note 368.
[458] Emily Steed, *supra* note 375.
[459] Id.
[460] Texas State University, San Marcos, *supra* note 373; Maureen Mecozzi, *supra* note 370.
[461] Texas State University, San Marcos, *supra* note 373; Steven Bardin, *Fish Biology: Largemouth bass*, *supra* note 367.
[462] Texas State University, San Marcos, *supra* note 373.
[463] Steven Bardin, *Fish Biology: Largemouth bass*, *supra* note 367.
[464] Texas State University, San Marcos, *supra* note 373.
[465] Id.
[466] James Davis and Joe Lock, *supra* note 366; Steven Bardin, *Fish Biology: Largemouth bass*, *supra* note 367; Emily Steed, *supra* note 375.
[467] Texas State University, San Marcos, *supra* note 373.

predators like bluegill.[468] Soon after spawning (within hours up to a couple of days), the female leaves or is chased away from the nest area.[469] Eager males yet to spawn harass "spawned out" females to the point that they move away from spawning areas causing some to suspend offshore and others to "move to or return to home ranges in deeper water" fairly quickly after they have spawned.[470]

Males are fiercely territorial and guard the nest vigorously against intruders.[471] While the males do not feed during this time, they can still be caught due to their aggressive behavior during which they will remove potential predators and artificial baits from the nest by carrying them in their mouths.[472] In contrast to females' muscle activity spiking on the day of the spawn, male muscle activity remains high during "nest excavation, shuddering, and post-spawn parental care activities," and male activity rises even after spawning "as a result of their engagement in parental care activities."[473] Males generally do not eat during spawning, and "many males die each year due to their poor body condition prior to the spawning period."[474]

Newly hatched bass are called fry and are transparent, are around 3 mm long, and have no mouth parts.[475] Mouth parts develop in around 18 hours.[476] They remain in the bottom of the nest for the first week or two until their yolk sac is absorbed.[477] Once the yolk sack is absorbed, the fry "swim up" from the bottom and congregate in a school feeding on zooplankton in the nest area which is being protected by the male from predators.[478] The male protects the nest and school of fry until they reach independence, which is usually for around 7 to 10 days (but can be up to 5 weeks) after all of the fry have

---

[468] Id.; James Davis and Joe Lock, *supra* note 366.
[469] S.J. Cooke, et al., *supra* note 381.
[470] Ralph Manns, *Life of bass: Size factors*, IN-FISHERMAN, March 28, 2019, available at https://www.in-fisherman.com/editorial/life-of-bass-size-factors/358997.
[471] Maureen Mecozzi, *supra* note 370.
[472] Texas State University, San Marcos, *supra* note 373.
[473] S.J. Cooke, et al., *supra* note 381.
[474] James Davis and Joe Lock, *supra* note 366.
[475] Steven Bardin, *Fish Biology: Largemouth bass*, *supra* note 367.
[476] Id.
[477] Maureen Mecozzi, *supra* note 370.
[478] Steven Bardin, *Fish Biology: Largemouth bass*, *supra* note 367; James Davis and Joe Lock, *supra* note 366.

hatched.[479] This confines the spawning males to a small range and shallow area.[480] These adult males are called "fry guarders" by fishermen.[481]

Once the adult male leaves, the fry school disperses.[482] The fry form swarms and may join swarms from 1 to 4 other nests to gradually form a school as they reach fingerling size.[483] Significant predation from other fish, birds, and aquatic animals means that the majority of fry do not make it to adulthood.[484]

From a fishing standpoint, males do not feed much while guarding their fry or guarding the nest, but they remain very catchable due to their aggressive behavior.[485] In contrast, females continue to feed with spawning activity, and the fact that males are not feeding means that there is more prey available to the larger females, which can make them harder to catch.[486] Females are larger than males and can also ingest larger shad, which are more abundant in springtime due to "size-differential mortality during the winter."[487]

The physical costs on male bass during the spawning period are high from nest building, mating, and guarding combined. Some have theorized that this is why males do not get as big as females. Males eat infrequently and opportunistically during the spawn.[488] Male bass are very active and constantly moving during this time, but this movement does not show up in large scale telemetry measures.[489]

---

[479] Emily Steed, *supra* note 375; Maureen Mecozzi, *supra* note 370; K.C. Hanson, et al., *Intersexual variation in the seasonal behaviour and depth distribution of a freshwater temperate fish, the largemouth bass*, CANADIAN J. ZOOLOGY 86: 801-811 (2008), available at http://fishlab.nres.illinois.edu/Reprints/Hanson%20et%20al%20CJZ%202008.pdf; James Davis and Joe Lock, *supra* note 366.
[480] K.C. Hanson, et al., *Intersexual variation*, *supra* note 479.
[481] Maureen Mecozzi, *supra* note 370.
[482] Id.
[483] Id.
[484] Id.
[485] S. Marshall Adams, et al., *Energy partitioning in largemouth bass under conditions of seasonally fluctuating prey availability*, TRANSACTIONS OF THE AMERICAN FISHERIES SOCIETY 111(5): 549-558, September 1982, available at https://afspubs.onlinelibrary.wiley.com/doi/10.1577/1548-8659%281982%29111%3C549%3AEPILBU%3E2.0.CO%3B2.
[486] Id.
[487] Id.
[488] K.C. Hanson, et al., *Intersexual variation*, *supra* note 479.
[489] Id.

In one study, researchers estimated that nest guarding males swim the equivalent of 30 miles (49 km) per day compared to only 7.5 miles (12 km) for females and non-nest-guarding males.[490] However, they remain in an isolated area, so their swimming activities are short bursts and do not cover as much distance as other bass.[491]

The time around the spawn is the best time to catch a giant bass. So, pay attention especially to the actions of the female in this chapter, as they are the bigger fish. Sex-specific differences are most obvious during the spawning period.[492]

Overview/Summary

The spawn is a major annual event in bass's lives and consumes a large amount of energy and focus during preparation, mating, and recovery. The timing varies by geographic latitude. For example, the largemouth bass spawning period lasts from mid-February to early May in most of Texas,[493] but is from mid-April to early July in Wisconsin.[494] In some locations, it is much shorter—like Pickwick Reservoir on the Tennessee River, where it is from March to mid-April.[495] In other locations, like Florida, it is much longer. At Toledo Bend, the spawn begins in January, but quite a few fish do not move up to spawn until April.[496]

Individual male bass are triggered to begin searching for nest sites when the water temperature reaches around 60°F. Once they find a nest site, they then spend hours building the nest during a very strenuous process. Individual males generally stay in the nest area for 2-4 weeks (if unsuccessful) or 4 to 6 weeks (if successful). So, during the spawning period, males are shallower, but not generally eating. However, they are catchable because they often attack out of aggression. Males are rarely over five pounds.

In contrast, prior to spawning, individual female bass wait nearby the nest in deeper water once they are ready to spawn. They

---

[490] Id.
[491] Id.
[492] Id.
[493] Texas State University, San Marcos, *supra* note 373; Emily Steed, *supra* note 375.
[494] Maureen Mecozzi, *supra* note 370.
[495] Texas State University, San Marcos, *supra* note 373.
[496] Ken Smith Fishing, Part 2, *supra* note 386.

are on the nest for a few hours up to a couple of days while spawning. Individual females stay in the general vicinity of the nests for 7 to 30 days to spawn over multiple nests (usually 2 or 3). During this time, they continue to eat and remain catchable although there is typically a lot of forage available since the males are not eating which can make it a tough female bite to get. They are also catchable when on the nest, except generally during the actual act of spawning. Females are generally the "lunkers."

After they are finished spawning, females leave the general spawning area and set up nearby in deeper water and away from harassing males or head back to their home range (if it is in a different area). Females are hungry and ready to eat during their individual post-spawn period; they have lost at least 10 percent of their body weight during the spawning process. Overall, most females and presumed females or unsuccessful males are thought to spend around 2 weeks to 1 month shallow in their spawning area.[497]

During the time around the spawn, it may make more sense to fish for either pre- or post-spawners depending upon how many weeks into the period you are fishing and your goals. If you want to catch the biggest fish, then fishing for pre-spawners or for bed fish is likely to be more productive for most of the period, but your odds of catching them decrease as the spawning season progresses and more and more bass become "post-spawn" (and at least 10% lighter). Bigger fish are likely to spawn in less visible places like deeper water in pressured lakes, so searching for less visible spawners can help increase the size of your catches.[498] One pro, Keith Combs, looks in 5 to 6 feet deep areas for beds that are harder to see for the average angler and also describes how he will "bed fish blind" by fishing baits very slowly around likely spawning locations like stumps on Lake Guntersville in 5 to 6 feet deep water.[499] He thinks "a great many bass spawn deeper than we can conceive of seeing them."[500] One technique for deep water bed fishing in clear water involves using a bathyscope or "Flogger," which is a "cone-shaped looking device that allows an angler to put his or her viewing pane below the surface of

---

[497] Ken Smith Fishing, Part 1, *supra* note 385.
[498] Pete Robbins, *Finding and Catching Deep Bedding Bass*, IN-FISHERMAN, March 21, 2022, available at https://www.in-fisherman.com/editorial/finding-and-catching-deep-bedding-bass/458913.
[499] Id.
[500] Id.

the water to watch a fish's behavior."[501] Using a team with one person watching and another fishing can be particularly effective.[502]

Combs also mentioned using "today's high-end sonar units" to "see some deeper bedding fish and analyze their behavior in real time."[503] Some researchers have noted that bass have been observed spawning in waters up to 25 feet deep.[504] Bass have also been observed spawning on wide limbs nowhere near the bottom in trees in deep water. These deeper spawners could represent a significant portion of the fish that are deemed "nonreproductive" in the scientific studies using telemetry discussed later in this chapter. If so, finding these less pressured fish might increase the size of your catches if you can learn to find and target them.

More scientific studies are needed to find out more about how many bass spawn shallow, deep, during spring, during fall, etc.—perhaps with bass telemetered with EMGi monitoring for longer periods of time to look for shuddering associated with spawning activities. Much remains to be answered about the spawning habits of largemouth bass in my opinion.

---

[501] Id.
[502] Id.
[503] Pete Robbins, *supra* note 498.
[504] James Davis and Joe Lock, *supra* note 366; Pete Robbins, *supra* note 498.

> **Question Box:**
> **How can you tell a male bass from a female bass?**
> Largemouth bass are not very sexually dimorphic in the way their bodies appear externally—so it is hard to tell the sexes apart.[1] Female bass are almost always the bigger fish on a nest; otherwise, the sexes are hard to distinguish! I could find no scientific support for the idea that males' lower jaws come to more of a point than females, even though a couple of my Lake Fork University guide professors said this was a valid way to tell the sexes apart. So, I think this is simply not true.[2] Researchers also say that it is "nearly impossible to manually strip eggs from [females] until immediately prior to spawning," so this is not a valid technique either.[3]
>
> According to researchers, the valid ways to tell the sexes apart include the "presence or absence of a swollen reddish genital papilla (89% accurate in spring, but only 48% in fall), the shape of the scaleless area surrounding the urogenital opening ('poor indicator'), and the depth and angle of probe penetration into the urogenital opening (90 to 94% accurate)."[4] But even these techniques in the hands of expert biologists were not 100% accurate—especially the farther you get away from the peri-spawn period.
>
> ---
> [1] Koji Yokogawa, Aquaculture Sci. **62**(4), 361-374 (2014).
> [2] G.W. Benz and R.P Jacobs, Practical field methods of sexing largemouth bass, Benz, 1986, G. W. Benz & R. P. Jacobs (1986): Practical Field Methods of Sexing Largemouth Bass, The Progressive Fish-Culturist, 48:3, 221-225
> [3] S.J. Cooke, et al., Physical activity and behavior of a centrarchid fish, Micropterus salmoides, during spawning, Ecology of Freshwater Fish 2001: 10: 227–237.
> [4] Benz, supra note 2.

Analytics of the Spawn

Many bass anglers and writers think of the spawn as an event where all the fish are pre-spawn, then spawning, and then post-spawn—all at the same time. So, a buddy of mine will see fish spawning on his home lake in mid-March, and two weeks later, he will tell me that the spawn is "over" on that lake, so he is now only fishing for post-spawners. However, that is not how the spawn works. The largemouth bass shallow spawning season is a 60-to-90-day (8 to 13 weeks) period in spring when water temperatures are between 55-

and 75°F—although there are exceptions at a few fisheries.[505] At any point during this period, some bass are indeed spawning, but a larger percentage are either pre- or post-spawn depending upon the week of the spawning cycle. In addition, some bass are "non-reproductive" and not participating at all.

Figure 1 is a depiction of a hypothetical 12-week spawning season in a hypothetical lake containing 100,000 bass with one week on each side of the spawn (making a total of 14 weeks depicted in the graph) before the spawn begins when all the bass are theoretically pre-spawn and after it is over when all the bass are theoretically post-spawn. The graphs show the number of fish in each phase of the spawn (i.e., pre-spawn, spawning, post-spawn, and non-spawners).

Figure 1: Number of bass in each stage of a hypothetical spawn of 100,000 bass during a 14-week spawning period (including weeks before the spawn starts and after completed).

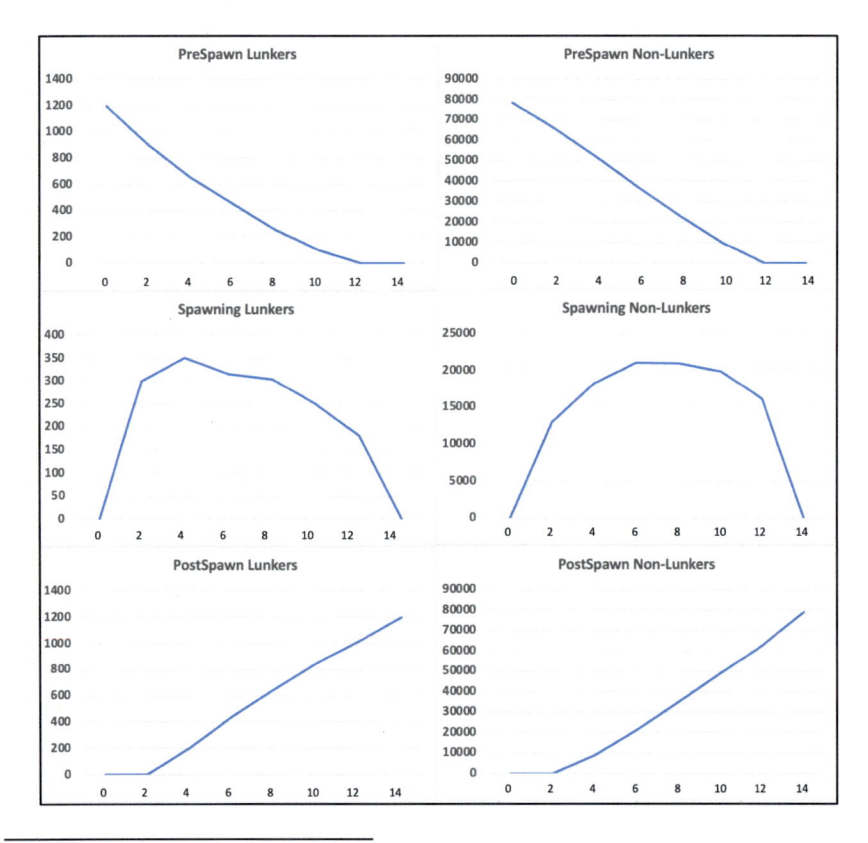

---

[505] SportsDay Staff, *supra* note 368.

Notice in the graphs in Figure 1 that some bass are at all stages throughout the spawning time period. Notice that there are more bass either pre- or post-spawn at all time periods during the "spawn" than bass spawning. So, on any one day from the beginning to the end of the spawning period, you could catch an individual bass that is pre-spawn, another that is post-spawn, another that is actively spawning on a bed, and another that is not participating in the spawn. The odds of catching a bass in each category change as the spawning period advances. Figure 2 is another depiction of the same hypothetical data to present it another way.

Figure 2: Two-dimensional area/line chart of the same data from Figure 1. Hypothetical spawning season at a hypothetical lake in Texas with 100,000 bass (lunkers are not broken out in this chart).

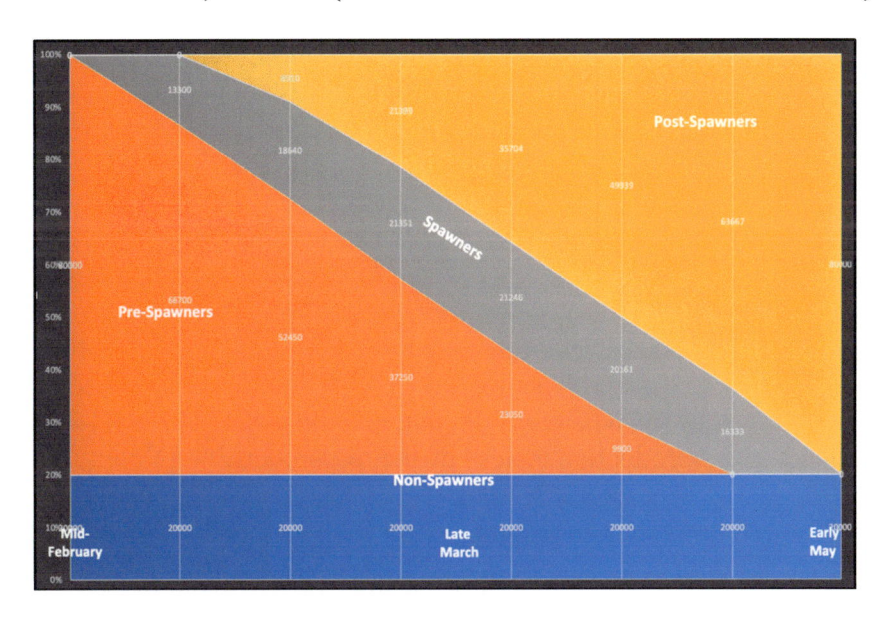

Looking at Figure 2, notice that in early March in this hypothetical southern lake, you are much more likely to catch a pre-spawner than a post-spawner. However, by early April, the opposite is true. Also note that the odds of finding a bass on a bed (a "spawner") remain stable throughout the spawning period, and there are fewer spawners than pre-and post-spawners throughout the spawning period. In reality, bass may bed in waves at some lakes throughout the period, but the overall numbers are likely fairly stable.

In addition, throughout the spawning period, you could catch a "pre-spawner," a "post-spawner," a bed fish, and a non-spawner all on the same day.

Depending on your goals, it may make more sense to fish for pre-spawners when more fish are in that mode and post-spawners when more fish are there. However, you could also choose to chase a pre-spawn giant before she "spawns out" at any point during the spawning season, but your odds of success simply decrease as the season progresses and fewer and fewer individual bass are in that pre-spawn phase.

What about the idea of "non-spawners" in my graphs above? Based upon several scientific articles (see discussion that follows) and observations of one of my Lake Fork University professor guides, I think some bass do not participate in the shallow spring spawn and perhaps do not spawn at all in a given year or maybe spawn in deeper water or spawn in the fall instead of spring.[506] I estimated the number of non-spawners to be 20% of the total population, which I explain below. Most likely, this 20% (or more) includes nonparticipants in the spawning ritual who stay home, deep spawners, fall spawners, and bass hanging out near the spawners but not participating.

As I was reviewing the literature to write this book, I noticed a pattern among the researchers that followed telemeter-tracked bass during the spring: *the researchers found that some bass did not move shallow and did not show any sign of participating in the spawn.* For example, in one study, researchers found that only 3 of 11 male bass followed in real time with acoustic telemetry built nests, received eggs, and raised fry, whereas 8 did not, and those 8 of 11 (73%) were deemed "nonreproductive males" by the researchers.[507] (Note: Calling them "nonreproductive" assumes that they have to move shallow and have to spawn in the spring to spawn, and either or both of these assumptions could be wrong if they spawn deep or spawn in the fall.).[508] So, in that study, only 27% of male bass behaved as classically believed during the spawn.

In another study, only 7/16 males spawned (43.75%), while only 5/8 females spawned (62.5%), which means 56.25% of males

---

[506] Steven Bardin, *Fish Biology: Largemouth bass*, *supra* note 367; SportsDay Staff, *supra* note 368 (noting that some female bass do not spawn each year).
[507] K.C. Hanson, et al., *Intersexual variation*, *supra* note 479.
[508] Steven Bardin, *Fish Biology: Largemouth bass*, *supra* note 367.

and 37.5% of females in that study were "nonreproductive."[509] In another study, out of 11 unsexed bass, none (0%) exhibited male spawning behavior.[510] A disappointing aspect of these findings is that none of the scientists comment on what is going on with the fish that are non-participants in the shallow spawn. So, I think there is an open question about exactly what percentage of bass move shallow to spawn in the spring. Hopefully, biologists will research this further by implanting EMGi monitors in tracked bass (preferably with real time telemetry for depth and location) to see what these bass are up to while a significant portion of the population moves shallow to spawn.

Looking at these numbers, it seems like most bass—especially male bass—may not actually move shallow to spawn during spring since less than 50% moved shallow to spawn in all the telemetered studies. However, I could not find any scientific literature even considering that possibility (most seemed to assume that all bass spawn shallow in the spring), so I had to pick a number of non-spawners for my projections. I chose 20% for "non-spawners" in the graphs in Figures 1 and 2 above as my best guess given the science available today. Researchers reported that around 20% of telemetered bass behaved in unexpected ways, so that seemed like the most acceptable number at this time.[511] In reality, I suspect that the number of bass that do not move shallow to spawn in spring may be much higher than 20% in many fisheries. At Lake Fork, I see many shallow spawners in the spring—they are everywhere! However, at my home lakes in Arkansas, I almost never see a nesting bass in shallow water at 2 out of 3 of the lakes that I regularly fish no matter how hard I look. So, something is different about the spawn at these lakes compared to Lake Fork. Due to the lack of scientific discussion on this topic, I want to keep my projections on the low end, and I think 20% "nonspawners" is a reasonable projection based upon currently available information.

Eventually, I think scientists may find that more bass than currently believed either spawn deep[512] or spawn in the fall[513] or do not spawn, and that there is much less than 100% participation in the

---

[509] S.J. Cooke, et al., *supra* note 381.
[510] Karle Woodward and Richard Noble, *supra* note 387.
[511] Ken Smith Fishing YouTube Channel, *Toledo Bend Telemetry Tracking Study Update Todd Driscoll TP&W Biologist Feb 2022.*
[512] Pete Robbins, *supra* note 498.
[513] Steven Bardin, *Fish Biology: Largemouth bass*, *supra* note 367.

classic shallow water spring spawn. Since telemetry just tracks movement, it would be difficult for researchers following telemetered bass to detect spawning activity in many studies without EMGi monitors or some other technique to detect the actual spawning act. So, I suspect there is much yet to be discovered about bass spawning habits.

Another reason I believe many bass do not participate in the shallow spring spawn is because one of my Lake Fork University guide professors who has worked on Lake Fork since it opened in the 1980s fished the same areas of the lake year-round (including spawning season) during the two years I spent fishing with him. When I asked him why, he told me that he believes some fish are "resident fish" and simply do not leave those areas with the seasons like many anglers believe. So, with him, we might fish shallow when all of the other anglers are fishing deep, and vice versa—including during spawning season. The areas he liked to fish for the "resident fish" tended to be more intermediate range in depth (maybe 7 to 15 feet on Lake Fork). I have no idea if this pattern holds on other lakes, but I do believe that he is right. These fish could be some of bass that the scientists deemed "non-reproductive" fish.

So, for now, the analytics of the spawn are simply best estimates because I think scientists still have a lot to learn about how largemouth bass spawn in the wild.

Sociological question: Is it okay to fish for bedding bass?
According to experts at Texas Parks and Wildlife Department, fishing for spawning bass in the southern United States "has little to no impact on production success at the population level" because female bass are very fertile and it does not "take a high percentage of brood success to adequately sustain population density."[1] The Texas experts say that "bed-fishing for bass is not a biological fisheries management issue in Texas."[2] When you think about the numbers, it is easy to understand why bed fishing has little impact—even in heavily pressured reservoirs like Lake Fork. Thousands of eggs are laid in each nest and only two fry would need to survive to adulthood per nest to replace the mating pair that produced them in the overall bass population.[3] Only around 0.02% of fry survive to adulthood due to heavy predation by other fish and by birds, so the size of the spawn rarely is the main factor that determines the size of the adult bass population.[4] Instead "suitable habitat, ample nutrients, availability of prey of suitable sizes, favorable water temperatures, and seasonal length and stability" determine the number of adult bass.[5]

---

[1] The Dallas Morning News Sportsday Staff, Sasser: Mating largemouth bass move to shallow areas, become easier to catch, March 3, 2014, available at https://www.dallasnews.com/news/2014/03/01/sasser-mating-largemouth-bass-move-to-shallow-areas-become-easier-to-catch/.
[2] Id.
[3] Ralph Manns, Infisherman, Life of Bass: Size Factors, March 28, 2019, available at https://www.in-fisherman.com/editorial/life-of-bass-size-factors/358997.
[4] Id.
[5] Id.

5

Study 2: Moon Phases and Big Bass

I think I have werewolf tendencies. A big ole' full moon in the night sky makes me especially excited to get on the water the next morning to chase big bass! My whole life I've heard over and over from fishermen everywhere that the days around full moons are the best time to catch big bass. But is that really true? Maybe more big bass (if that's even true?) are caught around full moons because fishermen like me have been told this story so long that we put in more effort on the days around full moons? Full moons enhance vision after the sun goes down because of the increased light available for creatures who rely upon sight.[514] Lots of studies of other animals have been done, and some have shown that full moons affect some animals' behavior—including humans.[515]

---

[514] Steve Quinn, *The effects of Solunar forces on bass fishing*, IN-FISHERMAN, July 13, 2021, available at https://www.in-fisherman.com/editorial/solunar-forces-on-bass-fishing/377272.
[515] Id.

But does the science really support a full moon effect for lunker bass? Are the moon phases and Solunar tables accurate for largemouth bass fishing? Are big bass more likely to bite around certain moon phases? Those are the questions I will try to answer in this chapter. This can be an emotional subject. Fishermen are so passionate about Solunar tables that at least two major fishing publications faced major backlash from angry readers for failing to include the tables in an issue.[516] Warning: I'm just the messenger here, so don't get angry with me if my results do not show what you expected!

Generalities and Prior Research

Many anglers believe the spawn peaks and waves are controlled by the moon phase and that largemouth bass feeding behavior is synchronized with the phases of the moon.[517] This idea was popularized by John Alden Knight in 1936 when he published his "Solunar" tables.[518] The Solunar tables predict times when the likelihood of fishing success is theoretically higher by predicting days and hours of increased fish feeding activity based on moon phase (and other factors for some tables).[519] Solunar tables are often published in fishing magazines and other wildlife publications recommending peak fishing days and times.[520] In this chapter, I will look at days based on moon phase; in a later chapter, I will look at time of day.

Scientists generally agree that "entrained endogenous rhythms associated with environmental cues, particularly in relation to the changing light conditions created by the differing lunar phases" affect the behavior and activity patterns of animals.[521] The Solunar effect is believed to be related to the influence on wildlife of the alignment of

---

[516] Id.
[517] Id.
[518] Mark Vinson and Ted Angradi, *Muskie lunacy: Does the lunar cycle influence angler catch of muskellunge?*, PLoS ONE 9(5): e98046, May 2014, available at https://www.researchgate.net/publication/262694023_Muskie_Lunacy_Does_the_Lunar_Cycle_Influence_Angler_Catch_of_Muskellunge_Esox_masquinongy.
[519] Id.
[520] K.C. Hanson, et al., *Effects of lunar cycles on the activity patterns and depth use of a temperate sport fish, the largemouth bass*, FISHERIES MANAGEMENT AND ECOLOGY 15(5-6): 357-364, December 2008, available at https://onlinelibrary.wiley.com/doi/abs/10.1111/j.1365-2400.2008.00634.x.
[521] Id.

the sun and the moon and said to be greatest when the sun and moon are aligned during the full and new moon.[522]

In marine environments, the moon phase affects both light conditions and tidal fluctuation related to the "moon's varying magnetic pull on the earth at different positions throughout the lunar cycle."[523] Behaviors of different species (including zooplankton, invertebrates, and fish) are affected by lunar cycles—including activities like predator avoidance, spawning behavior, and swimming activity.[524] Most research on lunar cycles has been done near the equator where the day length is more constant and the seasonal weather is less variable than northern and southern latitudes.[525] Research done near the equator (and on other species) may not translate to largemouth bass in non-equatorial locations like the United States.

In theory, fish depth is likely related to moonlight for several reasons. Generally, light from the moon affects vertical migration of fish at night.[526] Smaller fish and invertebrates like zooplankton migrate to deeper depths during times of increased moonlight to avoid visually oriented predators like largemouth bass.[527] Therefore, bass also migrate to those depths to follow their prey.[528] As levels of moonlight increase, the extended periods of light can help bass capture their prey using their vision, which is often better than their prey's vision in low light conditions.[529] Studies have shown that bass's efficiency of foraging at night is increased with the amount of moonlight.[530]

However, since most fishermen are fishing during daylight hours, moonlight penetration of the water column may or may not be relevant to daytime fishing. In a study discussed below, researchers found "nearly equal peaks in daytime catch during full and new moons" for a different fish species (the muskellunge) and concluded

---

[522] Mark Vinson and Ted Angradi, *supra* note 518.
[523] K.C. Hanson, et al., *Effects of lunar cycles*, *supra* note 520.
[524] Id.
[525] Id.
[526] Id.
[527] Id.
[528] K.C. Hanson, et al., *Effects of lunar cycles*, *supra* note 520.
[529] Id.
[530] Id.

that "lunar illumination per se does not account for variation in the muskellunge catch."[531]

In one study of largemouth bass, researchers followed telemetered, free-swimming largemouth bass in a lake in eastern Ontario, Canada and recorded swimming activity and depth distribution using three-dimensional acoustic telemetry array.[532] These researchers found that during spring and summer, bass inhabited greater depths on the 26-50% and 51-75% waxing moon.[533] A waxing moon is a moon that is going from new toward full. In other words, bass used deeper parts of the lake when the moon was 26-50% and 51-75% illuminated during the waxing phase of the moon cycle.[534] This supports the idea that bass are pursuing their prey to deeper depths when ambient light triggers zooplankton and small fish to descend to deeper depths.[535] Swimming activity and depth distribution of largemouth bass were affected by the "percent of lunar face shining and whether the moon was waxing or waning," but *consistent patterns were not detected throughout the year*.[536]

According to this study, lunar phase did appear to be a significant determinant of swimming activity, but *not in a uniform and repeatable way that could be tracked on a Solunar table*.[537] The only repeatable, uniform pattern was that depth distribution was affected by lunar phases in the spring and summer months.[538] So, it is possible during spring and summer months that if the moon drives bass to a depth where they are more catchable for some reason, the moon phase might matter. For instance, if bass are suspending at 15 feet, and there is a hump in deeper water that comes up to 15 feet, perhaps at this location bass may feed on that hump. However, daily movement distances showed no repeatable patterns in relation to the moon phases.[539]

---

[531] Mark Vinson and Ted Angradi, *supra* note 518.
[532] K.C. Hanson, et al., *Effects of lunar cycles*, *supra* note 520.
[533] Id.
[534] Id.
[535] Id.
[536] Id.
[537] K.C. Hanson, et al., *Effects of lunar cycles*, *supra* note 520..
[538] Id.
[539] Id.

Solunar tables typically predict the top fishing (and hunting) days to occur on the days of full or new moons.[540] Many outdoorsmen swear by them. Countless anecdotal articles about lunar cycle and fishing have been published.[541] However, the researchers in this acoustic telemetry study of largemouth bass found, "there appears to be *no conclusive scientific study* to support the claims that temperate sport fish behavior varies during certain times of the year in response to changing lunar periods in a manner that increases the likelihood of capturing fish via recreational angling."[542] These researchers found "*no evidence suggesting that activity levels of largemouth bass are affected by the lunar cycle in a repeatable manner throughout the year as suggested by Solunar calendars.*"[543] Overall, these researchers concluded that Solunar tables have "*little value for identifying peak fishing time.*"[544] They found no clear pattern of bass activity or depth distribution on an annual scale based on moon phase.[545]

One reason that lunar phase failed to support annual trends is the effect of the master abiotic factor—water temperature—on bass behavior and metabolism.[546] Water temperature has many effects on bass metabolism and swimming performance.[547] During spring and summer months, bass had five times greater movement distances than during winter.[548] During winter months, largemouth bass are quiescent, cease much foraging, and limit movements to a more localized area.[549] In northern latitudes where lakes are covered with ice and snow, moonlight cannot penetrate the water column, so the ambient light effects are minimized.[550]

In a different study with a different freshwater fish species, the muskellunge, researchers came to different conclusions.[551] In this

---

[540] See, e.g., Solunar Forecast and Predictions, *Best Fishing and Hunting Times Table*, available at https://solunarforecast.com.
[541] K.C. Hanson, et al., *Effects of lunar cycles*, *supra* note 520.
[542] Id.
[543] Id.
[544] Id.
[545] K.C. Hanson, et al., *Effects of lunar cycles*, *supra* note 520.
[546] Id.
[547] Id.
[548] Id.
[549] Id.
[550] K.C. Hanson, et al., *Effects of lunar cycles*, *supra* note 520.
[551] Mark Vinson and Ted Angradi, *supra* note 518.

study, the researchers compared fish catch records to lunar cycle.[552] Those researchers found that *the number of muskellunge caught strongly correlated to the lunar cycle* and that more fish were caught "around the full and new moon than at other times."[553] When night fishing, more muskellunge were caught around a full moon than a new moon.[554] *However, the overall maximum relative effect was less than 5%*, meaning that those anglers who fished only during peak lunar times would only catch 5% more muskellunge than anglers fishing on random days.[555] The effect varied by lake.[556] The effect of moon phase was stronger for larger muskellunge, stronger in midsummer (July, August), and stronger at more northern latitudes than southern ones.[557] Muskellunge are "sit-and-wait" predators, which is much different than largemouth bass where swimming activity may be a better indicator of feeding activity.[558] The authors concluded that for muskellunge there was a lunar synchronization in feeding around full and new moon cycles.[559]

However, there are several problems with this muskellunge study. First, it did not involve largemouth bass (and I could find no similar study for largemouth bass), and muskellunge are much different from largemouth bass as noted above. Secondly, the study is likely tainted by considerable bias since many fishermen believe that fishing is better around full and new moons, so angler activity increases during those times.[560] If there are more anglers on the water during full and new moons, then naturally, catch rates will almost certainly go up. While "angler catch of muskellunge is strongly related to the lunar cycle" in this study, it is possible that this is more a measure of angler behavior than fish behavior.[561] I know that I personally also tend to make sure that I am on the water near full and new moons because this has been passed along from other fishermen and in many fishing magazines over the years.

---

[552] Id.
[553] Id.
[554] Id.
[555] Id.
[556] Mark Vinson and Ted Angradi, *supra* note 518.
[557] Id.
[558] Id.
[559] Id.
[560] Id.
[561] Mark Vinson and Ted Angradi, *supra* note 518.

So, let's keep digging.

The Eight Moon Phases

There are eight phases to a lunar cycle that lasts approximately 29.5 days before beginning again. The phases represent a percentage of the moon illuminated and a trend toward either a full or new moon. The phases include (with the percent illumination and trend in parentheses) new moon (0% illumination), waxing crescent (1-49% illumination; trending toward a full moon), first quarter (50% illumination; trending toward a full moon), waxing gibbous (51-99% illumination; trending toward a full moon), full moon (100% illumination), waning gibbous (99-51% illumination; trending toward a new moon), third quarter (50% illumination; trending toward a new moon), and waning crescent (49-1% illumination; trending toward a new moon), and then the cycle starts over with new moon. Figure 1 shows this cycle.

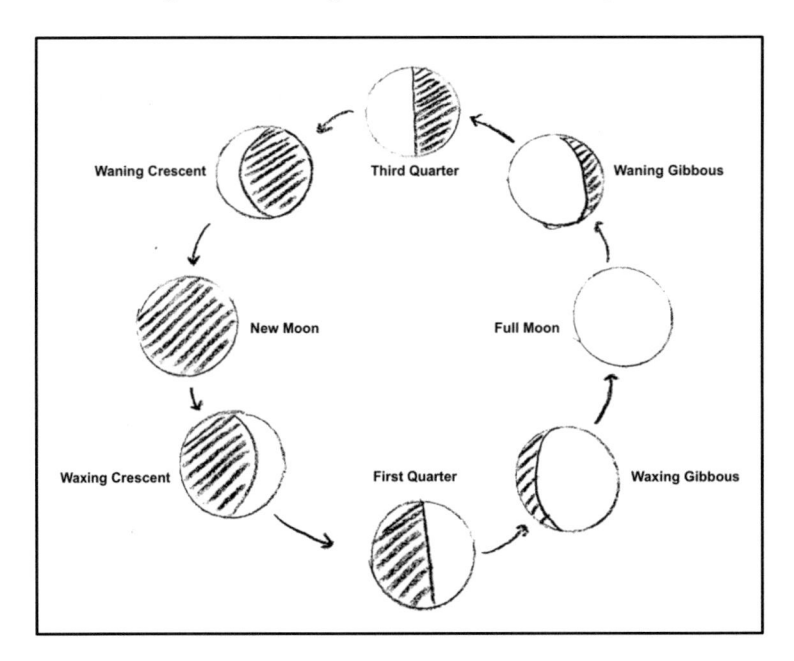

Figure 1: The phases of the lunar cycle.

On the night of a full moon, "the moon rises at about the time the sun sets and sets about when the moon rises."[562] In contrast, during a new moon, the moon "rises at daybreak and sets at sundown."[563] Around a week after a new moon, a half-moon appears mid-day and sets in the middle of the night.[564] Around a week after a full moon, a half-moon appears in the middle of the night and sets around mid-day.[565] When the half-moon appears, the lunar influence is greatest in the morning and evening, so some say these are the best fishing times during half-moons (i.e., first and third quarter moons).[566]

My ShareLunker Database Research

Background: To review, Texas Parks and Wildlife Department (TPWD) has a statewide program called the ShareLunker Program to develop big bass that has been discussed earlier in this book. Although some version of the program has been around since the 1980's, TPWD started the ShareLunker program year-round in 2018.[567] Since then, "anglers who reel in any largemouth bass at least 8 pounds or 24 inches can participate simply by entering their lunker catch information,"[568] which includes the bass's weight, length, location caught, date caught, and other information. Anglers are motivated to enter their fish because they receive a "Catch Kit" that includes a decal, merchandise, giveaways, and entry into drawings for larger prizes.[569] Plus, fish over 13 pounds may become legacy fish with offspring hatched and released into other Texas lakes.[570]

TPWD publishes an archive of all accepted lunkers over 8 pounds or 24 inches on their website, which is available to the

---

[562] Steve Quinn, *The effects of Solunar forces on bass fishing*, supra note 514.
[563] Id.
[564] Id.
[565] Id.
[566] Id.
[567] News Release, *Toyota ShareLunker Program begins new year-round season Jan. 1*, TEXAS PARKS AND WILDLIFE DEPARTMENT, September 29, 2017, available at https://tpwd.texas.gov/newsmedia/releases/?req=20170929a.
[568] TEXAS PARKS AND WILDLIFE DEPARTMENT, Toyota ShareLunker Program Texas Parks and Wildlife, available at https://texassharelunker.com.
[569] Id.
[570] Id.

public.[571] I used this public archive to analyze the data surrounding those catches to answer some common questions among bass fishermen. In the study in this chapter, I tried to answer the question: "What moon phase is best to catch a lunker bass?"

Moon Phases and 8+ Pound Bass Reported to TPWD in 2022

For this study, I focused on the data for one year, 2022. During 2022 a total of 511 lunkers over eight pounds were reported to TPWD through the ShareLunker program. The number of days the moon spent in each phase and different categories of illumination were counted for 2022 and are reported below. The number of lunkers expected if the moon had no effect was calculated based strictly on the percentage of days spent in each phase. The United States Navy database for moon phases at midnight Central Standard Time (Texas) was used to determine the percentage of moon illumination for each date a lunker was caught.[572]

The eight moon phases were defined as follows: New Moon (0% illuminated), Waxing Crescent (1-49% illuminated), First Quarter (50% illuminated), Waxing Gibbous (51-99% illuminated), Full Moon (100% illuminated), Waning Gibbous (99-51% illuminated), Third Quarter (50% illuminated), Waning Crescent (49-1%), and back to New Moon.

---

[571] TEXAS PARKS AND WILDLIFE DEPARTMENT, *Texas ShareLunker Archives*, available at https://texassharelunker.com/archives/.
[572] UNITED STATES NAVAL OBSERVATORY, Astronomical Applications Department, *Fraction of the Moon Illuminated*, available at https://aa.usno.navy.mil/calculated/moon/fraction?year=2022&task=00&tz=6&tz_sign=-1&tz_label=true&submit=Get+Data.

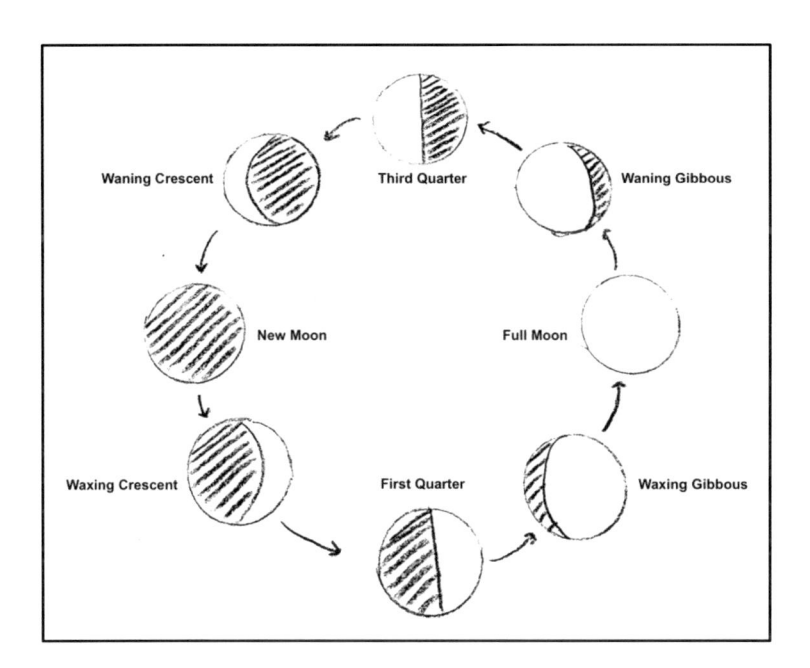

The moon spends very little time at exactly 50% illumination, and the definition of First and Third Quarters outside that range varies. There were only three catches when the moon was exactly First Quarter with 50% illumination. Therefore, the First Quarter category was eliminated, and these three catches were reclassified as Waxing Gibbous because that is the phase that the moon transitioned to during that night. There were no catches when the moon was exactly 50% illuminated in Third Quarter, so this category was also eliminated. These changes make the graphs and data less confusing given the varying definitions of quarter moon phases.

Results: There were 365 days in 2022 with a total of 17 New Moons, 89 Waxing Crescent Moons, 82 Waxing Gibbous Moons, 13 Full Moons, 80 Waning Gibbous Moons, and 84 Waning Crescent Moons. There were only 4 precise 50% illuminated quarter moons, and the three upon which lunkers were caught were reclassified as described above. The moon in 2022 spent 4.66% of its time in the New Moon phase, 24.38% in Waxing Crescent, 22.47% in Waxing Gibbous, 3.56% in Full Moon, 21.92% in Waning Gibbous, and 23.01% in Waning Crescent.

If the moon phase has absolutely no effect, the percentage of the 511 Texas 8+ pound lunker bass reported in 2022 during each moon phase should equal the percentage of days the moon spent in

109

that phase during the year. Using those percentages, there should have been 23.81 lunkers caught in New Moon phase, 124.58 during Waxing Crescent, 114.82 during Waxing Gibbous, 18.19 during Full Moons, 112.01 during Waning Gibbous, and 117.58 during Waning Crescent moons. Obviously, bass don't come in fractions/decimals, but I use the fractions/decimals to be precise in comparing actual to expected. Table 1 shows these numbers.

Table 1. Number and Percentage of 2022 Days in Each Moon Phase vs. Expected and Actual Number of 8+ lb. Lunkers Caught

Moon Phase	Number of 2022 Days	Percentage of 2022 Days	Expected Number of 8+ lb. Lunkers Out of 511 Caught	Actual Number of 8+ lb. Lunkers Caught
New Moon	17	4.66%	23.81	36
Waxing Crescent	89	24.38%	124.58	116
Waxing Gibbous	82	22.47%	114.82	120
Full Moon	13	3.56%	18.19	18
Waning Gibbous	80	21.92%	112.01	97
Waning Crescent	84	23.01%	117.58	124

Table 1 above includes the actual number of 8+ pound lunkers reported for each category in the far right-hand column. Notice that of the 511 eight plus pound lunkers caught in 2022, thirty-six lunkers were caught during new moons, 116 during waxing crescent, 120 during waxing gibbous, 18 during full moons, 97 during waning gibbous, and 124 during waning crescent moons.

To get the odds or chances of catching an 8+ pound lunker during each moon phase, let's simply divide the actual number caught by the number expected and multiplying times 100 to get the percentage of expected. Table 2 shows the results.

Table 2: Percentage of Bass Caught versus Expected During Each Moon Phase

Moon Phase	Expected Number of 8+ lb. Lunkers Out of 511 Caught	Actual Number of 8+ lb. Lunkers Caught	Percentage Actual vs. Expected	
New Moon	23.81	36	36/23.81 x 100 =	151.2%
Waxing Crescent	124.58	116	116/124.58 x 100 =	93.1%
Waxing Gibbous	114.82	120	120/114.82 x 100 =.	104.5%
Full Moon	18.19	18	18/18.19 x 100 =	99.0%
Waning Gibbous	112.01	97	97/112.01 x 100 =	86.6%
Waning Crescent	117.58	124	124/117.58 x 100 =	105.5%

Notice that during new moons, 151.2% of the expected number of lunkers were caught—or 51.2% more than expected—because 36 were caught, but only 23.81 were expected based on the number of days of 2022 spent in a new moon. So, in 2022, the *best* chances of an 8+ pound bass being reported to TPWD were on *new moon* days when the chances were 51.2% higher than expected.

In contrast, only 86.6% of the expected lunkers were caught during waning gibbous moons making it the worst performing moon phase in Texas in 2022 for reporting 8+ pound lunkers. Theoretically, therefore, anglers had a 13.4% lower than expected chance (100 percent minus 86.6 percent) of catching an 8+ pound lunker than an average day in 2022. Waxing gibbous and waning crescent were both better than expected, but only a little, with increased odds of 4.5% and 5.5%, respectively. In contrast, waxing crescent underperformed expectations with anglers catching only 93.11% of expected lunkers, meaning a 6.89% lower than expected shot. Full moon was closest to expected at 99% of expected because 18.19 were calculated as expected and 18 were caught. Figure 2 shows these numbers in graphical form.

Figure 2: **Percentage of Expected 8+ Pound Lunkers Caught During Each Moon Phase**

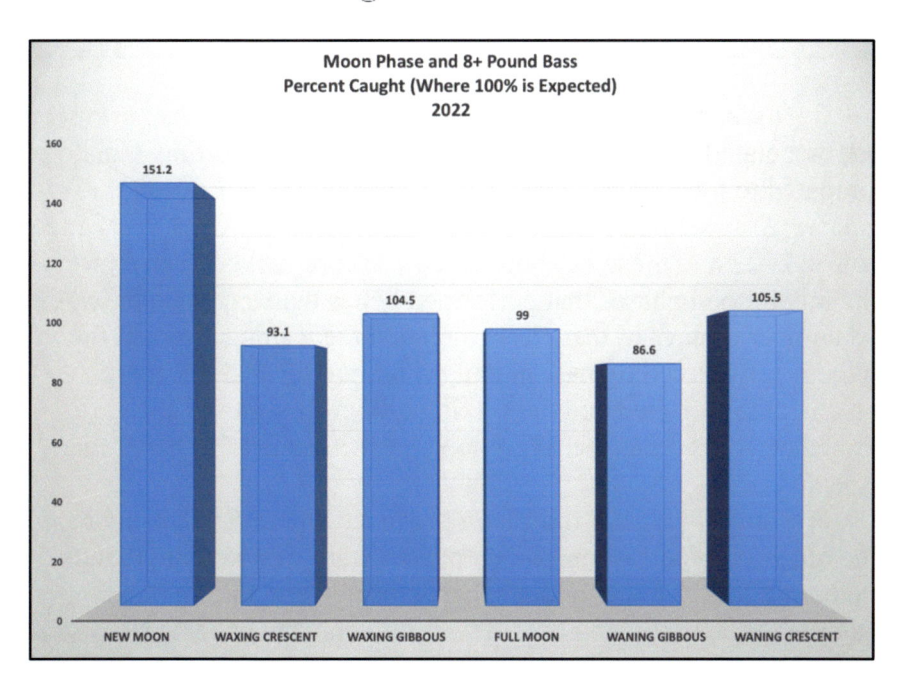

Figure 3 is another way of looking at the same data as the percentage increase or decrease in chances of catching an 8+ pound lunker during each moon phase.

Figure 3: Percentage increase or decrease in chances of reporting an 8+ pound lunker in Texas in 2022 based upon moon phase.

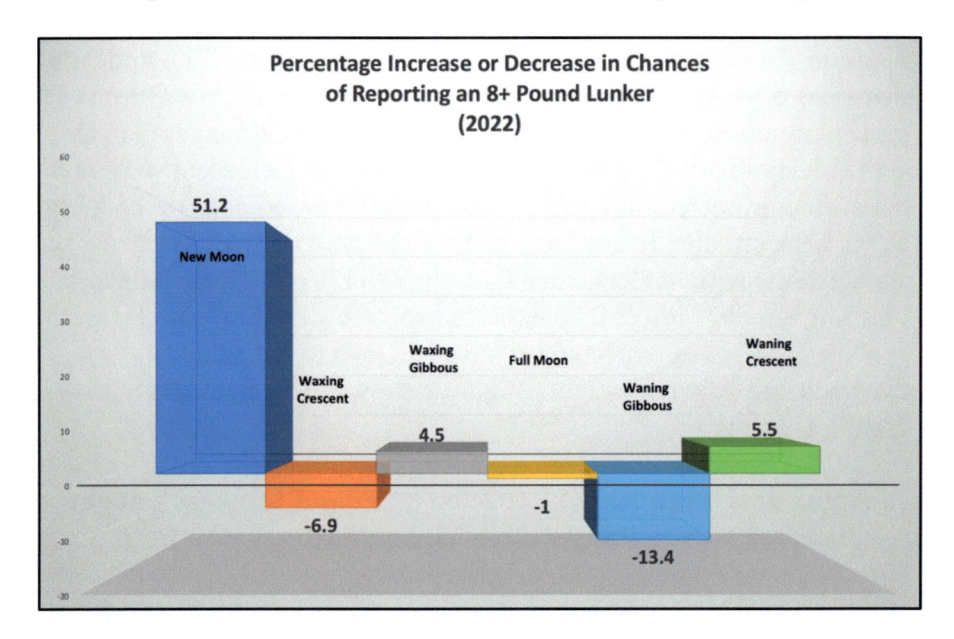

Percentage Increase or Decrease in Chances of Reporting an 8+ Pound Lunker (2022)

- New Moon: 51.2
- Waxing Crescent: -6.9
- Waxing Gibbous: 4.5
- Full Moon: -1
- Waning Gibbous: -13.4
- Waning Crescent: 5.5

    Notice that for 8+ pound bass in Texas in 2022, the new moon was associated with a 51.2% increased chance of reporting a lunker compared to the average day; so, *the new moon was the best time to catch an 8+ pound lunker in 2022 in Texas.* There were 17 new moon days in 2022 and those days produced 12 more lunkers than expected. The other moon phases that performed better than expected based on the number of days in that phase included the waning crescent moon immediately preceding new moons which produced 5.5% more lunkers than expected and the waxing gibbous moon which immediately precedes the full moon and produced 4.5% better than expected.

    Surprisingly, the full moon produced 1% LESS than average. The other underperforming moon phases were the waning gibbous producing 13.4% fewer lunkers than expected and the waxing crescent moon producing 6.9% fewer lunkers than expected.

From these findings, it is hard to find a definitive pattern, and the findings above may simply represent some random findings based on a statistical anomaly.

So, let's look at the data another way.

8+ Pound Lunkers Reported versus Percentage Moon Illumination

Let's look at the moon a different way—by percentage illumination—since many anglers believe this to be most important. We can start by comparing time spent around full moon and new moons, i.e, when the moon is almost full or new. For example, if the moon is 99% illuminated or 1% illuminated, is that also better than 50%. Technically, neither is a full or new moon, but both are close. So, does it matter?

To answer this question, I first looked at a graph to see how much time the moon spends near full or new. Figure 4 shows the number of days that the moon spent at each percentage of illumination in 2022.

Figure 4: Number of Days in 2022 the Moon was at Each Percentage of Illumination

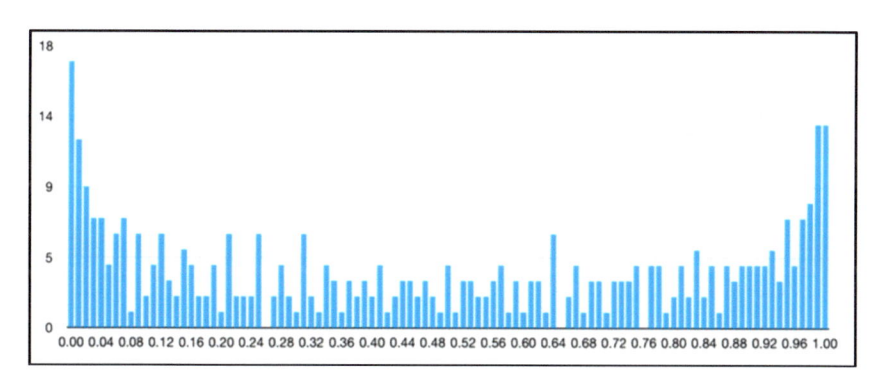

The chart above reveals that the moon spends a lot of time close to, but not exactly in, a full or new moon phase. So, I decided to divide the cycle into thirds to see if a pattern developed. The closest division to thirds meant dividing the phases into 0 to 25% illumination, 26 to 74% illumination, and 75 to 100% illumination. The number of days, percentage of days, expected number of lunkers, and actual number of 8+ pound lunkers for 2022 are shown in Table 3.

Table 3: Number and Percentage of 2022 Days in Each Moon Illumination Category vs. Expected and Actual Number of 8+ lb. Lunkers Caught

Moon Phase	Number of 2022 Days	Percentage of 2022 Days	Expected Number of 8+ lb. Lunkers Out of 511 Caught	Actual Number of 8+ lb. Lunkers Caught
0 – 25% Illumination	128	35.07%	179.21	195
26 – 74% Illumination	121	33.15%	169.40	143
75 – 100% Illumination	116	31.78%	162.40	173

These numbers show that when the moon was 0 to 25% illuminated, anglers fared the best and were 8.8% more likely to report an 8+ pound lunker because they caught 108.8% of expected (i.e., 195/179.21 x 100). The second-best time was when the moon was 75 to 100% illuminated when anglers reported 106.5% of expected (i.e., 173/162.40 x 100), which was 6.5% more than expected. Anglers fared the worst during the time that the moon was in between the full and new moons and was 26 to 74% illuminated because they only caught 84.4% of expected lunkers (i.e., 143/169.40 x 100), which is 15.6% below expectations. Thus, *more 8+ pound lunkers were caught nearer the full and new moon phases than during the periods in between.* These numbers are depicted in Figure 5 below.

Figure 5: Percentage of Expected 8+ Pound Lunkers Caught vs. Moon Illumination

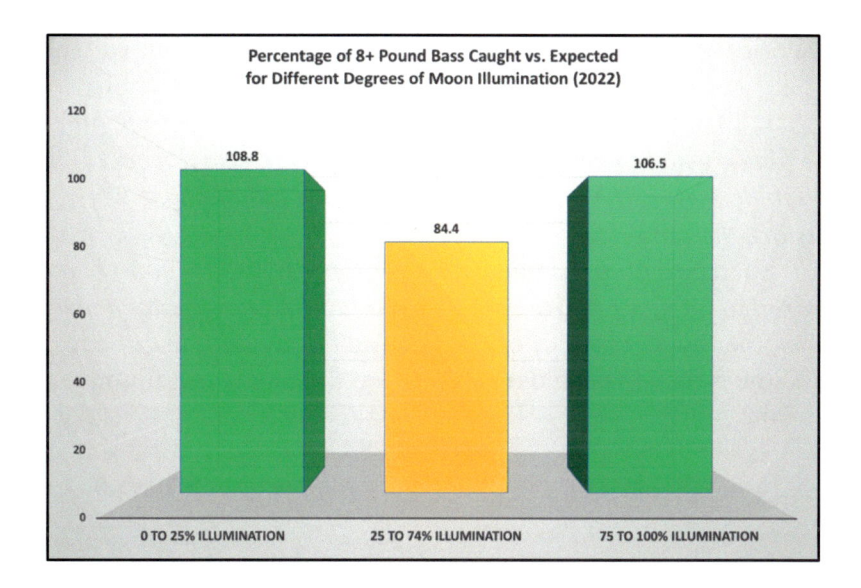

Figure 6 depicts the data a different way.

Figure 6: Percentage increase or decrease in chances of reporting an 8+ pound lunker in Texas in 2022 based upon moon illumination.

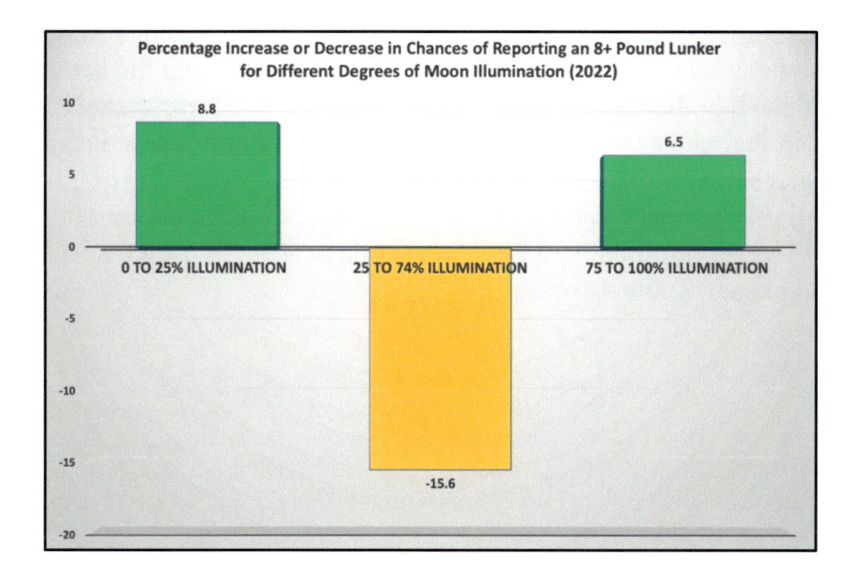

Note from Figures 5 and 6 that *the times around new (+8.8%) and full (+6.5%) moons were better than the interim times between new and full moons (-15.6%)*. These findings are more in line with the theories of the fishermen who advocate use of the Solunar tables. So, it is more likely that percentage moon illumination is more important than the specific moon phase, but surprisingly, *the full moon phase when there is more light at night for visual feeders like largemouth bass did NOT outperform the new moon phase when nights are the darkest.*

So, based on percentage moon illumination, *8+ pound lunkers appeared to be more active around both full and new moon phases.* On the other hand, chances of catching an 8+ pound lunker were 15.6% lower than expected on days when the moon was illuminated 26 to 74%.

Moon Phases and 13+ Pound Lunkers Reported to TPWD in 2022

Next, let's look at the giant 13+ pound ShareLunkers reported during each moon phase. Because these giants are rare, I looked at 5 years of data to get enough lunkers to evaluate. From 2018 through 2022, there were 87 bass over 13 pounds reported to TPWD. Sixty-three of these 87 giants (72.4%) were caught during the following months: Mar 2022, Jan – Mar 2021, Feb – Mar 2020, Mar 2019, and Mar 2018. Therefore, I counted days in each of the moon phases in those months to determine the expected number of lunkers during those dates to make the expectations more closely match the actual months when the biggest bass were being caught. There were 302 days in the relevant months counted. So, if the moon phase does not matter, then you would expect to catch a similar percentage of 13+ pound giants during each phase, i.e., the number of giants caught would be proportional to the number of days spent in each respective moon phase. Table 4 shows the results.

Table 4. Number and Percentage of 2018-2022 Days in Each Moon Phase During Relevant Months vs. Expected and Actual Number of 13+ lb. Lunkers Caught

Moon Phase	Number of Relevant. 2018-22 Days	Percentage of Relevant 2018-22 Days	Expected Number of 13+ lb. Lunkers Out of 87 Caught	Actual Number of 13+ lb. Lunkers Caught
New Moon	15	4.97%	4.32	1
Waxing Crescent	71	23.51%	20.45	25
Waxing Gibbous	70	23.18%	20.17	23
Full Moon	12	3.97%	3.45	7
Waning Gibbous	65	21.52%	18.72	12
Waning Crescent	69	22.85%	19.88	19

Based upon the above, only 1 of the 4.32 thirteen pound plus lunkers expected during new moons was caught, which is 23.15% of expected. In contrast, 7 thirteen pound plus lunkers were caught during full moons, while only 3.45 were expected, which means that 202.9% of expected was caught. In other words, *during a full moon, anglers were more than twice as likely to report catching a 13+ pound bass than expected* based on the number of full moon days. Table 5 shows percentage caught versus expected for all phases.

Table 5: Percentage of 13+ Pound Bass Caught versus Expected During Each Moon Phase

Moon Phase	Expected Number of 13+ lb. Lunkers Out of 87 Caught	Actual Number of 13+ lb. Lunkers Caught	Percentage Actual vs. Expected
New Moon	4.32	1	1 / 4.32 x 100 = 23.15%
Waxing Crescent	20.45	25	25/20.45 x 100 = 122.25%
Waxing Gibbous	20.17	23	23/20.17 x 100 = 114.03%
Full Moon	3.45	7	7/3.45 x 100 = 202.90%
Waning Gibbous	18.72	12	12/18.72 x 100 = 64.10%
Waning Crescent	19.88	19	19/19.88 x 100 = 95.57%

The results are depicted graphically in Figure 7 below.

Figure 7: Percentage of Expected 13+ Pound Lunkers Caught During Each Moon Phase

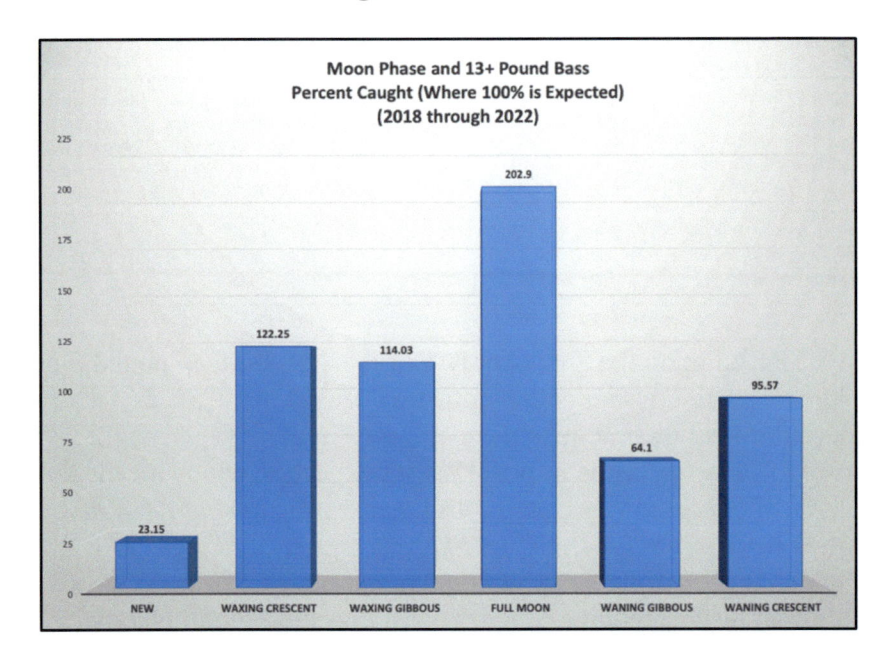

Moon Phase and 13+ Pound Bass Percent Caught (Where 100% is Expected) (2018 through 2022)

- NEW: 23.15
- WAXING CRESCENT: 122.25
- WAXING GIBBOUS: 114.03
- FULL MOON: 202.9
- WANING GIBBOUS: 64.1
- WANING CRESCENT: 95.57

Notice that the pattern here is different from the 8+ pound lunkers. *For 13+ pound lunkers, the full moon outperformed all the other moon phases and produced more than twice as many (202.9%) lunkers as would be expected based on the number of days spent in full moon phase.* New moons produced only 23.5% of the 13+ pound lunkers expected, which is markedly different from the findings for 8+ pound lunkers.

Also, *for 13+ pound bass, waxing moons outperformed waning moons.* The waxing moon phases (the phases that occur as a moon progresses from new to full) outperformed expectations for 13+ pounders with waxing crescent producing 22.25% more than expected and waxing gibbous producing 14.03% more than expected. In contrast, the waning moon phases (the phases that occur as the moon progresses from full to new) underperformed expectations with waning gibbous being the worst phase at 35.9% fewer than expected and waning crescent 4.43% under expectations.

So, for 13+ pound giants, the full moon was by far the best time and waxing moons clearly outperformed waning moons. Perhaps the true giants (13+ pounders) are nocturnal like big deer. Bass are

118

sight feeders. Maybe during full moons, the biggest bass are more actively feeding because they have more light at night.

Let's check the data another way, like we did for the 8+ pounders.

13+ Pound Lunkers Reported versus Percentage Moon Illumination

Now, let's look at the 13+ pound giants and percentage of moon illumination. A total of 87 thirteen pound plus lunkers were caught during the relevant days from 2018 through 2022 (see discussion above of "relevant days"). The numbers for each category are included in Table 6.

Table 6: Number and Percentage of 2018-2022 Days in Each Moon Illumination Category vs. Expected and Actual Number of 8+ lb. Lunkers Caught

Moon Phase	Number of Relevant 2018-22 Days	Percentage of 2022 Days	Expected Number of 13+ lb. Lunkers Out of 87 Caught	Actual Number of 13+ lb. Lunkers Caught
0 – 25% Illumination	103	34.1%	29.7	27
26 – 74% Illumination	102	33.8%	29.4	31
75 – 100% Illumination	97	32.1%	27.9	29

Based upon the data in Table 6, 27/29.7 or 90.9% of expected were caught from 0 to 25% illumination, 31/29.4 or 105.4% of expected from 26 to 74% illumination, and 29/27.9 or 103.9% of expected from 75 to 100%. These findings are depicted graphically in Figure 8.

Figure 8: Percentage of Expected 13+ Pound Lunkers Caught vs. Moon Illumination

Percentage of 13+ Pound Bass Caught vs. Expected for Different Degrees of Moon Illumination 2018 through 2022

- 0 TO 25% ILLUMINATION: 90.9
- 26 TO 74% ILLUMINATION: 105.4
- 75 TO 100% ILLUMINATION: 103.9

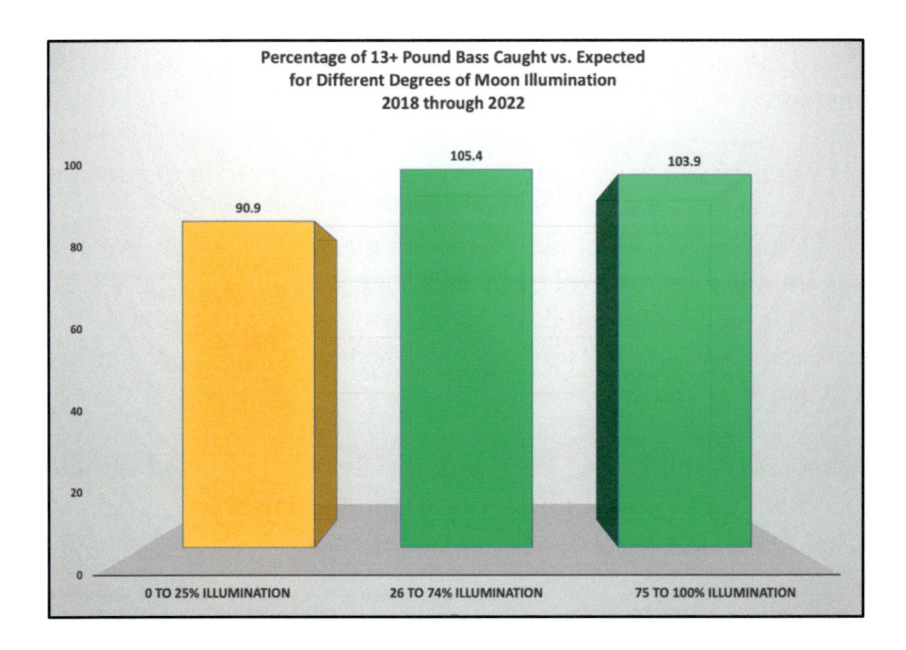

     Therefore, *the biggest bass (13+ pounds) tended to be caught less than expected when the moon was 25 percent or less illuminated but tended to be caught in higher-than-expected numbers above that range.* The graph shows anglers increased their chances of catching a 13+ pound bass between 3.9 and 5.4% by fishing when the moon is over 26% illuminated but decreased their chances by 9.1% by fishing when it is 25% or less illuminated. These would tend to support the theory that the biggest bass are more active during times when there is enough light to feed at night. Perhaps most 13+ pound bass are nocturnal feeders and mostly get caught during daytime when this feeding trickles over into the daylight hours. However, note that these effects for moon phase are relatively small compared to findings in some of the other studies in this book, so moon phase may be overwhelmed by other factors discussed in this book.

Individual Angler Results by Moon Phase

     The findings regarding moon phase above were small given the inconsistencies between the categories of bass studied. So, how much does moon phase matter for an individual angler (versus a large population in the study above). Let's look at my own personal biggest bass catches to see. Table 7 shows my 12 biggest bass and the moon phase and illumination when each was caught.

Table 7: My Top Twelve Bass with Moon Phase and % Moon Illumination

12 lbs. 9 oz.	Waning Crescent	33%
10 lbs.	Full Moon	100%
9 lbs. 7 oz.	New Moon	0%
9 lbs.	Waxing Gibbous	99%
8 lbs. 14 oz.	Waning Crescent	33%
8.45 lbs.	Waxing Gibbous	93%
8.34 lbs.	New Moon	0%
8.22 lbs.	Waning Gibbous	93%
8.02 lbs.	Waning Gibbous	81%
7 lbs. 11 oz.	Waxing Crescent	46%
7.61 lbs.	Waning Gibbous	71%
7.5 lbs.	Waning Gibbous	59%

So, for me personally, 3 (25%) of my 12 biggest bass have come on either new (2) or full (1) moons. Six have come on waning moons, and three have come on waxing moons, which is the opposite of my findings above. All my bass were caught during daylight hours, and most in the afternoons. Average illumination at midnight for my top 12 was 59% illumination with 5 out of 12 (42%) being caught with the moon more than 75% illuminated. This might support the idea that bigger fish prefer to feed when there is more nighttime illumination. Overall, in small numbers of most individual fishermen, the bigger patterns discussed in this and other studies may not hold. So, go fishing when you can and only take these types of considerations into account if you can go fishing whenever you want or whenever you need a good excuse to tell your fishing buddies when you get skunked!

Conclusion

The relationship between moon phases and illumination is more complicated than many authors and fishermen would have you believe and is *likely easily overwhelmed by other factors*. Moon phase and illumination is simply one factor to take into consideration when choosing flexible fishing dates. I suspect that moon issues can be easily overshadowed in largemouth bass behavior by many other factors like weather, barometric pressure, time of day, season, and water temperature. *But overall, lunkers tended to be more active around full and new moons based on the analysis of the TPWD data with 8+ pound lunkers seeming to prefer the new moon while the giant 13+ pound lunkers seemed to prefer the full moons.* This is surprising because as many authors and fishermen acknowledge, there is a bias toward fishermen being on the water during full moons because of the common belief that full moons are better—yet fewer 8+ pound lunkers were caught during those times despite the likely increased fishing pressure.

One Lake Fork guide noted that many anglers believe that the full moon brings on the spawn in waves, so anglers plan their trips around the full moons which can bias the outcomes of any studies of catches during that time.[573] Full moons may be better in common vernacular because fishermen believe it's better and go fishing more around a full moon.[574] So, fishing effort and communication around full moons may have more to do with perceived increased catches than any lunar effect. For example, on a recent trip to Lake Fork, I met a couple of fishermen from Colorado who were at Fork for their annual spring fishing trip. They were very excited that they had timed it "perfectly" because they believed a "wave" of bass had just moved up on beds as they predicted based on moon phase. There were indeed a lot of bass up on beds. However, I had been at Lake Fork a few weeks earlier during a different moon phase, and there were just as many bass up on beds then. So, even though they were convinced they had chosen wisely based on moon phase, I think a lot of bass were on beds throughout the spring at Lake Fork that year, and I personally did not see any difference based on moon phase during my two trips, even though the moon phases were vastly different. Therefore, I was less convinced.

The numbers in my study are fairly small, so there are likely inadequate samples to make serious scientific conclusions from

---

[573] Steve Quinn, *The effects of Solunar forces on bass fishing*, supra note 514.
[574] Larry Hodge, *March is big bass month*, TEXAS FISH AND GAME MAGAZINE, 2004, available at
https://tpwd.texas.gov/fishboat/fish/didyouknow/inland/bassinmarch.phtml.

observations of these trends in this study. However, my findings are supported by reports of some other analyses. One Lake Fork guide "examined catch dates and moon phase of Texas' 50 biggest bass and found that almost half of them were caught with at least 75% illumination."[575] He reported that 42% of his own top 50 bass were caught when the moon was at least 75% illuminated.[576] Again, almost twice as many of the 13+ pound bass as expected were caught during full moons, and these are the class of fish that closest to the Texas top 50. While my data do not confirm his regarding illumination of greater than 75%, my data are at least supportive when it comes to the full moon itself.

In another analysis of 346 thirteen pound plus lunkers in the ShareLunker data by a different author back in 2004, the researcher also found that the giant 13+ pound bass preferred full over new moons.[577] That researcher found that 22% of 13+ pounders were caught "within two days either side of a full moon."[578] In contrast, he found that only 14% of those 13+ pounders were caught within 2 days of a new moon.[579]

Any effect of moon phase appears to be relatively small compared to other factors like time of year, weather, and time of day studied elsewhere in this book. So, fish when you can! And don't worry too much about the moon phase unless you have werewolf tendencies or need an excuse for a tough day.

---

[575] Steve Quinn, *The effects of Solunar forces on bass fishing*, supra note 514.
[576] Id.
[577] Larry Hodge, *March is big bass month*, supra note 574.
[578] Id.
[579] Id.

123

6

Home Ranges & Personalities

  Think about your fishing buddies for a minute. Fishermen have different personalities on the water. Some fishermen like to camp on a single spot for hours and carefully fish the area slowly and methodically. Other fishermen have two or three favorite spots they will cover and rotate through repeatedly in a day. I am personally this kind of fisherman. I have 3 or 4 spots on most lakes that I like for each time of year, and I concentrate my efforts in those spots rotating through them repeatedly at different times of day. Still other fishermen roam the whole fishery "covering water" with high-speed, on plane rocket trips all over the lake burning tanks of gas and covering the fishery from top to bottom. These guys sometimes make no casts or just a few casts after briefly checking their graphs before flooring the hotfoot and heading off to the next spot.
  Largemouth bass are a lot like fishermen—they have individual personalities and tendencies too.[580] Some bass "move just

---

[580] K.C. Hanson, et al., *Intersexual variation in the seasonal behaviour and depth distribution of a freshwater temperate fish, the largemouth bass*, CANADIAN J.

15 minutes in an 8-hour day, while others swim for hours."[581] So, broad generalizations about bass behavior often miss the mark because they fail to consider the variations in individual bass personalities and behaviors. This is particularly true when telemetered bass are followed to determine their "home range." A "home range" is the "area over which an animal regularly travels."[582] Home ranges limit the distance bass travel but not necessarily the amount of movement and activity within that defined home range. Tracking studies reveal that individual bass have a wide range of home range preferences. Some bass "occupy discreet locations for extended periods," whereas others decide to make "lake-wide movements" during the exact same time periods and conditions that others stay in a single location—sometimes with total daily movements varying as much as 25-fold or more between individual bass on the same body of water on the same day.[583]

Researchers using tracking studies have identified three categories of largemouth bass home range behavior.[584] First, most bass are *homebodies* that live in discrete and singular, well-defined home ranges year-round. Fifty-five percent of the telemetered bass in one study fell into this category.[585] The size of the home ranges of these homebodies vary greatly with some bass having small home ranges around the size of half of a football field, while other bass in the same fishery have huge home ranges the size of 100 football

---

ZOOLOGY 86: 801-811 (2008), available at http://fishlab.nres.illinois.edu/Reprints/Hanson%20et%20al%20CJZ%202008.pdf.
[581] Steve Quinn, *Understanding Lunker Largemouths*, IN-FISHERMAN, 2022 Bass Guide, 18-22, Summer 2022.
[582] Andrea Sylvia, et al., *Influence of largemouth bass behaviors, angler behaviors, and environmental conditions on fishing tournament capture success*, Iowa State University, available at https://dr.lib.iastate.edu/server/api/core/bitstreams/0bf6e7c2-a0b3-44dc-9aa0-6967449d29ff/content.
[583] Kyle Hanson, et al., *Assessment of largemouth bass behavior and activity at multiple spatial and temporal scales utilizing a whole-lake telemetry array*, HYDROBIOLOGIA 582(1): 243-256 (May 2007), available at https://www.researchgate.net/publication/226543386_Assessment_of_largemouth_bass_Micropterus_salmoides_behaviour_and_activity_at_multiple_spatial_and_temporal_scales_utilizing_a_whole-lake_telemetry_array; K.C. Hanson, et al., *Intersexual variation*, supra note 580.
[584] Kyle Hanson, et al., *supra* note 583.
[585] Karle Woodward and Richard Noble, *Over-winter movements of adult largemouth bass in a North Carolina reservoir*, PROC. ANNU, CONF. SOUTHEAST ASSOC. FISH AND WILDL. AGENCIES 51:113-122 (1997).

fields.[586] Second, many bass are like human "snowbirds" that move to Florida for the winter from New York. These *snowbirds* live in one home range during part of the year and live in a different home-range during a different part of the year. Sometimes they may even have a 3rd home range. Typically, these bass have a primary home range and a winter home range that differs from their primary home range.[587] When they decide it's time to move to their second home range, these bass often change locations very quickly and can travel several miles in a short time period between home ranges.[588] In the study above, 36% of the bass tracked fell into this category. Finally, a few bass (9% in the study) are homeless *nomads* with no identifiable home range roaming the fishery continuously.[589] Nomad bass often cover large areas of a fishery within a single day.[590] They are present even on very productive fisheries with plenty of forage, so there is no obvious reason for them to roam so much.[591]

The figure below shows an estimate of the percentage of bass in each of the 3 home range categories.

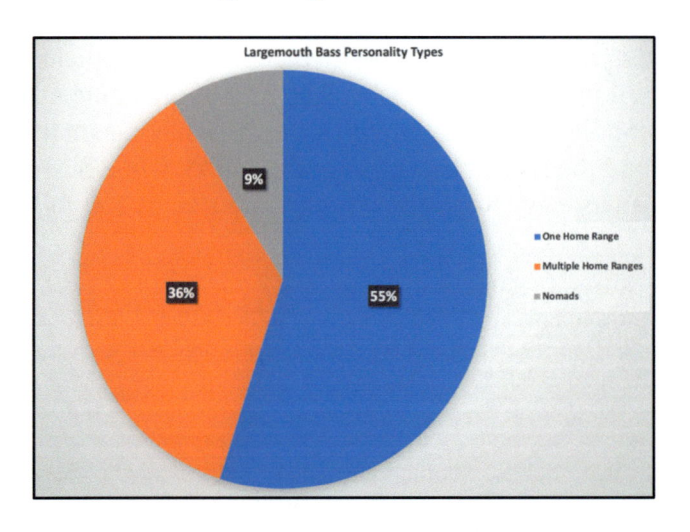

---

[586] Kyle Hanson, et al., *supra* note 583.
[587] Id.
[588] Id.
[589] Karle Woodward and Richard Noble, *supra* note 585.
[590] Kyle Hanson, et al., *supra* note 583.
[591] Ken Smith Fishing YouTube Channel, *Toledo Bend Telemetry Tracking Study Update Todd Driscoll TP&W Biologist Feb 2022 Part 5*, available at https://www.youtube.com/watch?v=f1sL9FZnS4g&list=PLLzhji805wVzkLnAA97I8VmdZpR8arB_Q&index=5.

Let's look at each home range personality type in more detail.

Single Home Range Bass (i.e., "Homebodies")

Most adult largemouth bass in tracking studies live a relatively "boring" life within a well-defined home range in an area where the bass spends its life and does not leave.[592] My Lake Fork University professor guides confirmed the "boring" life patterns of many bass. One Lake Fork guide and his clients have caught the same bass from the same flat over the years so many times that he finally named the bass. Another veteran Lake Fork guide told me that he considered many bass to be "resident" bass with small home ranges that live in a relatively small area year-round and do not migrate much with the seasons. I have friends who closely study their pictures of bass, and they have told me that they repeatedly catch the same fish in certain areas of the lakes they fish from year to year. If you fish the same lake or area annually, look back at some of your pictures and see if you have been catching the same fish repeatedly. You might be surprised.

Although the percentage varies in each study, these homebody bass are the clear majority with over half of the bass tracked exhibiting this pattern in the studies that I reviewed. For example, in an ongoing unpublished study of bass at Toledo Bend, the researcher considered the habits of 58% of the bass to be "boring" because they did not move much within a half-mile to one mile area—including a couple of bass larger than 6 pounds.[593] These homebody bass likely stay in areas that offer "the most food and best spawning opportunities" and "don't stray far from their spawning area unless they're forced away by changing water levels, lack of prey, or poor water quality."[594] Smaller home areas mean that they are "familiar with the structure and cover of their home area and may swim directly between their base and feeding grounds" without following cover or structure.[595]

---

[592] Karle Woodward and Richard Noble, *supra* note 585.
[593] Ken Smith Fishing YouTube Channel, *Toledo Bend Telemetry Tracking Study Update Todd Driscoll TP&W Biologist Feb 2022 Part 3*, available at https://www.youtube.com/watch?v=vBZBhEmkbAU&list=PLLzhji805wVzkLnAA97I8VmdZpR8arB_Q&index=3.
[594] Steve Quinn, *Understanding Lunker Largemouths*, *supra* note 581.
[595] Id.

The size of individual bass's home range varies greatly between individual bass and between bodies of water. Some bass have small home ranges, while others have much larger home ranges. For example, bass in one study in Lake Baldwin, Florida had home ranges that varied from 1.5 acres all the way up to nearly 100 acres.[596] Since one football field including end zones is 1.32 acres, one bass lived in an area that was only a little bigger than one football field, and another bass in the same lake lived in an area the size of 74 football fields! In another study in North Carolina, where the temperatures are colder than Florida, researchers found smaller home ranges than the Florida study averaging 5.21 acres (about 4 football fields) but ranging from 0.64 acres (a little less than half a football field) up to 19.35 acres (nearly 15 football fields).[597]

The characteristics of the fishery greatly influence the size and shape of home ranges. Prey density and competition from other fish affect bass activity level and home range size.[598] Some lakes have bigger home ranges because they have less prey density and not much vegetation, so the bass have to move over larger areas to find the food they need to survive; i.e., their foraging strategies are different than lakes covered in vegetation or in lakes more densely populated with prey.[599] For example, Lake Martin, Alabama had larger home ranges than other lakes in one study because "it is a relatively low productivity system with very little aquatic vegetation."[600] Lakes with vegetation often have different distributions of bass than lakes without such vegetation. During spring and summer, vegetation attracts forage fish that use the vegetation as food and cover, so largemouth bass are attracted and stay close to those areas because their food is nearby.[601]

Home ranges also vary in shape with some bass staying so close to shore year-round that their home range is better measured in

---

[596] Karle Woodward and Richard Noble, *supra* note 585.
[597] Id.
[598] Kyle Hanson, et al., *supra* note 583.
[599] Ryan Hunter and Michael Maceina, *Movements and home ranges of largemouth bass and Alabama spotted bass in Lake Martin, Alabama*, J. FRESHWATER ECOLOGY 23(4): 599-606 (2008), available at https://doi.org/10.1080/02705060.2008.9664247.
[600] Id.
[601] Kyle Hanson, et al., *supra* note 583.

length than area.[602] For example, in one study, a couple of telemetry tracked bass never got far from shore.[603] One had a home range length of around 900 yards (827 m) and another one's home range was around 820 yards (750 m) of shoreline.[604] Both were fish with multiple home ranges with one's winter home range being over 1300 yards (1210 m) long and the other's being around 370 yards (340 m) long, but neither ever got far from shore.[605]

Water temperatures can affect home range size because colder water temperatures generally decrease bass movement—so lakes farther north in colder areas may have bass with smaller home ranges than southern bass. For example, in one study in Florida, bass had home ranges from 1 to 74 football fields during one part of the year, while bass in colder areas in North Carolina had much smaller home ranges from 0.5 to 15 football fields during that same part of the year.[606] Similarly, bass can have smaller winter home ranges if prey concentrate in warmer areas related to inputs from springs or streams like they do at Watts Bar Reservoir.[607] So, bass can stay in these areas and maintain energy reserves while decreasing activity level during winter and be in better condition utilizing a smaller area than bass in the colder main lake areas.[608]

It is important to recognize that just because a fish has a home range does not mean that fish is not moving around during the day or year. Fish shift positions daily and by season based on conditions and can move from deep to shallow water and back within their individual home range. They move from cover to open water within their home range as well. So, as I discuss seasonal patterns later in this book, recognize that these patterns occur for individual bass within their home range area. In most lakes, an area the size of a football field, which is on the small end of bass home ranges, can have many

---

[602] Karle Woodward and Richard Noble, *supra* note 585.
[603] Id.
[604] Id.
[605] Id.
[606] Id.
[607] S. Marshall Adams, et al., *Energy partitioning in largemouth bass under conditions of seasonally fluctuating prey availability*, TRANSACTIONS OF THE AMERICAN FISHERIES SOCIETY 111(5): 549-558, September 1982, available at https://afspubs.onlinelibrary.wiley.com/doi/10.1577/1548-8659%281982%29111%3C549%3AEPILBU%3E2.0.CO%3B2.
[608] Id.

different types of habitats, depths, structure, and forage. So seasonal patterns are important, even if the individual bass has a small home range.

Bass with Multiple Home Ranges (i.e., "Snowbirds")

Some bass switch between home ranges depending upon the season. The most common pattern among bass with multiple home ranges is a primary home range and a winter home range—like the "snowbirds" who migrate south for winter. In one study, 36.4% of bass had multiple home ranges.[609] The author described this pattern as consisting "of a shift from an initial home range to a winter home range, and a subsequent return to the initial home range."[610] The winter home range moves were "toward larger portions of the impoundment and deeper water."[611] The distance between home ranges can be from 500 yards to several miles.[612] Multiple other researchers have reported similar findings.

For example, a 6 pound lunker named "Snowbird" had two home ranges—a primary home range and a spawning home range—that were 5 miles apart in Toledo Bend.[613] From July through December, Snowbird lived in a ¼ mile are near the shoreline in an area near a steep drop-off so that she could easily and quickly move between water that was 3 feet deep and water that was 25 feet deep.[614] During January, she made the five mile journey within 2 weeks to her second home range, but she evidently found the area too muddy to spawn during the month of February and quickly returned to her primary home range in early March.[615] Then, she traversed the same 5 miles back to her spawning home range in mid-April and stayed through May until the battery on her tracker died.[616] So, except for

---

[609] Karle Woodward and Richard Noble, *supra* note 585.
[610] Id.
[611] Id.
[612] Id.
[613] Ken Smith Fishing YouTube Channel, *Toledo Bend Telemetry Tracking Study Update Todd Driscoll TP&W Biologist Feb 2022 Part 2*, available at https://www.youtube.com/watch?v=vBZBhEmkbAU&list=PLLzhji805wVzkLnAA97I8VmdZpR8arB_Q&index=2.
[614] Id.
[615] Id.
[616] Id.

the quick five mile transits, she was always in very familiar areas in these two home ranges.[617]

Some bass even have more than two home ranges. For example, two bass in one study had "an initial home range, a winter home range, and an apparent spawning home area."[618] Neither bass spent more than a month in the spawning area.[619]

Researchers believe that these multiple home range bass "have either committed home range features to memory or mechanistic navigation cues (e.g., olfaction, vision, electrolocation, audition, water movement) may be independently identified year after year" to guide their migration, sometimes over miles of water that have changed from year to year due to flooding or drought.[620]

Bass with No Home Range (i.e., "Nomads")

Some bass are nomads that roam huge areas without a definable home range. These bass often travel great distances and are not bound to any particular area of the body of water. For example, in the Toledo Bend study, researchers found that 15.8% (3/19) of the tracked bass roamed so far that they did not even remain inside the 5.5 mile long and 1.45 mile wide embayment (totaling 4900 acres) where they were first found.[621] Nomad tendencies and the associated dispersal of gene pools are important for genetic diversity and help spread genes across the entire population of bass, even in large lakes—so there is likely an evolutionary advantage that has led to the persistence of these types of personalities among a few bass.[622] One such nomad, in the Toledo Bend study swam over 10 miles (7 miles "as the crow flies) during two weeks in January before being caught

---

[617] Id.
[618] Karle Woodward and Richard Noble, *supra* note 585.
[619] Id.
[620] Christopher Bunt et al., *Site fidelity and seasonal habitat preferences of largemouth bass in a temperate regulated reservoir*, HYDROBIOLOGIA 848: 2595-2608 (2021), available at https://doi.org/10.1007/s10750-021-04582-1.
[621] Ken Smith Fishing YouTube Channel, *Toledo Bend Telemetry Tracking Study Update Todd Driscoll TP&W Biologist Feb 2022 Part 1*, available at https://www.youtube.com/watch?v=DhCX1h6EN24&list=PLLzhji805wVzkLnAA97I8VmdZpR8arB_Q&index=1
[622] Karle Woodward and Richard Noble, *supra* note 585.

by an angler under a boat dock 7 miles from where it was released after tagging.[623]

Lunkers do not tend to be nomads. Some researchers have found that big bass tend to live in smaller home ranges and are less likely to be nomads.[624] Nomadic tendencies tend to decrease as bass get larger and older. Most nomads are of small or intermediate size.[625] For example, in one study, the only nomad was the smallest fish (12.95 inches).[626] In another study, on Table Rock Lake, the researcher noted that "the larger fish had smaller core home ranges, suggesting these larger fish may have sufficient foraging opportunities from a much smaller area."[627] Another researcher found that home range size was not correlated with bass's size, but all of the bass in this study were under 2 pounds.[628] I noticed that the nomads tended to be caught more often by anglers in these studies than the other types of fish. These fish may be so active, so mobile, and so curious, that perhaps they are the ones most easily tempted by fishing lures. This may be another reason that they are typically the smallest—they take more chances and just don't live long enough to reach large sizes, but more research is needed to make definitive statements about catchability and home range tendencies.

Conclusion

Lunker bass are likely to either have a single home range or to be snowbirds migrating between a couple of home ranges based upon the season. They spend their time in familiar surroundings as "creatures of instinct and habit" where they can easily navigate with full understanding of routes to deeper water, food, and/or cover.[629] They are so familiar with their home range that they "may swim

---

[623] Ken Smith Fishing, Part 2, *supra* note 613.
[624] Karle Woodward and Richard Noble, *supra* note 585.
[625] Id.
[626] Id.
[627] Jason Harris, Master of Science Thesis, *Habitat selection, and home range of largemouth bass following a habitat enhancement project in Table Rock Lake,* Missouri, University of Missouri MOspace, 2013, available at https://mospace.umsystem.edu/xmlui/bitstream/handle/10355/37945/research.pdf?sequence=2&isAllowed=y.
[628] Karle Woodward and Richard Noble, *supra* note 585.
[629] Steve Quinn, *Understanding Lunker Largemouths*, *supra* note 581.

directly between their base area and feeding grounds" without "following cover or structure."[630] They avoid "loud splashes, boat noises, and trolling motors associated with fishing."[631] The biggest bass is likely to be on the biggest hidden piece of cover on a nondescript flat that fishermen are likely to overlook.[632] They tend to hold "close to flats that offer() the most food and best spawning opportunities," and they "don't stray far from their spawning area unless they're forced away by changing water levels, lack of prey, or poor water quality."[633] Flats with big laydowns and stumps tend to be a favorite according to one biologist.[634] While they are rarely in the "middle of nowhere," they are often in "areas where there is little or no fishing pressure."[635] So, *fish where other fishermen are not*!

One question that remained unanswered in the home range studies that I reviewed is whether bass keep the same home range lifelong or switch to new home ranges from time to time in their lives. The studies are limited by the battery life of the tracking device implanted, so most of the studies are for a few months up to around a year and a half. For instance, do younger bass tend to live in certain types of home ranges while older larger bass tend to prefer a different type of home range. The closest answer that I could get is from a Lake Fork lunker named Missy.[636] Missy was implanted with a radio transmitter in 1986 after being entered into the ShareLunker program.[637] She was caught in 1992 a second time weighing 15 pounds, and a new transmitter was implanted.[638] She spent a month at the hatchery in Athens, Texas before being returned to Lake Fork.[639] When she was released back into Lake Fork, she "resumed her former movement and feeding patterns, working along the break-line around points and into creeks near where she'd spawned and first been caught."[640] Therefore, as old creatures of habit, lunker bass likely

---

[630] Id.
[631] Id.
[632] Ken Smith Fishing, Part 5, *supra* note 591.
[633] Steve Quinn, *Understanding Lunker Largemouths*, *supra* note 581.
[634] Ken Smith Fishing, Part 5, *supra* note 591; Steve Quinn, *Understanding Lunker Largemouths*, *supra* note 581.
[635] Ken Smith Fishing, Part 5, *supra* note 591.
[636] Steve Quinn, *Understanding Lunker Largemouths*, *supra* note 581.
[637] Id.
[638] Id.
[639] Id.
[640] Id.

maintain their same home range habits throughout their lifetime unless something changes that forces them to move.

  Does a bass released at a tournament site miles from its home range return to its original home range, or find a new home range? I don't think anyone really knows. Scientists do know that the released bass eventually disperse back out into the main part of the lake, but it may take them anywhere from a few hours to several months to do so, and it is not clear how many find their way back to their original home range.[641] Another question: could nomads just be young fish that have not yet found a home range that suits them? More research is needed to answer that question.

---

[641] Alice Abrams and A.J. Zolderdo, et al., *Dispersal patterns of largemouth bass and smallmouth bass following early-, mid-, and late-season fishing tournaments in an eastern Ontario lake*, NORTH AMERICAN J. FISHERIES MANAGEMENT: 41: 1454-1464, 2021.

7

Water Temperature: The Master Factor

Water temperature is called the "abiotic ecological master factor" or the "master environmental factor" determining largemouth bass behavior because it has a bigger impact than any other factor.[642] One researcher noted, "The average daily water temperature inhabited by largemouth bass was the best indicator of both activity and depth utilization across the entire year."[643] As you will see throughout this

---

[642] Helene Volkoff and Ivar Ronnestad, *Effects of temperature on feeding and digestive processes in fish*, TEMPERATURE 7(4): 307-320 (2020), available at https://www.ncbi.nlm.nih.gov/pmc/articles/PMC7678922/pdf/KTMP_7_1765950.pdf ; Tyler Peat et al., *Comparative thermal biology and depth distribution of largemouth bass and northern pike in an urban harbour of the Laurentian Great Lakes*, CANADIAN J. ZOOLOGY 94: 767–776 (2016); K.C. Hanson, et al., *Intersexual variation in the seasonal behaviour and depth distribution of a freshwater temperate fish, the largemouth bass*, CANADIAN J. ZOOLOGY 86: 801-811 (2008), available at http://fishlab.nres.illinois.edu/Reprints/Hanson%20et%20al%20CJZ%202008.pdf.
[643] K.C. Hanson, et al., *Intersexual variation*, *supra* note 642.

book, other factors affect bass behavior—like weather, light, turbidity, oxygen concentration, moon phase, etc.—but all of those factors' effects are dependent on water temperature.[644] This is because water temperature affects largemouth bass's metabolic, physiologic, and developmental processes.[645] Water temperature plays a huge role in bass behavior, which makes understanding water temperature very important to anglers aspiring to catch lunkers.[646]

Largemouth bass "cannot control their body temperatures with internal processes" like humans, so their body temperature is "barely above the temperature of the water in which they swim."[647] Therefore, scientists call them "ectotherms"; lay folks call them "cold blooded."[648] The only way bass can change their body temperature is to move to water of a different temperature, so scientists also call them "poikilotherms."[649]

An individual bass's temperature is less than 1.5°F (0.7-0.8°C) higher than the water temperature where it swims because bass do not have sufficient heat produced or retained from metabolic processes to maintain body temperature.[650] The graph below approximates the relationship between a bass's temperature and the water temperature where it is living:

---

[644] Id.
[645] Tyler Peat et al., *supra* note 642; K.C. Hanson, et al., *Intersexual variation*, *supra* note 642; Helene Volkoff and Ivar Ronnestad, *supra* note 642.
[646] Id.
[647] Steven Bardin, *Fish Biology: Largemouth bass: A comprehensive species guide*, Wired2Fish, January 28, 2023, available at https://www.wired2fish.com/fish-biology/largemouth-bass-a-comprehensive-species-guide/; Helene Volkoff and Ivar Ronnestad, *supra* note 642.
[648] Steven Bardin, *Fish Biology: Largemouth bass*, *supra* note 647; Helene Volkoff and Ivar Ronnestad, *supra* note 642.
[649] Helene Volkoff and Ivar Ronnestad, *supra* note 642.
[650] Tyler Peat et al., *supra* note 642; Helene Volkoff and Ivar Ronnestad, *supra* note 642; Steven Bardin, *Fish Biology: Largemouth bass*, *supra* note 647.

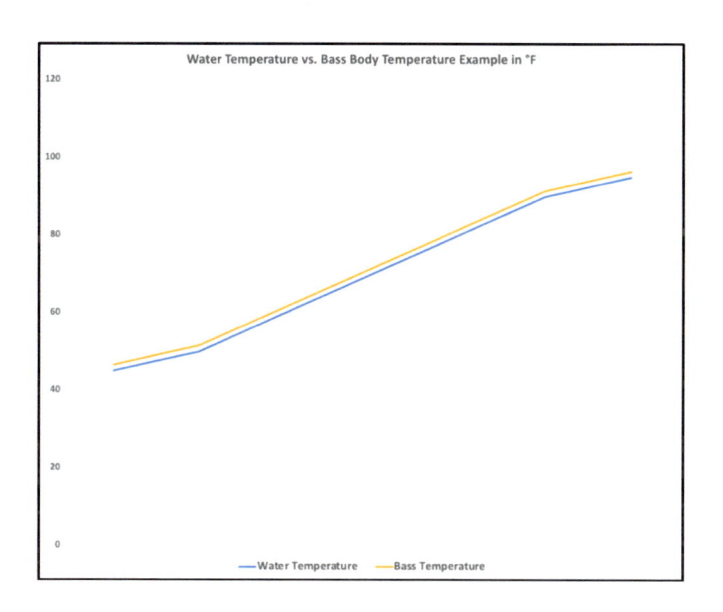

[Chart: Water Temperature vs. Bass Body Temperature Example in °F]

Water temperature affects catchability of bass. For example, one southern author who recorded his 8900 adult bass catches for 18 years found that bass bit progressively better as water temperature rose to an optimal temperature range and then slowed down above that range.[651] Specifically, he found the optimal water temperature range for the bass bite to be 69-78°F, which he described as conditions "that foster generally shallow bites in late spring and early fall in the Southeast."[652] He and his partners averaged 4.66 bass per outing at optimal temperatures, but only 1.87 bass per outing during the slowest bite which he found in cold water of 49-58°F.[653] At temperatures from 59-68°F, which were a little cooler than his optimal temperature, he caught 3.66 bass per outing.[654] At temperatures above his optimal range, he caught 3.2 bass per outing at 79-88°F and 3.77 bass per outing at temperatures above 88°F.[655] So, at the worst water temperatures (49-58°F) he caught only 40% of his catch rate at the best water temperatures (69-78°F). During the other temperature

---

[651] Ralph Manns, *Moon Magic Largemouth Bass*, IN-FISHERMAN, January 19, 2012, available at https://www.in-fisherman.com/editorial/moon-magic-largemouth-bass/154779.
[652] Id.
[653] Id.
[654] Id.
[655] Id.

ranges closer to the optimal range, he caught 69-81% of his catch rate during optimal water temperatures.

Differences in catch rates at different water temperatures are not surprising considering how much water temperature affects bass. Food consumption depends on bass having "adequate sensory perception and the capacity for locomotion" with feeding behavior dependent up steps "including food detection, capture, ingestion and ultimately swallowing"—all of which can be influenced by water temperature.[656] Water temperature has major effects on bass's (1) *metabolic processes* like digestion and oxygen consumption, (2) *physiologic processes* like nerve and muscle function, and (3) *developmental processes* like growth, maturation, and reproduction. Bass can adapt to some changes and extremes in water temperature, but not all. Let's look in more detail at how water temperature affects largemouth bass.

Metabolic Processes

Biochemical enzymatic reactions that determine the rate of metabolism for largemouth bass are primarily driven by water temperature.[657] To be more specific, a bass's standard metabolic rate (SMR) is the rate of metabolism required to maintain the bass's routine activity level and the processes necessary for life.[658] The largemouth bass's average standard metabolic rate *doubles or triples with every 18°F (10°C) increase* in water temperature, and likewise halves or thirds with drops of the same magnitude.[659] Big changes at lower temperatures have more effects than big changes at higher temperatures.[660] Some researchers report that bass's metabolic rate is exponentially related to temperature.[661]

Scientists generally say that bass have an optimal feeding temperature range with feeding diminishing both below and above

---

[656] Helene Volkoff and Ivar Ronnestad, *supra* note 642.
[657] Steven Bardin, *Fish Biology: Largemouth bass*, *supra* note 647.
[658] Helene Volkoff and Ivar Ronnestad, *supra* note 642.
[659] Id.
[660] Id.
[661] Daniel Lemons and Larry Crawshaw, *Behavioral and metabolic adjustments to low temperatures in the largemouth bass*, PHYSIOLOGICAL ZOOLOGY 58(2): March/April 1985, available at https://www.journals.uchicago.edu/doi/10.1086/physzool.58.2.30158564.

that range.[662] Between 50-68°F feeding rate increases rapidly as the water temperature rises.[663] Feeding remains high from 68°F up to at least 81-85°F, but declines as water temperatures rise above that level according to some researchers.[664] Some Florida bass have been observed simply remaining still in shaded areas when water temperatures were higher than 81°F, even though their stomachs were empty.[665]

    Not all researchers agree, so more research is needed on the effects of high temperatures on bass feeding.[666] Notice that in Manns' study mentioned earlier in this chapter, he found that he caught more bass at temperatures above 88°F than at the interval just below. I have personally caught many bass in a power plant lake at water temperatures way above 81°F (even over 100°F), so maybe they are feeding less than at 80 degrees, but they are still feeding and active at much higher temperatures than these scientists describe based on my personal experience. For example, below is a picture of my 2D sonar showing a group of 5- and 6-pound bass feeding on a ledge in mid-summer—notice the water temperature is 90.7°F. I caught several of these lunker bass, and they were very actively feeding.

---

[662] Charles Coutant, *Responses of bass to natural and artificial temperature regimes*, Presented at the National Symposium on the Biology and Management of Centrarchid Basses, Tulsa, Oklahoma, February 3-6, 1975, available at https://www.osti.gov/servlets/purl/4235116-bvKqQi/.
[663] Id.
[664] Id.
[665] Id.
[666] Id.

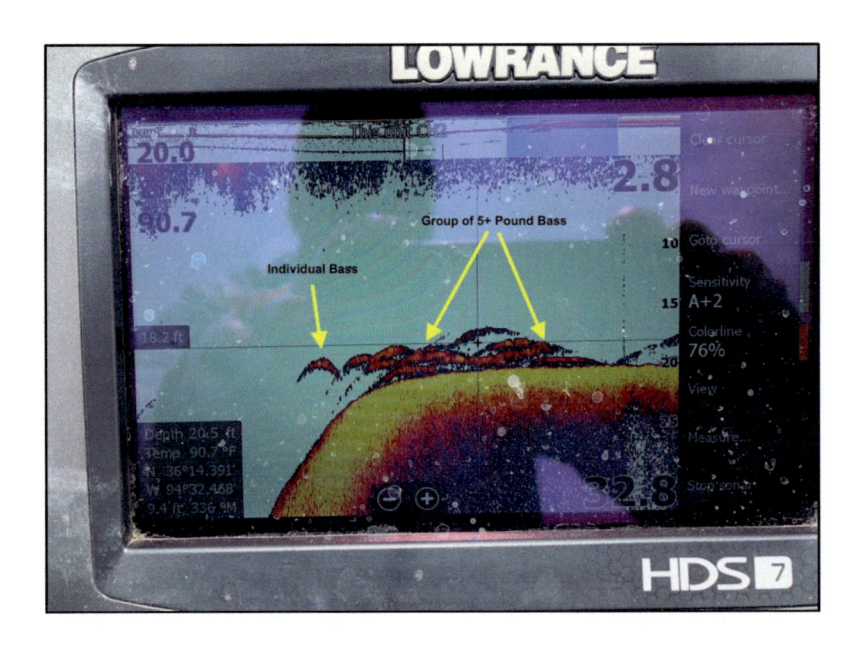

I have seen similar groups of bass on other lakes as well in the heat of summer with water temperatures in the upper 80s. So, I believe bass clearly eat at temperatures above 81-85°F reported by some researchers, and Manns' findings in his study quoted earlier also support that assertion.

Because bass's metabolic processes are slowed in cold temperatures, *digestive processes and enzymes* are also markedly slowed so that bass feed intermittently and go long periods between meals.[667] One researcher found that "there is little, if any, natural feeding by largemouth" bass when water temperature is below 50°F (10°C).[668] Another researcher also found that food intake "became negligible" below 50°F (10°C).[669] These researchers found that "an energy analysis reveals that food intake fails to meet even resting requirements at temperatures below 50°F (10C).[670] A meal that might take several hours to digest in summer can take several days in winter.[671] Over half of bass's stomachs are empty in winter when examined by researchers.[672]

---

[667] Charles Coutant, *supra* note 662.
[668] Id.
[669] Daniel Lemons and Larry Crawshaw, *supra* note 66.
[670] Id.
[671] Steven Bardin, *Fish Biology: Largemouth bass*, *supra* note 647.
[672] Id.

Bass acclimate biologically to survive during harsh winter conditions by "minimizing standard and active metabolic demands, by storing visceral fat [in the fall], and by maximizing growth during the fall."[673] Largemouth bass feed heavily in fall to maximize caloric intake to build up visceral fat for winter.[674] During times when they are minimally feeding, bass use the energy from their visceral fat for metabolic demands.[675] Use of energy from visceral fat was calculated to be less than 33% of bass's standard metabolic demands, so bass must have some food intake even during winter to survive.[676] Lunker bass have higher energy reserves (fat stores) and also have a higher metabolic rate due to their increased body mass—so they may have to eat either more or bigger meals than their smaller counterparts during winter.[677]

Changes in metabolic rate related to water temperature can cause major behavioral changes by affecting cellular respiration, oxygen consumption, and the bass's nervous system.[678] For example, *oxygen consumption* in one study of largemouth bass increased by 40% (from 48.8 to 69.4 mm O2/kg h) with a 23°F (13°C) rise in temperature from 68°F (20°C) to 91°F (33°C).[679] Such large changes in oxygen consumption can have a dramatic effect on bass behavior. Also, low water temperatures decrease the efficiency of the bass's heart reducing cardiac output "and may decrease the ability of a fish to uptake and transport oxygen."[680]

---

[673] S. Marshall Adams, et al., *Energy partitioning in largemouth bass under conditions of seasonally fluctuating prey availability*, TRANSACTIONS OF THE AMERICAN FISHERIES SOCIETY 111(5): 549-558, September 1982, available at https://afspubs.onlinelibrary.wiley.com/doi/10.1577/1548-8659%281982%29111%3C549%3AEPILBU%3E2.0.CO%3B2.
[674] Id.
[675] Id.
[676] Id.
[677] K.C. Hanson, et al., *Intersexual variation*, supra note 642.
[678] Helene Volkoff and Ivar Ronnestad, supra note 642.
[679] Fernando Diaz and Ana Denisse Re, *Temperature preference and oxygen consumption of the largemouth bass acclimated to different temperatures*, AQUACULTURE RESEARCH 38(13):1387-1394, August 2007.
[680] K.C. Hanson, et al., *Intersexual variation*, supra note 642.

Physiologic Processes

Physiologic performance of bass's muscles and nerves is maximized within a specific range of optimal temperatures and declines in temperatures outside that range.[681] At critical temperatures at the upper and lower ends of bass's thermal tolerance range, their physiologic performance goes to zero, and they eventually die.[682] Largemouth bass swim slower and swim less in cold water than in warm water. Scientists are unsure if these changes are due to physiologic effects on the fishes' muscles or nerves—both of which are important in propulsion of fish.[683]

Water temperature affects the *"sensitivity of sensory systems*, including vision, hearing, olfaction, and taste, likely affecting feeding behavior."[684] For example, light sensitivity of the retina, hearing sensitivity, and taste preferences have been shown to change with water temperature changes in some fish.[685] So, water temperature can affect bass feeding behavior by enhancing or impairing bass's senses used for feeding.

Water temperature affects bass's *nerves and brain function*. Bass behave differently at cold winter water temperatures because their central nervous system function declines at water temperatures below 45°F, which can make them appear "sluggish."[686] Extreme cold temperatures can disrupt bass's cognitive abilities "perhaps also disturbing their ability to forage for food."[687] The decreased cognitive effect of colder water may be present at temperatures higher than 45°F because one big bass specialist, Josh Jones, notes that lunker bass are easier to catch during winter months in Texas (where the water temperature is usually warmer than 45°F) when he catches a much higher percentage of the lunker bass that he sees on forward facing sonar compared to summer.[688] He speculates, "I'm no biologist, but I think their brain function or vision gets compromised

---

[681] Helene Volkoff and Ivar Ronnestad, *supra* note 642.
[682] Id.
[683] Id.
[684] Id.
[685] Id.
[686] Daniel Lemons and Larry Crawshaw, *supra* note 66.
[687] Helene Volkoff and Ivar Ronnestad, *supra* note 642.
[688] Steve Ryan, *The gathering legend of Josh Jones*, IN-FISHERMAN, 2023 Bass Guide, 42-45.

during those periods of rapid cooling, and they don't process as well that the lure they are about to eat is fake."[689] I think he is correct.

Cold water temperatures below 45°F (7°C) cause bass's central nervous system to decline in function, which can affect the fishes' locomotor ability as well as its cognitive function.[690] Cold temperatures also directly affect the function of bass's muscles that propel them. Excessively cold or hot water temperatures can reduce locomotor performance of bass to the point that they have difficulty capturing food.[691] However, the locomotor abilities of their prey are also affected evening the odds somewhat. [692]

The speed, distance, and amount of swimming activity of bass are directly related to water temperature. Swimming is "largely dependent on environmental temperature" according to researchers.[693] Bass spend a lot of time swimming in place holding position. During winter in eastern Ontario, bass spend over 95% of their time swimming in place (i.e., at speeds < 0.1 m/s).[694] In the same study, the researcher found that bass spend 80% of their time holding position during fall, but only 55% of their time holding position in spring.[695]

Bass *swim slower in cold water* than warm water. Laboratory studies confirm that largemouth bass swimming speeds decrease as water temperature falls.[696] In one study, maximum swimming speeds were lower at cooler temperatures reaching their lowest points during

---

[689] Id.
[690] Daniel Lemons and Larry Crawshaw, *supra* note 66; Helene Volkoff and Ivar Ronnestad, *supra* note 642.
[691] Id.
[692] Id.
[693] Caleb Hasler et al., *Effect of water temperature on laboratory swimming performance and natural activity levels of adult largemouth bass*, CANADIAN J. ZOOLOGY, 87(7): June 25, 2009, available at https://cdnsciencepub.com/doi/10.1139/Z09-044.
[694] Kyle Hanson, et al., *Assessment of largemouth bass behavior and activity at multiple spatial and temporal scales utilizing a whole-lake telemetry array*, HYDROBIOLOGIA 582(1): 243-256 (May 2007), available at https://www.researchgate.net/publication/226543386_Assessment_of_largemouth_bass_Micropterus_salmoides_behaviour_and_activity_at_multiple_spatial_and_temporal_scales_utilizing_a_whole-lake_telemetry_array.
[695] Id.
[696] Id.

early winter.[697] Cold water decreases maximum swim speeds "by decreasing the efficiency of biochemical reactions resulting in increases in the amount of time required for muscle contractions, which also reduces tail beat frequency as well as power output."[698] One researcher found that bass swim slowest in winter, 1.78 times faster in fall than winter, and 3.18 times faster in spring than in winter.[699] Another author estimated that bass swim at least 20% faster in fall than in winter.[700]

    Bass *swim shorter distances in cold water* than warm water. Swimming activity decreases as water temperature decreases in laboratory studies.[701] Fish in cold winter water are less able to swim distances as their locomotor functions are more impaired than in warmer conditions, so they may be forced to adapt to more erratic temperature fluctuations by downregulating metabolic activities.[702] The daily distance traveled and mean voluntary swimming activity by most bass decreases as water temperature decreases becoming lowest in winter.[703] Multiple studies have demonstrated the consistent theme of decreased swimming activity in colder months compared to warmer months with the specific quantification varying somewhat by body of water. In one study, researchers found that bass moved "up to 10.7 times farther on a daily basis in spring than winter, and up to 6.5 times farther in fall than winter."[704] Another researcher estimated that largemouth bass activity is 60% lower in winter than during the warm months.[705] Another researcher found that daily swimming activity was lowest in winter, was 1.2 times higher in fall, and 3.25 times

---

[697] Caleb Hasler et al., *Effect of water temperature*, *supra* note 693; Caleb Hasler, *Measuring the influence of winter conditions on largemouth bass behavior using both biotelemetry and laboratory studies*, Queen's University Thesis Submission, Kingston, Ontario, Canada, August 2007, available at https://qspace.library.queensu.ca/bitstream/handle/1974/818/Hasler_Caleb_T_2007 _08_MSc.pdf?sequence=1&isAllowed=y.
[698] K.C. Hanson, et al., *Intersexual variation*, *supra* note 642.
[699] Kyle Hanson, et al., HYDROBIOLOGIA, *supra* note 694.
[700] Id.
[701] Caleb Hasler, *Measuring the influence of winter conditions*, *supra* note 697.
[702] Helene Volkoff and Ivar Ronnestad, *supra* note 642.
[703] Kyle Hanson, et al., HYDROBIOLOGIA, *supra* note 694; Caleb Hasler et al., *Effect of water temperature*, *supra* note 693; Caleb Hasler, *Measuring the influence of winter conditions*, *supra* note 697.
[704] Kyle Hanson, et al., HYDROBIOLOGIA, *supra* note 694.
[705] K.C. Hanson, et al., *Intersexual variation*, *supra* note 642.

higher in spring.[706] Still another researcher found that the daily movement rates for largemouth bass were highest during summer months when water temperatures were higher than 77°F (25°C).[707] In one study, fish movements were five times higher in warmer months than in winter.[708]

Throughout the range of water temperatures, individual fish continue to show their personalities because daily movement rates vary "by as much as 25-fold among individual fish" under the same water temperature conditions.[709] In other words, some individual bass swim faster and farther than other bass year-round under the same conditions.

Developmental Processes

Water temperature affects developmental processes like how bass grow, mature, and reproduce. Largemouth bass have an optimal water temperature range for growth between 75°F (24°C) and 86°F (30°C) according to a couple of studies, with some studies suggesting juveniles grow better at the higher end of that range.[710] Bass grow from mid-March through mid-December in the southern U.S. when water temperatures are above 50°F (10°C).[711] When temperatures exceed optimal levels for extended periods, bass experience "decreased growth rates, higher metabolic costs, and increased natural mortality rates."[712] In lakes that do not reach optimal temperature ranges or only remain in the optimal temperature ranges for short periods of time, the bass will be smaller and less healthy.[713]

---

[706] Kyle Hanson, et al., HYDROBIOLOGIA, *supra* note 694.
[707] Ryan Hunter and Michael Maceina, *Movements and home ranges of largemouth bass and Alabama spotted bass in Lake Martin, Alabama*, J. FRESHWATER ECOLOGY 23(4): 599-606 (2008), available at https://doi.org/10.1080/02705060.2008.9664247.
[708] K.C. Hanson, et al., *Effects of lunar cycles on the activity patterns and depth use of a temperate sport fish, the largemouth bass*, FISHERIES MANAGEMENT AND ECOLOGY 15(5-6): 357-364, October/December 2008, available at https://onlinelibrary.wiley.com/doi/abs/10.1111/j.1365-2400.2008.00634.x.
[709] Kyle Hanson, et al., HYDROBIOLOGIA, *supra* note 694.
[710] Fernando Diaz and Ana Denisse Re, *supra* note 679.
[711] S. Marshall Adams, et al., *supra* note 673.
[712] Tyler Peat et al., *supra* note 642.
[713] Id.

Bass require a lot of forage to maintain their weight and to grow. Largemouth bass continue to grow throughout their lives and must eat five pounds of forage per pound of body weight each year just to *maintain* their body weight.[714] To *increase in size,* bass must "consume an additional 10 pounds of forage to gain 1 pound of body weight."[715] Bass grow in length the fastest during the first two years of life.[716] Under optimal conditions, biologists say that Florida bass can reach 14 inches in length at 2 years of age, are commonly 3 pounds after only three years, and often gain up to one pound per year thereafter.[717] Northern largemouth bass have a similar growth rate to Florida bass for the first three years, but grow substantially slower than Florida bass after 3 years of age.[718]

Water temperature also affects how bass mature and reproduce. Largemouth bass reach sexual maturity at around one year of age and 10 inches of length and they continue to mate until they are around 12 years of age.[719] They require different amounts of energy depending upon their sex.

Females require more energy for gonad development than males,[720] so they must time food intake in a way that gives their bodies plenty of energy for the spawning season. Water temperature changes guide their energy intake and energy storage.[721] Females eat the most in May and "reach their highest growth rate in June," according to one study.[722] Females' bodies accumulate visceral and liver fatty tissue in early spring into late fall.[723] Water temperatures

---

[714] Steven Bardin, *Fish Biology: Largemouth bass, supra* note 647.
[715] Id.
[716] Maureen Mecozzi, Wisconsin Department of Natural Resources, Bureau of Fisheries Management, *Largemouth Bass*, August 2008, available at https://dnr.wisconsin.gov/sites/default/files/topic/Fishing/Species_lmbass.pdf.
[717] Jason Kinner, *Creating trophy fishing opportunities in Kentucky with F1 largemouth bass*, Eastern Outdoors Media, December 16, 2021, https://www.easternoutdoorsmedia.com/creating-trophy-fishing-opportunities-in-kentucky-with-f1-largemouth-bass/.
[718] Id.
[719] Emily Steed, Animal Diversity Web, *Micropterus salmoides: American black bass*, U. Michigan Museum of Zoology, available at https://animaldiversity.org/accounts/Micropterus_salmoides/; Maureen Mecozzi, *supra* note 716; Steven Bardin, *Fish Biology: Largemouth bass, supra* note 647.
[720] S. Marshall Adams, et al., *supra* note 673.
[721] Id.
[722] Id.
[723] Id.

trigger the spawn and trigger female (and male) gonad development in fall and early spring.[724]

Males grow the fastest and store the most energy in summer and fall.[725] Males grow least in spring when they are busy with nest building and fry guarding without much food intake.[726] Both sexes have a summer depression in energy storage when temperatures reach their maximums, "which affects food intake and increases energy requirements."[727]

Water Temperature Adaptations and Limitations

Largemouth bass have temperatures to which they can acclimate, temperatures that are fatal, and temperatures that require genetic shifts. The optimal temperature for largemouth bass growth is 75F (24°C) to 86°F (30°C).[728] Florida bass have a different optimum temperature range and lethal temperature range than Northern largemouth bass. Northern largemouth bass can survive colder temperatures than Florida bass. In other words, Florida bass have a "winter temperature limitation" that limits how far north in latitude they can live.[729] That latitude is not as well defined as many biologists previously believed. Recently, a MLF study revealed two lunkers caught at Lake of the Ozarks in Missouri had 97.82% and 85% Florida genetics.[730] The bass that has over 95% Florida genetics is considered a Florida-genetic largemouth bass, which means that Florida bass may have a farther northern latitude tolerance than

---

[724] Id.
[725] S. Marshall Adams, et al., *supra* note 673.
[726] Id.
[727] Id.
[728] Fernando Diaz and Ana Denisse Re, *supra* note 679; Tyler Peat et al., *supra* note 642.
[729] Robert Montgomery, *Biologists refine the native range of Florida bass*, BASSMASTER, December 17, 2021, available at https://www.bassmaster.com/conservation-news/news/biologists-refine-the-native-range-of-florida-bass.
[730] Steven Bardin, *Two successful years of MLF lunker DNA initiative data has been analyzed*, MAJOR LEAGUE FISHING, February 16, 2023, available at https://majorleaguefishing.com/conservation/two-successful-years-of-mlf-lunker-dna-initiative-data-has-been-analyzed/.

previously believed or that some Florida bass have acclimated or evolved to live at more northern latitudes.[731]

    Major sudden water temperature changes can also have significant effects on the performance of bass's bodies. Sudden short term temperature variations can have drastic and even detrimental effects.[732] Timing, intensity, and duration of exposure and speed of temperature changes affect the response of fish to temperature.[733] Individual fish experiencing moderate changes in water temperature can usually adjust their preference/avoidance behavior to maintain close to optimal metabolic and physiologic performance.[734] Long term variations can give fish time to acclimate.[735] In some cases, their physiology adjusts over short time periods through acclimatization via reversible temporary physiologic adaptations that do not require genetic alterations.[736] So, bass who experience temperature changes may change their behavior to maintain optimal metabolic performance.[737] Even longer-term environmental variations can allow fish to acclimate via genetic changes over time.[738] In some lakes and rivers, exposure to longer term temperature changes over multiple generations can lead to genetic adaptions and evolutionary changes.[739] Neither of these types of adaptations allow fish to respond to sudden episodic changes like summer heat waves.[740]

    Bass can acclimate to some temperatures, but there is a limit.[741] For instance, in some lakes bass may be able to adjust to higher temperatures for a few days or a few weeks during unusually hot summers, even though those temperatures are not compatible with long term survival. In one study, largemouth bass movement dropped steeply when water temperatures were near 86°F (30°C) in a Florida lake, which suggested maximum thermal tolerance.[742] However, at

---

[731] Id.
[732] Helene Volkoff and Ivar Ronnestad, *supra* note 642.
[733] Id.
[734] Id.
[735] Id.
[736] Helene Volkoff and Ivar Ronnestad, *supra* note 642.
[737] Id.
[738] Id.
[739] Id.
[740] Id.
[741] Id.
[742] Jason Harris, Master of Science Thesis, *Habitat selection, and home range of largemouth bass following a habitat enhancement project in Table Rock Lake*,

Table Rock Lake, the highest monthly temperature of 87°F (30.7°C) coincided with the highest movement rates, which suggested that water temperatures of 86°F (30°C) did not impede bass movements in this midwestern reservoir and that these midwestern bass had acclimated.[743]

     Some temperatures are fatal for bass. The "ultimate lethal temperature" is "the highest temperature to which fish can acclimate."[744] Based on my experiences at a power plant lake in the hot Arkansas summer, I know it is somewhere above 100°F for some largemouth bass because some power plant lake bass seem to thrive in 95-100°F water temperatures for several weeks during Arkansas summers.[745] I caught a lot of bass in water over 100°F over several summers at that power plant lake. In fact, the two bass in the picture below were caught on the same cast near the warm water outlet in a power plant lake where the water was over 100°F; one was on the front treble hook of a big, deep-running crankbait, and the other was on the back treble hook.

Missouri, University of Missouri MOspace, 2013, available at https://mospace.umsystem.edu/xmlui/bitstream/handle/10355/37945/research.pdf?sequence=2&isAllowed=y.
[743] Id.
[744] Helene Volkoff and Ivar Ronnestad, *supra* note 642.
[745] However, after a recent summer when the whole lake (i.e., not just the area where the hot water entered the lake) was above 100°F there has been a precipitous drop in the number of 5 pound plus bass in the lake. Previously, the cove near the outlet would get up over 104°F each summer, which would overheat my electronics. I still fished in there sometimes and often caught some lunker bass in that hot water. But the main part of the lake was only usually up to around 92 to 95°F. Since the whole lake heated to over 100°F, the fishing has dramatically dropped off for lunker bass. I suspect that the lethal limit was reached for some fish and that they could no longer find any part of the lake below that temperature. Maybe in the past, they would move into the hot cove (over 104°F) for a few hours to feed and then move to cooler parts of the lake (but still over 90°F).

What about power plant lakes? Previous studies showed that "heated lakes exhibit alterations in phytoplankton peaks, larval fish abundance, and reduced zooplankton abundances, as well as altered mortality rate, lifespan, and growth rate of some fish species."[746] In one study, researchers compared metabolism, growth, and thermal tolerance of largemouth bass in heated power plant cooling lakes (aka, "thermally altered lakes") that reach "supra-optimum temperatures" above 85°F (30°C) to ambient temperature lakes.[747] The bass in power plant lakes had reduced metabolic rates compared to ambient lake bass at 85°F, and they showed "markedly increased growth rates" at 85°F compared to their ambient cousins.[748] Researchers found that largemouth bass can adapt to "lessen sublethal effects of warming by altering physiological processes to reduce the impact of warming on

---

[746] Dalon White and David Wahl, *Growth and physiological responses in largemouth bass populations to environmental warming: Effects of inhabiting chronically heated environments*, J. THERMAL BIOLOGY 88: 102467, February 2020, available at https://www.sciencedirect.com/science/article/abs/pii/S0306456519302943.
[747] Id.
[748] Id.

aerobic scope."[749] However, these changes are not passed along to their offspring, so future offspring have to adapt as well.[750] However, maximum thermal tolerance is not changed in power plant bass.[751] Even though the power plant lake bass lived in a heated environment for many years, their ultimate lethal temperature was not changed compared to the ambient lake bass—so these lakes can get too hot for bass survival.[752] Below is a picture of a power plant lake that I fish regularly; note the heat rising from the water.

Bass also have temperature limits for some bodily functions that are not necessarily fatal.[753]

---

[749] Id.
[750] Id.
[751] Id.
[752] Id.
[753] Helene Volkoff and Ivar Ronnestad, *supra* note 642.

Study 3: Barometric Pressure and Big Bass

Barometric pressure . . . admit it . . . you've used the "mother of all excuses" for a tough day on the water when that high pressure system or cold front moved in that day, the day before, or was about to move in.[754] Guides, tournament pros, celebrity fishermen, and amateur anglers all insist that cold fronts and the associated barometric pressure changes affect bass with all sorts of anecdotal evidence.[755] Some researchers have found that barometric pressure influences the migration time of rainbow trout, the depth and distribution of sauger (*Sander canadense*), and the vertical migration and movement rate of black crappies.[756] Whether or not largemouth bass respond to barometric pressure is another area of considerable

---

[754] Hal Schramm, *The effects of cold fronts on bass*, IN-FISHERMAN, available at https://www.in-fisherman.com/editorial/the-effects-of-cold-fronts-on-bass/154617.
[755] Id.
[756] Daniel VanderWeyst, *The effect of barometric pressure on feeding activity of yellow perch*, Aquatic Biology, Bemidjii State University, available at https://www.bemidjistate.edu/directory/wp-content/uploads/sites/16/2023/02/2014-VanderWeyst-D.-The-effect-of-barometric-pressure-on-feeding-activity-of-yellow-perch..pdf.

controversy and passionate fishing debate. Many bass fishermen say that falling barometric pressure is associated with the best fishing, while a rising barometric pressure is associated with relatively poor fishing.[757] They say that a "medium and stable" barometric pressure is in between.[758] So, let's see if there is any scientific truth to this analysis.

Previous Research

According to one respected fisherman biologist, researchers have been unable to prove a relationship between barometric pressure and the activity of largemouth bass.[759] In fact, Manns says, "Every scientific report we've seen, in which barometric pressure was studied, reached a similar conclusion: no direct relationship is evident."[760] He says this is because "no way has been found to isolate barometric pressure influences from simultaneous weather phenomena," and "significant barometric changes are rare without accompanying changes in wind, temperature, and sky conditions."[761] In addition, scientists have not seriously theorized a mechanism by which bass could directly detect barometric pressure changes.[762]

In Manns' study at Lake Travis in Texas, researchers tracking bass with radio devices as well as direct observation by divers "observed no obvious relationship between pressure readings or the nature of pressure changes and the behavior of largemouth bass."[763] No trends were found between bass proximity to cover and weather trends before and after front passage.[764] However, these researchers did find that at low barometric pressures bass were more likely to be feeding on the surface away from the shoreline than when barometric

---

[757] Erik Nyman, *What is the best barometric pressure for fishing*, Weather Station Advisor, July 20, 2022, available at https://www.weatherstationadvisor.com/best-barometric-pressure-for-fishing/.
[758] Id.
[759] Ralph Manns, *Barometric pressure and bass*, IN-FISHERMAN, October 24, 2017, available at https://www.in-fisherman.com/editorial/barometric-pressure-and-bass/153689.
[760] Id.
[761] Id.
[762] Id.
[763] Id.
[764] Ralph Manns, *Barometric pressure and bass*, *supra* note 759.

pressures were higher.[765] Manns found that bass were more likely to strike on low pressure days when 52% of the "bass struck lures during lows compared to only 39% during highs."[766] However, he noted that "the vast majority of our strikes took place when the barometer reading was neither particularly high nor low."[767] He concluded, "High or low barometric readings, by themselves, were not consistently indicative of bass activity or catchability."[768]

Manns also found that bass were more likely to strike on falling barometric pressure than rising and said "when the barometer was falling slowly (less than 0.21 inch per hour), 65% of the bass that were presented lures struck."[769] In contrast, "on a slowly rising barometer, only 30% struck."[770] But offshore, his findings were different. When they looked at a larger sample, "29% fed offshore on a slow rising barometer, while 24% fed offshore on both a slow falling and a steady barometer."[771] There were multiple confounding factors, however.[772]

In short, prior studies have failed to show a definite relationship between barometric pressure and bass feeding activity. Here, I'm not going to worry about whether it is the barometric pressure or the associated weather changes; instead, I will simply use barometric pressure as a possible direct cause for any changes as well as a proxy for weather.

What is Barometric Pressure?

The Earth is surrounded by layers of air called the atmosphere.[773] The five layers of the atmosphere are: exosphere,

---

[765] Id.
[766] Id.
[767] Id.
[768] Id.
[769] Ralph Manns, *Barometric pressure and bass*, supra note 759.
[770] Id.
[771] Id.
[772] Id.
[773] National Geographic, *Barometer: A barometer is a tool used to measure atmospheric pressure, also called barometric pressure*, available at https://education.nationalgeographic.org/resource/barometer/.

thermosphere, mesosphere, stratosphere, and troposphere.[774] The troposphere is the layer closest to earth.[775]

Barometric pressure is "the measure of the weight of Earth's atmosphere."[776] Barometers are the tools used to measure the pressure caused by the weight of these layers of atmosphere, so the air pressure is called barometric pressure or atmospheric pressure.[777] The Earth's gravity pulls the air toward the surface to give it the weight. In the U.S., barometric pressure is reported in inches of Mercury (inHg).[778]

The normal range of barometric pressure at sea level is from 29 inHg to 31 inHg and is usually in the range from 29.2 to 30.4 inHg.[779] Pressure decreases with altitude generally, but pressures reported are generally converted to "a value that would be observed if that instrument were located at sea level" where standard air pressure is 29.92 inHg, so if the reporting source is so adjusted, the numbers can be used for comparisons (I found sources reporting pressures both ways, however, so I will speak in terms of "low" and "high" as general terms for the altitude where you are fishing rather than absolute values).[780] Barometric pressure changes daily (and throughout the day) due to variables like wind patterns, air temperatures, air density, and the Earth's rotation.[781] Barometric pressure can be monitored with handheld barometers in your exact location or by using a weather app on your phone.[782]

---

[774] MasterClass, *How barometric pressure works: 4 impacts of atmospheric pressure*, June 7, 2021, available at https://www.masterclass.com/articles/how-barometric-pressure-works.
[775] Id.
[776] Id.
[777] National Geographic, *Barometer*, supra note 773; Erik Nyman, *supra* note 757; National Geographic, *Atmospheric pressure*, available at https://education.nationalgeographic.org/resource/atmospheric-pressure/.
[778] National Geographic, *Atmospheric pressure*, supra note 777.
[779] MasterClass, *How barometric pressure works*, supra note 774; Hal Schramm, *The effects of cold fronts on bass*, supra note 754.
[780] NATIONAL OCEANIC AND ATMOSPHERIC ADMINISTRATION, U.S. Department of Commerce, *Jetstream: An online school for weather*, available at https://www.weather.gov/jetstream/pressure.
[781] MasterClass, *How barometric pressure works*, supra note 774; Erik Nyman, *supra* note 757.
[782] Erik Nyman, *supra* note 757.

Direct Effects of Barometric Pressure on Bass

Many fishermen speculate that the barometric pressure affects bass feeding activity.[783] Some fishermen and authors venture that the barometric pressure directly affects bass by affecting the bass's swim bladder, which is an organ that helps bass regulate their buoyancy.[784] Bass's swim bladders are primarily used to "achieve neutral density and hold at constant depths."[785] The weightlessness provided by the swim bladder reduces the energy bass need to swim in place.[786] The bass's air bladder slowly and naturally adjusts pressure to stay in equilibrium if there are pressure changes or depth changes.[787]

Proponents of barometric pressure discomfort theories claim that bass's swim bladder responds to air pressure like a balloon and that increasing barometric pressure compresses the bass's swim bladder and that decreasing barometric pressure allows the bass's swim bladder to expand.[788] They say that fish have discomfort related to the fluctuations in their swim bladders related to barometric pressure changes and that this discomfort affects bass's feeding activity.[789] They liken it to scuba divers experiencing the "bends" when they come up too quickly from the depths, saying an inflated swim bladder will cause discomfort and balance difficulties.[790]

From a scientific standpoint, the theories of bladder expansion/deflation and discomfort are improbable because *air pressure likely has minimal effect on bass underwater.* Water is much heavier than air, so atmospheric pressure changes do not have near as much affect below the water's surface as above it.[791] Bass likely do sense some pressure changes with their swim bladders.[792] For instance, the bass may "notice that it's floating or sinking a *few inches* higher or lower in the water column in response to a change in air

---

[783] Id.
[784] Id.
[785] Ralph Manns, *Barometric pressure and bass*, supra note 759.
[786] Id.
[787] Id.
[788] Erik Nyman, *supra* note 757.
[789] Id.
[790] Id.
[791] Hal Schramm, *The effects of cold fronts on bass*, supra note 754.
[792] Id.

pressure."[793] However, bass regularly experience larger changes in pressure with depth changes while hunting prey or moving between locations.[794] A bass can simply adjust its depth by a few inches to reestablish equilibrium without the fish sensing much if any pressure change at all, so "depth changes likely override the perception of small changes in air pressure."[795]

More specifically, barometric pressure usually ranges from 29.2 to 30.4.[796] So, a large change in barometric pressure from very low to very high or vice versa is a change of only 4 percent.[797] The 4% pressure change at most that a bass experiences with the passage of a major weather event is the same amount of pressure change that a bass experiences by simply moving "about 16 inches deeper in the water column, a fraction of the depth change bass commonly undertake in their daily movements."[798] So, a largemouth bass only needs to "swim up or down a foot or two to experience as great or greater a pressure change than that created by all but the largest natural pressure changes of typhoons and hurricanes."[799] Therefore, it is highly unlikely that discomfort has anything to do with any changes in bass's behavior.[800]

Not much research exists on the direct effects of barometric pressure on fish and feeding. I found a study which researchers claimed was the "first study . . . that has attempted to relate feeding activity of fish to barometric pressure."[801] The study was on yellow perch in laboratory tanks, so it has limited usefulness in application to largemouth bass in the wild in my opinion, but I will mention it here anyway. These researchers did 12 trials with 5 at rising pressure, 5 at falling pressure, and 2 at stable pressure.[802] They concluded that barometric pressure had no "significant influence on how much

---

[793] Ralph Manns, *Barometric pressure and bass*, *supra* note 759.
[794] Id.
[795] Id.
[796] Hal Schramm, *The effects of cold fronts on bass*, *supra* note 754.
[797] Id.
[798] Id.
[799] Ralph Manns, *Barometric pressure and bass*, *supra* note 759.
[800] Hal Schramm, *The effects of cold fronts on bass*, *supra* note 754.
[801] Daniel VanderWeyst, *supra* note 756.
[802] Id.

yellow perch ate."[803] They note that other species "could react differently to pressure changes."[804]

Barometric Pressure and the Weather

Barometric pressure is a proxy for the general weather pattern, and most anglers agree that the weather affects bass fishing—so if you look at barometric pressure as simply a proxy for the weather, then it is not surprising that it could affect bass fishing. Barometric pressure is used "to predict short-term changes in the weather" with barometric pressure changes often signaling incoming changes in weather and cloud cover.[805]

Falling barometric pressure and low barometric pressure usually mean that clouds, precipitation, and wind are about to arrive.[806] When a low pressure system settles in place, clouds or storms follow because "there isn't enough force" in the air to push them away.[807] So, low pressure systems are usually "associated with cloudy, rainy, or windy weather."[808] Major factors creating clouds and weather changes include barometric pressure changes, air temperatures, and moisture content.[809]

Rising barometric pressure often means that a high pressure system is arriving, which usually signals sunny, clear weather is coming.[810] As barometric pressure rises the increasing pressure in the atmosphere pushes cloudy and rainy weather out, which clears the way for clear skies and dry air.[811] After a weather front passes, higher pressure and associated bright sunlight and clear skies typically follow.[812] A "cold front" is classically associated with rising barometric pressure, clear skies, wind, and falling temperatures, which bring conditions that many fishermen consider to be bad

---

[803] Id.
[804] Id.
[805] National Geographic, *Barometer*, *supra* note 773; Erik Nyman, *supra* note 757; Ralph Manns, *Barometric pressure and bass*, *supra* note 759.
[806] Ralph Manns, *Barometric pressure and bass*, *supra* note 759; Erik Nyman, *supra* note 757; National Geographic, *Atmospheric pressure*, *supra* note 777.
[807] National Geographic, *Barometer*, *supra* note 773.
[808] Id.; MasterClass, *How barometric pressure works*, *supra* note 774.
[809] Ralph Manns, *Barometric pressure and bass*, *supra* note 759.
[810] Erik Nyman, *supra* note 757.
[811] National Geographic, *Barometer*, *supra* note 773.
[812] Ralph Manns, *Barometric pressure and bass*, *supra* note 759.

fishing conditions of "high barometer, bright blue sky, sharply colder temperatures, and a strong north or northwest wind."[813] High pressure systems usually mean fair and calm weather, clear skies, and bright sunlight—proverbial "blue bird skies" many fishermen equate with poor fishing conditions.[814]

Barometric pressure rises and falls twice daily due to heating of the sun with the amount of daily cyclical changes being greater closer to the equator.[815] For example, in Texas there are daily barometric pressure changes because as the sun warms the water and land the barometric pressure drops after being high in the morning due to cooling overnight.[816]

My ShareLunker Database Research

Texas Parks and Wildlife Department (TPWD) has a statewide program called the ShareLunker Program that has been discussed earlier in this book. Although some version of the program has been around since the 1980's, the ShareLunker program became year-round in 2018.[817] Since then, "anglers who reel in any largemouth bass at least 8 pounds or 24 inches can participate simply by entering their lunker catch information,"[818] which includes the bass's weight, length, location caught, date caught, and other information. Anglers are motivated to enter their fish because they receive a "Catch Kit" that includes a decal, merchandise, giveaways, and entry into drawings for larger prizes.[819] Plus, fish over 13 pounds may become legacy fish with offspring hatched and released into other Texas lakes.[820]

TPWD publishes an archive of all accepted lunkers over 8 pounds or 24 inches on their website, which is available to the

---

[813] Hal Schramm, *The effects of cold fronts on bass*, supra note 754.
[814] National Geographic, *Atmospheric pressure*, supra note 777.
[815] NATIONAL OCEANIC AND ATMOSPHERIC ADMINISTRATION, supra note 780.
[816] Ralph Manns, *Barometric pressure and bass*, supra note 759.
[817] News Release, *Toyota ShareLunker Program begins new year-round season Jan. 1*, TEXAS PARKS AND WILDLIFE DEPARTMENT, September 29, 2017, available at https://tpwd.texas.gov/newsmedia/releases/?req=20170929a.
[818] TEXAS PARKS AND WILDLIFE DEPARTMENT, Toyota ShareLunker Program Texas Parks and Wildlife, available at https://texassharelunker.com.
[819] Id.
[820] Id.

public.[821] I used this public archive to analyze the data surrounding those catches to answer the question: "What effect does barometric pressure have on catching lunker bass?"

For this study, I limited the data to the year 2022. During 2022 a total of 511 lunkers over eight pounds were reported to TPWD through the ShareLunker program. A Plano, Texas based weather website publishes an archive of barometric pressures by date.[822] I used that archive to determine the barometric pressure on the day that each of these 511 lunkers were caught. Plano is centrally located in Texas, and after watching several Texas weather maps over time, the barometric pressure in central Texas is usually (but not always) reasonably close (for rough study purposes) to the barometric pressure in other areas of Texas—so I used the barometric pressure archive for all of the bass reported from lakes around Texas.[823] While imperfect because barometric pressure varies by location, my method a way to get a rough idea whether or not barometric pressure is associated with differences in big bass behavior since I cannot find pressures for each catch location by date. Due to the imperfections of my methods, I was surprised by the consistency of my results.

Barometric Pressure and 8+ Pound ShareLunkers in 2022

The average barometric pressure was 30.03 (Range 29.56-30.55) in central Texas in 2022 on the days the 511 lunkers were caught. The average barometric pressure for the whole year in central Texas was 30.04 (Range 29.56-30.78), so there was basically no difference in the average day and the average day that a lunker was caught.

Lunkers were caught at the lowest barometric pressure reported, but not quite the highest. I am going to demonstrate step-by-step how I did the calculations to reach the graphical depictions later in the chapter to "show my work" for any readers who are interested. Table 1 shows the barometric pressure distribution on the days when the 511 reported 8+ pound lunkers were caught.

---

[821] TEXAS PARKS AND WILDLIFE DEPARTMENT, *Texas ShareLunker Archives*, available at https://texassharelunker.com/archives/.
[822] Barometric Pressure Reports (inHg), Dallasdawg.com Weather, Plano, Collin County, Texas, USA, available at https://www.dallasdawg.com/wxbarodetail.php.
[823] Id.

Table 1: Number of 8+ Pound Lunkers Reported to TPWD in 2022 versus Barometric Pressure on Day Caught

Barometric Pressure (inHg)	# Lunkers Reported
<29.50	0
29.51-29.60	5
29.61-29.70	9
29.71-29.80	36
29.81-29.90	61
29.91-30.00	159
30.01-30.10	89
30.11-30.20	65
30.21-30.30	25
30.31-30.40	18
30.41-30.50	38
>30.50	6

It is tempting to simply look at the above table and draw conclusions based on these numbers alone, but doing so would ignore the fact that the number of days at a given barometric pressure varies greatly. For example, a lot more days are in the midrange (e.g., 29.91-30.00) and a lot more bass were caught during those days (159 bass), so the above distribution may simply represent the fact that there was a lot more fishing time available during times when the higher numbers of bass were recorded. So, the numbers must be analyzed considering the actual number of days in 2022 at each barometric pressure range. So, let's keep digging.

The 365 days of 2022 were each assigned the barometric pressure from the online central Texas weather station, and the number of days in each barometric pressure range were counted. Table 2 shows the number of days at each barometric pressure range for 2022 in central Texas and the percentage of days in 2022 spent in that range.

Table 2: Number of 2022 Days at Each Barometric Pressure and the Percentage of 2022 Days at Each Pressure

Barometric Pressure	Number of Days in 2022	Percentage of Days in 2022
<29.50	0	0
29.51-29.60	3	0.82
29.61-29.70	6	1.64
29.71-29.80	25	6.85
29.81-29.90	51	13.97
29.91-30.00	109	29.86
30.01-30.10	53	14.52
30.11-30.20	49	13.42
30.21-30.30	23	6.30
30.31-30.40	17	4.66
30.41-30.50	17	4.66
>30.50	12	3.29

If barometric pressure has no effect at all on big bass fishing, then the lunker bass reported to TPWD should be equally distributed across all days regardless of barometric pressure. For example, 30% of the 511 lunkers should be caught on 30% of the days regardless of barometric pressure; so, the percentage of lunkers caught should equal the percentage of days spent at each barometric pressure. For example, since only 3.29% of the days in 2022 were at barometric pressures over 30.50, only 3.29% of the 511 bass (which is 16.8 bass) would be expected to be caught on those days in 2022 if barometric pressure did not have an effect. Table 3 shows the barometric pressures versus, the percentage of days at each barometric pressure, and the expected number of lunkers of the 511 lunkers reported if barometric pressure had no effect.

Table 3: Barometric Pressure and Percentage 2022 Days at Each Range with Expected Number of Lunkers

Barometric Pressure	Percentage of 2022 days	Expected # of Lunkers Based on Percentage of Days (511 x %Days)
<29.50	0	0
29.51-29.60	0.82	4.19
29.61-29.70	1.64	8.38
29.71-29.80	6.85	35.00
29.81-29.90	13.97	71.39
29.91-30.00	29.86	152.58
30.01-30.10	14.52	74.20
30.11-30.20	13.42	68.58
30.21-30.30	6.30	32.19
30.31-30.40	4.66	23.81
30.41-30.50	4.66	23.81
>30.50	3.29	16.81

Now, let's look at the number of lunkers actually reported to TPWD at each barometric pressure range versus the expected number based upon the number of days in the year. Table 4 shows the number of expected lunkers at each barometric pressure range versus the actual number reported. In the fourth column, the percentage of expected is included.

Table 4: Actual versus Expected Number of 8 Pound Plus Bass Reported to TPWD in 2022

Barometric Pressure	Expected Lunkers	Actual Lunkers Reported	Actual versus Expected (in %)	
<29.50	0	0	0	
29.51-29.60	4.19	5	5/4.19 =	119.3%
29.61-29.70	8.38	9	9/8.38 =	107.4%
29.71-29.80	35.00	36	36/35 =	102.9%
29.81-29.90	71.39	61	61/71.39 =	85.4%
29.91-30.00	152.58	159	159/152.58 =	104.2%
30.01-30.10	74.20	89	89/74.20 =	119.9%
30.11-30.20	68.58	65	65/68.58 =	94.8%
30.21-30.30	32.19	25	25/32.19 =	77.7%
30.31-30.40	23.81	18	18/23.81 =	75.6%
30.41-30.50	23.81	38	38/23.81 =	159.6%
>30.50	16.81	6	6/16.81 =	35.7%

The results in Table 4 are depicted graphically in Figure 1.

Figure 1: Percentage of 8+ Pound Bass Reported to TPWD in 2022 at Each Barometric Pressure Range versus Expected (Based on # of Days in 2022 at that Pressure Range)

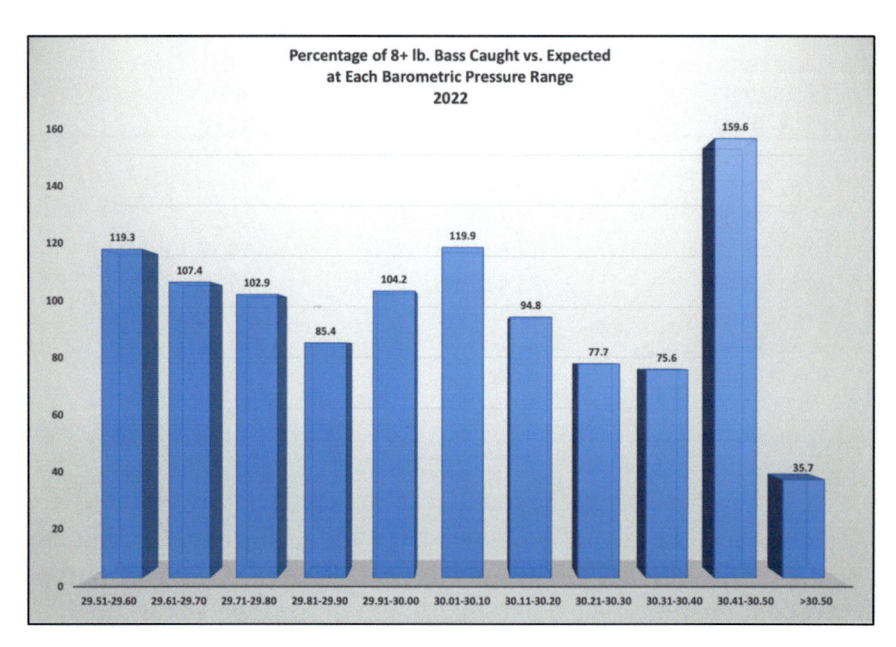

Percentage of 8+ lb. Bass Caught vs. Expected at Each Barometric Pressure Range 2022

Pressure Range	Percentage
29.51-29.60	119.3
29.61-29.70	107.4
29.71-29.80	102.9
29.81-29.90	85.4
29.91-30.00	104.2
30.01-30.10	119.9
30.11-30.20	94.8
30.21-30.30	77.7
30.31-30.40	75.6
30.41-30.50	159.6
>30.50	35.7

If you ignore the bar in Figure 1 at 30.41-30.50 for a moment, a trend toward catching more lunkers than expected at lower barometric pressure and fewer lunkers at higher barometric pressures than expected is evident because at almost all pressures below 30.10, more lunker bass were caught than expected whereas at pressures above 30.11, fewer big bass were caught than expected at almost all pressures.

For example, when fishing on days with a barometric pressure between 29.51 and 29.60, anglers reported 119.3% of the fish expected based on the number of days, whereas at barometric pressures from 30.31-30.40, anglers only reported 75.6% of the bass expected. Another way to look at this is that compared to average days in 2022, anglers were 19.3% MORE likely to catch a lunker when the barometric pressures was from 29.51-29.60, but were 24.4% LESS (100 minus 75.6%) likely to catch a lunker when the barometric

164

pressure was between 30.31-30.40. Fishing at pressures higher than 30.50 decreased the chance of catching a lunker by 64.3%. There was one exception. The barometric pressure in the high range from 30.41 to 30.50 was associated with a 59.6% increased chance; it is not clear why this result occurred and is most likely simply a statistical outlier or anomaly.

Averaging the data from the levels below 30.10 reveals a *6.5% increased chance of catching a bass over 8 pounds on days when the pressure was 30.10 or less compared to average days.* In contrast, averaging the data above 30.10, an angler would have *11.32% decreased chance of catching an 8+ pound bass on days with barometric pressures of 30.11 or greater. Overall, 8+ pound lunker bass were more likely to be caught at low barometric pressures than high barometric pressures,* which is in line with common fishing wisdom.

Now, let's look at the effect of falling, stable, and rising barometric pressures. For purposes of analysis, I defined a daily change of 0.10 inHg or more as rising or falling and anything less than that as stable.

Of the 511 eight plus pound lunkers reported in 2022, 137 were caught on falling days ($\geq$0.10 inHg drop compared to prior day), 281 on stable days (<0.10 change from prior day), and 93 on rising days ($\geq$0.10 inHg rise compared to prior day). That is 26.81%, 54.99%, and 18.2% respectively. In comparison, in 2022 overall there were 91 falling days, 199 stable days, and 75 rising days, which is 24.93%, 54.52%, and 20.55% respectively.

If barometric pressure has no effect, then we would expect the 511 lunkers to have been caught equally each day independent of barometric pressure, which means 24.93% or 127.39 lunkers would have been caught under falling pressure, 54.52% or 278.60 lunkers would have been caught under stable pressure, and 20.55% or 105.01 lunkers during rising pressure. Instead, there were 137 lunkers caught during falling pressure, 281 lunkers caught during stable pressure, and 93 lunkers caught during rising pressure.

This means that 107.54% (137/127.39 x 100) of the expected number of lunkers were caught when the pressure was falling, 100.86% (281/278.6 x 100) of expected under stable pressure, and 88.56% (93/105.01 x 100) of expected were caught under rising pressure. Thus, fishing on falling pressure days resulted in a 7.54%

increased chance above average for catching an 8+ pound lunker, while fishing when the pressure was rising was associated with a 11.44% decreased chance. Figure 2 shows the percentage of 8+ pound lunkers caught versus expected.

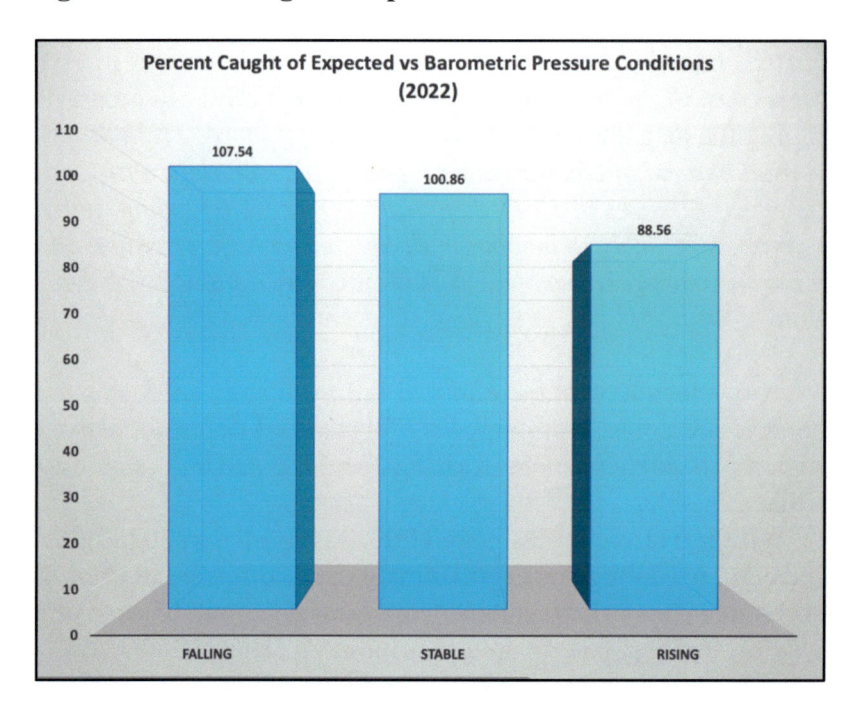

Figure 2. Percentage of Expected 8+ Pound Lunkers in 2022

Percent Caught of Expected vs Barometric Pressure Conditions (2022)

- FALLING: 107.54
- STABLE: 100.86
- RISING: 88.56

So, fishing on a falling barometric pressure increased the chances of an 8+ pound lunker being reported by 7.54%, and stable barometric pressure was associated with approximately the same number of lunkers as expected based upon the number of days. In contrast, rising barometric pressure was associated with an 11.44% decreased chance of reporting an 8+ pound lunker.

Barometric Pressure and 13+ Pound ShareLunkers

What about the giant 13+ pound ShareLunkers? Would barometric pressure have more or less effect on these even larger fish. For this part of the analysis, I looked at the barometric pressures on the dates that 87 largemouth bass were reported to TPWD from 2018 through 2022 that were 13 pounds or more in weight. These fish were typically caught during spring when barometric pressures are different from other times of the year, so I only included 302 days during the months that these fish were caught over those 5 years in the analysis of the percentage of 13+ pound lunker bass expected to be caught. For the relevant dates, I went through the same series of calculations demonstrated above in Tables 1 through 4. The percentage of actual catches versus expectations are shown in Figure 3.

Figure 3: Percentage of 13+ Pound Bass Reported to TPWD from 2018 through 2022 at Each Barometric Pressure Range versus Expected (Based on # of days at that Pressure Range During the Relevant Months)

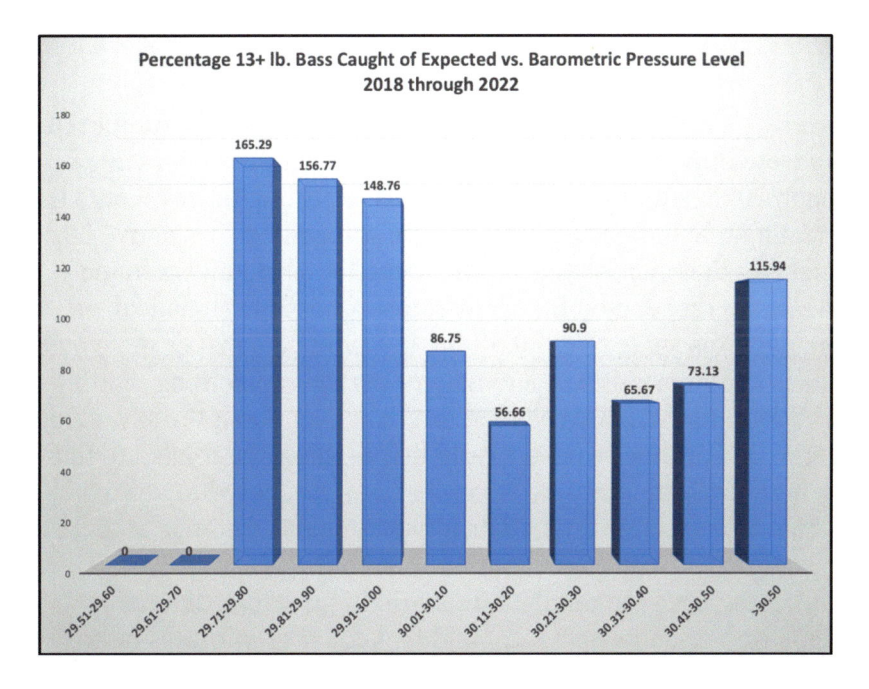

Percentage 13+ lb. Bass Caught of Expected vs. Barometric Pressure Level 2018 through 2022

Pressure Range	Percentage
29.51-29.60	0
29.61-29.70	0
29.71-29.80	165.29
29.81-29.90	156.77
29.91-30.00	148.76
30.01-30.10	86.75
30.11-30.20	56.66
30.21-30.30	90.9
30.31-30.40	65.67
30.41-30.50	73.13
>30.50	115.94

So, for 13 pound plus lunkers, there were none caught below a barometric pressure of 29.70, but then there were only 5 days below those pressures during the relevant periods over the five years when these giants were being caught from 2018 through 2022 because these very low barometric pressures appeared to be rare during the late winter/ early spring times when 13+ pound lunkers were generally caught.

The 13+ pound lunkers seemed to prefer pressures between 29.71 and 30.00, and also maybe the very high pressures over 30.50.

The giants did not like pressures between 30.01 and 30.50, with the catches being lower than expected for all those days/pressures.

Averaging the data from the levels below 30.10 reveals *a 39.4% increased chance of catching a bass over 13 pounds on late winter/early spring days when the pressure was 30.10 or less* compared to average late winter/early spring days (eliminating rare days in this time frame where pressure was below 29.70). In contrast, averaging the data above 30.10, an angler would have *19.54% decreased chance of catching a 13+ pound bass on days with barometric pressures of 30.11 or greater during late winter/early spring.* Overall, 13+ pound lunker bass were more likely to be caught at low barometric pressures than high barometric pressures just like *8+ pounders,* which is in line with common fishing wisdom.

So, *like 8+ pound lunker bass, the 13+ pound lunker bass were more likely to be caught at lower pressures than higher pressures.* The findings below 29.70 are difficult to interpret because there were only 5 such days during the relevant times from 2018 through 2022, so I make no conclusions regarding those levels. It is interesting that there is a high-pressure spike in catches above 30.50. Remember that there was a similar spike for 8+ pounders in the 30.41-30.50 range, which I dismissed as a possible statistical anomaly. This spike over 30.50 for 13+ pounders makes me wonder if this is another statistical anomaly or perhaps something worth considering further. Maybe there is something about the sky, cloud cover, wind, or other weather issue that is somehow related to these very high-pressure days; however, I cannot find anything to which to attribute these seemingly statistically anomalous findings at this time.

Now, let's look at the effect of falling, stable, and rising barometric pressures on 13+ pound lunkers. For purposes of analysis, I defined a daily change of 0.10 inHg or more as rising or falling and anything less than that as stable.

Over the five years from 2018 through 2022, there were 87 bass over 13 pounds reported to TPWD. Of those 87 bass, 35 (40.23%) were reported on falling barometric pressure days, 33 (37.93%) were reported on stable barometric pressure days, and 19 (21.84%) were reported on rising pressure days. During the relevant months, 35.1% of the days had falling barometric pressure, 34.77% had stable pressure, and 30.13% had rising pressure.

Comparing the number of bass reported to the expected number based on number of days, 114.60% (35/30.54) of expected were caught on falling barometric pressure days, 109.09% (33/30.25) of expected on stable pressure days, and only 72.49% (19/26.21) of expected on rising pressure days. Figure 4 depicts these findings graphically.

Figure 4. Percentage of Expected Reported for 13+ Pound Lunkers from 2018 through 2022

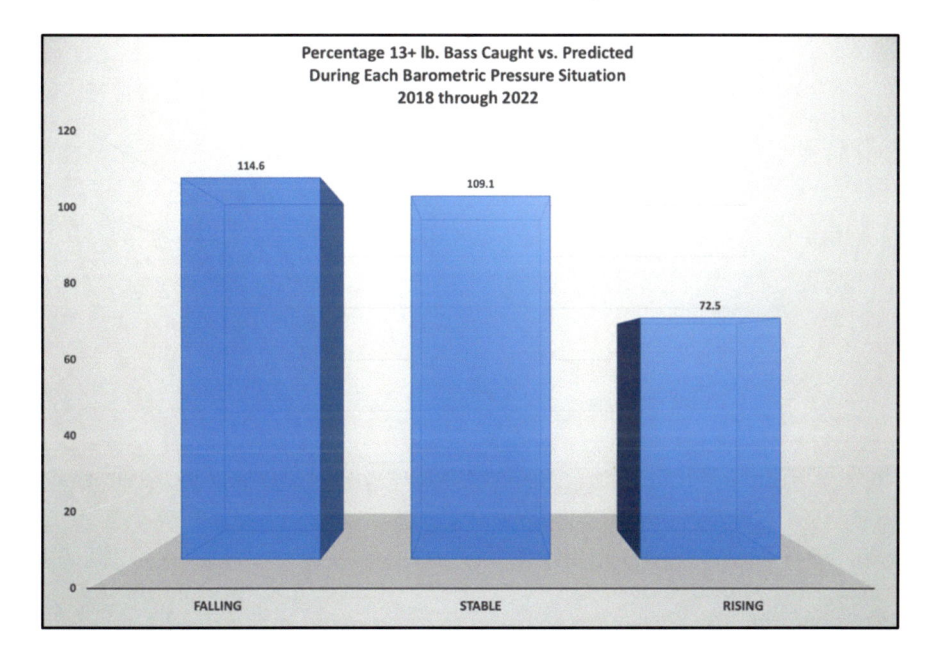

So, *13+ pound giants were more likely to be reported when the barometric pressure was falling or stable, just like their 8+ pound buddies.* They were also less likely to be reported when the barometric pressure was rising. *The effect was greater for the 13+ pounders than for the 8+ pounders.* Figure 5 shows the findings for 8+ and 13+ pound lunkers in one graph.

Figure 5. Percentage Increased or Decreased Chance of Reporting an 8+ or 13+ Pound Lunker Under Changing Barometric Pressure Scenarios

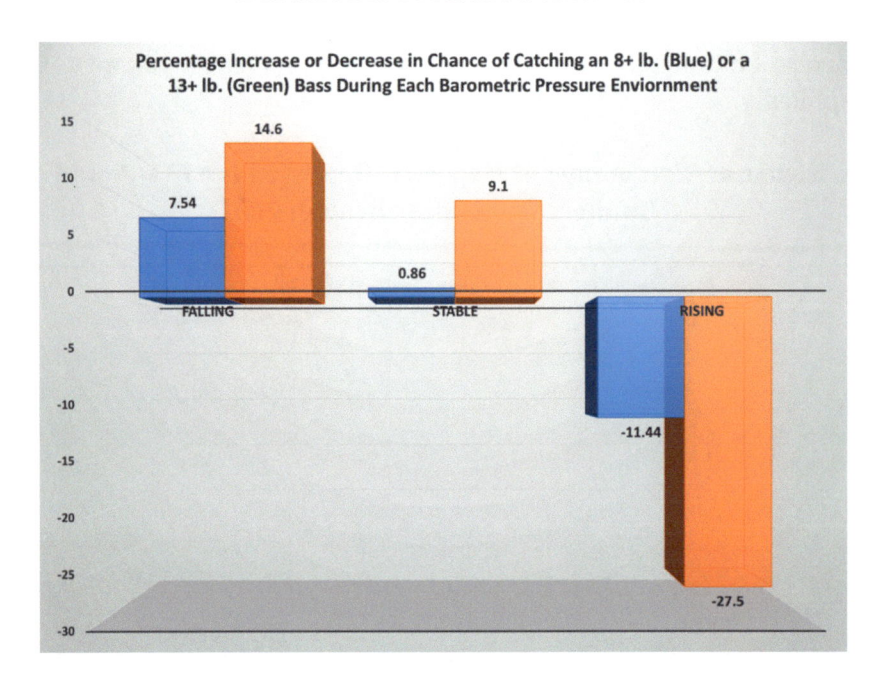

Percentage Increase or Decrease in Chance of Catching an 8+ lb. (Blue) or a 13+ lb. (Green) Bass During Each Barometric Pressure Enviornment

Pressure	8+ lb	13+ lb
FALLING	7.54	14.6
STABLE	0.86	9.1
RISING	-11.44	-27.5

Note in Figure 5 that *changing barometric pressure had more of an effect on the reporting rate of the biggest lunkers (13+ pounders) compared to the smaller lunkers (8+ pounders).* Look back at Figures 1 and 3 for specific barometric pressure ranges, and notice that *the effects of specific ranges also appear to be greater for the 13+ pounders compared to the 8+ pound lunkers.*

Individual Angler Results by Barometric Pressure

So, what are the likely implications of barometric pressure for an individual angler? Here are my top 12 biggest bass and the barometric pressure in my location on the days when and where they were caught.

1. 12 lbs. 9 oz.   29.98   Stable
2. 10 lbs.   30.02   Stable
3. 9 lbs. 7 oz.   30.02   Falling
4. 9 lbs.   29.94   Stable
5. 8 lbs. 14 oz.   29.98   Stable
6. 8.45 lbs.   29.98   Rising
7. 8.34 lbs.   30.13   Stable
8. 8.22 lbs.   29.60   Falling
9. 8.02 lbs.   30.13   Rising
10. 7 lbs. 11 oz.   29.78   Rising
11. 7.61 lbs.   30.22   Stable
12. 7.5 lbs.   30.22   Stable

So, for my biggest 12 bass, 7 were caught on stable pressure days, 3 on rising pressure days, and 2 on falling pressure days. All were caught below pressures of 30.25. Only one was caught below pressure of 29.90. Notice that all but one of my fish was caught in the midrange of pressures as shown in Figure 6. None of my fish was over 13 lbs. (although one was close!), so they were likely less affected than the biggest fish.

Notice that I caught 3 of my biggest lunkers on rising pressure days, but only 2 on falling pressure days, which is opposite of the general trend. I like offshore fishing and rarely fish casting toward the bank. In one study, researchers found that bass "mostly moved offshore under bright sunlight."[824] It is possible that my preferred methods of fishing (offshore, deep) simply put me in a spot more often where lunkers cross my path on rising or high barometric pressure days than average. So, your individual fishing tendencies may influence how much barometric pressure affects your results.

---

[824] Ralph Manns, *Barometric pressure and bass*, *supra* note 759.

Figure 6: Oval shows the pressure ranges where all but one of my fish were caught [Graph is from Figure 1].

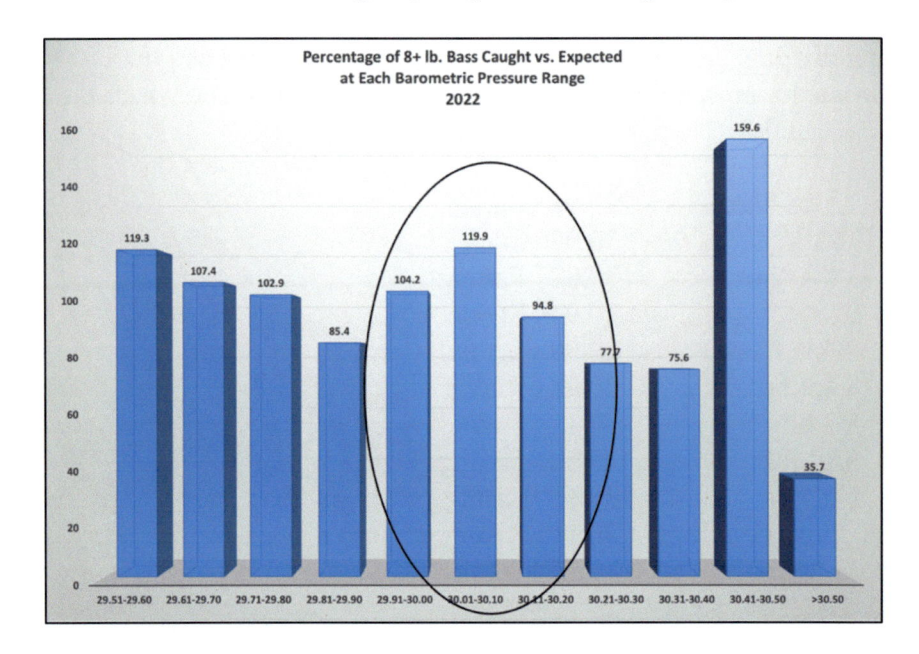

Percentage of 8+ lb. Bass Caught vs. Expected at Each Barometric Pressure Range 2022

Range	Value
29.51-29.60	119.3
29.61-29.70	107.4
29.71-29.80	102.9
29.81-29.90	85.4
29.91-30.00	104.2
30.01-30.10	119.9
30.11-30.20	94.8
30.21-30.30	77.7
30.31-30.40	75.6
30.41-30.50	159.6
>30.50	35.7

A little over 60 percent of the days of 2022 were in the pressure range in the oval area in Figure 6 (which is likely similar to the years when I caught my fish). Therefore, I caught most of my biggest bass on days when the pressure was simply within its most likely range because more days simply fall within that range. I am, however, surprised by the fact that only one of my fish (1/12 = 8.3%) fell outside the common range, given that I often fish in all kinds of extreme weather. This may have something to do with my fishing preferences (offshore, deep) as discussed above.

Conclusion

The chances of catching a lunker were higher on days when the barometric pressure was low. The effect was more dramatic as the bass got bigger, with 13+ pound lunkers showing higher tendencies to be reported on low pressure and on falling pressure days than 8+ pound lunkers.

Lunkers were most likely to be reported on falling barometric pressure days. Lunkers were more likely than average to be reported on stable pressure days as well; but on rising barometric pressure days, the chances of reporting a lunker were below average. Specifically, 13+ pound bass were more likely to be reported by 14.6% on falling pressure days and 8+ pounders 7.54% more likely, while 13+ were 27.5% less likely to be reported on rising pressure days and 8+ pounders 11.44% less likely. Thus, *the effect of rising versus falling pressure appears to be more than double on 13+ pounders versus 8+ pounders.*

Barometric pressure is a proxy or signpost for weather with low and/or falling pressure signaling present or approaching clouds, wind, and rain, and high and/or rising barometric pressure signaling present or approaching calm weather and bluebird skies. One researcher concluded that it was "likely more accurate to consider weather and sky conditions rather than barometric pressure in explaining fish activity and inactivity."[825] This may very well be true, but barometric pressure is a quantifiable factor that can be evaluated and easily checked by fishermen with the understanding that it may reflect changing weather conditions.

Since my review of the ShareLunker data showed that lunkers likely preferred low or falling barometric pressures, this would suggest that more lunkers were caught on days when clouds, wind, and rain were already present or rapidly approaching. Biologists postulate that "clouds, waves, and changes in lighting affect hunting success by predators, by favoring species with eyes sensitive to low light levels."[826] Largemouth bass are mostly visual feeders. So, "wind, clouds, rain, or low light make hunting more successful" for largemouth bass when feeding.[827] Therefore, the findings in my study are consistent with expectations.

Weather changes like frontal passages with their associated "overcast skies, wind, rain, and temperature changes, often seemed to turn bass on."[828] As a cold front approaches, declining pressures and the associated weather changes may trigger fish to feed; however, once the front sets in, the stable and rising pressure with associated changes in the weather may shut off the bite.[829] The reason for these

---

[825] Id.
[826] Id.
[827] Steve Quinn, *Bass Strike Savvy*, IN-FISHERMAN, October 13, 2021, available at https://www.in-fisherman.com/editorial/bass-strike-savvy/395799.
[828] Ralph Manns, *Barometric pressure and bass*, supra note 759.
[829] Sanibel-Captiva Conservation Foundation, *Fishing: Where should I fish today?*, available at https://recon.sccf.org/sport-fishing.

effects is a mystery as biologists have reported "no biological explanation for cold fronts affecting bass behavior" even as numerous professional bass fishermen attest that cold fronts increase their success rates.[830]

Wind is also an important factor associated with barometric pressure. Barometric pressure is often highly predictive of wind with low or falling barometric pressure bringing in or increasing the speed of wind and high or rising barometric pressure having the opposite effect. Wind makes a difference in fishing results with wind speed usually being more important than direction depending upon the specifics of the fishery. In Manns' study of 8900 bass catches, he found that wind direction did not have much effect although he noted that "breezes from the south or southeast, or north or northeast accompanied slightly better results."[831] In contrast, he found wind speed had a significant effect on his catches with "average catch per trip rising from 2.85 in calm conditions (0-3 mph), to 3.60 per trip in light wind (4-8 mph), to 3.71 in medium wind (8-15 mph), and to 3.77 per trip in strong winds."[832]

Calm weather and bluebird skies are usually associated with rising or high barometric pressure. For my personal fishing style of offshore preferences, high or rising pressure days may be some of my best days as shown by my 12 biggest lunkers. Remember, blue bird days are not always bad. In fact, Manns found in his tracking and diving study that there was more feeding under clear skies than partly cloudy skies (although overcast days were best).[833] Some argue that "the maximum brightness of clear skies, which creates optimum feeding opportunities for plankton-eating prey, likely encourages maximum preyfish activity, which in turn may stimulate increased predation" by largemouth bass.[834] The idea that "bright sun hurts bass' eyes" is not true.[835] If it did, bass would not spawn shallow or chase bait fish shallow.[836] Bright light is not an important biologic

---

[830] Hal Schramm, *The effects of cold fronts on bass*, supra note 754.
[831] Ralph Manns, *Moon Magic Largemouth Bass*, IN-FISHERMAN, January 19, 2012, available at https://www.in-fisherman.com/editorial/moon-magic-largemouth-bass/154779.
[832] Id.
[833] Ralph Manns, *Barometric pressure and bass*, supra note 759.
[834] Id.
[835] Hal Schramm, *The effects of cold fronts on bass*, supra note 754.
[836] Id.

issue.[837] The ideas that high pressure "makes bass uncomfortable" or "hurts their inner ear" are also false for reasons discussed earlier in this chapter.[838]

In summary, fishermen were more likely to report lunkers under low and/or falling barometric pressure conditions and were least likely to report lunkers under high and/or rising barometric pressure conditions. These effects were greater on the biggest lunkers. However, your individual fishing tendencies may alter these results. Fish when you can! And if you get skunked, remember this chapter and you can use barometric pressure as a valid excuse—or at least present a good argument to your fishing buddy!

---

[837] Id.
[838] Id.

9

Feeding Mechanisms and the Senses

The "Large Mouth" Feeding Mechanics

    Largemouth bass swallow their prey whole instead of biting off parts and eating it a piece at a time.[839] Largemouth bass are described as "powerful suction feeders" with a mouth that functions in a way that creates a "rapid vacuum-cleaner attack."[840] Bass capture prey by quickly opening their mouth and flaring their gills creating a void that results in a vacuum in the water column in the open space inside their mouths which causes water and prey to be forcefully

---

[839] Steven Bardin, *Fish Biology: Largemouth bass: A comprehensive species guide*, Wired2Fish, January 28, 2023, available at https://www.wired2fish.com/fish-biology/largemouth-bass-a-comprehensive-species-guide/.

[840] James Gorman, *How it Works: The Large Mouth of the Largemouth Bass*, NEW YORK TIMES, December 26, 2017, available at https://www.nytimes.com/2017/12/26/science/largemouth-bass-jaw.html.

drawn in due to suction.[841] Suction feeding is the most common way that fish capture prey because suction is always generated when a fish opens its mouth in the water.[842] When the bass eats, the water flows in one direction—"in the mouth and out the opercular cavity" (basically backwards out the gills down and toward the tail).[843] Therefore, a bass can take in even more water than the size of its mouth cavity.[844] If you've even had a fish suck down a frog or other topwater bait you are aware that bass are suction feeders because sometimes it sounds like a toilet flushing as the water (and hopefully your frog) rapidly fills the void created by the bass's open mouth and gill flare.[845] Imagine the open space in the water created when a big mouth like the one below opens quickly!

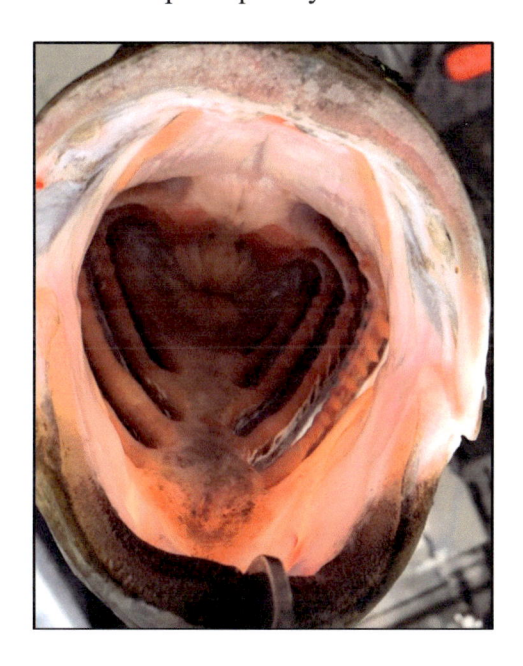

---

[841] Steven Bardin, *supra* note 839; Jayne Gardiner and Phillip Motta, *Largemouth bass switch feeding modalities in response to sensory deprivation*, ZOOLOGY 115(2), 78-82, April 2012.
[842] Jayne Gardiner and Phillip Motta, *supra* note 841.
[843] T.E. Higham, *Feeding Mechanics*, ENCYCLOPEDIA OF FISHING PHYSIOLOGY: FROM GENOME TO ENVIRONMENT 1: 597-602, 2011, available at https://biomechanics.ucr.edu/Higham%202011%20Fish%20Physiology.pdf.
[844] Id.
[845] Id.

Engineers and researchers used x-ray videography and CT scans to study and describe the way a bass's mouth works as a "four-bar linkage—four rigid sections linked by flexible joints."[846] The design of a bass's mouth allows it to move with three degrees of freedom, which means that it can move more like your shoulder or hip joint (ball-and-socket joints) than your elbow or knee (hinge joints with one degree of freedom).[847]

Feeding mechanics of largemouth bass have been studied using digital particle image velocimetry (DPIV) and computational fluid dynamics as well.[848] The speed of the water sucked into an open bass's mouth is highest in the center of its open mouth making it most effective when the prey is immediately in front of its mouth.[849] If the prey is more than 1 to 1.25 mouth diameters away, the suction is minimally effective.[850] So bigger bass can suck in its prey from farther away than small bass due to the bigger diameter of their mouths.[851] The suction force generated when a bass opens its mouth depends on how fast the bass opens its mouth (i.e., buccal cavity) and how wide the bass opens its mouth with a faster opening and a bigger mouth both resulting in a greater suction force.[852]

Largemouth bass are also ram feeders.[853] A pure ram feeder "uses a rapid, whole-body acceleration to overtake and engulf the completely stationary prey."[854] When a bass is swimming forward, it will ingest more water than if it is not moving and will ingest an area farther in front of its mouth.[855]

Bass, like most fish, use a combination of suction and ram feeding.[856] Ram feeding requires the bass move fast enough to overtake the prey, which means that the bass must have enough room to accelerate to high attack speeds.[857] As the bass swims faster, the water area taken in is more elongated and further out in front of the

---

[846] James Gorman, *supra* note 840.
[847] Id.
[848] TE Higham, *supra* note 843.
[849] Id.
[850] Id.
[851] Id.
[852] Jayne Gardiner and Phillip Motta, *supra* note 841.
[853] Id.
[854] Id.
[855] TE Higham, *supra* note 843.
[856] Jayne Gardiner and Phillip Motta, *supra* note 841.
[857] Id.

bass's rapidly moving mouth.[858] An individual largemouth bass has a "maximum swimming speed of 2.5 times its body length per second making chasing down and capturing forage a viable option at any time."[859] The way a bass's mouth works means that "each bass has an area to the front and slightly to each side within which it's likely to make a successful attack" called the "strike window" by one biologist.[860] The size of the strike window increases as bass move faster and become more active.[861] For an inactive bass, the strike window can be very small.[862] Cruising bass in clear water have a strike window of "about 6 feet" that "increases to 10 feet or more at full speed."[863] As their speed increases, however, they are less able to turn their heads to the side to eat, so the strike window is a more narrow area directly in front of the fish.[864]

The size of a bass's prey greatly influences the fluid dynamics of the suction mechanism.[865] The peak force with which a bass can suck in its prey occurs when the prey is around 33% of the bass's mouth diameter, which "has important implications for prey selection."[866] In other words, a bass may be able to inhale a shad 1/3 of the size of its mouth diameter more quickly and easier than a larger or smaller shad; so bigger bass might favor bigger shad and smaller bass favor smaller shad based on this ratio.[867] Although less efficient than the 1/3 ratio, a bass can eat a forage fish that is not wider than the width of its mouth because it swallows it whole.[868]

Bass swallow their prey whole, which limits the size of meal they can consume. One of my Lake Fork guide professors who catches a lot of lunker bass told me that a bass can eat another bass up to 1/3 of its weight; so a 6 pound bass can eat a 2 pound bass, which seems about right based on my experience with mouth sizes and fishing big baits—but I have not found any science to confirm those

---

[858] TE Higham, *supra* note 843.
[859] Steven Bardin, *supra* note 839.
[860] Steve Quinn, *Bass Strike Savvy*, IN-FISHERMAN, October 13, 2021, available at https://www.in-fisherman.com/editorial/bass-strike-savvy/395799.
[861] Id.
[862] Id.
[863] Id.
[864] Id.
[865] TE Higham, *supra* note 843.
[866] Id.
[867] Id.
[868] Steven Bardin, *supra* note 839.

numbers, other than maybe the 33% of mouth diameter rule quoted above.[869]

Largemouth bass will selectively choose to eat fish near their maximum consumable size when given a choice in holding tanks.[870] For example, in one study, bass ate bluegill preferably over tilapia because bluegill size and morphology made them closer to maximum consumable size than tilapia giving them more "bang for their buck" in energy rewards with each meal.[871] However, if no prey were around near maximum consumable size, then the bass preferred the tilapia.[872]

Sometimes bass overestimate their ability to eat a big meal and "bite off more than they can chew." One day while I was fishing a six-pound lunker floated to the surface with a 2-pound catfish stuck in its throat. Catfish have heads that are disproportionately large for their bodies compared to largemouth bass, and this lunker bass had overestimated its ability to swallow the catfish's head. The lunker was thrashing around on the surface, so I netted it and removed the catfish from its throat. It survived and swam away quickly when released. The catfish was not so lucky. I have seen quite a few dead bass floating with other bass stuck in their mouths like the one in the picture below that apparently "bit off more than it could [swallow]." Lunker bass like big meals (and big baits).

---

[869] TE Higham, *supra* note 843.
[870] Harold Schramm and Alexander Zale, *Effects of Cover and Prey Size on Preferences of Juvenile Largemouth Bass for Blue Tilapias and Bluegills in Tanks*, TRANSACTIONS OF THE AMERICAN FISHERIES SOCIETY, 114 (5) 725-731, 1985.
[871] Id.
[872] Id.

Bass have "pharyngeal teeth" deep in their throats, sometimes called "crushers" that hold their forage in a way that allows the prey to slowly be pushed down the esophagus and into the stomach.[873] Bass swallow other fish (like bream, shad, other bass) head first and sometimes flip the fish around in their mouth (if they caught it from behind) before swallowing to make the prey's fins and scutes pass more easily in their pharynx and digestive system. Shad have spiney scales called scutes along their bellies with sharp edges pointing toward their tails that you can feel if you run your finger from the tail toward their head.[874] These scutes have sharp edges that could injure the bass or cause it to get stuck in the bass's mouth, so they eat them head first.[875] Therefore, you see a shad's tail instead of its head sticking out of a bass's throat when you catch a bass that has just eaten a shad.

Hunting and Schooling Behavior

Largemouth bass are not technically "ambush feeders" most of the time, even though many fishing articles describe them as such. Bass ambush their prey if an opportunity presents itself, but overall "ambush is an inefficient tactic for bass" and is "not their preferred feeding tactic."[876] Fish that use ambush as their primary method of feeding—like halibut, rockfish, sculpin, and sole—are typically "bulky, camouflaged, sit on bottom, and move only inches when they strike."[877] These types of fish also typically have relatively small and non-muscular bodies (much different from largemouth bass) with big heads and mouths because they often "wait many days between feedings."[878] Largemouth bass have streamlined bodies that are slim, muscular, and strong making them adept at making short dashes to

---

[873] Steven Bardin, *supra* note 839.
[874] MISSOURI DEPARTMENT OF CONSERVATION, *Gizzard shad: Field guide*, available at https://mdc.mo.gov/discover-nature/field-guide/gizzard-shad.
[875] Id.
[876] Ralph Manns, *Ambush is the wrong word*, POND BASS MAGAZINE, January 27, 2011.
[877] Id.
[878] Id.

capture forage fish.[879] This is in marked contrast to the body characteristics of ambush-feeding fish.

Bass "move almost constantly when active."[880] Actively feeding bass are usually on the move and either cruise alone or "form schools with bass of similar sizes."[881] They cruise back and forth "fairly steadily along edges of cover to flush forage fish" or to chase forage into open water.[882] Cruising bass will "flush" their prey such that forage fish are eaten that get too close or dart the wrong way.[883] Inactive bass rarely form schools (move synchronously) and are hesitant to strike forage or baits.[884] By leaving cover and cruising, hungry bass have a better chance of encountering forage fish than if they simply stayed put in ambush position in most environments where forage fish are not overly abundant.[885] Forage fish hide in cover to avoid being eaten by bass, so bass are naturally often caught near the edges of cover because that is where forage fish gather and are most likely to be flushed.[886]

Bass also cruise the open waters in schools or small wolf packs to work together to flush and herd prey. According to Texas biologists, many largemouth bass—including a lot of lunkers—are pelagic (or out in the open water) most of the time chasing shad.[887] Largemouth bass associations like schools appear to be driven by visual cues because they occur primarily during daylight hours with over 97 times more associations occurring during day than at night in one study.[888]

Some aggressively feeding lunkers form small schools that many bass anglers call "wolf packs," especially during late spring,

---

[879] Id.
[880] Id.
[881] Ralph Manns, *Ambush is the wrong word*, *supra* note 876.
[882] Id.
[883] Id.
[884] Id.
[885] Id.
[886] Ralph Manns, *Ambush is the wrong word*, *supra* note 876.
[887] Ken Smith Fishing YouTube Channel, *Toledo Bend Telemetry Tracking Study Update Todd Driscoll TP&W Biologist Feb 2022 Part 4*, available at https://www.youtube.com/watch?v=yna85FwrzzE&list=PLLzhji805wVzkLnAA97I8VmdZpR8arB_Q&index=4.
[888] Caleb Hasler, et al., *Frequency, composition and stability of associations among individual largemouth bass at diel, daily and seasonal scales*, ECOLOGY OF FRESHWATER FISH 16: 417–424 (2007).

summer, and early fall to hunt more efficiently than cruising alone.[889] Wolf packs are usually groups of 4 to 8 similarly-sized bass (often lunkers) stalking the banks in a pocket or out in the open water together hunting as a group.[890] May through September is the best time of year to target wolf packs with a "peak in May and June and another smaller peak in September."[891] Wolf pack bass "tend to be females," especially during the post-spawn period when one author says, "They're worn out from spawning, so they'd rather get into a small pack to patrol the bank and corner prey."[892] By working together they "exert half the energy and feast on bluegill and baitfish in the shallows" or shad in the open waters.[893]

Wolf packs have mostly been described as shallow water phenomenon, but I have seen similar activity on forward-facing sonar in deeper water with wolf packs suddenly appearing and chasing shad balls. I have caught several lunker bass in wolf packs in open water. The 8+ pounder in the picture below was in a wolf pack from which I also caught a 7 pounder and a 6.5 pounder; interestingly, all three lunkers only bit when my bait was retrieved from west to east, even though I casted from other directions as I circled the pack (before trolling motors would lock you in place) feeding on a group of shad in a small pocket:

---

[889] Rob Newell, *Wolf-pack bass: The Advanced Course*, FLW OUTDOORS MAGAZINE, September 9, 2011, available at https://majorleaguefishing.com/archives/2011-09-09-wolf-pack-bass-the-advanced-course/.
[890] Id.
[891] Id.
[892] Walker Smith, *How to catch wolf pack bass in the early summer*, Wired2Fish, May 22, 2020, available at https://www.wired2fish.com/spring-fishing-tips/how-to-catch-big-wolf-pack-bass-in-the-early-summer/#slide_2.
[893] Id.

According to biologist scuba divers, some areas of cover that look impenetrable from the surface have open pathways beneath them that allow actively feeding bass to repeatedly pass back and forth to catch forage fish.[894] So, actively feeding bass are also found in what appears to be thick cover to the angler, but the cover's unseen passageways allow the bass to move about to feed. Sometimes actively moving/feeding bass will stop temporarily in cover where the cover stops or structure changes, and those bass are also catchable with well-placed or repeated casts.[895]

Inactive Bass and Feeding

While bass are often *located* in cover, they are not usually actively feeding inside that cover. A hungry or feeding bass typically does not hide in cover thick enough to limit its vision or limit its ability to chase down its prey.[896] Bass are adept at accelerating rapidly from their cruising speed to quickly strike vulnerable prey.[897]

---

[894] Ralph Manns, *Ambush is the wrong word*, supra note 876.
[895] Id.
[896] Id.
[897] Id.

Adult bass holding their position in heavy cover are usually neutral or inactive, resting, or digesting a recent meal and are not looking to feed.[898] Bass move into and out of cover to rest undisturbed by larger threats (like anglers), "rather than to feed."[899] Neutral and semi-active bass resting inside cover are catchable bass, but you may have to put the lure right in front of their noses or arouse them by repeated casts.[900]

    Direct observations by scuba divers of bass "immobile inside cover and apparently asleep" reveal that some inactive bass do not feed or strike baits even when forage fish or lures swim right in front of their mouths.[901] These truly inactive bass "tend to sleep alone."[902] Similarly, bass tracked electronically that hold in position for long periods without moving are usually not catchable because they will not feed or respond to lures or baitfish.[903] I have personally casted several different types of lures at a few suspended bass and watched on forward-facing sonar as the bass never budged no matter what lure I ran past it. Bass that are digesting a large meal are inactive because most of their blood is in their stomach for digestion purposes which leaves less blood for the nervous system to use in further feeding movements—so "it's physically difficult for them to feed, even if opportunity arises."[904]

    Unlike some inactive bass, neutral and semiactive bass in open water are catchable. Neutral bass are simply hanging out, maybe swimming in place, and not actively feeding. Life is hard for bass because prey can be hard to find and to catch, so bass can go extended periods without a meal with multiple studies showing that about half of bass have nothing in their stomachs at any one time.[905] Therefore, bass must conserve energy and chase prey only when their chances of success are good.[906] A favorable feeding opportunity occurs when the bass gains more energy from the meal than it loses from the chase.[907]

---

[898] Id.
[899] Ralph Manns, *Ambush is the wrong word*, supra note 876.
[900] Id.
[901] Id.
[902] Id.
[903] Ralph Manns, *Ambush is the wrong word*, supra note 876.
[904] Steve Quinn, *supra* note 860.
[905] Id.
[906] Id.
[907] Id.

So, bass are usually hungry, "but in a nonfeeding mode while conserving energy as they await the opportunity to feed when success is more likely."[908]

Researchers found that during winter bass spend 90-95% of their time swimming in place or holding position (swim speeds less than 0.30 body lengths per second).[909] In fall, they still spend most of their time (80 percent) swimming in place.[910] Neutral bass often "drift around rather than holding in one place."[911] They often form nonactive groups with other bass, but "don't synchronize their movements or hold close together."[912] These groups that do not synchronize movements are called "aggregations" by scientists and not schools.[913] Interestingly, forage fish seem to know when bass are on the prowl and when they are not because forage fish are often nearby to these aggregations of neutral bass, "but stay at least 3 feet away and remain constantly wary."[914] Neutral bass will "strike forage fish that blunder too close."[915] To catch neutral bass, precise placement of casts is often necessary.[916]

Fishermen often talk about "reaction" or "reflex" strikes by inactive bass, so let's consider the science. When a doctor strikes your knee in the right spot (i.e., the patellar tendon) with a reflex hammer, a signal is sent immediately to the spinal cord and back, and the knee jerks forward without the brain having to do any work at all. This is called a "reflex." Your body has numerous other reflexes to provide a quick response to some stimuli without your brain having to think about the response. I can find no research documenting a similar "reflex" reaction for bass when it comes to feeding. In contrast, reflex or reaction strikes require the bass to make a very

---

[908] Id.

[909] Kyle Hanson, et al., *Assessment of largemouth bass behavior and activity at multiple spatial and temporal scales utilizing a whole-lake telemetry array*, HYDROBIOLOGIA 582(1): 243-256 (May 2007), available at https://www.researchgate.net/publication/226543386_Assessment_of_largemouth_bass_Micropterus_salmoides_behaviour_and_activity_at_multiple_spatial_and_temporal_scales_utilizing_a_whole-lake_telemetry_array.

[910] Id.

[911] Ralph Manns, *Ambush is the wrong word, supra* note 876.

[912] Id.

[913] Id.

[914] Id.

[915] Id.

[916] Ralph Manns, *Ambush is the wrong word, supra* note 876.

quick, but conscious decision. In most places, "bass can't afford to pass up a good feeding opportunity."[917] The reaction strike is usually "motivated by the instinct to feed" not really a "reaction feed."[918] Some reaction strikes are probably more about a bass being agitated by and reacting violently to the sudden appearance (or re-appearance for multiple casts) of a wounded prey rather than a true reflex mediated by the bass's nervous system. So, the idea of "reflex strikes" is a misnomer.

Vision

Bass are primarily sight feeders that rely heavily on their eyesight for feeding.[919] Scientists describe largemouth bass as a "visually oriented top predator in many freshwater systems."[920] Among the bass's senses, the "most prominent role in prey/food detection" is played by vision.[921] In addition to feeding, eyesight is important for spawning, aggregating/schooling behaviors, avoiding predation, and many other bass behaviors.[922] Bass have excellent eyesight which makes presentation of the baits important because their vision is good enough to detect fakes, especially in clear water or high visibility conditions, such as calm days, clear skies, and clear water.[923]

Bass use eyesight to evaluate "location, size, color, shape, flash, and action" at a distance to decide whether to strike a forage

---

[917] Steve Quinn, *supra* note 860.
[918] Id.
[919] *Bass Eyesight: Good enough to see prey, lures, lines, bait and you*, Bass Fishing and Catching article, available at https://www.bassfishingandcatching.com/bass-eyesight.html; Fishing and Tech, *Hot fishing tips: 5 scientific facts about largemouth bass*, 2022, available at https://www.fishingandtech.com/post/hotfishingtips-5scientificfactsaboutlargemouthbass.
[920] Lisa Mitchem, et al., *Seeing red: Color vision in the largemouth bass*, CURRENT ZOOLOGY 65(1): 43-52, February2019, available at https://academic.oup.com/cz/article/65/1/43/4924236.
[921] Helene Volkoff and Ivar Ronnestad, *Effects of temperature on feeding and digestive processes in fish*, TEMPERATURE 7(4): 307-320 (2020), available at https://www.ncbi.nlm.nih.gov/pmc/articles/PMC7678922/pdf/KTMP_7_1765950.pdf.
[922] Lisa Mitchem, et al., *supra* note 920.
[923] Fishing and Tech, *supra* note 919.

fish or bait.[924] Generally bass will "seek to get the biggest reward for the least exertion of energy."[925] However, real or artificial prey that "poses a threat of injury or which may be beyond its ability to handle in a struggle" will deter them.[926] Bass instinctively look for long and slender shapes as prey.[927]

Visual Field: As you can see in the picture below, bass's eyes protrude away from their head and are located on the slightly forward and upper part of the head.

Note that the bass's eyes in the picture above are bulbous and protrude out away from its head like goggles, or "goggle eyes."[928] This allows bass to have a larger field of vision than humans so that bass can see in all directions except directly behind or below them.[929] Bass do not have eyelids.[930]

In addition to eye position, bass have an "exceptionally wide lateral field of view" (out to the sides of their bodies) because the lens

---

[924] Bass Eyesight, *supra* note 919.
[925] Id.
[926] Id.
[927] Id.
[928] Id.
[929] Fishing and Tech, *supra* note 919.
[930] Bass Eyesight, *supra* note 919.

in their eyes extends through the pupil, unlike humans' eyes where the lens is completely behind the pupil.[931] Also, bass have lenses that are spherical in shape like a ball, whereas humans' lenses are flattened or ovoid like a magnifying glass.[932] Bass's spherical lenses help them focus their eyes better underwater than humans.[933]

Bass use one eye to see objects on each side of their body (i.e., their side vision is monocular).[934] The position of their eyes on the sides of their heads and the shape of their eyes' lenses allows bass to see in almost a 360-degree circle around their bodies by using monocular vision on each side of their body and binocular vision in front of their body.[935] In other words, each eye can see the area on almost the whole side that eye sets on, and the two eyes together can see in front.[936] Bass can see up to 50 feet to the sides in clear water and can distinguish fine details with sharp visual acuity to the sides.[937]

In front of their heads and directly above them, the two lateral visual fields overlap to give bass two-eyed (i.e., binocular), three-dimensional vision with better depth perception.[938] They can focus roughly 5 to 12 inches in front of them.[939] Bass use this binocular vision to study their prey after locating the prey laterally and moving closer for the strike.[940] By changing position or focus, bass can see up to 30 or 40 feet with their binocular vision—including seeing fisherman above the surface of the water.[941] Sometimes they will even strike lures as soon as they hit the water, demonstrating that they can see the lure flying in the air and track it with their eyes before it lands in some conditions.[942] Motion detection is used by bass for hunting their prey.[943] Things that move are generally living in their environment, so they are explored as possible food.[944]

---

[931] Id.
[932] Fishing and Tech, *supra* note 919.
[933] Id.
[934] Bass Eyesight, *supra* note 919.
[935] Id.
[936] Id.
[937] Id.
[938] Id.
[939] Bass Eyesight, *supra* note 919.
[940] Id.
[941] Id.
[942] Id.
[943] Id.
[944] Bass Eyesight, *supra* note 919.

The location and characteristics of their eyes give bass a couple of small blind spots in their vision directly behind them and directly below them.[945] Because they are aware of their blind spots they often will back into cover to protect their back or sit near the bottom to protect their blind spot below.[946] Bass's blind spots are mitigated by their other senses including their "ability to sense vibration and changes within the water body using its lateral line."[947]

Color Vision: The color vision of largemouth bass was studied as early as 1937 when researchers "trained bass to approach pipettes painted with particular colors (red, yellow, green, white, black, gray, etc.) using a food reward when bass approached target colors and mild electric shocks when bass approached the non-target colors."[948] In that study, researchers "found that bass could readily discern both red and green from all other colors, but often had problems discerning yellow from white and blue from black colors."[949]

More recent studies show that largemouth bass eyes, like human eyes, contain different kinds of photoreceptor cells known as rods and cones.[950] Cones are color sensitive.[951] Researchers have shown that "bass use chromatic (i.e., color) cues in making visual-based decisions."[952] In other words, bass have color vision and use it to make decisions—like whether to bite your lure. Specifically, bass have dichromatic vision which means their eyes are tuned to two colors because they have only two types of cone cells: red and green.[953] Bass's cone cells are green sensitive (maximum sensitivity of 535 nm) and red sensitive (maximum sensitivity of 614 nm).[954] This means that *bass probably see four "colors"*: *red, green, dark* (black to dark shades of grey), *and light* (white to light shades of grey).

---

[945] Id.
[946] Id.; Steven Bardin, *supra* note 839.
[947] Steven Bardin, *supra* note 839.
[948] Lisa Mitchem, et al., *supra* note 920.
[949] Id.
[950] Technological Angler, *Research reveals bass color preferences*, available at https://www.technologicalangler.com/bass-color-vision.
[951] Id.
[952] Lisa Mitchem, et al., *supra* note 920.
[953] Id.
[954] Id.

Researchers found that bass can make highly selective decisions based upon distinguishing red from green and distinguishing either from "achromatic alternatives" (i.e., white, black, and greys).[955] In contrast, bass cannot make selective decisions requiring them to distinguish between dark colors like black and blue or requiring them to distinguish between light colors like white and yellow.[956] Red is particularly easy for bass to identify.[957] Studies showed that largemouth bass have a "strong preference for red coloration over blue or black"; but it is hard to say how this would translate to fishing lures.[958] Bass can distinguish green from black and grays, but they have difficulty telling green from blue.[959] Researchers say that bass have more difficulty associating meaning to achromatic cues like white and black (and yellow for bass).[960]

For lure selection, the science of bass color vision likely means that bass place much less emphasis on color than fishermen—so colors outside of greens, reds, whites, and blacks are likely more effective to attract fisherman than bass. So, if your buddy is catching fish on blue fleck plastic worms and you don't have any of that exact color, you can likely get away with a different color worm because bass do not see blue the same as humans. Since blue is closest to green on the visible spectrum, I suspect bass may see it more as green; and since it is a "fleck" worm and likely has flecks of color or sparkle in it—I would probably choose a green pumpkin candy worm from my tackle box and assume the bass will see it similarly. Since bass struggle to distinguish blue from black as well, then a black worm with flecks of color/sparkle might also be a good choice.

I admit that my tackle box is full of many colors that bass cannot distinguish. I often "stock up" on the latest hot color at my local lake, only to rarely use that color ever again. The bottom line is to probably that fishermen should try variations of green, red, white, or black (dark) when switching between bait colors to see what the fish are biting on a particular day. Color definitely matters, but switching from blue to green or from white to chartreuse probably doesn't have much effect in the bass's eyes. However, switching from

---

[955] Technological Angler, *supra* note 950; Lisa Mitchem, et al., *supra* note 920.
[956] Technological Angler, *supra* note 950.
[957] Lisa Mitchem, et al., *supra* note 920.
[958] Id.
[959] Id.
[960] Id.

green to red or from white to black might make a big difference to bass. My favorite plastic worm color is "plum," which means different things from different manufacturers with some "plum" colors looking almost black while others look kind of blue—so some scientific measurements might be necessary to figure out exactly what the bass are seeing with regard to different "plum" colors. The bluish ones might be greenish or blackish to bass and the darker ones might be dark grey or black to bass. At any rate, they work for me, which may be more related to my confidence than the color the bass are seeing.

For comparison, humans have three different types of cones cells—red-, green-, and blue-sensitive cones—compared to bass only having two.[961] This means that humans have "trichromatic vision" sensitive to three different colors, including their many different shades and combinations.[962] Researchers believe there is no significant variation in visual sensitivity between the Florida bass and Northern largemouth bass.[963]

Digging a little deeper: Largemouth bass have an "offset, dichromatic" visual system that gives them an advantage as an underwater predator because "one photoreceptor optimally perceives the background illumination spectrum, and one photoreceptor contrasts the background spectrum."[964] This system "creates high contrast between background lighting and prey illuminated by overhead sun."[965] Underwater "long wave-lengths (orange-red spectrum) are reflected in background lighting, whereas short wavelength (blue-green spectrum) contrasts that background."[966] Thus, the largemouth bass's dichromatic red/green visual system gives them a predatory advantage in underwater conditions.[967]

---

[961] Lisa Mitchem, et al., *supra* note 920.
[962] Id.
[963] Lisa Mitchem, et al., *supra* note 920.
[964] Id.
[965] Id.
[966] Id.
[967] Id.

> **Question Box:**
> **Can bass tell chartreuse from white or light grey?**
> **How about blue from black?**
>
> Bass have dichromatic vision and can only discern red and green. According to scientists, this means that to bass "chartreuse yellow should appear similar to white . . . because chartreuse yellow equally stimulates both the green and red cone cells at similar frequencies," so there is "no opponency resulting from chartreuse yellow."[1] Bass tested in behavioral assays "were incapable of distinguishing white from chartreuse yellow and vice versa."[2] Therefore, researchers say that there is "strong support for the idea that chartreuse yellow appears similar to white in the bass visual system."[3]
>
> Researchers similarly find that bass are "incapable of distinguishing between black and blue colors" for the same reasons and using the same tests.[4]
>
> ---
> [1] Lisa Mitchem, et al., Seeing red: color vision in largemouth bass, *Current Zoology* 65(1), February 2019, pp. 43-53, available at https://academic.oup.com/cz/article/65/1/43/4924236.
> [2] Id.
> [3] Id.
> [4] Id.

Low Light and Night Vision: Bass also have rod cells in their eyes. Rod cells are responsible for night and low light vision, but do not help much with color vision.[968] Bass rod cells are maximally sensitive at 528 nm.[969] Bass can detect small movements from far away and in very dim light.[970] In addition to rods for night vision, bass eyes have an extra structure not found in human eyes called the tapetum lucidum that contains a layer of tissue that "amplifies the incoming light."[971] Even so, bass decrease their activity, socialization, and feeding at night because their vision is diminished considerably compared to daytime. However, bass may prefer to feed in low light conditions possibly because their vision is better than the vision of their prey under low light conditions.

Sight Variations: To the bass, the same colors may look different in one fishery compared to another. The visual environment

---
[968] Technological Angler, *supra* note 950.
[969] Lisa Mitchem, et al., *supra* note 920.
[970] Fishing and Tech, *supra* note 919.
[971] Id.

is much different under water than in air and is "highly variable based on time of day, depth, and shade."[972] A bass's visual perception is complicated by "the fact lighting environments vary dramatically in aquatic habitats" based on the "effects of water depth, algae, turbidity, dissolved organic matter, and time of day," as well as water clarity.[973] All of these factors can alter "(1) the visual backgrounds against which objects are viewed, (2) the irradiance spectrum that illuminates objects and determines the inherent radiance reflected from an object, and (3) the transmission of the reflected radiance between an object and the viewer."[974] Differences in these factors between different bodies of water help explain why bass seem to prefer certain colors of baits at one lake but different colors at another.

Hearing

Hearing helps bass detect prey, avoid predators, and participate in other essential activities.[975] Bass have hearing organs within their bodies, but no external ears.[976] Bass ears are located entirely inside their skulls, unlike humans.[977]

Sound travels through water in waves that are measured in terms of intensity (decibels) and frequency (hertz).[978] Sound travels through water almost 4.5 times faster than it travels through air—specifically, at around 5,000 feet per second through water versus only 1,125 feet per second through air.[979]

Bass inner ears include an upper section for equilibrium called the semicircular canals, a middle section, and a lower section called the labyrinth.[980] Hearing occurs mostly in the labyrinth, which has three sensory patches (a.k.a., the maculae) called the utricule, saccule, and lagena.[981] Each of these three sensory patches contain a special

---

[972] Lisa Mitchem, et al., *supra* note 920.
[973] Id.; Steven Bardin, *supra* note 839.
[974] Lisa Mitchem, et al., *supra* note 920.
[975] Fishtales, *What can bass really hear?*, Bixxel Media, available at https://bixxel.media/new-page-98.
[976] Fishing and Tech, *supra* note 919.
[977] Fishtales, *What can bass really hear?*, *supra* note 975.
[978] Id.
[979] Id.
[980] Id.
[981] Id.

kind of hearing cell called a "hair cell" with tiny calcified ear stones laying on top of them on a thin membrane.[982] When sound reaches the bass's inner ear, "the stones move across the (sensory patches) and stimulate the hair cells that send a message to the brain."[983] When the sound "is received in the brain, the bass goes thru three phases: an initial arousal and evaluation phase, a search phase, and a close-up analytical evaluation phase."[984]

Sound is transmitted as "both a pressure wave and particle displacement" under water.[985] The particle displacements associated with sound dissipate rapidly as they move through water away from the source.[986] So, particle motion associated with sound and detected by bass's ears and their lateral line (see discussion below) travel only a short distance.[987] As a result, bass in shallow water close to a boat will likely hear people talking in the boat, but fish 20 feet deep may not.[988] In addition, sound originating in air is refracted and reflected by the water's surface so that on days with lots of waves the sound waves are refracted in many different directions which disrupts transmission, but on calm days, sound travels farther across the lake so that you can hear people talking from farther away on the lake.[989]

Bass's hearing allows them to detect and be spooked by unnatural vibrations on the surface such as a boat motor idling.[990] At Toledo Bend, researchers found that the sound of an outboard motor idling above them in a figure of eight pattern caused bass to move locations 42% of the time—especially in water less than 10 feet deep.[991] Even in water 10 feet or deeper, 25% of bass moved in

---

[982] Fishtales, *What can bass really hear?*, *supra* note 975.
[983] Id.
[984] Id.
[985] Joachim Mogdans, *Sensory ecology of the fish lateral-line system: Morphological and physiological adaptations for the perception of hydrodynamic stimuli*, J. FISH BIOLOGY 95(1): 53-72, July 2019, available at https://onlinelibrary.wiley.com/doi/10.1111/jfb.13966.
[986] Id.
[987] Id.
[988] Fishtales, *What can bass really hear?*, *supra* note 975.
[989] Id.
[990] Fishing and Tech, *supra* note 919.
[991] Ken Smith Fishing YouTube Channel, *Toledo Bend Telemetry Tracking Study Update Todd Driscoll TP&W Biologist Feb 2022 Part 5*, available at https://www.youtube.com/watch?v=f1sL9FZnS4g&list=PLLzhji805wVzkLnAA97I8VmdZpR8arB_Q&index=5.

response to the motor, and at 20 feet or deeper, 20% moved.[992] Researchers think it might be the biggest fish that spooks first, but have not been able to prove that.[993] So, a stealthy approach is important for lunker chasing.

Lateral Line

The lateral line is a mechanosensory system (somewhat similar to human's sense of touch) that allows bass to "detect motion relative to the surface" of their skin by perceiving water particle movements in the hydrodynamic environment around them.[994] It measures the relative movements between a bass's body and the water.[995] The lateral line helps bass "feel what is going on in the neighborhood," which bass use in behaviors like schooling, orienting their bodies in current (i.e., rheotaxis), sensing change in the objects around them (hydrodynamic imaging), courtship communication, detecting prey, and avoiding predators.[996] The lateral line system can "feel" small scale pressure changes that are almost impossible for humans to measure.[997]

The lateral line consists of a "series of pores which open into a canal-like system that run from the gill plate to the tail and also across the bass' head and face."[998] The system contains thousands of hair-like sensors called *neuromasts* that detect water movement within the pore system.[999] Neuromasts "provide the bass a sense of direction and a sense similar to 'touching' something from a distance" and can be distributed across a bass's body, but are concentrated along the lateral lines.[1000]

---

[992] Id.
[993] Id.
[994] Joachim Mogdans, *supra* note 985; Fishing and Tech, *supra* note 919; Matthew Weeg and Andrew Bass, *Frequency response properties of lateral line superficial neuromasts in a vocal fish, with evidence for acoustic sensitivity*, J. NEUROPHYSIOLOGY 88(3), September 1, 2002, available at https://journals.physiology.org/doi/full/10.1152/jn.2002.88.3.1252.
[995] Joachim Mogdans, *supra* note 985.
[996] Fishing and Tech, *supra* note 919; Matthew Weeg and Andrew Bass, *supra* note 994.
[997] Joachim Mogdans, *supra* note 985.
[998] Fishtales, *What can bass really hear?*, *supra* note 975.
[999] Joachim Mogdans, *supra* note 985.
[1000] Fishing and Tech, *supra* note 919; Joachim Mogdans, *supra* note 985.

Neuromasts consist of a macula with sensory hair cells, supporting cells, and mantle cells.[1001] Hair cells are similar to those found in the auditory (hearing) and vestibular (balance) system of humans.[1002] Ciliary bundles of the hair cells "are embedded in a gelatinous dome-like structure, the cupula."[1003] Water movements cause the cupula to move resulting in "shearing of the ciliary bundles" causing changes in the hair cells' membrane potential—and thus a stimulus to which fish can react.[1004]

The lateral-line system is divided into superficial neuromasts and canal neuromasts.[1005] Superficial neuromasts are on the skin surface, and canal neuromasts are in canals beneath the skin surface (i.e., subdermal) connected to the superficial pores.[1006] Superficial neuromasts are velocity detectors with responses proportional to the velocity of the water flowing across them; they are arranged on the head, trunk and tail fin in lines or clusters.[1007] In contrast, canal neuromasts are in canals on the head and trunk and contact the water through canal pores; they function as pressure gradient and acceleration detectors.[1008]

Two classes of nerve fibers innervate neuromasts with one class sensitive to accelerations and responding to 30 to 200 Hz frequencies, while the other class is sensitive to velocity and responds best to frequencies below 30 Hz.[1009] Afferent nerve fibers contact the hair cells of neuromasts and transmit their impulses to the brainstem where additional ascending fibers communicate with the midbrain and forebrain.[1010] Thus, the lateral line system is perceived at all levels of the bass's central nervous system.[1011] In my view, this means that actions that are reflexes (if present in fish; see discussion on reaction strikes earlier in this chapter), as well as actions that require a decision, are influenced by the lateral line system.

[1001] Joachim Mogdans, *supra* note 985.
[1002] Id.
[1003] Id.
[1004] Id.
[1005] Id.; Matthew Weeg and Andrew Bass, *supra* note 994.
[1006] Matthew Weeg and Andrew Bass, *supra* note 994.
[1007] Joachim Mogdans, *supra* note 985.
[1008] Id.
[1009] Matthew Weeg and Andrew Bass, *supra* note 994.
[1010] Joachim Mogdans, *supra* note 985.
[1011] Id.

The lateral line system is *important for several functions*. It is especially important for detecting prey and predators under low light conditions.[1012] Predators and prey cause vibrations that cause water molecules to move causing a "hydrodynamic disturbance" when they are near a bass; the strength of the resultant lateral line stimulus depends upon the frequency, water displacement, acceleration, and velocity of the disturbance in the water.[1013] Bass can use the signal strength to identify what type of prey or predator is approaching.[1014] The lateral line system is also important in telling bass how to orient their bodies in currents (i.e., rheotaxis) because it allows them to distinguish natural background currents from currents related to surrounding organisms.[1015] So, the lateral line is important in helping fish find current seams.

By combining hearing with the lateral line system, bass can detect an unseen lure from as far as fifty feet away.[1016] The lateral line system can detect low frequency vibrations outside the range of the bass's hearing, and the bass's hearing can detect higher frequency vibrations outside the range of the bass's lateral line system; so, the bass's hearing and lateral line capabilities work together to extend the range of water movements, vibrations, and sounds that are detectable by bass.

The lateral line system is *especially important to assist bass with low light and night feeding.* The lateral line helps bass localize their prey from a distance, even in low light conditions. With fewer visual cues in low light, bass switch from primarily ram feeding (i.e., gaining velocity to overtake and engulf prey) to more reliance on suction feeding to capture prey.[1017] In other words, in dim light bass "approach prey slowly but open their mouths more rapidly, which has been shown to result in greater buccal pressure, causing their prey to move a greater distance at a more rapid velocity as they are being drawn into predators' mouths."[1018] Even though bass are primarily visual feeders, when necessary, bass detect and localize their prey

---

[1012] Id.
[1013] Fishtales, *What can bass really hear?*, *supra* note 975.
[1014] Joachim Mogdans, *supra* note 985.
[1015] Id.
[1016] Fishing and Tech, *supra* note 919.
[1017] Jayne Gardiner and Phillip Motta, *supra* note 841.
[1018] Id.

from a distance and can strike accurately in total darkness or if blind by using information from the lateral line system.[1019]

Smell

Largemouth bass are primarily visual feeders, so smell and taste are secondary in the process of getting a bass to inhale your bait. Smell is a form of chemoreception in which bass sense chemical molecules in the water like hazard molecules, pheromones and other hormones, bile acids, sugar, salt, amino acids, bitter substances, and other chemicals in the water.[1020] Authors believe that bass use smell to detect predator or prey, to help find a mate, and to detect pollutants.[1021]

Largemouth bass have four nostrils or nares (two on each side) with one sitting slightly in front of the other on each side of the head just in front of the eyes.[1022] Bass nostrils are not for breathing; i.e., they are exclusively for smell.[1023] Largemouth bass nostrils are not connected to the throat like humans, so bass's senses of smell and taste are not interconnected.[1024] The anterior (i.e., front) nostril protrudes above the skin and is a tubular structure with a circular opening.[1025] The posterior (i.e., back) nostril has a more angular or oval opening and is flat to the skin.[1026] The location of the anterior and posterior nostrils are shown in the picture below:

[1019] Id.
[1020] Hyun Tae Kim, et al., *Anatomy, ultrastructure and histology of the olfactory organ of the largemouth bass Micropterus salmoides, Centrarchidae*, APPLIED MICROSCOPY, 49:18, December 2019, available at https://www.ncbi.nlm.nih.gov/pmc/articles/PMC7818377/; Fishtales, *What can bass smell*, Bixxel Media, available at https://bixxel.media/new-page-19.
[1021] Fishtales, *What can bass smell?*, *supra* note 1020.
[1022] Steven Bardin, *supra* note 839.
[1023] Fishtales, *What can bass smell?*, *supra* note 1020.
[1024] Id.
[1025] Hyun Tae Kim, et al., *supra* note 1020.
[1026] Id.

Posterior Nostril

Anterior Nostril

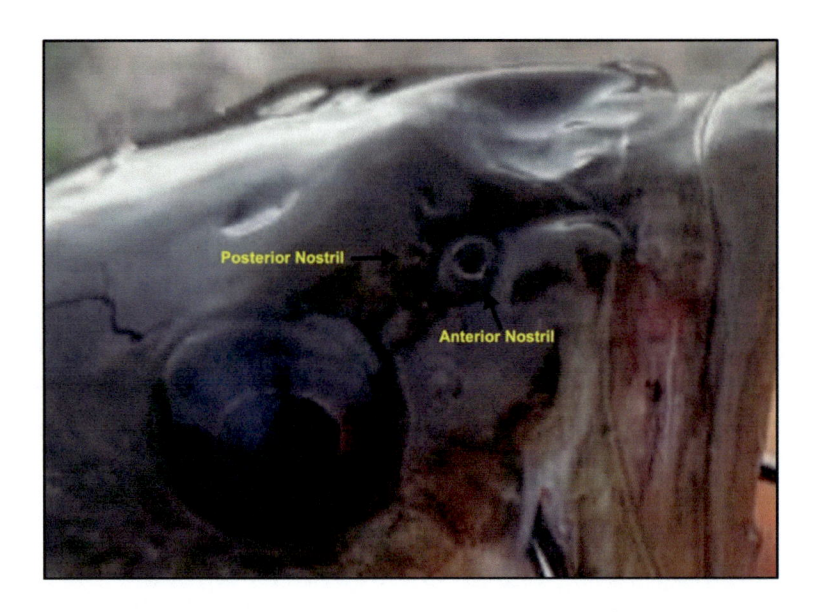

    Water flows in the anterior nostril and out the posterior nostril through the olfactory chamber across a folded membrane called the "olfactory rosette."[1027] Bass's olfactory (i.e., smell) organs have been examined by stereo microscopy, light microscopy, and even scanning electron microscopy.[1028] The olfactory rosette is "a folded membrane that contains thousands of chemoreceptor cells that detect waterborne biological or chemical scent molecules."[1029] Five types of cells are found inside the olfactory chamber including "olfactory receptor neurons, supporting cells, basal cells, lymphatic cells and mucous cells."[1030] When a scent is detected by cells in the olfactory rosette, a signal is sent via nerves (called olfactory receptor neurons) to the brain, which then decides what the scent represents.[1031] The olfactory chamber includes small accessory nasal sacs that are used for intentional water ventilation of the olfactory chamber—kind of like a fish "blowing its nose."[1032]

    Fish attractants are a highly competitive, multi-billion-dollar industry, so most of the research in this area has been done by the

---

[1027] Fishtales, *What can bass smell?*, *supra* note 1020; Fishing and Tech, *supra* note 919.
[1028] Hyun Tae Kim, et al., *supra* note 1020.
[1029] Fishtales, *What can bass smell?*, *supra* note 1020.
[1030] Hyun Tae Kim, et al., *supra* note 1020.
[1031] Fishtales, *What can bass smell?*, *supra* note 1020.
[1032] Hyun Tae Kim, et al., *supra* note 1020.

companies that profit from their research and keep it mostly proprietary.[1033] As a result, there is not a lot of unbiased scientific research available on the taste and smell abilities of largemouth bass. I am trying to avoid literature that is conducted by industry to avoid possible financial biases in the results; for example, scientists working for a company that manufactures lure scents are highly motivated to prove that their scents work, which can bias the results. Therefore, I will concentrate on data and information with less potential bias.

The olfactory rosette grows as bass grow and becomes proportionally larger and stronger.[1034] So, some say that for larger bass, scent is more important when choosing baits/lures.[1035] I'm not sure that makes any more sense than saying people with big noses have a keener sense of smell. I did not find scientific support for either notion.

Some authors report that bass use smell to determine whether potential prey is edible and that correct smells can attract bass while wrong smells can deter them.[1036] A former industry biologist says that, "Presently, there is no evidence linking bass repulsion with human odor."[1037] He notes, however, that detergents, soaps, DEET (in bug spray), and many food and lotion preservatives (especially if containing benzene) are offensive scents to largemouth bass.[1038] He says that DEET can stay on your hands for 90 minutes after application and transfer to your baits can repel bass and other fish.[1039] Surprisingly, he also notes that, "Neither gas nor oil is repulsive to bass."[1040] He says that this is because oil and oil based attractants are not water-soluble, which means bass cannot smell them.[1041]

In many species, smell is used to detect the most distant stimuli while touch and taste are used for the closest stimuli.[1042] I could not find unbiased scientific data to support the conclusion that

---

[1033] Fishtales, *What can bass smell?*, *supra* note 1020.
[1034] Fishing and Tech, *supra* note 919.
[1035] Id.
[1036] Id.
[1037] Fishtales, *What can bass smell?*, *supra* note 1020.
[1038] Id.
[1039] Id.
[1040] Id.
[1041] Id.
[1042] Helene Volkoff and Ivar Ronnestad, *supra* note 921.

smell plays as prominent of a role for largemouth bass as it does for other species (e.g., whitetail deer).

Taste

Unlike in humans, bass's sense of taste and smell are completely separate because the bass's nasal passages do not connect with its oral cavities. Bass have thousands of taste buds located inside their mouth, throat, pharynx, tongue, and lips.[1043] Taste is important for bass in "the ultimate acceptance or rejection of potential food items."[1044] Vision is used to make the initial decision to inhale a food item, but taste helps determine how long a bass holds onto an item and whether it is swallowed or expelled. If a bass decides not to swallow an item it has in its mouth because of the item's taste, the item is typically *expelled within 3 seconds and sometimes so fast that an angler would never know he or she had a bite.*

Bass have "six major pads of caniform teeth" in their pharynx with many taste buds surrounding these teeth.[1045] Depending upon the food item, these teeth are used for food processing by "mastication, crushing or tearing prior to swallowing" (e.g., bass swallow other fish whole, but may expel undigestible parts of a crawfish and some scales from fish before swallowing).[1046] The fact that teeth and taste buds are in proximity suggests that food processing and tasting occur together at this location, and "that together these processes determine whether a potential food item is swallowed."[1047]

In one study, food balls were used to feed bass in tanks, and these food balls were "inhaled with equal frequency" regardless of whether or not they had a tasty feeding stimulant in them or not—so the bass relied primarily upon vision, not taste or smell, to decide whether or not to inhale the food.[1048] The scientists noted that bass ingest food in three steps: "(1) inhalation of the food into the oral

---

[1043] Steven Bardin, *supra* note 839; Fishing and Tech, *supra* note 919.
[1044] P.J. Linser, et al., *Functional significance of the co-localzation of taste buds and teeth in the pharyngeal jaws of the largemouth bass*, BIOL. BULL. 195(3):273-81, 1998, available at https://pubmed.ncbi.nlm.nih.gov/9924772/.
[1045] Id.
[1046] Id.
[1047] Id.
[1048] Id.

cavity, (2) passage through the pharyngeal cavity, and (3) swallowing."[1049] Gustation or tasting occurs once the food is in the oral cavity and passing through the pharyngeal cavity before swallowing and is very important in decision making before swallowing for bass.

Scientists tested taste sensation of bass by feeding them food balls with and without a feeding stimulant (a shrimp flavored mixture that the bass had been conditioned to eat).[1050] They videotaped and directly observed the bass eating the food balls.[1051] Food balls with the feeding stimulant were swallowed, "whereas food balls without a feeding stimulant were promptly expelled" out of their mouths; this shows that taste plays a "major role in stimulating swallowing."[1052] More specifically, food balls without any feeding stimulant were spit out after being held in the mouth for a few seconds," whereas "food balls containing a feeding stimulant were swallowed within 30 seconds."[1053]

Food balls were swallowed in proportion to the amount of feeding stimulant they contained; so, food balls with more stimulant were swallowed more frequently than those with less stimulant.[1054] However, even the food balls with hardly any feeding stimulant (>0.05% of one stimulant) "were swallowed more frequently than those without the stimulant."[1055] Therefore, *taste "appears to play a major role in the decision to swallow or reject a food ball, whereas vision is the primary sense affecting its initial inhalation."*[1056]

Interestingly, during this experiment (which also involved bass eating goldfish), "bass were occasionally observed to inhale goldfish, hold them in the oral cavity for several seconds, and then release them unharmed."[1057] So, inhalation is clearly different from swallowing because "the decision to swallow a food item occurred only after the object was in the mouth."[1058]

[1049] P.J. Linser, et al., *supra* note 1044.
[1050] Id.
[1051] Id.
[1052] Id.
[1053] Id.
[1054] P.J. Linser, et al., *supra* note 1044.
[1055] Id.
[1056] Id.
[1057] Id.
[1058] Id.

So how long do you have to set the hook on a bait the bass decides to reject? *Bass took an average of "about 3 seconds after inhalation" to eject an item out of its mouth that it rejected.*[1059] Another author reported that, "Scuba divers have reported seeing bass inhale and exhale soft plastics so quickly anglers didn't feel anything."[1060]

In short, largemouth bass make decisions to inhale a food item or lure based primarily upon visual cues.[1061] However, once the item is in the bass's mouth, taste strongly modulates the bass's decision whether or not to swallow the item.[1062] Feeding studies have also shown that "food was located by vision, because odorants introduced into the water did not serve as attractants or stimulate feeding behavior" of largemouth bass fry.[1063]

Attractants that give a bass taste have the potential to make the fish hold on to the bait longer, giving the angler a better chance of landing a hook set. Attractants might also serve to mask nonnatural tastes and smells that bass find repellent like detergents, soaps, and DEET. Salt, garlic, "baitfish," "crawdad," and others are common scents and attractants on the market.[1064] Given their potential to add a believable taste to a plastic lure (assuming they stay with the lure long enough), some of these products are likely to lead to fewer missed connections on hooksets than a tasteless piece of plastic.

Electroreception?

Bass may be able to sense changes in electrical current in the water, which could be more important than we realize today. Bass have an internal electrical detection system called the ampullae of Lorenzini, which include canals in the skin containing sensory cells.[1065] Muscle contractions of struggling prey in the water near bass may cause a voltage change in the water that bass might be able to

---

[1059] Id.
[1060] A.J. Hauser, *How do largemouth bass taste?*, The Minimalist Fisherman, 2022, available at https://theminimalistfisherman.com/how-do-largemouth-bass-taste/.
[1061] P.J. Linser, et al., *supra* note 1044.
[1062] Id.
[1063] Id.
[1064] A.J. Hauser, *supra* note 1060.
[1065] Fishing and Tech, *supra* note 919.

sense.[1066] Electroreception could also help bass navigate under low light conditions or at night.[1067] More study is needed in this area, so I only mention it briefly for completeness.

[1066] Id.
[1067] Id.

10

Prey

Forage quality and quantity help determine the size of bass in a fishery.[1068] More and higher energy food make fish grow faster.[1069] Largemouth bass will "grow continuously throughout their lives" with adequate forage consumption.[1070] To maintain their body weight, largemouth bass must consume five pounds of forage per pound of body weight each year as a maintenance diet; for example, a 5 pound bass needs to eat 25 pounds of forage over a year to remain at 5 pounds.[1071] To gain one pound each year, they need to eat an additional 10 pounds of forage; so, for a 5 pound bass grow into a 6

[1068] Wes Neal, *Unraveling the Bass Genetic Code for Pondmeisters*, Bass Resource, July 21, 2016, available at https://www.bassresource.com/fish_biology/bass-genetic-code.html.
[1069] Id.
[1070] Steven Bardin, *Fish Biology: Largemouth bass: A comprehensive species guide*, Wired2Fish, January 28, 2023, available at https://www.wired2fish.com/fish-biology/largemouth-bass-a-comprehensive-species-guide/.
[1071] Id.; James Davis and Joe Lock, *Largemouth bass biology and life history*, Southern Regional Aquacultural Center SRAC Publication No. 200, August 1997.

pound bass in one year, it will need to consume a total of 35 pounds of forage in total during that year.[1072]

Adult bass feed about every 14 to 24 hours most of the year depending upon the size of their meal.[1073] Largemouth bass choose their prey for several reasons including hunger, but also "defense, curiosity, reaction, [and] aggression."[1074] Prey size depends on what prey items live in the particular body of water and which prey are vulnerable to predation, which can vary by season.[1075]

As largemouth bass get bigger, their meals get bigger and more diverse.[1076] The most common meals for lunker bass include crayfish, shad, and sunfish (bream), so those will be the topics of this chapter, along with a brief discussion of the worm.[1077]

Crayfish

Crayfish are an important food source for largemouth bass.[1078] In one study, researchers found that largemouth bass were on the bottom of the fishery 77% of the time—especially in shallow water.[1079] Bass were even on bottom 67% of the time in water 10 feet deep and 61% of the time in water 20 feet deep.[1080] Since crayfish are bottom dwellers, they are a nearby source of food for bass, so lunker fishermen can increase their odds of catching bass by understanding crayfish.

In the food chain, crayfish are important bioprocessors and predators, so they can be very important for moving energy up the

---

[1072] Steven Bardin, *Fish Biology: Largemouth bass*, *supra* note 1070; James Davis and Joe Lock, *supra* note 1071.
[1073] James Davis and Joe Lock, *supra* note 1071.
[1074] Steven Bardin, *Fish Biology: Largemouth bass*, *supra* note 1070.
[1075] Id.
[1076] Id.
[1077] Id.
[1078] Peter Mathieson, *Understanding bass forage: Crawfish*, BASSMASTER, December 10, 2019, available at https://www.bassmaster.com/how-to/news/understanding-bass-forage-crawfish/.
[1079] Ken Smith Fishing YouTube Channel, *Toledo Bend Telemetry Tracking Study Update Todd Driscoll TP&W Biologist Feb 2022 Part 5*, available at https://www.youtube.com/watch?v=f1sL9FZnS4g&list=PLLzhji805wVzkLnAA97I8VmdZpR8arB_Q&index=5.
[1080] Id.

food chain.[1081] Crayfish are opportunistic feeders that tend to feed at night when they use their antennae to feel and taste in the dark.[1082] They eat almost any plant or animal, dead or alive.[1083] Adult crayfish prefer plants as food (herbivores) and eat "aquatic plants, leaves, and woody debris."[1084] Young crayfish are more carnivorous and prefer "aquatic insects, tadpoles, snails, fish, and salamanders."[1085]

In many fisheries, crayfish are the "most important link in the aquatic food chain" because they "eat algae, waterweeds, and aquatic animals, and are in turn, eaten by over 240 species of wild animals."[1086] In addition to bass and other fish, crayfish are eaten by racoons, otters, herons, and other wildlife.[1087] Crayfish are so important in ecosystems that in some ponds, lakes, and rivers, they can make up more than half of the macroinvertebrate biomass (i.e., much of the food source for largemouth bass).[1088]

Crayfish (a.k.a., crawfish) are in the same scientific *order* (Decapoda) as crabs, lobsters, and shrimps.[1089] They are invertebrates that belong to the same scientific *group* (Arthropoda) as insects, spiders, centipedes, and scorpions.[1090] They are in the *subphylum* Crustacea like lobsters and crabs and are covered with a protective shell or exoskeleton that they must shed periodically to allow them to grow.[1091]

[1081] Louis Helfrich and Robert DiStefano, *Sustaining America's aquatic biodiversity—Crayfish biodiversity and conservation*, Virginia Cooperative Extension, 420-524 (CNRE-82P), March 24, 2020, available at https://www.pubs.ext.vt.edu/420/420-524/420-524.html; Peter Mathieson, *Understanding bass forage: Crawfish*, *supra* note 1078.
[1082] Louis Helfrich and Robert DiStefano, *supra* note 1081.
[1083] Id.
[1084] Id.
[1085] Id.
[1086] Id.
[1087] Louis Helfrich and Robert DiStefano, *supra* note 1081; Christopher Taylor, et al., *A reassessment of the conservation status of crayfishes of the United States and Canada after 10+ years of increased awareness*, FISHERIES 32(8):372-389, August 2007, available at https://www.researchgate.net/publication/233308728_A_Reassessment_of_the_Conservation_Status_of_Crayfishes_of_the_United_States_and_Canada_after_10_Years_of_Increased_Awareness.
[1088] Christopher Taylor, et al., *supra* note 1087.
[1089] Id.
[1090] Louis Helfrich and Robert DiStefano, *supra* note 1081.
[1091] Id.

Crayfish live in freshwater streams, lakes, ponds, marshes, and swamps with water temperatures primarily between 55°F and 85°F.[1092] Like largemouth bass, crayfish are ectotherms or "cold blooded," so water temperature has a major influence on crayfish behaviors. At water temperatures below 45°F, crayfish are inactive and bury themselves in mud burrows or rock crevices.[1093]

Crayfish are native to freshwater ecosystems on every continent except Antarctica and Africa.[1094] Their presence is often an "important indicator of water quality and environmental health" because they "flourish in clean waters and perish in polluted waters."[1095] Crayfish live on the bottom of the water body spending the majority of their lives "walking on stream and lake bottoms (largely at night), but quickly burrow under rocks and logs to avoid predators."[1096] Burrowing crayfish dig holes in the banks of streams and in moist soils creating "chimneys" of mud excavated by burrowing tunnels 1 to 5 feet deep or to the water table to find moist soil.[1097]

Crayfish are agile and fast due to their flexible jointed segments.[1098] Their bodies have two segments: (1) the cephalothorax which includes the head and chest, and the (2) abdomen or rear half of the body.[1099] The cephalothorax is covered by the shell and the rear half is "covered by seven jointed segments of a large, fan-like tail."[1100] They have two eyes supported on stalks.[1101] They have two kinds of antennae.[1102] They have ten legs including one pair of claws and 4 slender pairs of walking legs.[1103] Crayfish have pincers used for defense, mating, burrowing, egg laying in females, and feeding.[1104] They can regenerate their limbs if broken off, but the

---

[1092] Id.
[1093] Peter Mathieson, *Understanding bass forage: Crawfish*, *supra* note 1078.
[1094] Christopher Taylor, et al., *supra* note 1087.
[1095] Id.
[1096] Louis Helfrich and Robert DiStefano, *supra* note 1081; Peter Mathieson, *Understanding bass forage: Crawfish*, *supra* note 1078.
[1097] Louis Helfrich and Robert DiStefano, *supra* note 1081.
[1098] Id.
[1099] Id.
[1100] Id.
[1101] Id.
[1102] Louis Helfrich and Robert DiStefano, *supra* note 1081.
[1103] Id.
[1104] Id.

new ones are often smaller or misshapen.[1105] Typically, crayfish walk forward on the bottom with their legs, but rapidly flip their tail to swim backwards if startled or to escape danger.[1106] They breath using internal gills like fish, but can remain out of water for long periods of time in humid conditions.[1107]

Over 350 species of crayfish live in the United States, which gives the U.S. the richest diversity of crayfish in the world.[1108] Almost all North American crayfish are in the *family* Cambaridae.[1109] Crayfish come in a variety of colors including blue, red, brown, gray, yellow, and white.[1110] They also come in a range of shapes and sizes from 1 to 6 inches in length.[1111] Red swamp crayfish and White River crayfish "are the two most commonly cultured species" and "make up over 90% of the total crawfish cultured in the US, with red swamp crawfish, … typically comprising 70-80% of the total catch."[1112]

Crayfish Spawn: Crayfish spawn in the spring and fall. Most crayfish live only 2 to 4 years and begin mating their second year.[1113] When water temperatures first top 50°F in spring, male crayfish emerge from crevices in rocks and venture out into the open to look for females.[1114] This is typically begins sometime between February and May depending upon latitude.[1115] For about a two week period in spring, males walk on top of rocks and other hard substrates clear of silt and mud, exposing themselves to bass and other predators.[1116] So, during this time period, rocky areas from 3 feet deep to 30 feet deep have the highest concentrations of exposed crayfish, which attracts large numbers of feeding bass.[1117] Crayfish can spawn in mud, but

---

[1105] Id.
[1106] Id.
[1107] Louis Helfrich and Robert DiStefano, *supra* note 1081.
[1108] Id.
[1109] Christopher Taylor, et al., *supra* note 1087.
[1110] Louis Helfrich and Robert DiStefano, *supra* note 1081.
[1111] Id.
[1112] Texas A&M AgriLife Extension, *Aquatic Fisheries and Pond Management, Crawfish*, available at https://fisheries.tamu.edu/pond-management/species/crawfish/.
[1113] Louis Helfrich and Robert DiStefano, *supra* note 1081.
[1114] Peter Mathieson, *Understanding bass forage: Crawfish*, *supra* note 1078.
[1115] Id.
[1116] Id.
[1117] Id.

prefer clean rocky areas if available.[1118] Penetrating sunlight and relatively clear water are important.[1119] Fall is also mating season for most species.[1120] The fall mating cycle is more intense than the spring, especially at southern latitudes.[1121]

Females lay eggs in the spring for most species.[1122] Females may carry 20-700 eggs on their abdomen for up to 10 months before they hatch and are termed "in berry" because the eggs "look like a bunch of blackberries attached to the female's abdomen."[1123] The eggs become lighter in color closer to hatching.[1124] After hatching, the young stay attached and close to the female for up to 4 months before becoming independent.[1125]

Crayfish Color: As crayfish grow, they outgrow their hard outer shell approximately 1 to 3 times per year as adults.[1126] Therefore, they must regularly shed their shell (i.e., "molt") to allow them to continue growing.[1127] During molting, "a new soft shell develops beneath the old one" before the old shell splits and the whole crayfish emerges through this split in the old shell.[1128] The new shell is typically soft for 2 to 4 days, so they hide during this time.[1129]

Crayfish color is important for bass fishermen who hope to "match the hatch." Color provides important camouflage for crayfish to protect them from predation from visual feeders like largemouth bass. There is not much scientific research on the color of crayfish.[1130] Most crayfish are either greenish brown or brownish green to blend in with their surroundings on the bottom to hide from

---

[1118] Id.
[1119] Peter Mathieson, *Understanding bass forage: Crawfish*, supra note 1078.
[1120] Louis Helfrich and Robert DiStefano, *supra* note 1081.
[1121] Peter Mathieson, *Understanding bass forage: Crawfish*, supra note 1078.
[1122] Louis Helfrich and Robert DiStefano, *supra* note 1081.
[1123] Id.
[1124] Id.
[1125] Id.
[1126] Id.
[1127] Louis Helfrich and Robert DiStefano, *supra* note 1081.
[1128] Id.
[1129] Id.
[1130] Guenter Schuster, *Review of crayfish color patterns in the Family Cambaridae (Astracoidea), with discussion of their possible importance*, ZOOTAXA, 4755(1): 23, March 2020, available at https://www.biotaxa.org/Zootaxa/article/view/zootaxa.4755.1.3.

predators.[1131] Variations in color often result from differences in background color of their environment, but also from diet, molt stage, and age.[1132]

One researcher found that in almost all cases, crayfish color generally resembled the environment in which it lived.[1133] In other words, crayfish colors typically match the bottom of the lake, pond, river, or stream in which they live. Some anglers go so far as to set traps for crayfish to determine lure colors in bodies of water where they regularly fish. Generally, bodies of water with deeper water and muddy bottoms are more likely to have crayfish in darker colors (except when molting).[1134]

Another source of color change in crayfish is molting. The molt changes their color from "a camouflage olive/brown, to a bright orange or red cast, making them an easy visual target for bass."[1135] After mating, the males "molt," so red crayfish imitators may be more effective after the spring and fall crayfish mating cycles—especially in the southeastern United States.[1136] Red crayfish are also more likely to be present in shallow streams (even if they do not match their environment) and shallow waters because many crayfish contain a pigment that turns red with sunlight exposure according to some researchers.[1137] Also, young crawfish tend to be red during the first 2 or 3 months of life in some environments.[1138]

Color also likely plays a role as a biologic signal related to mating, communication, and territoriality to other crayfish because crayfish have multichromatic color vision.[1139] Base colors vary among individual crayfish, and distinct color patterns can emerge because of contrasting color differences on appendages.[1140] Spots, stripes, and/or bands can also be present on larger body regions.[1141]

[1131] Louis Helfrich and Robert DiStefano, *supra* note 1081.
[1132] Guenter Schuster, *supra* note 1030.
[1133] W.J. Kent, *The Colors of the Crayfish*, THE AMERICAN NATURALIST 35(419):933-936, 1901.
[1134] Id.
[1135] Peter Mathieson, *Understanding bass forage: Crawfish*, *supra* note 1078.
[1136] Id.
[1137] W.J. Kent, *supra* note 1133.
[1138] Id.
[1139] Guenter Schuster, *supra* note 1030.
[1140] Id.
[1141] Id.

Shad

"Shad" is a general term for the many different species of "silvery, flat-sided fish."[1142] Shad are important links in the food chain because they consume tiny organisms like algae and plankton and then themselves become food for larger fish, "herons, seagulls, cormorants, watersnakes, racoons, and many, many more" predators.[1143] Shad are so vital to most ecosystems that the survival of many fish and animals depends upon shad.[1144] In addition to linking tiny to large organisms in the food chain, shad help keep populations of larval insects, zooplankton, and other microscopic animals under control.[1145]

Shad population health can be an indicator of water quality and the health of bass populations so that when shad thrive, bass also thrive, but when shad struggle, so do bass.[1146] Because there are so many different types of shad that space limits an encyclopedic account, in this section I will concentrate on two of the most important shad used as forage by largemouth bass—the gizzard shad and the threadfin shad, which are common in lunker fisheries.

Shad have a row of "sharp-edged, spiny scales (or scutes) along the middle of the belly" directed backwards (posteriorly) which is why fish and birds eat them headfirst to allow them to pass smoothly into their gut.[1147]

Appearance: Gizzard (*Dorosoma cepedianum*) and threadfin (*Dorosoma petenense*) shad are very similar in appearance. Gizzard shad are members of the herring family and are also called "skipjacks" because they often skip along the surface of the water on their sides.[1148] Gizzard shad have a silvery blue dorsal surface with a silvery side that gradually becomes nearly white on the lower sides

---

[1142] MISSOURI DEPARTMENT OF CONSERVATION, *Field Guide: Gizzard Shad*, available at https://mdc.mo.gov/discover-nature/field-guide/gizzard-shad.
[1143] Id.
[1144] Id.
[1145] Id.
[1146] Peter Mathiesen, *Understanding bass forage: shad*, BASSMASTER, December 17, 2019, available at https://www.bassmaster.com/how-to/news/understanding-bass-forage-shad/.
[1147] MISSOURI DEPARTMENT OF CONSERVATION, *Gizzard Shad*, supra note 1142.
[1148] TEXAS PARKS AND WILDLIFE DEPARTMENT, *Gizzard Shad (Dorosoma cepedianum)*, available at https://tpwd.texas.gov/huntwild/wild/species/gsh/.

and belly.[1149] The more dorsal part of their sides may have some horizontal dark streaks.[1150] Gizzard shad are similar to the threadfin shad in appearance, but have a rounded, blunt snout that protrudes beyond their lower jaw unlike threadfin shad.[1151] In other words, the lower jaw in gizzard shad is small and does not project beyond the tip of the shad's snout, as shown in the picture below.[1152]

If you run your finger from underneath the mouth forward and your fingernail catches on the upper jaw opening the mouth, then you are almost always looking at a gizzard shad and not a threadfin.[1153]

[1149] TEXAS PARKS AND WILDLIFE DEPARTMENT, *Gizzard Shad*, supra note 1148; MISSOURI DEPARTMENT OF CONSERVATION, *Gizzard Shad*, supra note 1142.
[1150] MISSOURI DEPARTMENT OF CONSERVATION, *Gizzard Shad*, supra note 1142.
[1151] U.S. Geological Survey, *Nonindigenous aquatic species: Dorosoma cepedianum (Gizzard shad)*, available at https://nas.er.usgs.gov/queries/FactSheet.aspx?speciesID=492; MISSOURI DEPARTMENT OF CONSERVATION, *Field Guide: Threadfin Shad*, available at https://mdc.mo.gov/discover-nature/field-guide/threadfin-shad.
[1152] MISSOURI DEPARTMENT OF CONSERVATION, *Gizzard Shad*, supra note 1142.
[1153] TEXAS PARKS AND WILDLIFE DEPARTMENT, *Gizzard Shad*, supra note 1148; U.S. Geological Survey, *Gizzard Shad*, supra note 1151; MISSOURI DEPARTMENT OF CONSERVATION, *Gizzard Shad*, supra note 1142; TEXAS PARKS AND WILDLIFE DEPARTMENT, *Threadfin Shad (Dorosoma petenense)*, available at https://tpwd.texas.gov/huntwild/wild/species/threadfinshad/.

Gizzard shads' bodies are "moderately deep" (meaning fairly wide from dorsal to ventral surface).[1154] They have a "large lustrous dark or purple spot (may be faint in adults) just behind the upper end of the gill cover."[1155] Gizzards usually have 14 or fewer principle rays in their dorsal fin including a last ray that consists of a long, slender filament.[1156] Gizzard shads' anal fins usually have 29-35 rays.[1157] Their tails are deeply forked.[1158] Gizzard shads' fins are dusky and do not have prominent yellow colors (unlike threadfin shad).[1159] Gizzard shads' "eyelids" are "composed of fat storing adipose tissue."[1160] Their scales are thin, circular, smooth-edged and uniform (i.e., "cycloid) and usually there are 55 or more lateral line scales.[1161] Gizzard shad often grow 9 to 14 inches in length.[1162] The Texas record gizzard shad weighed almost 3 pounds and was longer than 20 inches.[1163] Here is a picture of a 13 inch gizzard shad that I snagged with a crankbait:

[1154] TEXAS PARKS AND WILDLIFE DEPARTMENT, *Gizzard Shad*, *supra* note 1148; U.S. Geological Survey, *Gizzard Shad*, *supra* note 1151.
[1155] MISSOURI DEPARTMENT OF CONSERVATION, *Gizzard Shad*, *supra* note 1142.
[1156] Id.
[1157] Id.
[1158] Id.
[1159] Id.
[1160] U.S. Geological Survey, *Gizzard Shad*, *supra* note 1151.
[1161] Id.
[1162] TEXAS PARKS AND WILDLIFE DEPARTMENT, *Gizzard Shad*, *supra* note 1148.
[1163] Id.

215

Threadfin shad look a lot like gizzard shad, but in contrast to gizzard shad, threadfins lower jaw projects out beyond their upper jaw so their snout is not as prominent, and their fins have a yellowish tint unlike gizzards.[1164]

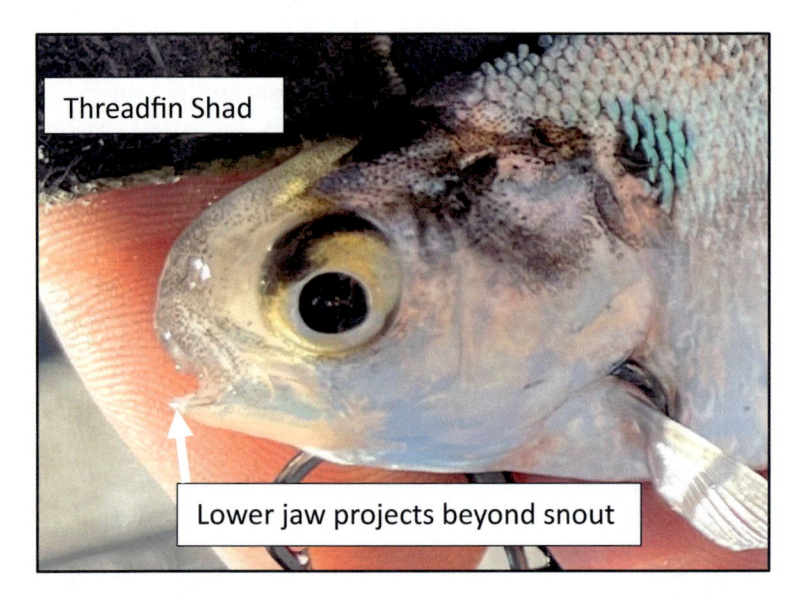

Threadfin Shad

Lower jaw projects beyond snout

Threadfin shad fins (except the dorsal fin) have a yellowish tint including their tail.[1165] If you are looking at a shad with yellowish fins, it is probably a threadfin and not a gizzard.[1166] I think the shad in the picture below is a very large threadfin shad based upon its lower jaw projecting and its fin colors:

[1164] Billy Higginbotham, *Forage species: Range, description, and life history*, Oklahoma Cooperative Extension Service, Southern Regional Aquaculture Center, SRAC-140-2, Oklahoma State University, March 2017, available at https://extension.okstate.edu/fact-sheets/forage-species-range-description-and-life-history.html; MISSOURI DEPARTMENT OF CONSERVATION, *Gizzard Shad*, supra note 1142; TEXAS PARKS AND WILDLIFE DEPARTMENT, *Threadfin Shad*, supra note 1153; MISSOURI DEPARTMENT OF CONSERVATION, *Gizzard Shad*, supra note 1142.
[1165] TEXAS PARKS AND WILDLIFE DEPARTMENT, *Threadfin Shad*, supra note 1153; MISSOURI DEPARTMENT OF CONSERVATION, *Gizzard Shad*, supra note 1142.
[1166] TEXAS PARKS AND WILDLIFE DEPARTMENT, *Gizzard Shad*, supra note 1148; TEXAS PARKS AND WILDLIFE DEPARTMENT, *Threadfin Shad*, supra note 1153; MISSOURI DEPARTMENT OF CONSERVATION, *Threadfin Shad*, supra note 1151.

Threadfins have black pigment speckled in the floor of their mouth and on their chins that gizzard shad do not.[1167] They are generally smaller than gizzard shad and are rarely longer than 6 inches in length.[1168] Their anal fins are shorter than gizzards and only have 20-25 rays usually.[1169] Threadfins have many similarities to gizzards including their silver-blue coloring along the dorsal surface gradually transitioning to almost white on their sides and bellies,[1170] dusky dorsal fins with an elongated filament for the last ray,[1171] and a dark or purplish spot behind their gill plate.[1172]

      Gizzard shad and threadfin shad are very similar in appearance and can be difficult to distinguish. I doubt bass are examining their prey's jaws, looking for black pigment on their chins, or counting the scales on their sides or rays in their fins. Bass are primarily sight feeders, so the biggest difference on quick glance is the yellowish tint to the fins of threadfins, but not the gizzards. However, bass may not be able to distinguish yellow colorations from other light colors (like

---

[1167] TEXAS PARKS AND WILDLIFE DEPARTMENT, *Threadfin Shad*, supra note 1153.
[1168] Id.
[1169] Id.; MISSOURI DEPARTMENT OF CONSERVATION, *Gizzard Shad, supra* note 1142.
[1170] TEXAS PARKS AND WILDLIFE DEPARTMENT, *Threadfin Shad*, supra note 1153; MISSOURI DEPARTMENT OF CONSERVATION, *Gizzard Shad, supra* note 1142.
[1171] MISSOURI DEPARTMENT OF CONSERVATION, *Threadfin Shad, supra* note 1151.
[1172] MISSOURI DEPARTMENT OF CONSERVATION, *Gizzard Shad, supra* note 1142.

white) as discussed in the vision section of Chapter 9. The other primary difference between gizzards and threadfins affecting bass feeding is size, with threadfins being smaller targets. Threadfins are smaller and are therefore a more accessible meal for most bass. However, gizzards get larger and may be a more enticing meal for a lunker bass. Both have scutes on their lance-like bodies, so bass will try to swallow them headfirst. So, look inside the mouths of fish that you catch, and you may see a tail sticking out.

As an example of how knowledge of shad populations can affect fishing, let's look at Lake Fork. According to the 2021 Lake Fork survey by TPWD, threadfin shad are much more prominent in Lake Fork than gizzard shad. My Lake Fork University guide professors almost universally preferred chartreuse yellow crankbaits for deep offshore cranking, which is more likely to match the color of a threadfin shad than a gizzard shad. I have adopted my guides' preference and fish chartreuse crankbaits on Lake Fork also. Here is a 7-pound 11-ounce bass I caught on a chartreuse crankbait at Lake Fork in 2022:

Whether chartreuse "matches the hatch" of threadfin shad making it better than white at Lake Fork is debatable given bass's color vision (see Question Box in Chapter 9). However, chartreuse colored crankbaits were the clear preference of my guide professors and TPWD says threadfins predominate at Lake Fork, so it makes me wonder if bass somehow distinguish chartreuse in this specific fishery. Of course, it's possible that my preferences and the preferences of other fishermen may lead to significantly increased fishing effort with chartreuse and artificially raise the success rate. Regardless, knowledge of the shad population in your fishery and "matching the hatch" might help you land a lunker!

Distribution: Both gizzard and threadfin shad are found in most lunker bass waters.[1173] In most southern and midwestern states, gizzard and threadfin shad are in almost every lake and stream.[1174] Both live in a variety of rivers, lakes, ponds, and many other freshwater environments.[1175]

Both threadfins and gizzards are limited in their northern range due to cold weather tolerance limitations.[1176] Threadfin shad are a little more susceptible than gizzard shad to winter kill, as some biologists report that they are very sensitive and die off at low temperatures such that "45°F is about all they can take" before a large "winterkill," "die off," or "shad kill" occurs.[1177] With dramatic temperature drops, large shad kills have been seen in southern areas like northern Alabama on the Tennessee River—so shad kills are not limited to threadfins' northern range.[1178] However, threadfin populations are resilient and usually recover quickly after shad kills.[1179] Despite their cold sensitivity, some survive and they replenish rapidly, so "threadfin shad flourish throughout warmwater southern reservoirs and into some midwestern lakes."[1180] In addition,

---

[1173] TEXAS PARKS AND WILDLIFE DEPARTMENT, *Gizzard Shad*, *supra* note 1148.
[1174] See, e.g., MISSOURI DEPARTMENT OF CONSERVATION, *Gizzard Shad*, *supra* note 1142.
[1175] U.S. Geological Survey, *Gizzard Shad*, *supra* note 1151; MISSOURI DEPARTMENT OF CONSERVATION, *Gizzard Shad*, *supra* note 1142; TEXAS PARKS AND WILDLIFE DEPARTMENT, *Threadfin Shad*, supra note 1153; U.S. Geological Survey, *Nonindigenous aquatic species: Dorosoma petenense (Threadfin shad)*, available at https://nas.er.usgs.gov/Queries/FactSheet.aspx?speciesID=493.
[1176] U.S. Geological Survey, *Gizzard Shad*, *supra* note 1151; Billy Higginbotham, *supra* note 1164.
[1177] Peter Mathiesen, *Understanding bass forage: shad*, *supra* note 1146; TEXAS PARKS AND WILDLIFE DEPARTMENT, *Threadfin Shad*, supra note 1153; Billy Higginbotham, *supra* note 1164.
[1178] Peter Mathiesen, *Understanding bass forage: shad*, *supra* note 1146.
[1179] Id.
[1180] Id.

some states regularly help replenish their numbers with stocking programs.[1181]

Gizzard shad populations also fluctuate in numbers in response to low temperatures below 39°F, which can result in winter "shad-kills" or "die-offs."[1182] Researchers found that gizzard shad "mortality was high in water less than 39°F," but low above 45°F in New York.[1183] Gizzard shad populations are generally resilient and bounce back quickly after a shad kill. During severe winters, gizzard shad survive in some cold-water lakes by finding areas of uncharacteristic warmth, like industrial warm-water discharge areas or other areas that are artificially warmed.[1184]

Gizzard shad generally prefer water temperatures between 72 and 84°F (22-29°C).[1185] However, they also thrive in a local power plant heated lake that reaches temperatures over 100°F that I fish regularly, where I have found some very large gizzard shad like the 13-incher shown in a picture earlier in this chapter.

Gizzards are native to eastern North America from Quebec to Mexico and have naturally expanded their range since at least the 1600s.[1186] The native range of the threadfin shad is controversial because they first appeared to scientists in Tennessee River impoundments in 1948 and in the Ohio River tributaries in Illinois in 1957, and prior to that had only been found in "rivers and streams flowing into the Gulf of Mexico, from Florida to Mexico.[1187] In all of these locations there had been numerous samplings prior to the dates they were first discovered, so scientists are unsure if the threadfins came from dispersal from other waters naturally, or if they came from prior stockings.

[1181] Id.
[1182] U.S. Geological Survey, *Gizzard Shad*, supra note 1151; David Slone, *Fish kill likely caused by harsh winter, biologist says*, TIMES UNION ONLINE, March 29, 2019, available at https://timesuniononline.com/Content/Local-News/Local-News/Article/Fish-Kill-Likely-Caused-By-Harsh-Winter-Biologist-Says/2/453/119165.
[1183] Rob Neumann, *Science of shad winterkill*, IN-FISHERMAN, August 8, 2013, available at https://www.in-fisherman.com/editorial/science-of-shad-winterkill/153824.
[1184] U.S. Geological Survey, *Gizzard Shad*, supra note 1151.
[1185] Id.
[1186] TEXAS PARKS AND WILDLIFE DEPARTMENT, *Gizzard Shad*, supra note 1148; U.S. Geological Survey, supra note 1151.
[1187] U.S. Geological Survey, *Threadfin shad*, supra note 1175.

Both gizzard and threadfin shad have been extensively transplanted and introduced across the country as forage fish, which has increased their ranges greatly. Today, both species are prominent across the country in bass fisheries either naturally or by stocking programs as forage fish.[1188] The simple fact is that they are there, so as a fisherman, how they got there matters less at this point, so I won't dig deeper here.

Behavior: Gizzard and threadfin shad usually live and travel in "large, constantly moving schools."[1189] During times when they are near the surface, they frequently jump clear out of the water or skip along the surface on their sides, which is why they have the common name, "skipjack," in some locales.[1190] Gizzards prefer quieter areas above the thermocline in open waters (i.e., the pelagic zone).[1191] They will stay in areas where the thermocline meets low light structure like humps and ledges during summer months.[1192] For fishing purposes, notice that gizzards get just above or at the thermocline on humps and ledges in the summer, so you will find largemouth bass on those same humps and ledges.[1193]

Threadfins also spend most of their time in schools in the pelagic (i.e., open water) zone like gizzard shad.[1194] However, threadfins like water with noticeable current in the upper five feet of the water column with the current often created by wind.[1195]

Both threadfin and gizzard shad prefer fertile and productive waters ranging from very clear to moderately turbid or silty.[1196] Depth preferences depend upon the specific lake characteristics like clarity, turbidity, and presence of plankton and algae.[1197] Gizzard

---

[1188] U.S. Geological Survey, *Gizzard Shad*, supra note 1151; TEXAS PARKS AND WILDLIFE DEPARTMENT, *Gizzard Shad*, supra note 1148; Peter Mathiesen, *Understanding bass forage: shad*, supra note 1146; Billy Higginbotham, supra note 1164.; TEXAS PARKS AND WILDLIFE DEPARTMENT, *Threadfin Shad*, supra note 1153.
[1189] TEXAS PARKS AND WILDLIFE DEPARTMENT, *Gizzard Shad*, supra note 1148; MISSOURI DEPARTMENT OF CONSERVATION, *Gizzard Shad*, supra note 1142.
[1190] Id.
[1191] U.S. Geological Survey, *Gizzard Shad*, supra note 1151.
[1192] Peter Mathiesen, *Understanding bass forage: shad*, supra note 1146.
[1193] Id.
[1194] Billy Higginbotham, supra note 1164.
[1195] TEXAS PARKS AND WILDLIFE DEPARTMENT, *Threadfin Shad*, supra note 1153.
[1196] MISSOURI DEPARTMENT OF CONSERVATION, *Gizzard Shad*, supra note 1142; U.S. Geological Survey, *Gizzard Shad*, supra note 1151.
[1197] Peter Mathiesen, *Understanding bass forage: shad*, supra note 1146.

shad are usually absent in water with less than 2 mg/L of dissolved oxygen.[1198] Gizzards move deep enough to "stay out of the direct sunlight, yet the water must have enough light to produce algae and plankton."[1199] At night, gizzard shad often move into shallow areas and coves.[1200] They are usually most active during the night and at dusk.[1201]

Food and growth: Adults of both species filter small food items from the water by "using long, close-set gill rakes."[1202] Gizzards and threadfins are "planktivores, straining minute organic particles with their gill rakes into their pharyngeal organ which is thought to concentrate and process food for swallowing."[1203] Their diet includes "algae, phytoplankton, zooplankton, and plant debris" as well.[1204] Gizzard shad also "feed heavily on detritus found on bottom sediments."[1205] A single gizzard shad "can consume an average of 13% of their wet weight biomass in dry sediment each day."[1206]

Gizzard shad grow much faster than threadfin shad. After hatching, young gizzards travel in compact schools until fall when they disperse.[1207] Gizzard shad grow rapidly in fertile waters with long growing seasons (e.g., southern reservoirs) and may be up to 7 inches at one year of life making them too big for many predators.[1208] In Missouri, gizzard shad are around 5 inches long at the end of their first year.[1209] They reach reproductive maturity at 2 or 3 years of age.[1210] By three years of age, gizzard shad in Missouri are around 11

[1198] U.S. Geological Survey, *Gizzard Shad*, supra note 1151.
[1199] Peter Mathiesen, *Understanding bass forage: shad*, supra note 1146.
[1200] Id.
[1201] MISSOURI DEPARTMENT OF CONSERVATION, *Gizzard Shad*, supra note 1142.
[1202] TEXAS PARKS AND WILDLIFE DEPARTMENT, *Gizzard Shad*, supra note 1148.
[1203] U.S. Geological Survey, *Gizzard Shad*, supra note 1151; TEXAS PARKS AND WILDLIFE DEPARTMENT, *Gizzard Shad*, supra note 1148; Billy Higginbotham, *supra* note 1164.
[1204] U.S. Geological Survey, *Gizzard Shad*, supra note 1151; Billy Higginbotham, *supra* note 1164.
[1205] U.S. Geological Survey, *Gizzard Shad*, supra note 1151.
[1206] Id.
[1207] Id.
[1208] Id.
[1209] MISSOURI DEPARTMENT OF CONSERVATION, *Gizzard Shad*, supra note 1142.
[1210] U.S. Geological Survey, *Gizzard Shad*, supra note 1151.

inches in length.[1211] Most adult gizzard shad are 9-14 inches long and weigh less than a pound.[1212] The maximum size recorded is 20 inches and 3 pounds 7 ounces.[1213] Typical northern gizzards live 5-7 years, but some have been reported up to 10 or 11 years old.[1214] Gizzards are eaten by 17 game fish species, including walleye, white bass, largemouth bass, crappies, some trout species, catfish, gar, and others.[1215] Various waterfowl also eat gizzard shad.[1216]

Threadfin shad growth rates are different from gizzard shad.[1217] After hatching in late spring, most of the newly hatched threadfin will be around 2 inches by late summer and reach 3 to 4 inches by fall.[1218] Most threadfin end up being around 4 or 5 inches in length and rarely live longer than 2 to 3 years.[1219] The maximum size for a threadfin shad is around 7 to 8 inches.[1220]

"Shad Spawn": The "shad spawn" of gizzard and threadfin shad (and other shad depending on location and details) has a major effect on the feeding patterns of largemouth bass. Both gizzard and threadfin spawns are triggered by water temperature, and the gizzard shad spawn occurs earlier in the year than the threadfin shad spawn. The gizzard shad spawn bite can be pre- and post-spawn for largemouth bass, whereas the threadfin shad spawn is more of a post-spawn bite for largemouth bass. Unlike the threadfin shad spawn, the gizzard shad spawn occurs throughout the day at most locales and is not limited to dawn. Shad spawns are believed to increase around full and new moon phases.[1221]

The *gizzard shad spawn generally occurs when the water temperature is from 64 to 69°F* and begins when the water reaches the lower end of this range on a warming trend in late spring in shallow

---

[1211] MISSOURI DEPARTMENT OF CONSERVATION, *Gizzard Shad*, supra note 1142.
[1212] Id.
[1213] Id.
[1214] U.S. Geological Survey, *Gizzard Shad*, supra note 1151.
[1215] Id.
[1216] Id.
[1217] Peter Mathiesen, *Understanding bass forage: shad*, supra note 1146.
[1218] Id.
[1219] Billy Higginbotham, supra note 1164; Peter Mathiesen, *Understanding bass forage: shad*, supra note 1146.
[1220] Billy Higginbotham, supra note 1164.
[1221] David Brown, *How to find and fish the shad spawn for bass*, Wired2Fish, April 27, 2015, available at https://www.wired2fish.com/spring-fishing-tips/how-to-find-and-fish-the-shad-spawn-for-bass.

protected water in pockets, coves, bays, and inlets.[1222] In Texas this is typically from mid-March until mid-May, while in Missouri it is usually in early April throughout May.[1223] The US Geological Service, which must be looking at more northern lakes, says that the gizzard shad spawn is "random and occurs from mid-May to mid-June."[1224]

During the gizzard shad spawn, adult males and females gather and intermix in a school in protected shallow water and eject sperm (milt) and eggs into the water without any apparent regard for individual mates.[1225] As they spawn, the male and female shad "roll and tumble about each other in a mass near the water's surface."[1226] One female can produce over 250,000 to 300,000 eggs per year on average.[1227] Once released by the female, the sticky eggs sink and attach to the first object they touch—usually on the bottom, but can be to vegetation, etc.[1228]

Gizzards often spawn along shallow points in relatively open water, so bass will push them up into areas along shallow points to feed. At Lake Fork, you can see wolf packs of lunker bass chasing gizzards mostly in April, but from early march through mid-May. This occurs all day and is not limited to a morning bite. Wolf packs typically only chase them for a few weeks around and during the gizzard shad spawn at some lakes.[1229]

After 2 to 7 days, the eggs hatch and gizzard shad fry emerge.[1230] After hatching, "for the first 2 days after hatching, they persistently swim upward and sink back for about the same distance."[1231] The fry are very slender and delicate until they get to be

---

[1222] TEXAS PARKS AND WILDLIFE DEPARTMENT, *Gizzard Shad, supra* note 1148; MISSOURI DEPARTMENT OF CONSERVATION, *Gizzard Shad, supra* note 1142.
[1223] MISSOURI DEPARTMENT OF CONSERVATION, *Gizzard Shad, supra* note 1142.
[1224] U.S. Geological Survey, *Gizzard Shad, supra* note 1151.
[1225] Id.; TEXAS PARKS AND WILDLIFE DEPARTMENT, *Gizzard Shad, supra* note 1148.
[1226] MISSOURI DEPARTMENT OF CONSERVATION, *Gizzard Shad, supra* note 1142.
[1227] Id.; U.S. Geological Survey, *Gizzard Shad, supra* note 1151.
[1228] MISSOURI DEPARTMENT OF CONSERVATION, *Gizzard Shad, supra* note 1142; TEXAS PARKS AND WILDLIFE DEPARTMENT, *Gizzard Shad, supra* note 1148; U.S. Geological Survey, *Gizzard Shad, supra* note 1151.
[1229] Peter Mathiesen, *Understanding bass forage: shad, supra* note 1146.
[1230] MISSOURI DEPARTMENT OF CONSERVATION, *Gizzard Shad, supra* note 1142; U.S. Geological Survey, *Gizzard Shad, supra* note 1151; TEXAS PARKS AND WILDLIFE DEPARTMENT, *Gizzard Shad, supra* note 1148.
[1231] MISSOURI DEPARTMENT OF CONSERVATION, *Gizzard Shad, supra* note 1142.

around 1.25 inches long.[1232] Fry are described as "slender, transparent fish, quite different in appearance from adults."[1233] The same is true of other herrings, like threadfin shad.[1234] Gizzard shad begin to take their typical adult shape once they are around 1.25 inches long."[1235] Young gizzards feed on plankton, microscopic organisms, and small insect larvae.[1236] By mid-summer they are from 1.5 to 2 inches long, but by fall, they may often be 5 inches long.[1237] Under ideal conditions, they may have a second spawn in the fall.[1238]

The *threadfin shad spawn* occurs later in the year than the gizzard shad spawn and *usually begins when water temperatures reach 70°F and continues into the summer.*[1239] Threadfins may have a second spawn in early fall.[1240] The threadfin spawn is a *low light early morning event each day.*[1241] During the morning shad spawns, the water is shimmering with enough activity that in quiet areas you can actually hear the shad splashing around like rain on the water.[1242] These are short-lived events each day that occur first thing in the morning under low light conditions and *end within an hour or two each day once the sunlight level is up.*[1243] Once the sun is fully up, it's over.[1244] You need to be there at daybreak to target bass feeding on the threadfin shad spawn.[1245]

When the spawn begins inside the shimmering school, each threadfin female is accompanied by several males while spawning.[1246] Female threadfins lay from 2,000 to 24,000 eggs each.[1247] The eggs are adhesive and attach to the first surface they touch—including

---

[1232] TEXAS PARKS AND WILDLIFE DEPARTMENT, *Gizzard Shad, supra* note 1148.
[1233] MISSOURI DEPARTMENT OF CONSERVATION, *Gizzard Shad, supra* note 1142.
[1234] Id.
[1235] Id.
[1236] TEXAS PARKS AND WILDLIFE DEPARTMENT, *Gizzard Shad, supra* note 1148.
[1237] Peter Mathiesen, *Understanding bass forage: shad, supra* note 1146.
[1238] Id.
[1239] TEXAS PARKS AND WILDLIFE DEPARTMENT, *Threadfin Shad, supra* note 1153.
[1240] Billy Higginbotham, *supra* note 1164.
[1241] Id.
[1242] David Brown, *supra* note 1221.
[1243] Id.
[1244] Id.
[1245] Id.
[1246] TEXAS PARKS AND WILDLIFE DEPARTMENT, *Threadfin Shad, supra* note 1153.
[1247] Billy Higginbotham, *supra* note 1164.

"submerged and floating objects."[1248] Threadfin spawning occurs around structures where eggs can attach like grass lines (especially on points), marinas, bridges, flooded bank grass, over vegetation or logs in open water, etc.[1249] Bass are often found post-spawn (for the bass) feeding in these areas near the mouths of creeks.[1250] A light wind is good, but a high wind can disrupt the shad spawn.[1251]

If you want to "match the hatch," you need to recognize which shad spawn you are fishing. Hopefully, this chapter will help. If you live in an area where other types of shad are prominent (e.g., blueback herring), then do some online research on the shad spawn prevalent in your fishery and use the information to your advantage!

Bluegill Sunfish (Lepomis macrochirus)

Largemouth bass feed on several different types of sunfish. Here, I will discuss the bluegill sunfish (*Lepomis macrochirus*), which is one of the most common and best known, and its habits can be generalized to most of the other species.[1252] But as always, check the specifics of your particular fishing location for species to fine tune your fishing; maybe catch a few sunfish, take pictures, and determine the exact species.

The bluegill sunfish is closely related (in the same genus, Lepomis) as several other forage species for bass including the pumpkinseed sunfish, redear sunfish, green sunfish, longear sunfish, and others.[1253] Subspecies of bluegill sunfish include northern, coppernose, handpaint, and eastern sunfish.[1254] Nicknames include "perch, bream, sunfish, sunnies, panfish, slabs and coppernose."[1255]

Bluegill sunfish are present throughout the United States thanks to massive stocking programs (especially of northern and

---

[1248] Id.
[1249] David Brown, *supra* note 1221; U.S. Geological Survey, *Threadfin shad*, *supra* note 1175.
[1250] David Brown, *supra* note 1221.
[1251] Id.
[1252] Billy Higginbotham, *supra* note 1164.
[1253] Steven Bardin, *Bluegill sunfish: a comprehensive species guide*, Wired2Fish, February 23, 2023, available at https://www.wired2fish.com/crappie-fishing/bluegill-sunfish-a-comprehensive-species-guide/.
[1254] Id.
[1255] Id.

coppernose sunfish subspecies) due to their adaptability, popularity as a sport fish, and popularity as a forage species because they spawn several times each year.[1256] They have also been stocked outside the U.S. in countries ranging from Japan to South Africa to Iran to Venezuela.[1257] Their native range was west of the Rockies to the southeastern states including Florida up to Virginia along the coast and from Mexico up to southern Canada in the Midwest.[1258]

Adult bluegill generally prefer static or low current, clear water, near the shore around cover like fallen trees, weed beds, aquatic vegetation, etc.[1259] They prefer slow moving water with lots of rock or vegetation.[1260] They can adapt to almost any water quality and temperatures to 95 degrees or higher and low oxygen at 5 ppm.[1261]

Bluegill live near the shore where sunlight reaches the bottom for the majority of the year.[1262] During fall and winter, they will often move offshore for winter in deep water.[1263] They are almost always in schools ranging from 6 fish to 100s.[1264] They rely on the school for protection and for foraging.[1265] They eat insects and almost anything else (omnivores) including "zooplankton, crawfish, amphibians, eggs and small fishes."[1266] They also eat aquatic vegetation, which can be 20% of their diet when insect supplies are low.[1267] They also eat the eggs and fry of other species—including the largemouth bass, which is why bass are particularly aggressive toward bluegill during bass's spawning period.[1268]

Spawn: For largemouth bass fishermen, knowledge of bluegill's spawning habits can work in the fisherman's favor. Bluegills often become feeding targets for big bass during the bass's post-spawn because once bass leave spawning areas, bluegills move

---

[1256] Id.; Billy Higginbotham, *supra* note 1164.
[1257] Steven Bardin, *Bluegill sunfish*, supra note 1253.
[1258] Id.; Billy Higginbotham, *supra* note 1164.
[1259] Billy Higginbotham, *supra* note 1164.
[1260] Steven Bardin, *Bluegill sunfish*, supra note 1253.
[1261] Id.
[1262] Id.
[1263] Id.
[1264] Id.
[1265] Steven Bardin, *Bluegill sunfish*, supra note 1253.
[1266] Id.
[1267] Id.; Billy Higginbotham, *supra* note 1164.
[1268] Id.

into the same areas and start their spawn.[1269] Unlike bass, bluegill beds are close together, setting up a smorgasbord of potential food for big bass.[1270] Big bass often find ambush points to pick off bluegills during this time period and will fall for bluegill baits.[1271] These spots are typically "shoreline points on either side of a spawning cove, shoreline pockets, the front and sides of a downed tree, dock, or any kind of large structure near the bluegill beds."[1272] If you can find some early season bluegill beds, bass will be nearby.[1273]

Water temperature is again the master abiotic factor here. *Active bluegill spawning season is initiated during springtime when water temperatures reach 65 to 75 degrees.*[1274] The bluegill spawn *continues during spring, summer, and fall*, except that it may shut down for a while if water temperatures go above *85 degrees*, then resume in the fall when the water temperature drops back below 85°F.[1275]

Bluegill sunfish are colony spawners, meaning the males form schools in the spring to select *community nesting sites* as a group in close proximity to each other (unlike largemouth bass) and together form a pattern "similar to a honeycomb" on the bottom of the body of water.[1276] There may be 50 or more individual nests in the colony—each made and protected by an individual male.[1277] This pattern and proximity allows them to guard nests, protect eggs, and protect fry as a community.[1278]

The community nesting site is typically close to the shoreline in an area with some type of hard substrate bottom with aquatic vegetation or some type of hard structure nearby.[1279] Each male fans out an oval or circular shaped nest by clearing silt from the bottom using its fins and tail in the selected area to expose the hard bottom in

---

[1269] Tom Cece, *Largemouth bass by calendar*, On The Water, December 20, 2022, available at https://www.onthewater.com/largemouth-bass-calendar.
[1270] Id.
[1271] Id.
[1272] Id.
[1273] Id.
[1274] Steven Bardin, *Bluegill sunfish*, supra note 1253; Billy Higginbotham, *supra* note 1164.
[1275] Id.
[1276] Steven Bardin, *Bluegill sunfish*, supra note 1253.
[1277] Billy Higginbotham, *supra* note 1164.
[1278] Steven Bardin, *Bluegill sunfish*, supra note 1253.
[1279] Id.

water that is one to five feet deep.[1280] When complete, each nest is around 7 to 15 inches in diameter.[1281] These bluegill bedding areas make distinctive honey-comb patterns on side-imaging sonar.

Males use their bright coloration and territorial behavior to attract individual females to their nests.[1282] Males keep trying to court multiple females into a single nest which can end up with more than 100,000 eggs.[1283] The eggs stick to the nests. The number of eggs from a particular female is proportionate to her size.[1284] Females lay 2,000 to 20,000 eggs per spawning attempt.[1285] Individual females can produce up to 80,000 eggs per year.[1286] Depending upon water temperature, fertilized eggs hatch in 3 to 5 days.[1287]

After spawning, males stick around for 10 days until the fry swim up.[1288] The females leave the nest area after spawning and go back to areas to feed "until more eggs become ripe."[1289] Females may come back to the nest area several times during the spawning season, which lasts several months.

Some species' that are similar to bluegill, such as the redear sunfish (Lepomis microlophus), have slightly different spawning habits and especially may not have as prolonged of a spawning period or may spawn a little deeper.[1290] So, the predominant spawning pattern in your particular body of water may depend on exactly which type of sunfish is present—so some specific research on your body of water can be helpful to "match the hatch."

Color: Coloration varies with sex, with males being more colorful than females.[1291] Males are darker during their spawning

---

[1280] Billy Higginbotham, *supra* note 1164; Steven Bardin, *Bluegill sunfish*, supra note 1253.
[1281] Steven Bardin, *Bluegill sunfish*, supra note 1253.
[1282] Id.
[1283] Id.
[1284] Id.
[1285] Id.
[1286] Steven Bardin, *Bluegill sunfish*, supra note 1253.
[1287] Billy Higginbotham, *supra* note 1164.
[1288] Steven Bardin, *Bluegill sunfish*, supra note 1253.
[1289] Id.
[1290] Billy Higginbotham, *supra* note 1164.
[1291] Steven Bardin, *Bluegill sunfish*, supra note 1253.

season.[1292] Colors vary somewhat with water quality, but "normally several vertical bars are visible along the sides."[1293]

Growth: Males usually mature faster than females.[1294] Males generally grow larger, but don't live as long.[1295] In the south, they can be mature in the first year, but in the north it can take 4-6 years to reach maturity.[1296] Growth rates are controlled by temperature and food availability.[1297] At 1.25 inches, they look like adults.[1298] In the south, they reach 2-3 inches after the first year, then grow around 2 to 4 inches per year.[1299] They grow faster in water over 85 degrees, mostly because they stop spawning and concentrate on foraging.[1300] In cooler temperatures, they are around 2 inches the first year, and then grow 1 to 2 inches per year afterward.[1301] Bluegills have a short

---

[1292] Id.
[1293] Billy Higginbotham, *supra* note 1164.
[1294] Steven Bardin, *Bluegill sunfish*, supra note 1253.
[1295] Id.
[1296] Id.
[1297] Id.
[1298] Id.
[1299] Steven Bardin, *Bluegill sunfish*, supra note 1253.
[1300] Id.
[1301] Id.

lifespan because almost all fish eat them. Most southern bluegill live 5 years, and northern bluegill live around 10 years.[1302]

Worms

Worms, like earthworms and nightcrawlers, do NOT make up a significant part of a bass's natural diet.[1303] Worms live on land burrowing in soil and are not aquatic animals.[1304] They are also lousy swimmers, so they are not naturally swimming around in the water where bass can encounter them.[1305] Heavy rains do occasionally wash worms into streams and lakes, but "a bass could go its whole life without seeing one" naturally.[1306] Yet, bass love plastic worms. Berkley labs found that "bass do not need experience with real worms to appreciate the plastic versions" because "even totally naïve bass . . . with no natural food experience will eagerly attack real or plastic worms at first sight."[1307] Soft plastics, including plastic worms, accounted for 45% of the 13+ pound lunkers reported to TPWD in a 2004 study—more than any other bait.[1308] In the TPWD 2004 study, soft plastics even accounted for 72% of the ShareLunkers in April— one of the top big bass months (see Chapter 3).[1309] Even in the hands of scientists in scientific experiments, the plastic worms outperformed the other lures in a couple of experiments with a wacky rigged watermelon worm accounting for 57/92 "fish captures."[1310] In another experiment, a green plastic worm accounted for 17/25 "capture events."[1311]

[1302] Id.
[1303] Berkley Fishing, *Worms: What are bass thinking?*, available at https://www.berkley-fishing.com/berkley-ae-worms-what-are-bass-thinking.
[1304] Id.
[1305] Id.
[1306] Id.
[1307] Id.
[1308] Larry Hodge, *March is big bass month*, TEXAS FISH AND GAME MAGAZINE, 2004, available at https://tpwd.texas.gov/fishboat/fish/didyouknow/inland/bassinmarch.phtml.
[1309] Id.
[1310] Michael Louison, et al., *Hormonal responsiveness to stress is negatively associated with vulnerability to angling capture in fish*, J. OF EXPERIMENTAL BIOLOGY 220: 2529-2535 (2017).
[1311] Michael Louison, et al., *Quick learning, quick capture: largemouth bass that rapidly learn an association task are more likely to be captured by recreational*

So, why do bass strike plastic worms? One Lake Fork guide theorizes that "really big fish are less aggressive by nature, or more wary, or a combination of the two," and a "slow-moving bait does not make a lot of noise" and "will penetrate that fish's zone."[1312] He thinks those are the reasons that soft plastics are better for big bass.[1313] One bait company attributes bass's attraction to plastic worms to their natural instinct to strike "objects with the long body style of prey fish like minnows or shad," with "anatomical details, such as surface markings or placement of appendages, likely play[ing] a secondary role."[1314] Bass primarily feed on "long, horizontally oriented prey fish" which can resemble plastic worms in the bass's eyes.[1315] In short, as far as the experts can guess, plastic worms "fit pre-established visual criteria" for which bass are looking, and plastic worms penetrate areas in a slow-moving, quiet way where big bass live without alarming wary lunkers.[1316]

Other Prey

Adult bass feed heavily on "fishes including threadfin shad (*Dorosoma petenense*), gizzard shad (*Dorosoma cepedianum*), various minnows (*Cyprinidae*), sunfishes (*Centrarchidae*), and darters (*Percidae*), while continuing to consume aquatic insects (especially large insects such as dragonfly larvae."[1317] Regional delicacies for bass include blue back herring, alewife, golden shiner, fathead minnows, and many others. For example, the Alewife is a small herring primarily living along the Atlantic Coast north of South Carolina and the Great Lakes with a "dark dorsal side, bluish to greenish, and light sides with horizontal darker stripes" with some unique seasonal and spawning habits that can be used to locate

---

anglers, BEHAVIORAL ECOLOGY AND SOCIOBIOLOGY 73, Article 23 (2019), available at https://link.springer.com/article/10.1007/s00265-019-2634-7.
[1312] Larry Hodge, *March is big bass month*, *supra* note 1308.
[1313] Id.
[1314] Berkley Fishing, *Worms: What are bass thinking?*, available at https://www.berkley-fishing.com/berkley-ae-worms-what-are-bass-thinking.
[1315] Id.
[1316] Id.
[1317] Texas State University, San Marcos, Department of Biology, *Texas Freshwater Fishes: Micropterus salmoides, largemouth bass*, available at http://txstate.fishesoftexas.org/micropterus%20salmoides.htm.

feeding bass.[1318] Another example, the golden shiner (*Notemigonus crysoleucas*) is a member of the minnow family with "large silver or gold-colored scales" that prefers ponds and shallow streams and spawns in the summer.[1319] If you are fishing in a fishery with Alewife, golden shiner, blueback herring, or any other specific species of largemouth bass forage, then spending some time reviewing the life cycle and spawning habits of the forage in your fishery could pay off in a big way.

[1318] U.S. Geological Survey, *Nonindigenous aquatic species: Alosa pseudoharengus (Alewife)*, available at https://nas.er.usgs.gov/queries/FactSheet.aspx?speciesID=490.
[1319] Billy Higginbotham, *supra* note 1164.

11

Study 4: Time of Day

The best time of day to catch big bass is controversial. In one poll, 37% of bass anglers chose late afternoon, 32% early morning, 17% midday, 5% early afternoon, 4% night, and 4% late morning as the "best bass bite."[1320] My Lake Fork University guide professors gave me several different answers as well. One guide said the best time to catch a giant is around noon when all the other guides and fishermen go in for lunch—but I think he may have adopted this philosophy because he didn't want to take the boat in for a lunch break like the other guides. However, on a busy lake like Lake Fork, it is certainly possible that the temporary decrease of fishing pressure at lunch time each day could sync up with some big bass's feeding habits. Some guides swear the best time is at night around the lights on boat docks. Although some scientists say bass are more active at

---

[1320] Freshwater Fishing Advice, *Best time of day to catch bass (every season)*, available at https://freshwaterfishingadvice.com/best-time-day-bass-fishing/.

dawn and dusk, another big bass guide told me that he and his clients almost never catch the biggest bass early in the morning (and are off the water before dusk). Given bass's reliance on vision for feeding, he might be right that they bite better with sunlight. Solunar theorists say that major and minor periods of bass feeding vary by day based on moon position. One thing is clear to me: the experts do not agree on the best time of day to catch a big bass.

What time of day is best to target lunker bass? Are the Solunar tables accurate with their daily major and minor peaks? Is it better to go fishing early, mid-day, or late? What about fishing at dusk or even at night? Those are some of the questions I will try to answer in this chapter.

Solunar Tables and the Moon

Solunar theory is a popular theory that daily major and minor bass feeding times are synchronized with the relative position of the moon to the location where you are fishing. The idea that wildlife activity is synchronized with moon position was popularized by John Alden Knight when he published his "Solunar" tables in 1936.[1321] The Solunar tables predict times when the likelihood of fishing success is higher by predicting hours of increased fish feeding activity termed "major periods."[1322] In Solunar theory, major periods of wildlife activity usually last about 2 hours and occur when the moon is directly overhead or directly underfoot at a specific location, while minor periods of wildlife activity are shorter than majors and occur when the moon is 90 degrees from a given location.[1323] In other words, Solunar theorists say that "major periods occur when the moon is directly overhead or directly below a reference longitude," and "minors occur when it's positioned at 90 degrees to either side."[1324] The Solunar tables also take into account the moon phase each day

---

[1321] Mark Vinson and Ted Angradi, *Muskie lunacy: does the lunar cycle influence angler catch of muskellunge?*, PLoSONE 9(5):e98046, May 2014, available at https://www.researchgate.net/publication/262694023_Muskie_Lunacy_Does_the_Lunar_Cycle_Influence_Angler_Catch_of_Muskellunge_Esox_masquinongy.
[1322] Id.
[1323] Ralph Manns, *Moon Magic Largemouth Bass*, In-Fisherman, June 23, 2023, available at https://www.in-fisherman.com/editorial/moon-magic-largemouth-bass/154779.
[1324] Id.

and typically predict the top fishing (and hunting) days to occur around the days of full or new moons.[1325] Moon phases are discussed in Chapter 5.

Solunar tables are regularly published in fishing and wildlife magazines.[1326] Fisherman are so passionate about Solunar tables that at least two fishing publications faced major backlash from angry readers for failing to include the tables in an issue.[1327]

Different versions of Solunar tables are published with individual authors' adjustments based upon factors like sunrise and sunset times and the time of year.[1328] Numerous versions are available with various spins, including some that are apps for your phone.[1329] I studied a few examples and found that generally the major periods peak around noon and midnight on full and new moons in the ones that I reviewed. Then the major periods move forward or backward by around 45 minutes each day between full and new moons until reaching the next full or new moon when they return to around noon or midnight. So, over the month, the specific hours of the day in major periods are represented almost equally overall. In other words, a time like 10 am or 2 pm, for example, is just as likely to occur at a "major" period as 7 am or 6 pm or any other time.

Generally speaking, major activity is believed to peak when the moon is directly overhead or underfoot and minor periods occur when it is ninety degrees to either side of a specific location.[1330] Major and minor Solunar periods are roughly 6 hours apart.[1331] Solunar theorists believe that the moon's position creates a gravitational pull that differs depending upon its position around the earth and this difference in gravitational pull affects wildlife in a

---

[1325] Solunar Forecast and Predictions, *Worldwide solunar best hunting and fishing times*, available at https://solunarforecast.com.
[1326] K.C. Hanson, et al., *Effects of lunar cycles on the activity patterns and depth use of a temperate sport fish, the largemouth bass*, FISHERIES MANAGEMENT AND ECOLOGY 15(5-6):357-364, October/December 2008, available at https://onlinelibrary.wiley.com/doi/abs/10.1111/j.1365-2400.2008.00634.x.
[1327] Steve Quinn, *The effects of Solunar forces on bass fishing*, IN-FISHERMAN, July 13, 2021, available at https://www.in-fisherman.com/editorial/solunar-forces-on-bass-fishing/377272.
[1328] Id.
[1329] Id.
[1330] Id.
[1331] Ralph Manns, *Moon Magic Largemouth Bass*, *supra* note 1323.

predictable way each day.[1332] Some authors say that the moon's gravitational pull varies by as much as 20 percent because its path brings it closer and farther from the Earth at various times each day.[1333]

The pull of the moon certainly has some visible effects on the ocean, but not as much as most people think—especially with regard to the timing of tides.[1334] According to the National Oceanic and Atmospheric Administration (NOAA), "tides are very long-period waves that move through the ocean in response to forces exerted by the moon and sun, BUT "these gravitational forces do NOT control when high or low tide events occur."[1335] Instead, NOAA says that regional forces like "the geography and shape of the Earth" control the timing of high and low tides.[1336] In short, NOAA says, "High tides do NOT coincide with the location of the moon."[1337]

Tides are obviously not present in inland waterways, so moon position likely has even less of an effect on freshwater fisheries where largemouth bass live. However, some people believe that freshwater fish have genetically retained some of the instincts of their sea dwelling ancestors—remember that earlier in this book (see Chapter 2) I mentioned that largemouth bass are believed to be related to seabass and are believed to have evolved from two seabass species over 64 million years ago.[1338]

One avid angler and fisheries biologist, Ralph Manns, analyzed his catches over 10,466 hours of fishing during 2500 trips over 18 years from 1992 through mid-2010.[1339] He found that his

---

[1332] Steve Quinn, *The effects of Solunar forces on bass fishing*, supra note 1327.
[1333] Id.
[1334] Id.
[1335] National Ocean Service, NATIONAL OCEANIC AND ATMOSPHERIC ADMINISTRATION, *Are tides higher when the moon is directly overhead? High tides do not coincide with the location of the moon*, available at https://oceanservice.noaa.gov/facts/moon-tide.html#:~:text=High%20tides%20do%20not%20coincide,high%20or%20low%20tides%20occur.
[1336] Id.
[1337] Id.
[1338] Chengfei Sun, et al., *Chromosome-level genome assembly for the largemouth bass Micropterus salmoides provides insights into adaptation to fresh and brackish water*, MOLECULAR ECOLOGY RESOURCES 21(1):301-315, January 2021, available at https://onlinelibrary.wiley.com/doi/10.1111/1755-0998.13256.
[1339] Ralph Manns, *Moon Magic Largemouth Bass*, supra note 1323.

overall catch rates were higher during the two hours following the midpoint of Solunar majors, the Solunar minor hour, and the hour following the minor hour.[1340] He reported that "minor periods may actually exert greater effect on bass feeding than major periods, and should at least be weighted equally."[1341] His lowest catch rates occurred during the hours just before major and minor Solunar periods.[1342] However, *for lunker bass* consisting of 371 bass weighing 5 pounds or more, *he found no statistically significant pattern with regard to the Solunar periods.*[1343] He tended to catch more lunkers during the hour leading up to major Solunar periods and 2 hours after minor Solunar periods, but overall he concluded that "bass over 5 pounds were not as influenced by moon position."[1344] He concluded that baitfish activity and "other forces such as light conditions and weather often overwhelm effects of moon position as postulated by Solunar theory."[1345]

Manns claims that "the lunar influence on bass fishing seems to be more potent in waters where the food web is based on invertebrates and sunfish, rather than shad."[1346] This theory makes sense since "plankton and invertebrates seem most influenced by lunar forces," which might trigger bass activity; but, again, the effects on lunker bass are questionable at best.[1347] Manns suggested that Solunar theory might be more predictive of bass activity in ponds and small power plant lakes, but not on reservoirs—so the size and characteristics of the fishery may contribute to any effect.

[1340] Id.
[1341] Id.
[1342] Id.
[1343] Id.
[1344] Ralph Manns, *Moon Magic Largemouth Bass*, *supra* note 1323.
[1345] Id.
[1346] Id.
[1347] Id.

Dawn and Dusk

Another common theory is that bass are more active at dawn and dusk, so many fishermen feel it is vital to be on the water at the crack of dawn and as the sun goes down at dusk to catch the most and biggest bass. There is some scientific merit to this theory. Researchers who have monitored largemouth bass movements with tracking devices repeatedly report that bass "exhibit crepuscular activity peaks," which means the peaks occur in the low light conditions of dawn and dusk.[1348] Multiple studies show that largemouth bass are "more active during daylight hours than during night," and several studies show the "activity was the highest around dusk and dawn."[1349]

[1348] Kyle Hanson, et al., *Assessment of largemouth bass behavior and activity at multiple spatial and temporal scales utilizing a whole-lake telemetry array*, HYDROBIOLOGIA 582(1): 243-256 (May 2007), available at https://www.researchgate.net/publication/226543386_Assessment_of_largemouth_bass_Micropterus_salmoides_behaviour_and_activity_at_multiple_spatial_and_temporal_scales_utilizing_a_whole-lake_telemetry_array.

[1349] Ryan Hunter and Michael Maceina, *Movements and home ranges of largemouth bass and Alabama spotted bass in Lake Martin, Alabama*, J. FRESHWATER ECOLOGY

Experts theorize that the low light conditions associated with dawn and dusk (and heavy cloud cover) tilt the scales more in favor of largemouth bass by making their prey more vulnerable because bass's eyes generally have better sensitivity to low light conditions than their prey.[1350] Manns found that dusk was better than dawn adding that "tournaments are scheduled to end way too soon for the best bite."[1351]

Another possible reason that bass might theoretically be easier to catch around dawn and dusk is that they simply are closer to shore and in shallower water where anglers can target them better. Anglers generally tend to prefer to fish shallow and cast toward the bank, so dawn and dusk may simply bring more bass into the area where anglers prefer to fish resulting in more catches simply because bass in shallow waters cross paths with more anglers during those times. In one study, during fall and winter, bass tended to shift offshore from midday through early afternoon from around 11 am until 3 pm.[1352] Specifically, in November in one study, the bass averaged 80 feet (25 m) offshore in the mornings, then moved to an average of 130 feet (40 m) offshore during the afternoon, and then back to 33 feet (10 m) offshore during the evening.[1353] However, a different study at a different lake found that nearness to shore and structure selection was similar for both day and night, so patterns may be lake specific.[1354] During spring, bass tend to stay closer to shore throughout the day at most lakes.[1355]

A third theory that would make bass bite better at dawn is the fact that the threadfin shad spawn occurs during the first couple of

---

23(4): 599-606 (2008), available at https://doi.org/10.1080/02705060.2008.9664247.

[1350] Ralph Manns, *Barometric pressure and bass*, IN-FISHERMAN, October 24, 2017, available at https://www.in-fisherman.com/editorial/barometric-pressure-and-bass/153689.

[1351] Steve Quinn, *The effects of Solunar forces on bass fishing, supra* note 1327.

[1352] Karle Woodward and Richard Noble, *Over-winter movements of adult largemouth bass in a North Carolina reservoir*, PROC. ANNU, CONF. SOUTHEAST ASSOC. FISH AND WILDL. AGENCIES 51:113-122 (1997).

[1353] Id.

[1354] Jason Harris, Master of Science Thesis, *Habitat selection, and home range of largemouth bass following a habitat enhancement project in Table Rock Lake*, Missouri, University of Missouri MOspace, 2013, available at https://mospace.umsystem.edu/xmlui/bitstream/handle/10355/37945/research.pdf?sequence=2&isAllowed=y.

[1355] Karle Woodward and Richard Noble, *supra* note 1352.

hours of daylight and puts largemouth bass into a feeding mood during the time of year when the shad spawn is going on. During the shad spawn time period on many fisheries, dawn is undoubtedly a good time to catch fish of any size.

Night Bite

Largemouth bass are led by visual cues to initiate foraging activity leading to "increased movement during day and low light hours with decreased movement during night."[1356] In one study of 70 radio-tagged bass tracked for 13 months, largemouth bass nighttime movements were only 17% of their daytime movements in July and only 73% of their daytime movements in December.[1357] However, bass can still feed at night, and some argue that night time is the best time. Bass "have better night vision than humans and see well enough in clear water to attack prey a few feet away."[1358] In contrast, the "eyes of shad, bluegills, perch, and other preyfish aren't adapted for night vision, so they become more vulnerable after dark."[1359]

Bass are likely less active at night due to the darkness limiting the use of visual cues to feed, form groups, and socialize. Most bass are social fish that hang out in groups. These social tendencies also make them more vulnerable to angling with researchers noting, "Schooling and aggregating behaviors are apparently associated with increased feeding and vulnerability to angling."[1360] In one study, aggregations of largemouth bass occurred primarily during daylight hours with over 97 times more associations of two bass or more together occurring during daytime than nighttime, which suggested to researchers that visual cues were important for bass to form relationships.[1361] They quote prior research showing that bass disperse at night and reassemble the aggregations during the day.[1362]

[1356] Jason Harris, supra note 1354.
[1357] Id.
[1358] Steve Quinn, *Understanding lunker largemouths*, IN-FISHERMAN, 2022 Bass Guide, 18-22, 2022.
[1359] Id.
[1360] Ralph Manns, *Barometric pressure and bass*, *supra* note 1350.
[1361] C.T. Hasler, et al., *Frequency, composition and stability of associations among individual largemouth bass at diel, daily and seasonal scales*, ECOLOGY OF FRESHWATER FISH 16: 417–424 (2007).
[1362] Id.

So, bass tend to feed alone at night close to cover because they "have trouble staying in a group when it's dark."[1363]

Manns found in 702 night-time trips that his average number of bass caught per hour of fishing was about 60% of the number he caught each hour during the daylight.[1364] He reported that the bite was better on nights when the moon was bright, which again suggests the importance of vision to feeding bass.[1365] Other researchers have reported that bass are shallower and closer to shore at night than during the day, which might make them more catchable to many anglers under bright moonlight conditions.[1366] Also, use of lights to attract fish can play a role in predictably concentrating some big fish near dock lights at night on some lakes, like Lake Fork. In spite of those potential tricks, I did not find much support for the idea that nighttime was the best time to catch lunker bass from scientific sources.

My Online Database Research

To help answer the questions above, the online public database of catches from a series of big bass tournaments with hourly weigh-ins centering prizes around the biggest bass was analyzed. Specifically, the Sealy Outdoors Big Bass Splash tournament archives including 44 tournaments over the nine years from 2014 through 2022 were studied.[1367]

The Sealy Outdoors Big Bass Splash is an annual series of amateur largemouth bass fishing tournaments on southeastern lakes with large prizes for the biggest bass at hourly weigh-ins.[1368] Anglers can trailer their boat and launch wherever they want on the specific lake.[1369] The first cast daily is allowed at 6 am and the last weigh in is

---

[1363] Steve Quinn, *Understanding lunker largemouths*, supra note 1358.
[1364] Ralph Manns, *Moon Magic Largemouth Bass*, supra note 1323.
[1365] Id.
[1366] Jason Harris, supra note 1354.
[1367] Big Bass Splash, *Tournament results*, Sealy Outdoors, available at https://sealyoutdoors.com/results/#1668546067647-68ff909f-b38e.
[1368] *Sealy Outdoors Big Bass Splash: Where amateurs win like the pros!*, Sealy Outdoors, available at https://sealyoutdoors.com.
[1369] Big Bass Splash, *Official tournament rules*, Sealy Outdoors, available at https://sealyoutdoors.com/rules/.

at 2 pm.[1370] Fish are weighed in each hour beginning at 7 am until 2 pm, and the biggest few fish each hour win cash awards with the biggest few fish in the tournament winning even larger prizes.[1371] Anglers pay entry fees and are motivated by large prizes to catch big bass, to fish from 6 am to 2 pm, and generally to weigh them in sometime close to when they caught them (since the fish might die and be disqualified if it stays in the livewell too long).[1372]

Archives were publicly available online for 44 of these tournaments over nine years, and bass over 8 pounds were caught in all but two. The tournaments were held between March and the end of October each year. The tournaments were at Rayburn (15 times), Toledo Bend (9 times), Lake Fork (8 times), Guntersville (8 times), Chickamauga (2 times), and Kentucky Lake (2 times). I became familiar with the tournament by talking to anglers at Lake Fork.

A total of 514 bass 8 pounds or over were caught in these tournaments between 6 am and 2 pm.[1373] These bass were weighed in at hourly weigh-ins beginning at 7 am with the last weigh-in between 1 and 2 pm, and the hourly time that they were weighed in was included in the tournament archives.[1374]

Table 1 shows how many of the 514 bass 8 pounds or over were weighed in during each hour of the tournament.

[1370] Id.
[1371] Id.
[1372] Id.
[1373] Big Bass Splash, *Tournament results*, Sealy Outdoors, available at https://sealyoutdoors.com/results/#1668546067647-68ff909f-b38e (note that 8 bass were eliminated from this study because they were weighed in during the 2-3 pm times at one of the early tournaments with weigh ins from 2 to 3 pm.).
[1374] Id.

Table 1. Number of 8+ pound bass weighed during each hour & percentage of the total number of 8+ pound bass weighed during each hour.

Weigh-in Time	Number of 8+ lbers.	Percentage of Total (514) 8+ lbers.
7:00 to 7:59 AM	59	11.48%
8:00 to 8:59 AM	124	24.12%
9:00 to 9:59 AM	71	13.81%
10:00 to 10:59 AM	53	10.31%
11:00 to 11:59 AM	35	6.81%
12:00 to 12:59 PM	93	18.09%
1:00 to 2:00 PM	79	15.40%

If all times were equally productive for bass over 8 pounds, then each hour would have the same number of bass reported, but you can see in Table 1 that is not the case. Note that more bass (a total of 124) over 8 pounds were weighed in between 8 am and 9 am than any other time by far. The next closest time was from noon to 1 pm with 93 bass, which is only 75% as many as the 8 to 9 am hour. Notice there were 3.5 times as many 8+ pound lunkers weighed in from 8 to 9 am as from 11 am to noon. So, clearly there were some major differences in the number of lunkers weighed in during each hour. The results are depicted graphically in Figure 1.

Figure 1. Percentage of 8+ pound bass weighed in during each hour

```
Percentage of 8+ Pounders Weighed Each Hour

25
        24.12
20
                                                18.09
                                                        15.4
15                13.81
     11.48
                        10.31
10
                                6.81
 5
 0
   7AM-8AM 8AM-9AM 9AM-10AM 10AM-11AM 11AM-12PM 12PM-1PM 1PM-2PM
```

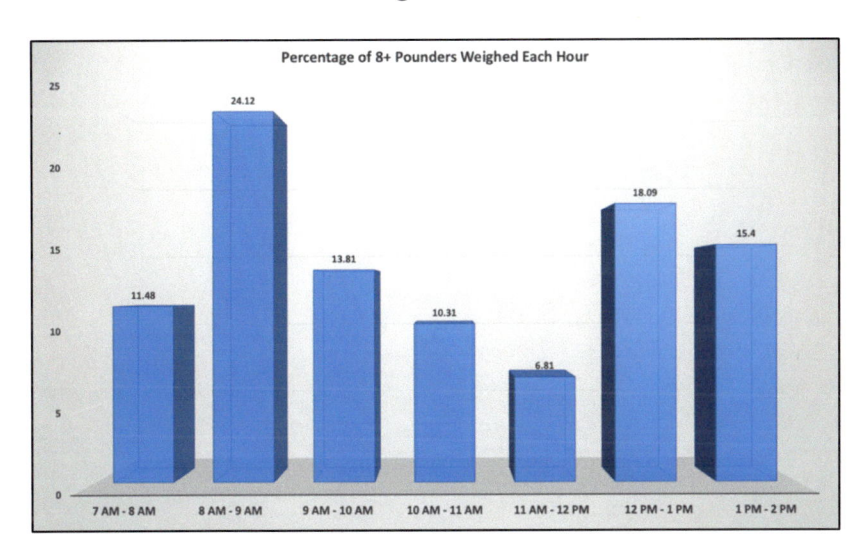

    So, these numbers appear to indicate that the highest percentage of the biggest bass were caught in the first few of hours of the tournament. In fact, almost 36% of the 8+ pound lunkers were weighed in during the first two hours of weigh-ins.

    Let's look at the numbers another way. Let's break the tournament day's weigh-ins into early morning (7 am to 9 am), late morning (9 am to 11 am), and mid-day (11 am to 2 pm). Of the bass over 8 pounds, 183 were weighed in before 9 am, 124 were weighed in between 9 am and 11 am, and 207 were weighed in from 11 am to 2 pm. Figure 2 shows the increased or decreased chance of weighing in an 8+ pound bass during the tournaments at early morning, late morning, and mid-day.

Figure 2: Percentage increase or decrease in chances of weighing in an 8+ pound bass by tournament weigh-in categories.

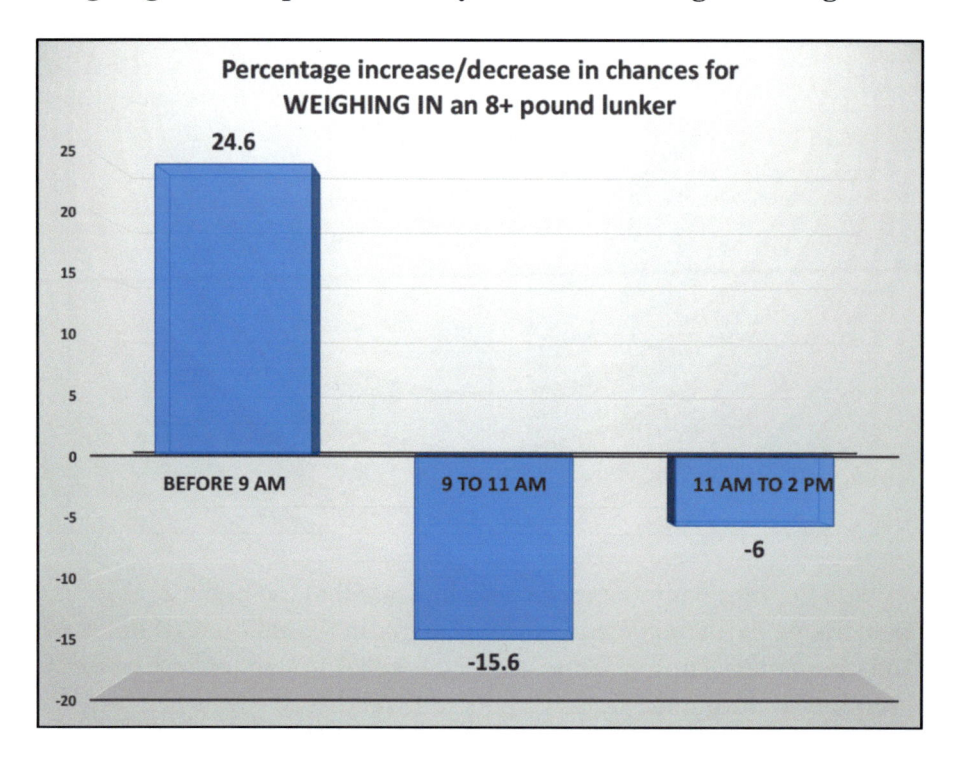

Percentage increase/decrease in chances for WEIGHING IN an 8+ pound lunker

- BEFORE 9 AM: 24.6
- 9 TO 11 AM: -15.6
- 11 AM TO 2 PM: -6

There is one obvious flaw in this methodology. Look back at the tournament rules mentioned in the beginning of this section. Notice that first cast is at 6 am. While there were only 7 weigh-ins, the fishermen actually started fishing at 6 am, but there was no 6 am to 7 am weigh-in. *This means that it is possible that the early morning showed better results simply because there was an extra hour of fishing that was not used in the calculations. The above data is very useful for anyone fishing a big bass tournament and choosing a weigh-in time, so I included it. However, we need to also account for the 6 am to 7 am hour to get a better idea of hourly catch odds (instead of weigh-in odds).*

So, let's redo the data.

Breaking down the 514 lunkers over 8 hours (instead of 7) means that 64.25 lunkers per hour would be expected. Of the bass over 8 pounds, 183 were weighed in before 9 am, 124 were weighed in between 9 am and 11 am, and 207 were weighed in from 11 am to 2 pm. During the THREE hours from 6 am to 9 am, 192.75 would be an expected average (i.e., 3 hrs. x 64.25). During the two hours from 9 to 11 am, 128.5 would be the expected average (i.e., 2 hrs. x 64.25). During the three hours from 11 am to 2 pm, 192.5 would be expected. So, from 6 am to 9 am, there were 183 of the expected 192.75 weighed in, which is 94.9% of expected. From 9 to 11 am, there were 124 of 128.5 expected, which is 96.5% of expected. From 11 am to 2 pm, there were 207 of 192.75 expected, which is 107.4% of expected. Suddenly, the graph looks much different by simply adding in the extra hour from 6 am to 7 am when there was no weigh-in with the early morning weigh-ins showing minus 5.1% chances, the late morning showing minus 3.5% chances, and the mid-day showing the best chances of +7.4%. These results are depicted graphically in Figure 3.

Figure 3: Percentage increase or decrease in chances of catching an 8+ pound bass by tournament weigh-in categories.

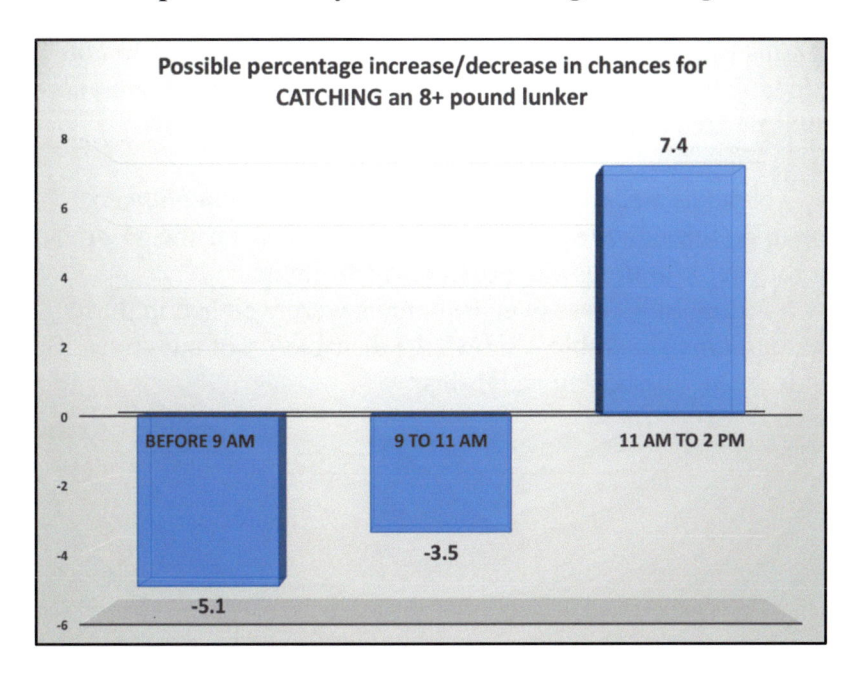

Overlooking subtle differences in data can lead fishermen to draw questionable conclusions. On the surface, more lunker bass are weighed in during the early morning hours than late morning and mid-day. However, the chances of actually catching a giant bass *appear to me to be fairly even throughout the tournament* when you factor in the early start and lack of an early weigh-in along with the fact that many anglers may keep the lunker in the livewell for a significant amount of time before going in for the weigh-in resulting in more lunkers being weighed in later in the day distant from the time actually caught. I think the livewell time likely accounts for the appearance of lower chances early in the tournament day and increased chances later in the day. It seems likely that the mid-day increased chances may simply be bass that stayed in the livewell from earlier in the day and could also be some gamesmanship as anglers try to guess the best time to weigh-in a big bass to cash in on an hourly prize since clearly more big bass per hour were weighed in during the earlier hours.

So, based upon this study, I would conclude that time of day had little effect on 8+ pound lunker bass catches. I would speculate that 8+ pound lunkers were as likely to be caught at 6 am as at 1 pm. However, because the amount of time bass spent in livewells before weigh-ins is unknown in this study and the catch times were not recorded, I can only say that no definite pattern emerged, and more study is needed.

Now, *let's consider the double-digit 10+ pound lunkers*. I'm going to go through the numbers the same way as for the 8+ pounders both for weigh-in times and possible catch times.

A total of 43 bass over 10 pounds were weighed in during these tournaments. Table 2 shows the distribution of bass over 10 pounds during the hourly weigh-ins.

Table 2. Number of 10+ pound bass weighed in each hour & percentage of the total number of 10+ pound bass weighed in each hour.

Weigh-in Time	Number of 10+ lbers.	Percentage of Total (43) 10+ lbers.
7:00 to 7:59 AM	3	6.98%
8:00 to 8:59 AM	17	39.53%
9:00 to 9:59 AM	3	6.98%
10:00 to 10:59 AM	5	11.63%
11:00 to 11:59 AM	0	0%
12:00 to 12:59 PM	10	23.26%
1:00 to 2:00 PM	5	11.63%

The pattern for the 10+ pounders was similar to, but more pronounced than, the pattern for 8+ pounders. *Almost 40 percent of the 10 pound plus bass were weighted in during the 8 o'clock hour between 8 and 9 am*, which is a considerably higher percentage than for the 8 pound plus bass. And *almost half of the double-digit bass (46.5%) caught in these tournaments were weighed in by 9 am.* The second most common hour was during the noon hour, which is similar to the 8+ pounders. Figure 4 depicts these findings graphically.

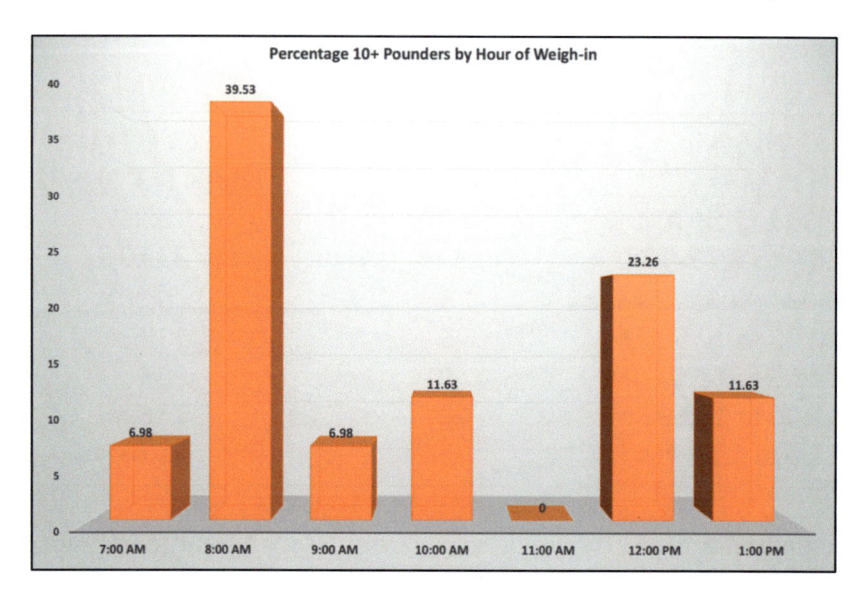

Figure 4. Percentage of 10+ pound bass by hour of weigh-in

Percentage 10+ Pounders by Hour of Weigh-in

Hour	Percentage
7:00 AM	6.98
8:00 AM	39.53
9:00 AM	6.98
10:00 AM	11.63
11:00 AM	0
12:00 PM	23.26
1:00 PM	11.63

Let's look at the numbers another way like we did for the 8+ pounders Let's break the tournament day's weigh-ins into early morning (7 am to 9 am), late morning (9 am to 11 am), and mid-day (11 am to 2 pm). Of the bass over 10 pounds, 20 were weighed in before 9 am, 8 were weighed in between 9 am and 11 am, and 15 were weighed in from 11 am to 2 pm. Figure 5 shows the increased or decreased chance of weighing in a 10+ pound bass during the tournaments.

Figure 5: Percentage increase or decrease in chances of weighing in an 10+ pound bass by tournament weigh-in categories.

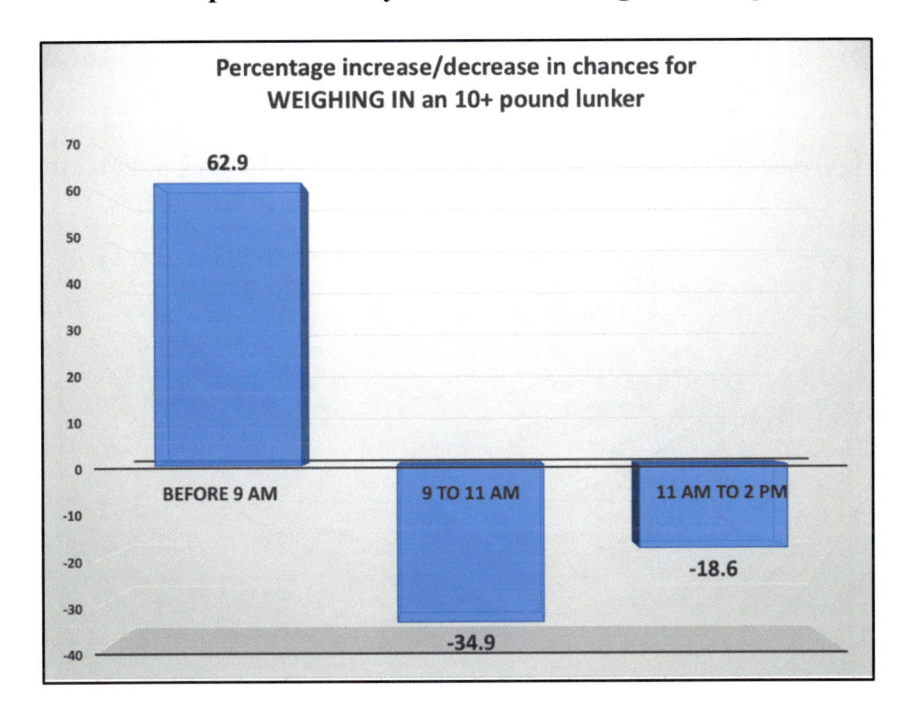

Percentage increase/decrease in chances for WEIGHING IN an 10+ pound lunker

- BEFORE 9 AM: 62.9
- 9 TO 11 AM: -34.9
- 11 AM TO 2 PM: -18.6

There is *one obvious flaw* in this methodology, just like with the data for the 8+ pounders. Remember that the first cast was at 6 am, but there was no 6 am to 7 am weigh-in. Thus, the *extra hour* of fishing without a weigh-in may have tainted the results.

So, let's redo the data while accounting for the extra hour of fishing.

Breaking down the 43 lunkers over 8 hours (instead of 7) means that 5.375 lunkers per hour would be expected. Of the bass over 8 pounds, 20 were weighed in before 9 am, 8 were weighed in between 9 am and 11 am, and 15 were weighed in from 11 am to 2 pm. During the THREE hours from 6 am to 9 am, 16.125 would be expected. During the two hours from 9 to 11 am, 10.75 would be expected. During the three hours from 11 am to 2 pm, 16.125 would be expected. So, from 6 am to 9 am, there were 20 of the expected 16.125 weighed in, which is 124.0% of expected. From 9 to 11 am, there were 8 of 10.75 expected, which is 74.4% of expected. From 11 am to 2 pm, there were 15 of 16.125 expected, which is 93.0% of expected. So, the graph looks much different by adding in the extra hour from 6 am to 7 am when there was no weigh-in with the early morning weigh-ins showing +24.0% chances, the late morning showing -25.6% chances, and the mid-day showing the best chances of -7.0%. These results are depicted graphically in Figure 6.

Figure 6: Percentage increase or decrease in chances of catching a 10+ pound bass by tournament weigh-in categories.

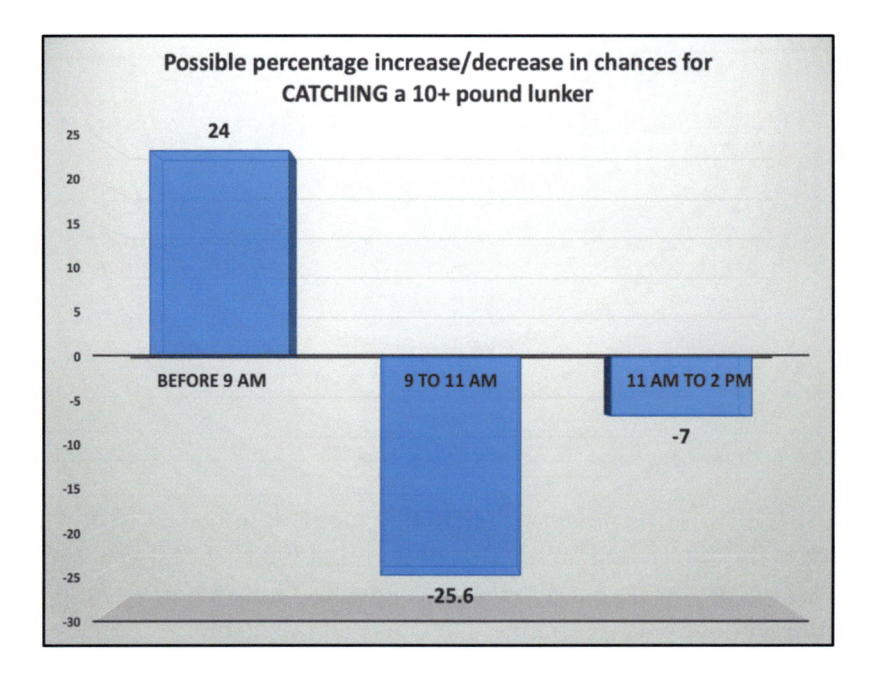

Possible percentage increase/decrease in chances for CATCHING a 10+ pound lunker

- BEFORE 9 AM: 24
- 9 TO 11 AM: -25.6
- 11 AM TO 2 PM: -7

So, a trend appears to be present toward catching more double-digit bass earlier in the morning than the rest of the day. To drive that point home, let's compare the number weighed in before 9 am to the number weighed in after 9 am. Before 9 am, 20 of the 43 double digit bass were already weighed in after just 3 hours of fishing (really probably more like 2.5 hours of fishing to allow time to travel to the weigh in site). In other words, *by 9 am 47% of the double-digit bass had already hit the scales after just 3 hours of fishing.* After 9 am, the remaining 23 (or 53%) were weighed in over a 5-hour period. On a per hour basis, this means that the chances of catching a 10+ pound lunker were much higher before 9 am than after. Specifically, 124% of expected 10+ pound lunkers were caught before 9 am (and possibly even more that were simply kept in the livewell and weighed in later). In contrast, over 5 hours, 23 of the expected 26.88 doubled digit bass were weighed in which is 85.6% of expected (or a 14.4% decreased chance). These numbers are shown graphically in Figure 7.

Figure 7: Percentage increase or decrease in chances of catching a 10+ pound bass before versus after 9 am.

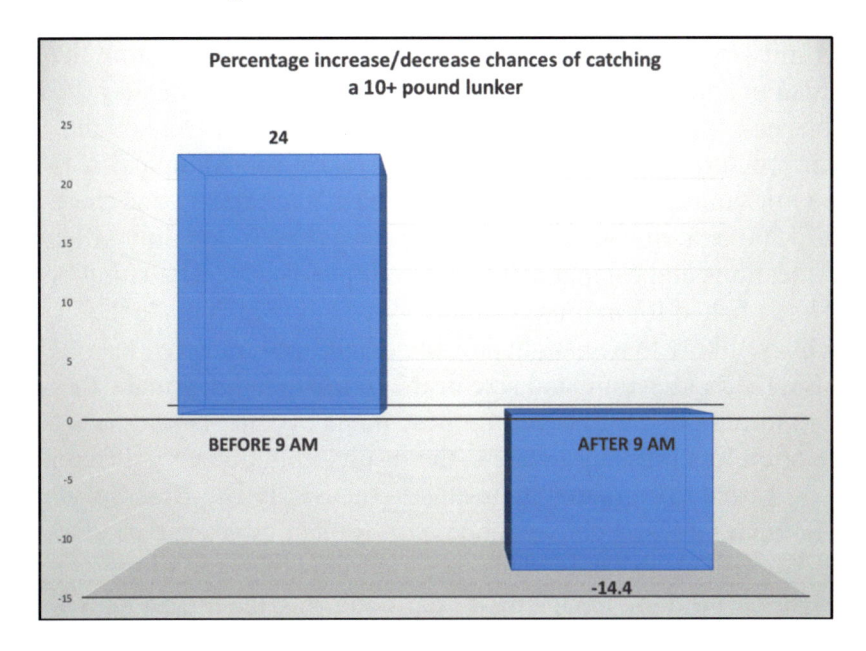

Thus, in this big bass tournament series, the chances of catching a 10+ pound lunker were much higher before 9 am than after 9 am. In fact, the chances are likely even more skewed than the data demonstrate because some of the double-digit bass may have been held in the fishermen's livewells and weighed in during an hour later than when they were caught.

So, this study suggests that when picking between hours from 6 am until 2 pm, the highest odds of catching a 10+ pound lunker are during the first few morning hours and possibly from 6:00 until 8:30 am. Therefore, for double digit bass fishing, the early morning hours seem to be best during the tournament times.

The numbers are much less clear for 8+ pound lunkers. Overall, time of day did not demonstrate a clear pattern for lunkers 8+ pounds or larger with a *high likelihood that 8+ pound bass were equally likely to be caught at any time throughout the tournament day.*

There are a few obvious limitations to my study. First, it ends at 2 pm, so most of the afternoon, dusk, and night are not included, and these are times that some authors suggest are best to catch big bass. Remember that Ralph Manns found that dusk was a better time than dawn. Second, anglers were not required to weigh in the fish when they catch them, so it is possible that some fishermen carry their catches around in the livewell and wait to weigh them in, losing proximity to the time caught. Third, the fishing pressure from the tournament anglers could decrease the big bass bite as the day wears on because these are huge tournaments with many anglers on the water pressuring the fish on busy public lakes; for example, I was on Lake Fork during one March 2023 big bass tournament, and there were 1500 entrants on the water competing, which certainly affected fish locations and catchability—for example, bass on spawning beds had been fished for numerous times by 10 am, which made them much less likely to be caught and some had been removed to weigh-in. So, the mere nature and size of the tournament may make the early morning hours best during these mega events. During less busy time or on less pressured waters, the results might be very different.

I tried to compare the results of the Seally Big Bass Splash to the Solunar tables. I chose a couple of Solunar tables and tried to correlate fish catch times to the major periods. Several of the tournaments did not have a major period during the tournament hours, so those were eliminated. Also, several tournaments only had a partial major period toward the end of the tournament times, which made assessment less valid, which is why I did not pursue this in more detail. But before I quit analyzing, I found that of 102 bass sampled, only 27.5% were caught during a major period, while the remaining 72.5% were not caught during the predicted major period time frame. So, I did not see any evidence of a pattern developing in the limited review that I was able to perform with regard to Solunar major periods.

Individual Angler Results by Time of Day

My personal best twelve fish did not follow any pattern except that I seemed to catch more at mid-day, including 3 of my top 12 at 1:40 pm specifically. I am rarely on the water at dusk because I typically am home for dinner with my family. So, I have not adequately tested the dusk time frame. Table 3 shows the times of my top 12 catches:

Table 3. My top 12 bass with time and date.

1.	12 lbs. 9 oz.	2:30 pm	6/29/16
2.	10 lbs.	11:00 am	5/26/21
3.	9 lbs. 7 oz.	1:40 pm	1/13/21
4.	9 lbs.	1:40 pm	4/26/21
5.	8 lbs. 14 oz.	10:20 am	6/29/16
6.	8.45 lbs.	1:00 pm	1/4/23
7.	8.34 lbs.	7:15 pm	6/29/22
8.	8.22 lbs.	1:40 pm	6/8/20
9.	8.02 lbs.	4:45 pm	5/23/19
10.	7 lbs. 11 oz.	6:25 pm	6/7/22
11.	7.61 lbs.	11:00 am	5/31/21
12.	7.5 lbs.	3:00 pm	3/27/19

Figure 8 depicts these numbers graphically.

Figure 8. Catch times of my top twelve bass

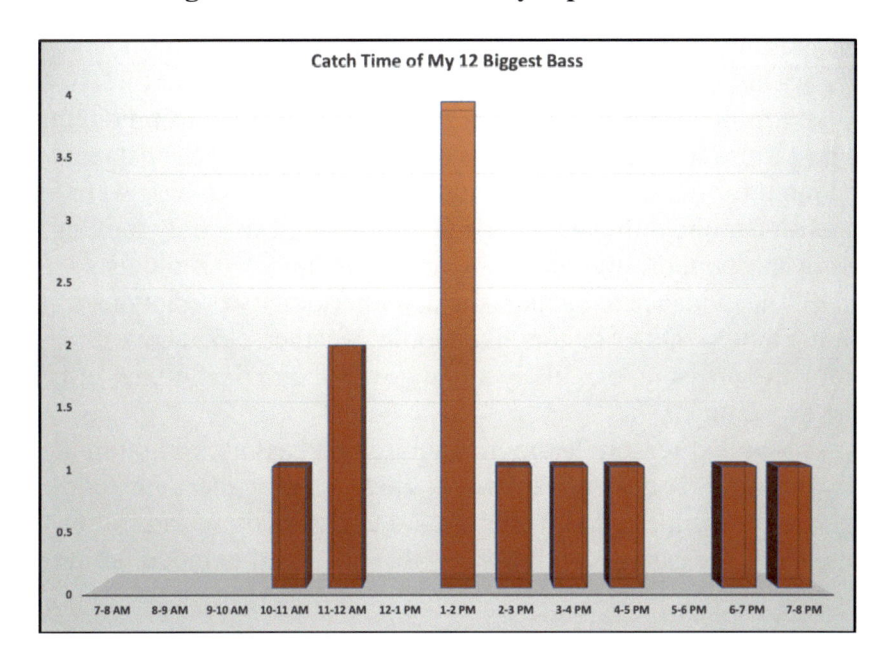

Individual angler fishing style and preferences likely affect when they catch their biggest fish. I prefer deep offshore fishing, and numerous studies suggest that the biggest bass shift offshore during the middle of the day. So, my results are not surprising. Note none of my biggest bass were caught before 10:20 am, even though I have spent countless early morning hours fishing, caught many fish early, and seen many sunrises on the same lakes as where I caught these fish. Oddly 3 of my biggest fish were caught at exactly 1:40 pm, so you can bet I will try to always be on the water during that time after reviewing this data! My catches suggest the afternoon hours are pretty good for my fishing style since 9 of my 12 biggest fish were caught after noon. This surprises me a little, as I was unaware until putting this chapter together and because I have spent so may sunrises on the water.

Conclusion

During tournaments, the early morning hours are likely the best time to catch double-digit bass—especially during mega tournaments with hundreds of tournament anglers on the water. This is likely because tournament anglers educate the biggest bass early of their presence making them harder to catch. Bass in the 8+ pound category are more evenly spread over the tournament hours.

Limited support is available for the Solunar tables predicting the best times to catch lunker bass in my evaluation of the data and the literature. Manns found among his catches that big bass were less responsive to the Solunar table peaks, and since I was only looking at bass over 8 pounds, my results are not surprising.[1375] Biologists found little evidence to support the daily periodicity predictions of the Solunar tables. Other factors like month, weather, cloud cover, barometric pressure, etc. likely simply overwhelm the Solunar effect most of the time.[1376]

Another reason that more double digit bass are caught in the early mornings at big tournaments is likely because most amateur anglers in these mega-tournaments tend to fish shallow and follow the contours of the banks. Studies show that bass tend to move farther

---

[1375] Ralph Manns, *Moon Magic Largemouth Bass*, *supra* note 1323.
[1376] Id.

offshore in the middle of the day.[1377] For example, in one study, researchers found that bass "mostly moved offshore under bright sunlight."[1378] In addition, during late spring and early summer, bass are drawn into the shallow water areas for the threadfin shad spawn, which ends each day once the sun gets up. So, more double digit bass are simply in the path of amateur anglers during the early morning hours leading to more catches. I think that the lunkers were still just as likely to bite in the middle of the day, but fewer anglers were in places to put lures in front of them offshore. If bass shift offshore during the middle of the day, unless the same number of anglers follow them offshore, it is unlikely that as many will be caught. So, any early morning or dusk pattern noted by anglers may be due to increased overlap of anglers and lunkers in shallow waters during those times, and the lunker bass are just as likely (or more likely if less pressured) to bite offshore mid-day as early in the morning. This would likely explain the pattern for my biggest bass being caught mid-day because I prefer offshore fishing and do not spend much time fishing shallow—even early in the mornings.

If you are a shallow water fisherman, then be on the water in the early mornings and just before dark to have the best chance of catching a double digit lunker. If you are an offshore fisherman, then I think your chances of landing a lunker are just as high in the middle of the day as the dawn and dusk time frames.

Finally, note that the effect of time of day appears to be greater on the biggest bass, i.e., those over 10 pounds because a clear pattern developed with more of those giants being weighed in before 9 am. In contrast, for the lunkers over 8 pounds, the data were less clear and no significant pattern was likely once the extra hour of early morning fishing was included in the calculations. This is similar to the outcome of my other studies in this book where barometric pressure (or weather) and month (or time of year) appeared to have a bigger effect on the 13+ pound giants than the more common 8+ pound lunkers. So, *the biggest bass in the fisheries may be the most sensitive to factors like time of day, barometric pressure/weather, and month/season* based on the overall findings in my studies in this book combined.

[1377] See, e.g., Jason Harris, supra note 1354; Karle Woodward and Richard Noble, *supra* note 1352; Kyle Hanson, et al., *supra* note 1348.
[1378] Ralph Manns, *Barometric pressure and bass*, *supra* note 1350.

12

Seasonal Patterns

Generalities

    Lunker largemouth follow seasonal patterns of behavior that influence catchability. For instance, anglers were over 7 times more likely to catch an 8+ pound lunker during the springtime in March than during the fall in November (see Chapter 3). For giant 13+ pound lunkers the effect was even more dramatic with anglers being 32 times more likely to catch a giant 13+ pound lunker during springtime in March than during summertime in June or July (see Chapter 3). In this chapter, I will discuss what scientists believe bass are doing during each season.

    Catchability "depends on the ability of anglers to successfully locate areas where fish are present."[1379] So, anglers are more

---

[1379] Andrea Sylvia, et al., *Influence of largemouth bass behaviors, angler behaviors, and environmental conditions on fishing tournament capture success*, Iowa State University, available at https://dr.lib.iastate.edu/server/api/core/bitstreams/0bf6e7c2-a0b3-44dc-9aa0-6967449d29ff/content.

successful if they can "selectively target areas where fish reside."[1380] In one study, researchers tracked tournament fishermen simultaneously with telemetered largemouth bass to see if the anglers were fishing where the bass were hanging out.[1381] As you would expect, they found that anglers caught more bass when they were in areas where the bass were located.[1382] Surprisingly, a lot of anglers were fishing in areas where fish were NOT located.[1383] Hopefully, this chapter will help you better understand seasonal patterns so that you spend more time fishing in the areas where lunker bass are present.

Water temperature changes associated with the changing seasons trigger bass to change their behavior to maintain optimal metabolic, physiologic, and developmental performance.[1384] Bass prefer living in the depth range from 5 to 25 feet and within 100 feet of shore in most fisheries year-round.[1385] Bass also stay in their "home-ranges" ranging from the size of half of a football field up to around 75 football fields as discussed in Chapter 6 throughout the year. So, when I say they are deeper and farther offshore during a particular season, I do not mean 60 feet deep and 300 yards offshore—just deeper and farther offshore than during other seasons within their home range. As a young fisherman reading fishing magazines, I once thought "deep" in winter meant jigging a spoon 80 feet deep and 500 yards offshore on a large lake near my home—so, I wanted to clarify from the start.

In broad terms, active bass are found in greater numbers during the spring in shallow coves and flats near spawning areas, during the summer in deeper water on offshore structure, during fall back in the coves and on flats, and during winter back in the deeper

---

[1380] Id.
[1381] Id.
[1382] Id.
[1383] Id.
[1384] Helene Volkoff and Ivar Ronnestad, *Effects of temperature on feeding and digestive processes in fish*, TEMPERATURE 7(4): 307-320 (2020), available at https://www.ncbi.nlm.nih.gov/pmc/articles/PMC7678922/pdf/KTMP_7_1765950.pdf.
[1385] Jason Harris, Master of Science Thesis, *Habitat selection, and home range of largemouth bass following a habitat enhancement project in Table Rock Lake*, Missouri, University of Missouri MOspace, 2013, available at https://mospace.umsystem.edu/xmlui/bitstream/handle/10355/37945/research.pdf?sequence=2&isAllowed=y.

water. They tend to be shallowest and closest to shore in springtime around the spawn and deepest and farthest from shore during wintertime.[1386] For example, at Toledo Bend, the average depth of the bass tracked in one study was 8 feet during spring, but 17 feet during winter.[1387] The details of each season are discussed below. In addition to water temperature, other factors like season, weather conditions, water clarity, and length of day influence behavior as well.

To help make this chapter easier to interpret across different geographic regions, the seasons are defined by water temperature (the master factor). "Winter" includes months when the water temperature is below 45 to 50 degrees Fahrenheit, "spring" between 55 and 75 degrees, "summer" above 80 degrees, and fall when the temperature is falling from 75 to 55 degrees. Note that I have left a vague 5-degree area between these seasons because the transitions are not always obvious and can vary considerably between different geographic regions and even between similar bodies of water in the same region.

[1386] K.C. Hanson, et al., *Intersexual variation in the seasonal behaviour and depth distribution of a freshwater temperate fish, the largemouth bass*, CANADIAN J. ZOOLOGY 86: 801-811 (2008), available at http://fishlab.nres.illinois.edu/Reprints/Hanson%20et%20al%20CJZ%202008.pdf.
[1387] Ken Smith Fishing YouTube Channel, *Toledo Bend Telemetry Tracking Study Update Todd Driscoll TP&W Biologist Feb 2022 Part 5*, available at https://www.youtube.com/watch?v=f1sL9FZnS4g&list=PLLzhji805wVzkLnAA97I8VmdZpR8arB_Q&index=5.

Winter (Water Temperature <45 to 50°F)

Lunker Statistics: Largemouth bass are generally less catchable in winter because at colder water temperatures their metabolism slows, their activity diminishes, and they eat fewer meals (see Chapter 7). So, no matter how much you learn about largemouth bass behavior, your catch rates are likely to be lower during winter than other times of the year. Specifically, one author who recorded 8900 bass catches over 18 years found the bite was the slowest in winter when water temperatures were between 49-58°F (his coldest category) when he and his partners caught less than two (1.87) bass per outing compared to almost five (4.66) bass per outing when the water temperature was in his best category from 69-78°F.[1388] Even so, if you can locate a big winter aggregation of bass, you can occasionally catch large numbers—even during winter.

Factors other than water temperature also affect bass behavior and spatial distribution—including food, sunlight, wind, vegetation, and oxygen availability.[1389] For example, forage fish availability

---

[1388] Ralph Manns, *Moon Magic Largemouth Bass*, IN-FISHERMAN, January 19, 2012, available at https://www.in-fisherman.com/editorial/moon-magic-largemouth-bass/154779.

[1389] Daniel Lemons and Larry Crawshaw, *Behavioral and metabolic adjustments to low temperatures in the largemouth bass*, PHYSIOLOGICAL ZOOLOGY 58(2): March/April 1985, available at https://www.journals.uchicago.edu/doi/10.1086/physzool.58.2.30158564; Caleb Hasler, *Measuring the influence of winter conditions on largemouth bass behavior using both biotelemetry and laboratory studies*, Queen's University Thesis Submission, Kingston, Ontario, Canada, August 2007, available at https://qspace.library.queensu.ca/bitstream/handle/1974/818/Hasler_Caleb_T_2007_08_MSc.pdf?sequence=1&isAllowed=y.

undergoes major decreases during winter in many freshwater fisheries because threadfin shad, gizzard shad, and other prey fish often have "heavy winter mortality" at low water temperatures resulting in a "shad kill."[1390]

In spite of the low water temperature and other factors negatively impacting fishing, winter can be one of the most likely times to catch a giant bass. Over 40% (36/87) of the 13+ pound ShareLunkers reported from 2018 through 2022 in my study in Chapter 3 were caught during winter months (December, January, and February in Texas) which was a much higher percentage than the summer (4.6%) and fall (8 %) months. For comparison, spring (March, April, and May in Texas) was only a little better than winter for 13+ pounders and accounted for 46% of the 13+ pounders in my study. Interestingly, winter was still a good time to catch 8+ pound lunkers in Texas in my study in Chapter 3, but only half as good as for 13+ pounders, since it only accounted for 22% (468/2124) of the 8+ pounders in 2022.

So, for some reason, the biggest bass may be the most catchable during winter months; perhaps their extra weight gives them more insulation allowing them to adapt better to cold temperature giving them a competitive advantage in chasing bait fish that are even more affected by the cold temperatures. Big bass may also be easier to catch in cold water because they might not be as able to distinguish lures from baitfish. One big bass specialist who has spent countless hours observing lunker bass behavior on forward facing sonar, Josh Jones, says that during summer he catches only about 1 of every 100 double digit bass that he sees on forward facing sonar, but in "winter, it's a different story."[1391] He says, "I'm no biologist, but I think their brain function or vision gets compromised during those periods of rapid cooling, and they don't process as well that the lure they are about to eat is fake."[1392] He also believes the "cold makes the shad and bluegills become lethargic and the big bass can feed much

---

[1390] S. Marshall Adams, et al., *Energy partitioning in largemouth bass under conditions of seasonally fluctuating prey availability*, TRANSACTIONS OF THE AMERICAN FISHERIES SOCIETY 111(5): 549-558, September 1982, available at https://afspubs.onlinelibrary.wiley.com/doi/10.1577/1548-8659%281982%29111%3C549%3AEPILBU%3E2.0.CO%3B2.
[1391] Steve Ryan, *The gathering legend of Josh Jones*, IN-FISHERMAN, 2023 Bass Guide, 42-45.
[1392] Id.

easier.[1393] They don't have to exert as much energy to eat. They just go wild."[1394]

Temperature Stratification: Thermal gradients develop in lakes over the seasons and can lead to significant stratification of the water column based upon temperature.[1395] Lakes are either isothermal (i.e., their temperature is the same throughout the depths) or thermally stratified (i.e., different temperatures at different depths) at different times during the year, depending on air temperature, season, rainfall, and other environmental factors specific to the individual body of water. Thermal stratification is an "annual occurrence at a majority of southern reservoirs."[1396] Cold water is more dense than warmer water.[1397] As water temperature falls, it reaches its maximum density at 4°C (39.2°F) before it starts forming ice crystals (in northern lakes generally).[1398]

Most lakes are isothermal during the winter months, meaning that the water temperature in most parts of the lake is the same within a degree or two from the surface to the bottom. For example, in a study of a deep Texas reservoir, Possum Kingdom, the water temperature varied less than 1 degree (47.0°F to 47.5°F) at depths from 3 feet deep to 80 feet deep in many places on the lake during January, and it remained isothermal from November through February.[1399]

When a lake is isothermal, it generally means that the lake water is mixing well across the depths. Isothermal temperatures vary

---

[1393] Id.
[1394] Id.
[1395] WaterCenter.org, *Water temperature patterns in lakes*, available at http://www.watercenter.org/physical-water-quality-parameters/water-temperature/temperature-ranges-in-lakes/.
[1396] Todd Driscoll, *Reservoir Stratification, Thermoclines, and Turnover*, Ken Smith Fishing, January 5, 2022, available at http://www.kensmithfishing.com/blog/reservoir-stratification-thermoclines-and-turnover/.
[1397] *About water temperatures*, The Concord Consortium, available at https://staff.concord.org/~btinker/GL/web/water/water_temperatures.html.
[1398] Todd Driscoll, *supra* note 1396; *About water temperatures*, *supra* note 1397; WaterCenter.org, *supra* note 1395.
[1399] Donald Leifeste and Barney Popkin, *Quality of water and stratification of Possum Kingdom, Whitney, Hubbard Creek, Proctor and Belton Reservoirs*, U.S. Geological Survey, Texas Water Development Board, available at https://www.twdb.texas.gov/publications/reports/numbered_reports/doc/R85/R85.pdf.

by lake location and specific lake characteristics. For example, among four Florida lakes, one had winter isothermy at 62°F (17°C) and another at 55°F (13°C), while more southern ones were isothermal at 66°F (19°C).[1400] In northern lakes where the surface layer is frozen during winter, the layer just below the ice can become supercooled (32.9°F/0.5°C) and less dense (as it begins to form ice crystals) than the rest of the lake (which will be at 39.2°F/4°C) forming a thermocline between the 39.2°F/4°C deeper layer and the supercooled surface layer.[1401] However, since bass fishermen are not generally fishing ice covered lakes for lunkers, I will cover thermoclines elsewhere (see summer section below).

Depth and Location: In most fisheries largemouth bass are deeper and farther offshore during winter than at other times of year.[1402] Numerous studies of telemetry tracked bass have shown winter bass prefer deeper water within the meaning of "deep" for a given fishery and bass's home range.[1403] For example, in one study, telemeter tracked bass "selected deeper positions in the water column during the winter period."[1404] In most lakes, except in special circumstances (see below) shallow water just does not hold many bass

---

[1400] Jaime Escobar, et al., *Thermal stratification, mixing, and heat budgets of Florida lakes*, Fundamental and Applied Limnology 174(4): 283-293, May 2009, available at https://www.researchgate.net/publication/233615553_Thermal_stratification_mixing_and_heat_budgets_of_Florida_lakes.

[1401] *About water temperatures, supra* note 1397.

[1402] Kyle Hanson, et al., *Assessment of largemouth bass behavior and activity at multiple spatial and temporal scales utilizing a whole-lake telemetry array*, Hydrobiologia 582(1): 243-256 (May 2007), available at https://www.researchgate.net/publication/226543386_Assessment_of_largemouth_bass_Micropterus_salmoides_behaviour_and_activity_at_multiple_spatial_and_temporal_scales_utilizing_a_whole-lake_telemetry_array; Karle Woodward and Richard Noble, *Over-winter movements of adult largemouth bass in a North Carolina reservoir*, Proc. Annu. Conf. Southeast Assoc. Fish and Wildl. Agencies 51:113-122 (1997); Tyler Peat et al., *Comparative thermal biology and depth distribution of largemouth bass and northern pike in an urban harbour of the Laurentian Great Lakes*, Canadian J. Zoology 94: 767–776 (2016); K.C. Hanson, et al., *Intersexual variation, supra* note 1386; Jason Harris, *supra* note 1385.

[1403] K.C. Hanson, et al., *Intersexual variation, supra* note 1386; BassFishingAndCatching.com, *What are largemouth bass fishing patterns?*, available at https://www.bassfishingandcatching.com/bass-fishing-patterns.html.

[1404] K.C. Hanson, et al., *Intersexual variation, supra* note 1386.

during winter.[1405] "Deep" is relative to typical depths in the specific fishery. In Toledo Bend, researchers found that telemetry tracked bass averaged 17 feet in depth during winter.[1406] In some fairly deep lakes that I usually fish, "deep" means 15 to 30 feet (not 60 feet), which is the depth some researchers have reported as well.[1407] In one shallow lake where I fish, the deepest parts are 15 feet deep, so in that lake "deep" means 10 to 15 feet. In some deeper lakes, bass will suspend during winter at these "deep" depths around vertical surfaces like "bluffs, deep creek channels, ditches and even standing submerged trees."[1408] In other lakes, bass are more likely to be on bottom in "deep" water for that lake. My home lakes do not have as much of the vertical cover, so I have had more success catching bass on bottom during winter.

Bass also tend to be further offshore during winter months. For example, researchers found that as water temperature decreased, the telemetry tracked bass moved farther offshore meaning they found a negative correlation (or inverse relationship) between water temperature and distance offshore.[1409] Around midday in one study the telemetered bass tended to be further offshore than in the mornings or afternoons—with them averaging 131 feet (40 m) offshore around midday compared to 82 feet (25 m) in the morning and 33 feet (10 m) in the evening.[1410] There are a few special situations that can create exceptions and opportunities for fishermen discussed below.

Activity Level: Bass are less active in cold winter water, swimming less and moving shorter distances at slower speeds.[1411] Generally, bass movement rates are positively correlated with water temperature so that as water temperature decreases, the rates and distances of movement by bass likewise decrease.[1412] Even though

---

[1405] BassFishingAndCatching.com, *supra* note 1403.
[1406] Ken Smith Fishing YouTube Channel, Part 5, *supra* note 1387.
[1407] BassFishingAndCatching.com, *supra* note 1403.
[1408] Id.
[1409] Karle Woodward and Richard Noble, *supra* note 1402.
[1410] Id.
[1411] K.C. Hanson, et al., *Intersexual variation*, *supra* note 1386; Ryan Hunter and Michael Maceina, *Movements and home ranges of largemouth bass and Alabama spotted bass in Lake Martin, Alabama*, J. FRESHWATER ECOLOGY 23(4): 599-606 (2008), available at https://doi.org/10.1080/02705060.2008.9664247.
[1412] Jason Harris, *supra* note 1385.

bass do not move as much in winter, largemouth bass are not sedentary or "dormant" in winter, as some authors suggest.[1413] Instead, bass stay in a more confined area during winter compared to other seasons, but they "still undertake significant localized movements, at times swimming at speeds up to 5 feet/second (1.6 m/s)."[1414] Specifically, in one study, telemetry-tracked bass moved an average of almost 1000 feet (298 meters) per week (i.e., over three football field lengths per week) during winter.[1415] However, they moved twice as far in spring, so their movement was diminished during winter compared to spring.[1416] In another study at a different lake, the bass moved less than one tenth as far on average in winter compared to spring and less than one sixth as far compared to fall.[1417]

Bass spend most of their time in the cold winter water swimming in place holding their position. Specifically, during winter over 95% of bass's time is spent holding position at swim speeds between 0 and 0.3 feet/second (0.1 m/s) according to one study.[1418] Holding position may be an energy conservation strategy (to prepare for the spawn or due to limited foraging opportunities), behavioral thermoregulation, or could be due to hypoxia in some locations.[1419]

Bass are less active during winter. In one study, researchers reported that activity level was 60% lower in winter than during summer months.[1420] Some biotelemetry studies show that "swimming activities increase in late winter, possibly suggesting acclimatization,"[1421] or possibly indicating pre-spawn activities like traveling to a spawning area.

The reason bass swim less and at slower speeds in winter is physiologic. Researchers note that low water temperature decreases the speed of muscle contractions by decreasing the efficiency of the underlying biochemical reactions causing the bass to have a lower

---

[1413] Caleb Hasler, et al., *Frequency, composition and stability of associations among individual largemouth bass at diel, daily and seasonal scales*, ECOLOGY OF FRESHWATER FISH 16: 417–424 (2007).
[1414] Kyle Hanson, et al., *Assessment of largemouth bass behavior*, supra note 1402.
[1415] Karle Woodward and Richard Noble, *supra* note 1402.
[1416] K.C. Hanson, et al., *Intersexual variation*, supra note 1386.
[1417] Kyle Hanson, et al., *Assessment of largemouth bass behavior*, supra note 1402.
[1418] Id.
[1419] Id.; K.C. Hanson, et al., *Intersexual variation*, supra note 1386.
[1420] K.C. Hanson, et al., *Intersexual variation*, supra note 1386.
[1421] Caleb Hasler, *Measuring the influence of winter conditions*, supra note 1389.

"tail beat frequency" and a lower "power output."[1422] In addition, low water temperature reduces bass's cardiac output "and may decrease the ability of a fish to uptake and transport oxygen."[1423] The net result is that bass swim slower and less in cold water.

Schooling/Aggregating Behavior: "Aggregations" are groups of fish that are not moving synchronously; if the fish are moving synchronously, the group is considered a "school."[1424] Individual pairings between fish within a few feet of each other for an hour or more are called "associations."[1425] Largemouth bass tend to form stable groups during winter "enter(ing) large aggregations and mak(ing) localized movements"—which can lead to occasional days with significant numbers of catches for fishermen.[1426] Winter aggregating behavior is described as "extremely prominent" for bass with the vast majority of bass (80% in one study) participating in aggregations with other bass during winter.[1427] Winter aggregations are much more stable than aggregations during the spring.[1428]

Largemouth bass were in associations with other bass for an average of over 9 hours each day averaging around 3 different bass per hour during winter.[1429] In other words, bass are social butterflies hanging around other bass most of the time and mingling with several bass in a group.[1430] Male-female associations occurred statistically more frequently than expected, and researchers speculated that these winter associations might be important during spring spawning season.[1431] Overall, winter associations were more stable (i.e., longer periods of time in association with other fish) but involved fewer other fish each day compared to spring associations.[1432]

Associations and aggregations of winter bass likely often occur out of necessity due to limited areas of optimum winter habitat with favorable food, water temperature, and oxygen content because

---

[1422] K.C. Hanson, et al., *Intersexual variation*, supra note 1386.
[1423] Id.
[1424] Caleb Hasler, et al., *Frequency, composition and stability*, supra note 1413.
[1425] Id.
[1426] Kyle Hanson, et al., *Assessment of largemouth bass behavior*, supra note 1402.
[1427] Caleb Hasler, et al., *Frequency, composition and stability*, supra note 1413.
[1428] Id.
[1429] Id.
[1430] Id.
[1431] Id.
[1432] Caleb Hasler, et al., *Frequency, composition and stability*, supra note 1413.

in one study fish tended to concentrate in limited areas so that 95% of associations were in only a "few, relatively small areas" in the lake studied.[1433] Thus, these associations may be driven by necessity and limited habitat because the associations become shorter and more transient when water quality improves in spring.[1434] During spring, "the lake has more available suitable habitat because the water is warmer, dissolved oxygen levels are 'normal,' and there is more area of the lake available for the fish to disperse to."[1435]

Special situations: Active winter bass may seek out specific areas like warming pockets, newly flooded trees and bushes, and areas with better oxygen content that can make them more catchable during winter.

a. *Warming Pockets:*

Warming pockets are areas of a fishery that accumulate and store heat so that the water is a few degrees higher in temperature, especially in late winter as spring approaches. Wind currents on warm days and unique lake features can create these pockets of warmer water that may be unique to the specific day, wind, or lake and can be transient, changing day to day.[1436] These areas can be especially productive for fishing. Bass in colder water often go to areas where warmer water is available, especially in early spring during the pre-spawn. A lake's characteristics and nuances can lead to the development of gathering points with warmer water for largemouth bass during these times. For example, "prey appear to concentrate in warm areas of Watts Bar Reservoir where inputs from springs or streams maintain these refuges 5-10°F (3-6°C) above main reservoir temperatures."[1437] Largemouth bass "take advantage of this concentration of prey by periodically feeding in these refuges during winter."[1438]

[1433] Id.
[1434] Id.
[1435] Id.
[1436] Caleb Hasler, *Measuring the influence of winter conditions*, supra note 1389.
[1437] S. Marshall Adams, et al., *supra* note 1390.
[1438] Id.

Sometimes a "warming pocket" can be 5-10°F warmer than another area based solely on its environmental characteristics.[1439] Finding these areas can be especially important during early spring for chasing pre-spawn lunkers. *Clues to their presence can be shallow water, protection from the north wind, unshaded, and presence of rocks or other heat storing structure.*[1440] Northern pockets on a body of water with high banks or a forest of trees blocking the wind are a good place to look for warmer water temperatures.[1441] If these areas are near deeper water, then they are more ideal because they allow the lunker bass to stay near deeper water.

b. *Newly Flooded Trees and Bushes:*

Sometimes bass are found surprisingly shallow in the middle of winter—at least in southern reservoirs. One time that this is especially true is during periods of high water when shoreline bushes and trees become newly flooded. One researcher noted that fish "inundate" flooded shorelines before December 1 or after January 20th in Florida in water temperatures as low as 43°F (6.2C); this researcher reported that almost 20 percent of their tracked fish went into these inundated areas during high water; however, between December 1 and January 20, they found that only 4.5% moved into the flooded shoreline.[1442] Bass can find cover important, even during cold winter water temperatures.

c. *Better Oxygenated Waters:*

Oxygen dissolved in the water is an important environmental factor for winter bass because it is important for bass's physiological processes since it is necessary in energy-producing pathways and aerobic metabolism required for the fish to survive.[1443] During winter, some lakes have areas with diminished oxygen content, which can severely limit the location and health of fish in the fishery. For example, some Florida lakes are completely oxygenated throughout

---

[1439] Jason Sealock, *How to target warming pockets for the best spring bass fishing*, Wired2Fish, April 10, 2019, available at https://www.wired2fish.com/spring-fishing-tips/how-to-target-warming-pockets-for-the-best-spring-bass-fishing/.
[1440] Id.
[1441] Id.
[1442] Karle Woodward and Richard Noble, *supra* note 1402.
[1443] Caleb Hasler, *Measuring the influence of winter conditions*, *supra* note 1389.

the water column during winter isothermy, while others are completely depleted of oxygen in deep waters.[1444]

Deoxygenation happens because the surface water's oxygenation is diminished by mixing of deeper water that has lost its oxygen due to accumulation of types of ions (reduced ions) in deeper layers (i.e., the hypolimnion) during summer that consume oxygen.[1445] Researchers tracked bass and compared their locations to "the distribution of dissolved oxygen throughout the lake at numerous times throughout the winter" in one study.[1446] Bass avoid habitat in fisheries with an "environmental oxygen level of approximately 2 mg/L of dissolved oxygen" or less.[1447]

In general, *areas of a fishery that have more wind or turbulence that can act to aerate the water are less likely to be depleted of oxygen.* Recent rain can also increase oxygen levels. Other factors like plant presence, water temperature, and water clarity can have varying effects on oxygenation depending upon the specifics. Multiple environmental factors influence winter behavior, so bass do not necessarily seek out the most optimally oxygenated waters, but they will avoid deoxygenated areas.[1448] Bass may be more oxygen sensitive during winter as well because low water temperatures reduce cardiac output "and may decrease the ability of a fish to uptake and transport oxygen."[1449] Oxygen level can be a particularly important issue for bass in lakes located at higher altitudes in winter.[1450] In northern lakes, hypoxia can especially be an issue due to "ice cover, low light intensity, reduction in photosynthetic biomass, benthic decomposition, and crowding of fish."[1451]

[1444] Jaime Escobar, et al., *supra* note 1400.
[1445] Id.
[1446] Caleb Hasler, *Measuring the influence of winter conditions*, *supra* note 1389.
[1447] Id.
[1448] Id.
[1449] K.C. Hanson, et al., *Intersexual variation*, *supra* note 1386.
[1450] Caleb Hasler, *Measuring the influence of winter conditions*, *supra* note 1389.
[1451] Id.

Spring (Water Temperatures 55 to 75°F)

Largemouth bass are generally the most catchable during the spring because they move shallow, are active, are in predictable places, and are eating before and after they spawn. The water temperature is favorable to bass activity in spring. See Chapter 4 for an in-depth discussion of the spawn. Manns caught the most bass per outing (4.66 per outing) in his 18-year study of 8900 catches when the water temperatures were from 69 to 78F, which correlates with late spring.[1452] He also recorded some of his highest numbers per outing (3.66 bass per outing) when water temperatures were from 59 to 68F, which correlates with early- to mid-spring as well.[1453]

Spring is the best time to catch a lunker bass in most fisheries. In my study (see Chapter 3), the months of March, April, and May accounted for 46% (976/2124) of the 8+ pound Texas ShareLunkers and also 46% (40/87) of the 13+ pound Texas ShareLunkers, which was the most of any season of the year. More specifically, March was the best month to catch a lunker bass by far (see Chapter 3). Because bass lose at least 10 percent of their body weight after spawning, there are statistically fewer lunkers to be caught after the spawn. In addition, the shallow location of bass during spring makes them more accessible to many fishermen.

[1452] Ralph Manns, *Moon Magic Largemouth Bass*, *supra* note 1388.
[1453] Id.

Temperature Stratification: Most largemouth bass fisheries in the southern U.S. are isothermal throughout the spring with the water temperature throughout the water column within a degree or two from a few feet below the surface to the bottom. In lakes that were frozen during the winter, the supercooled upper few feet mix with the deeper layers in spring when the ice thaws resulting in a "spring overturn," and those lakes become isothermal as well.[1454] The timing and duration of the spring overturn in these northern dimictic lakes depends on local weather conditions and can last for several weeks.[1455]

In late spring, the "first several feet of water (on the surface) begin to warm."[1456] This warm water layer floats temporarily on top of the cooler water below.[1457] The denser lower layers do not mix well with the less dense upper layer, so the lake becomes stratified horizontally at times during the spring.[1458] In some lakes, a relatively shallow and temporary thermocline can form—especially with sudden increases in air temperature over a short time. For example, see the thermocline forming at 9 feet deep (yellow arrows) in the image from my LiveScope below at Lake Atkins in Arkansas after the surface temperature was warmed by sudden warm weather raising the surface temperature from 62°F to 77°F in just two weeks in early May 2023.

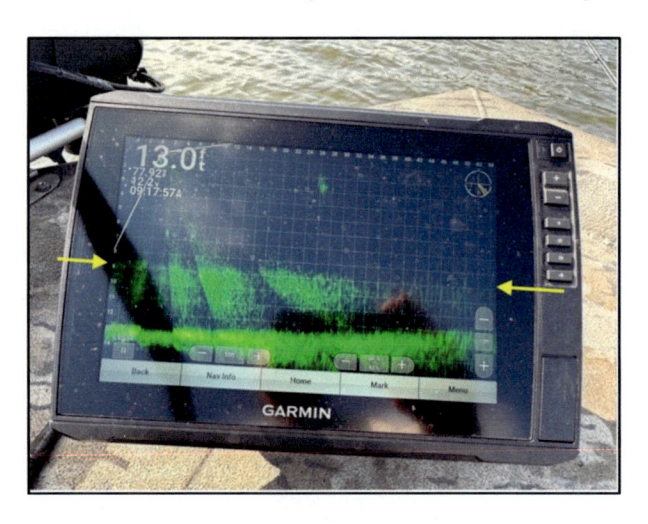

[1454] *About water temperatures, supra* note 1397; WaterCenter.org, *supra* note 1395.
[1455] WaterCenter.org, *supra* note 1395.
[1456] Todd Driscoll, *supra* note 1396.
[1457] Id.
[1458] WaterCenter.org, *supra* note 1395.

Wind and waves mix the two temporary layers efficiently in most lakes throughout spring because the temperature difference does not get substantial enough between the upper and lower layers to separate the layers; therefore, most lakes remain isothermal throughout the spring.[1459]

Depth and Location: In spring, large numbers of largemouth bass are closer to shore and shallower than other times of the year.[1460] Bass are typically less than 8 feet deep and within 65 feet of the shore during much of spring in many lakes.[1461] For example, 43% of tracked bass in Toledo Bend were on the shoreline (<30 ft. from shore) during spring.[1462] The average depth of tracked bass was 8 feet on Toledo Bend during the spring, which was the shallowest average of the year.[1463] Keep in mind that this is an average with many bass much shallower offsetting the bass that are staying out deep. Similarly, in another lake, most of the tagged bass migrated to the shallow section of the lake during spring.[1464]

In late spring, when the water reaches 70°F, the post-spawn roughly begins.[1465] Both male and female largemouth gradually resume feeding as they "slowly make their way out to deeper water (remember that "deep" is relative to other depths in the lake) where they will ultimately reside during the heat of summer."[1466] So, in late spring, the average depth inhabited by bass begins to increase.

Activity Level: Bass activity levels increase dramatically when water temperatures increase in spring. Activity levels have been positively correlated with feeding behaviors.[1467] During spring,

---

[1459] Todd Driscoll, *supra* note 1396; *About water temperatures*, *supra* note 1397; WaterCenter.org, *supra* note 1395.
[1460] Kyle Hanson, et al., *Assessment of largemouth bass behavior*, *supra* note 1402; K.C. Hanson, et al., *Intersexual variation*, *supra* note 1386.
[1461] Kyle Hanson, et al., *Assessment of largemouth bass behavior*, *supra* note 1402; Jason Harris, *supra* note 1385; K.C. Hanson, et al., *Intersexual variation*, *supra* note 1386.
[1462] Ken Smith Fishing YouTube Channel, Part 5, *supra* note 1387.
[1463] Id.
[1464] Caleb Hasler, et al., *Frequency, composition and stability*, *supra* note 1413.
[1465] BassFishingAndCatching.com, *supra* note 1403.
[1466] Id.
[1467] K.C. Hanson, et al., *Effects of lunar cycles on the activity patterns and depth use of a temperate sport fish, the largemouth bass*, FISHERIES MANAGEMENT AND

individual variations in activity level are at their highest with some bass being very active while others remain inactive. Specifically, some bass moved 25 times more in distance than other bass during one study of bass tracked during spring in April; notably by comparison the most active bass were only 3 times more active than the least in January.[1468]

The differences in home ranges discussed in Chapter 6 likely contribute to the individual movement differences with some bass staying within their home range to spawn, some traveling miles to a secondary home to spawn, and some simply roaming as nomads during the spawn. Also, once individual bass begin the spawning process, their overall movement distances drop significantly as males stay near and guard a specific nest for weeks.[1469] Spawning females also lurk in the area near nests with marked decreases in overall distances moved on a weekly basis.[1470] In one study, bass moved the least daily distances in February (the coldest month) and in April (corresponding to the spawn at that lake).[1471]

The studies can become somewhat confusing during spring. A study may say that bass move less making them seem less active during spring because the researchers measure the distance a bass moved over a week, for example, when they checked its location on one day and then rechecked it a week later finding it in the same location. However, during that week, that bass was likely very active during spring. Even though they are not traveling distances, males are very active throughout this time with one researcher estimating that males swim around the nest enough performing their duties to be the equivalent of 30 miles (49 km) per day, which is over 4 times more than females (7.5 miles; 12 km) during this time period.[1472]

Males' guarding activities make them vulnerable to being caught because they are very aggressive during this time. After the spawn, bass are more actively feeding and cruise for food more.

Ecology 15(5-6): 357-364, December 2008, available at https://onlinelibrary.wiley.com/doi/abs/10.1111/j.1365-2400.2008.00634.x.
[1468] Kyle Hanson, et al., *Assessment of largemouth bass behavior*, supra note 1402; K.C. Hanson, et al., *Intersexual variation*, supra note 1386.
[1469] K.C. Hanson, et al., *Intersexual variation*, supra note 1386; Caleb Hasler, et al., *Frequency, composition and stability*, supra note 1413.
[1470] Jason Harris, *supra* note 1385.
[1471] Id.
[1472] K.C. Hanson, et al., *Intersexual variation*, supra note 1386.

While some bass are spawning, others are either pre- or post-spawn. The same lake that had the lowest movement rates in April, recorded higher movement rates in March and May, and researchers observed that increased movement rates in March and May likely corresponded to the increase activities associated with pre- and post-spawn feeding.[1473] So, springtime is a smorgasbord of different bass activity levels. Remember the graph below from Chapter 4.

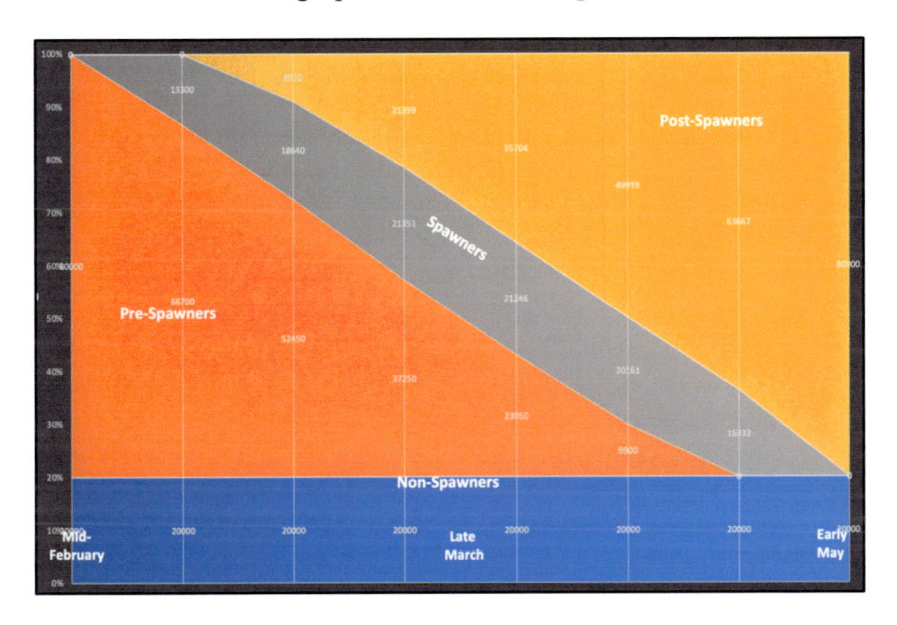

Not all bass are doing the same thing at the same time—so fishermen may catch individual bass at different phases of the spawn throughout spring.

Factors other than water temperature also affect bass activity level during spring. For example, before vegetation fully emerges, bass may need to be very active and move around a lot to find areas to feed, whereas once vegetation is fully grown in, activity levels may decline if the bass can stay in more localized areas while foraging for food.[1474]

Schooling/Aggregating Behavior: Bass continue to aggregate and associate with other bass in spring, but in different ways than in winter. Around 70% of bass associate with other bass during the

---

[1473] Jason Harris, *supra* note 1385.
[1474] Kyle Hanson, et al., *Assessment of largemouth bass behavior*, *supra* note 1402.

spring,[1475] but the associations are fewer, do not last as long (often lasting less than an hour, versus 6 hours in winter), and are more sporadic than in winter.[1476]

Special Situations: Spring is a time of great activity for bass and for their prey, so there are many opportunities to increase your odds of catching a lunker. Here, I will discuss just four: bedding bass, shad spawns, the bluegill spawn, and shell beds.

a. Bed Fishing: See Chapter 4.

b. Shad Spawns: See Chapter 10.

c. Bluegill Spawn: See Chapter 10.

d. Shell Beds:

Shell beds are an almost year-round great place to find fish. But they can be especially productive in spring and summer. A "shell bed" is an aggregation of freshwater mussels on the bottom of the fishery densely covering the area with either living mussels or their spent shells.

Shell beds are common and often unrecognized by fishermen who mistake shell beds for a rocky bottom when dragging baits over them.[1477] If you feel your football jig or Texas rigged worm clicking across the bottom of your lake or river on hard bottom, it might be on a shell bed. Sometimes shell beds are small. In some lakes, I have found shell beds as small as 6 feet by 6 feet where I have caught a lot of bass, but only if I put my bait in the specific 6 x 6 shell bed. I know it was a shell bed because I have caught some of the shells as shown in the examples below of shells caught on crankbaits dragging through hard bottomed areas:

[1475] Caleb Hasler, et al., *Frequency, composition and stability*, *supra* note 1413.
[1476] Id.
[1477] Garrett Hopper, et al., *Freshwater mussels alter fish distributions through habitat modifications at fine spatial scales*, FRESHWATER SCIENCE 38(4): December 2019, available at https://www.journals.uchicago.edu/doi/abs/10.1086/705666?af=R.

"Shell beds" are "dense, multi-species aggregations" of freshwater mussels that are 10 to 100 times denser in shells or living mussels than areas outside the beds.[1478] Beds can persist for years in a particular spot and can provide stable and healthy conditions for other organisms.[1479] Shell beds are a sign of bait and quality water to draw in largemouth bass.[1480] The presence of shell beds indicates quality water and fish habitat because "mussels are very sensitive to changes in their environment" and pollutants.[1481]

Freshwater mussels are important to aquatic ecosystems because they provide a vital link between the open water (pelagic zone) and the bottom (benthic zone) of the body of water.[1482] Live shell beds increase nutrients and other resources in the water column food web, which draws in the whole food chain—including

---

[1478] Id.
[1479] Id.
[1480] Marsha May, *Freshwater mussels play key role for bass*, TEXAS PARKS & WILDLIFE MAGAZINE, FISH & GAME, January/February 2022, available at https://tpwmagazine.com/archive/2022/jan/scout11d_r3/index.phtml.
[1481] Id.
[1482] Jeff Grabarkiewicz and Wayne Davis, *An introduction to freshwater mussels as biological indicators*, U.S. ENVIRONMENTAL PROTECTION AGENCY, EPA-260-R-08-15, November 2008, available at https://www.researchgate.net/publication/286418562_An_Introduction_to_Freshwater_Mussels_as_Biological_Indicators.

277

largemouth bass.[1483] Shell beds benefit other organisms by cleaning the water, by providing shelter, and by excreting important nutrients.[1484] Unionoids are burrowers, and the burrowing activity releases nutrients and oxygenating substrates into the water column.[1485] The spent shells of dead mussels and the shells of living mussels provide shelter from predators and increase the diversity of the bottom of the body of water.[1486] They act as habitat both for some fish and for their prey.[1487] Shells can house fish, crustaceans, mollusks, macroinvertebrates, and a variety of other creatures.[1488] Some larger aquatic predators like green sunfish have been noted to "wedge themselves horizontally" between shells "to avoid detection."[1489] Active sunfish nests are regularly observed within mussel beds.[1490]

Shell beds attract "benthic macroinvertebrates," which is a fancy term for bottom dwelling, very small animals that do not have backbones—including crayfish, snails, worms, mayfly larvae, aquatic insects, dragonflies, and damselflies, among others.[1491] Small bass, bream, bluegills, and other small fish eat benthic macroinvertebrates.[1492] Bigger bass feed on smaller fish, as well as crayfish, frogs, salamanders, and other organisms that are drawn to the area by the shell bed.[1493]

Freshwater mussels live nearly worldwide including all continents, except Antarctica.[1494] They are called bivalves because there are two sides to their shells.[1495] The vast majority of freshwater mussels in North America are in the family Unionidae.[1496] There are approximately 300 species in the United States with the highest

---

[1483] Garrett Hopper, et al., *supra* note 1477.
[1484] Id.
[1485] Jeff Grabarkiewicz and Wayne Davis, *supra* note 1482.
[1486] Garrett Hopper, et al., *supra* note 1477; Jeff Grabarkiewicz and Wayne Davis, *supra* note 1482.
[1487] Garrett Hopper, et al., *supra* note 1477.
[1488] Jeff Grabarkiewicz and Wayne Davis, *supra* note 1482.
[1489] Garrett Hopper, et al., *supra* note 1477.
[1490] Id.
[1491] Marsha May, *supra* note 1480.
[1492] Id.
[1493] Id.
[1494] Jeff Grabarkiewicz and Wayne Davis, *supra* note 1482.
[1495] Id.
[1496] Id.

number and diversity of species occurring in the Southeastern United States. Alabama, for example, is home to 175 different species, while Tennessee has 131 and Georgia has 99. For comparison, Texas has 53,[1497] New York has 30, Minnesota 44, Washington state 5, California 4, and Arizona 1.[1498]

Freshwater mussels, also called pearly mussels, naiads, or clams, have a unique and interesting life cycle that includes a parasitic larval stage requiring a fish host.[1499] When fully grown, mussels can measure from less than an inch up to 12 inches in length and live more than 50 to 100 years in some conditions, although some species with thin shells live only 5 or 6 years.[1500] The color, shape, size, and texture of their shells varies by species. Shell beds typically are made up of several different types of species in the same shell bed.[1501] Animals like racoons, muskrats, birds, fishes, and otters feed on mussels and may toss their spent shells along the shores or in the water.[1502] Mussels spend most of their lives buried in the sediments on the bottom as sedentary suspension feeders.[1503]

During the 1800s, freshwater mussels were harvested to make pearl buttons from their shells and by people pursuing fortune through freshwater pearls, which led to some areas of overharvest.[1504] Commercial musselers may still collect freshwater mussels in the cultured pearl industry.[1505] Cultured pearls are made by "taking a round core from the shell of some of our larger species of freshwater mussels and inserting that core into a clam" to make a "freshwater pearl."[1506] Some freshwater pearls are also made by a few species

---

[1497] Marsha May, *supra* note 1480.
[1498] Jeff Grabarkiewicz and Wayne Davis, *supra* note 1482 (see Figure 1).
[1499] Id.
[1500] Id.; TEXAS PARKS AND WILDLIFE DEPARTMENT, *Texas mussel watch: Texas freshwater mussel biology*, Wildlife Diversity Program, available at https://tpwd.texas.gov/huntwild/wild/wildlife_diversity/texas_nature_trackers/mussel/biology/.
[1501] TEXAS PARKS AND WILDLIFE DEPARTMENT, *Texas mussel watch*, *supra* note 1500.
[1502] Jeff Grabarkiewicz and Wayne Davis, *supra* note 1482.
[1503] Id.
[1504] Id.
[1505] TEXAS PARKS AND WILDLIFE DEPARTMENT, *Texas mussel watch*, *supra* note 1500.
[1506] Id.

such as the Tampico pearly mussel which produces the rare Concho River Pearl.[1507]

Freshwater mussels have been described as "the vacuum cleaners of the aquatic ecosystem" and "feed by filtering algae and small particles from the water."[1508] They "feed by filtering microscopic organisms and debris out of the water, cleaning streams in the process."[1509] Their huge gills allow them to filter water constantly.[1510] Researchers estimate that one mussel can clean 10 to 20 gallons of water every day and can remove harmful algae, bacteria, and metals from the water.[1511] In one study, researchers found that freshwater mussels filtered about 14 billion gallons of water a day on one 298 mile stretch of the Mississippi River.[1512] This is more than many large wastewater treatment plants can filter. Healthy populations of freshwater mussels lead to more pure water for humans and many plants and animals.[1513] Because they are sensitive, they are often the first living species to disappear if environmental conditions change or worsen, so they can be good indicators of the quality of the environment in some bodies of water.[1514]

As filter feeders, mussels stimulate primary and secondary production by excreting nitrogen and by biodeposition of other materials—feces and pseudofeces.[1515] They remove materials from the water like bacteria, phytoplankton, organic matter, and sediment via a siphoning mechanism.[1516] Filtering rate depends on the species, temperature, particle concentration, flow regime, and mussel size.[1517]

Freshwater mussels' reproductive cycle is unique and may involve largemouth bass as a host fish. Reproduction is initiated with "an upstream male releases sperm into the water column and a

---

[1507] Id.
[1508] Id.
[1509] Benji Jones, *The strange, savage life of a freshwater mussel*, October 27, 2022, available at https://www.vox.com/down-to-earth/2022/10/27/23424362/freshwater-mussels-fish-lure-extinction.
[1510] Id.
[1511] Id.
[1512] Id.
[1513] TEXAS PARKS AND WILDLIFE DEPARTMENT, *Texas mussel watch*, *supra* note 1500.
[1514] Id.
[1515] Garrett Hopper, et al., *supra* note 1477.
[1516] Jeff Grabarkiewicz and Wayne Davis, *supra* note 1482.
[1517] Id.

downstream female collects it via the incurrent aperture."[1518] Fertilization occurs internally, and the embryo develops within gill pouches (marsupia).[1519] Larvae called "glochidia" are brooded several months by the female.[1520] Eventually larvae are released by the female mussel and must find a suitable host, usually a specific fish species, or die.[1521] Once released, the larvae are obligate parasites that must find a suitable host (a fish) to survive.[1522] They attach to the fish's gills or fins and hang on for a few weeks or months.[1523] This process rarely harms the host fish.[1524] Some mussel species can use many different fish species as hosts, but others require specific species of fish as suitable hosts.[1525] Larvae attach to fish's fins, skin or gills and feed on host tissue as they develop.[1526] Eventually, the larvae "excyst and drop off" as juveniles falling back to the bottom.[1527]

Fish are attracted to shell beds, and shell beds need fish to survive—so the two are closely linked. Mussels depend on fish hosts for their larvae, so mussels are "only abundant and diverse where fish are abundant and diverse."[1528] The increased density of benthic macroinvertebrates and higher water quality around shell beds is key to attracting fish.[1529] In one study on the Kiamichi River in southeast Oklahoma, researchers using remote underwater recordings found more fish in areas with live mussel beds and with fake mussel beds ("sham treatments") than in areas with only sediment on bottom.[1530] This led these researchers to conclude that "habitat provided by mussel shells may be the primary benefit to fishes that occur with

---

[1518] Id.
[1519] Id.
[1520] Id.
[1521] TEXAS PARKS AND WILDLIFE DEPARTMENT, *Texas mussel watch, supra* note 1500.
[1522] Jeff Grabarkiewicz and Wayne Davis, *supra* note 1482.
[1523] TEXAS PARKS AND WILDLIFE DEPARTMENT, *Texas mussel watch, supra* note 1500.
[1524] Id.
[1525] Jeff Grabarkiewicz and Wayne Davis, *supra* note 1482.
[1526] Id.
[1527] Id.; TEXAS PARKS AND WILDLIFE DEPARTMENT, *Texas mussel watch, supra* note 1500.
[1528] Garrett Hopper, et al., *supra* note 1477.
[1529] Id.
[1530] Id.

mussels."[1531] In other words, the spent shells provide homes for things that fish like to eat—like crayfish and other benthic macroinvertebrates. Other studies have also found that mussel beds increase algae and invertebrates near them, which helps attract the food chain as well.[1532] In lakes, where there is less water flow than rivers, this effect may be especially important.[1533]

The invasive zebra mussel is an example of mussel filtration working too well and damaging the environment.[1534] When zebra mussels invaded Lake Erie in the 1980s, they proliferated until there were thousands per square foot in some areas of the lake.[1535] Researchers estimate that the zebra mussel population "can filter the entire volume" of Lake Erie "in less than a month and have made its water 600 percent clearer," which is not good for many of Lake Erie's native animals and fishes.[1536] The zebra mussels are filtering so much plankton that other organisms in the food chain do not have enough left to survive.[1537]

Below is a picture of a beer can I caught on a plastic worm at O.H. Ivie that is covered and filled with zebra mussels:

[1531] Id.
[1532] Id.
[1533] Garrett Hopper, et al., *supra* note 1477.
[1534] Benji Jones, *supra* note 1509.
[1535] Id.
[1536] Id.
[1537] Id.

The beer can ate a redbug-colored 12-inch plastic worm and put up a decent fight . . . in case you want to fish for beer cans. ☺ Notice the intact zebra mussels on the inside of the can.

Summer (Water Temperatures >80°F)

Lunker Statistics: By summer, largemouth bass have been through a spawning season that places major stressors on both sexes and leads to loss of at least 10 percent of total body weight.[1538] In my opinion, based on some summertime catches, I think the weight loss is significantly higher for many bass. So, there are less lunkers around during summertime than during spring. The number of 13+ pound ShareLunkers dropped off dramatically during the summer (June, July, and August) in my study in Chapter 3 accounting for only 4.6% (4/87) of the 13+ pound ShareLunkers from 2018-2022. In contrast, the number of 8+ pound ShareLunkers reported during summer months from 2018 through 2022 (See Chapter 3) remained fairly high accounting for 20.1% (427/2124), but still below the overall average for a 3-month period. The number of 8+ pounders dropped off from

---

[1538] James Davis and Joe Lock, *Largemouth bass biology and life history*, Southern Regional Aquacultural Center SRAC Publication No. 200, August 1997.

month to month as the summer progressed from 196 in June, to 133 in July, to only 98 in August out of 2124 caught throughout the five years in the study. Fishing effort may drop off to account for some of this drop as the air temperatures can get dangerously high in late summer in Texas leading more anglers to stay home or fish only in early morning or at dusk.

Interestingly, the 13+ pound statistics follow the idea that the bass reach their lowest weights in the summer months before beginning to put weight back on in the fall. In contrast, the 8+ pound bass remained more catchable than average through June. This might be because 8+ pound bass in Texas can find more contemporaries to form schools and wolfpacks with which to improve their hunting proficiency thru the summer—especially chasing shad in the pelagic zone of the lake, whereas the 13+ pounders simply have less colleagues with which to school and so are less efficient at maintaining their body weights through the summer. Perhaps the 13+ pounders are better able to hunt in the colder water in winter when their prey may be more affected by the cold temperatures than the larger/more insulated giant 13+ pounders.

Temperature Stratification: Lakes are most stratified by temperature during summer.[1539] During summer stratification, lakes develop a temperature barrier called the *thermocline* where the water temperature drops in a pronounced way over just a few feet of depth separating a deep cold layer without much oxygen from a warmer upper layer that is well oxygenated.[1540]

Thermal stratification occurs because "the density of water varies inversely with temperature."[1541] In other words, water at low temperature (i.e., cold water) is denser than water at high temperature (i.e., warm water).[1542] As the water gets colder, it gets denser, causing the cold water to sink to the bottom and the warm water to remain near the surface.[1543]

Sunlight heats the surface water layers much more than the deeper layers because water is a poor conductor of heat and requires a lot of energy to raise its temperature.[1544] In fact, only a little bit of

---

[1539] WaterCenter.org, *supra* note 1395.
[1540] Todd Driscoll, *supra* note 1396.
[1541] WaterCenter.org, *supra* note 1395.
[1542] *About water temperatures*, *supra* note 1397.
[1543] Id.
[1544] Id.

sunlight reaches the deeper levels enough to heat up the water at all.[1545] By the time 7 feet (2 m) of depth is reached, 98 percent of the energy from sunlight has been absorbed and converted to heat.[1546] So, instead of via sunlight, heat reaches the lower levels of lakes, ponds and rivers due to circulation of the water by wind and current causing the top layer to mix with the lower layers.[1547]

The summer sun and heat warm the surface layer so fast that the deeper water remains significantly colder and denser than the surface water.[1548] When the temperature difference between the upper layer and the lower layer gets large enough, the two layers stop mixing efficiently and the cold water stays on bottom while the upper layer continues to mix and circulate above it. A transition zone develops between the warm upper layer and the cold lower layer known as the thermocline.[1549] The thermocline is a layer that is usually only a few feet across where the water temperature changes rapidly with small increases in depth.[1550]

So, by mid-June in many lakes in the southern United States, the fishery is stratified into three layers: (1) an upper isothermal layer (i.e., same warmer temperature throughout the layer) known as the *epilimnion* consisting of warm well-mixed surface water that is less dense than the deeper layer,[1551] (2) the *thermocline* layer, which is a temperature transition zone and a strong water density/temperature barrier layer that is only a few feet in width where the temperature drops dramatically from the warm upper layer to the cold deep layer and acts as a wall between the layers,[1552] and (3) the deep isothermal layer (i.e., same colder temperature throughout the layer) called the *hypolimnion* consisting of cold dense water that is relatively undisturbed because it is not mixing with the upper layers (which are in contact with air and oxygen) and thus, has little to no oxygen.[1553]

[1545] Id.
[1546] Id.
[1547] *About water temperatures, supra* note 1397.
[1548] Todd Driscoll, *supra* note 1396; WaterCenter.org, *supra* note 1395; *About water temperatures, supra* note 1397.
[1549] *About water temperatures, supra* note 1397.
[1550] Id.
[1551] WaterCenter.org, *supra* note 1395.
[1552] Todd Driscoll, *supra* note 1396; WaterCenter.org, *supra* note 1395; *About water temperatures, supra* note 1397.
[1553] Todd Driscoll, *supra* note 1396; WaterCenter.org, *supra* note 1395.

Once a thermocline is established, "almost no exchange of water . . . takes place" between the layers.[1554] In the thermocline, which can be a few feet in width, the water temperature decreases from 0.5 to 6°F per foot of depth change.[1555] Above the thermocline, the temperature in the epilimnion (upper layer) is "nearly uniform" throughout due to the mixing of the waters in this layer by forces like wind, waves, rain, inflows from feeder creeks, etc.[1556] Below the thermocline, the water temperature is also isothermal (i.e., the same throughout) but at a significantly colder temperature than the water above the thermocline. Hydrogen sulfide gas can collect in the lower layer (hypolimnion) due to anoxia since the lower layer has no contact with air, so discharge from deep water lakes may smell like rotten eggs if it is coming from the lower layer.[1557] The lower layer is uninhabitable for largemouth bass in many lakes.[1558] The drawing below shows the layers, as well as some sources of oxygenation, mixing, and heat for the upper layer:

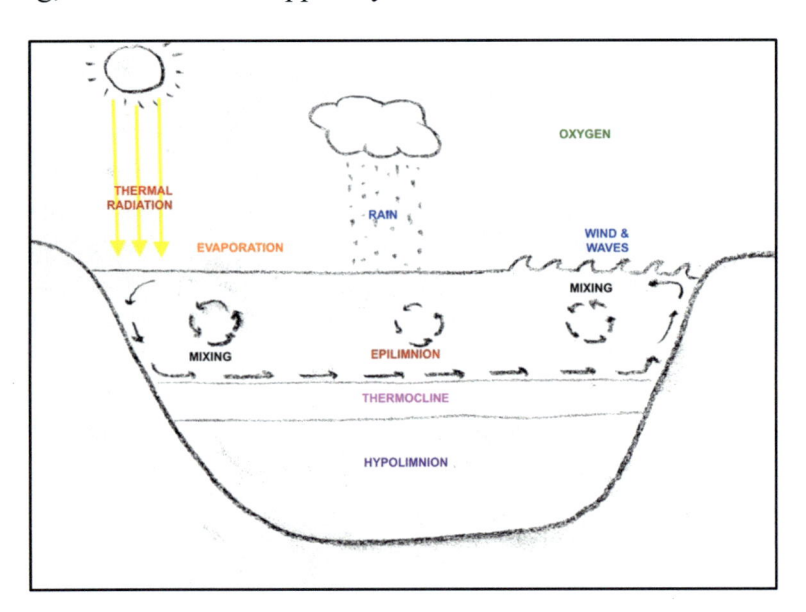

[1554] *About water temperatures, supra* note 1397.
[1555] WaterCenter.org, *supra* note 1395; Donald Leifeste and Barney Popkin, *supra* note 1399.
[1556] WaterCenter.org, *supra* note 1395.
[1557] Todd Driscoll, *supra* note 1396.
[1558] Id.

For example, in one Texas lake (Possum Kingdom), the upper layer (i.e., epilimnion) was uniformly 80°F from 3 feet to 20 feet and the lower layer starting around 25 feet and below was 53-56°F on one summer day.[1559] In between, the thermocline (depending upon the site measured) was around a five feet deep area (starting around 20 feet deep and ending around 25 feet deep) between the upper and lower layers with an almost 30 degree drop from upper to lower layers in temperature on that same day.[1560] Note that the uppermost 3 feet or so (and similar depth shallow water areas) of surface water can vary somewhat from the overall temperature of the epilimnion based upon sudden changes in air temperature. So, *the temperature sensor mounted on the bottom of your boat or on your trolling motor may not be quite deep enough to reflect the true temperature of the upper layer (epilimnion) in some instances.*

The thermocline is an important layer to recognize during the summer because it is often at a level where baitfish and bass will hold because it is the deepest layer above the anoxic deep cold layer. It is basically the "bottom" of the habitable part of the lake during summer in some lakes. Therefore, *it is important to fish above the thermocline during the summertime in many lakes*. Late in the summer (e.g., in August in the South) and on early summer mornings, bass may have a tendency to "feed up" instead of "feeding down" in some lakes—so don't forget to try the topwater bite during these times. Dragging a bait on bottom below the thermocline is unlikely to be as productive, even though fish occasionally will temporarily go down to pick up a bait off the bottom below the thermocline. However, dragging a bait at or just above the thermocline can be especially productive.

Thermocline timing, location, and development differs between bodies of water because many factors influence heat distribution in the water column including "air temperature, rainfall, cloudiness, wind, basin morphometry (e.g., depth, fetch), hydrologic residence time, and water clarity (i.e. concentrations of dissolved and particulate substances)."[1561] The thermocline usually forms around early to mid-summer "and is prevalent when the water is at its absolute hottest" with the spiking temperatures helping to create the

---

[1559] Donald Leifeste and Barney Popkin, *supra* note 1399.
[1560] Id.
[1561] Jaime Escobar, et al., *supra* note 1400.

thermocline.[1562] Air temperature and wind speed are important factors in determining a lake's thermal stratification timing and depth specifics. Wind speed is a huge factor more important than air temperature in determining a lake's thermal stratification in some lakes.[1563] Bigger lakes with larger surface areas usually have more surface momentum from wind resulting in greater mixing of the water layers, so they tend to have more variability in water temperature and in stratification patterns than smaller lakes with variability increasing the most in lakes with the greatest wind speeds.[1564]

In one study, lakes with lower wind speeds had higher temperatures in the upper layer (epilimnion) and more pronounced stratification (i.e., bigger temperature differences between the upper and lower layers) than lakes with higher wind speeds.[1565] Similarly, in another study, lakes with lower wind speeds had longer periods of stratification than lakes with higher wind speeds.[1566] Morphological factors of the lake also play a role in determining stratification specifics (including depth, duration, and timing) including factors like mean depth, total surface area, and overall volume because all of these factors play a role in how efficiently the lake water layers can mix.[1567]

The thermocline generally becomes deeper as the summer progresses and the sun effectively warms even deeper areas of the water column. During the earliest parts of the summer, the thermocline is relatively close to the water's surface[1568]; I remember feeling my upper body warm and my feet cold and below the thermocline while swimming in Greers Ferry Lake in central Arkansas sometimes in the early summer as a teenager. As summer progresses, the thermocline gets deeper—so the epilimnion increases in size and the hypolimnion decreases in size.[1569] For example, one

---

[1562] BassBlog Staff, *What is a thermocline, and how does it affect bass?*, August 12, 2022, available at https://www.bassblog.org/thermocline-affect-bass/.

[1563] Madeline Magee and Chin Wu, *Response of water temperatures and stratification to changing climate in three lakes with different morphology*, HYDROL. EARTH SYST. SCI., 21, 6253–6274, 2017, available at www.hydrol-earth-syst-sci.net/21/6253/2017/.

[1564] Id.
[1565] Id.
[1566] Id.
[1567] Id.
[1568] WaterCenter.org, *supra* note 1395.
[1569] Id.

biologist reported that the thermocline typically starts at around 25 feet at Sam Rayburn and Toledo Bend reservoirs in early summer and increases in depth to around 40 feet at mid-summer.[1570] The epilimnion is fairly constant in temperature and the hypolimnion also remains fairly uniform throughout although it will decline as it approaches the bottom (in northern lakes, to 4°C).[1571] In one lake that I fish regularly, the thermocline starts at around 20 feet in mid-June and gradually migrates to around 27 feet by the end of summer. Another lake I fish regularly is only around 15 feet deep over all but a very small area, and I usually do not detect a thermocline in that lake (except possibly over a very small area of a few acres that is around 25 feet deep).

Thermal stratification of lakes can lead to major differences in oxygen content by depth. In one study, water temperature and oxygen profiles on four relatively deep (17-24 m) Florida lakes were measured.[1572] All were "strongly stratified thermally in summer and weakly stratified or isothermal during winter."[1573]

Depth and Location: Summer bass location and depth depends upon the nature of the fishery. More bass tend to migrate into deeper water in summer than most of the rest of the year. During the early summer, a lot of bass will be scattered and suspended in deep water when they first reach their summer haunts.[1574] For example, in one study at Table Rock Lake, largemouth bass "occupied locations with deeper water during daylight hours throughout the summer months" at water depths of 13-23 feet (4-7 m) within 80 feet (<25 m) of shore often associated with structure like wood or docks.[1575] Bass move deeper during summer partially because the shallow water areas warm up too much during the heat of the day, so bass as ectotherms move out in schools around "deep structure like rock piles, humps and saddles."[1576] The hot, shallow water also has less oxygen content than the deeper water during the hot summer

---

[1570] Todd Driscoll, *supra* note 1396.
[1571] WaterCenter.org, *supra* note 1395.
[1572] Jaime Escobar, et al., *supra* note 1400.
[1573] Id.
[1574] BassFishingAndCatching.com, *supra* note 1403.
[1575] Jason Harris, *supra* note 1385.
[1576] BassFishingAndCatching.com, *supra* note 1403.

days.[1577] "Deep" typically means around the depth of the thermocline in many lakes.

    Bass also go deeper in summer because the water is "more stable" with regard to temperature and oxygen levels.[1578] Shad likewise go deeper, and the bass will follow them as well.[1579] The depth selected depends on the lake and the thermocline.[1580] Generally, the "larger, older bass haunt the depths of reservoirs in summer, really year-round."[1581]

    Some bass are still shallow, especially at certain times, throughout summer. At night, early morning, dusk, and during cooler spells in summer when the shallow water areas have an opportunity to cool many bass will move into shallow water to feed.[1582] Some bass stay shallow during the day by finding shaded areas where the water temperature does not get as hot. In some northern "natural lakes," however, "largemouth don't find it necessary to retreat to deep water as they do farther south in deeper reservoirs."[1583] In these natural lakes, an "abundance of aquatic vegetation [and relatively milder temperatures] provides ample oxygen in shallow areas of natural lakes throughout the summer."[1584] Even in southern reservoirs like Lake Fork, there will be a population of bass that remain shallow all summer according to one of my Lake Fork guide professors who has fished the lake with much success since it opened.

    In addition to these large moves related to seasonal changes in temperature and daylight hours, bass make other less predictable and shorter (both in time and distance) moves intermittently throughout the day that center on finding food and better water with more oxygen and better temperature.[1585] These types of moves tend to occur along "old road beds, tree lines or twisting, turning river channels."[1586] Checking these routes intermittently on hot summer days can lead to

---

[1577] Id.
[1578] David Hart, *How seasons and temperature affect bass*, BASSMASTER, April 2, 2018, available at https://www.bassmaster.com/how-to/news/how-seasons-and-temperature-affect-bass/.
[1579] Id.
[1580] Id.
[1581] BassFishingAndCatching.com, *supra* note 1403.
[1582] Id.
[1583] Id.
[1584] Id.
[1585] Id.
[1586] BassFishingAndCatching.com, *supra* note 1403.

schools of bass moving on short feeding excursions and be very productive.[1587] Because these are transient movements, the productivity typically doesn't last for more than a couple of hours.[1588]

Activity Level: Bass tend to be more active in the warm water of summer, swim faster, and swim farther each day than the rest of the year.[1589] For example, one study found that "daily distance traveled . . . was highest . . . during . . . the warmest months."[1590] In Table Rock Lake, for example, movement rates were highest among 70 radio-tagged largemouth bass during the daytime hours of June and July when they averaged 91 yards per hour (83.5 m/h)—that's almost the length of a football field every hour.[1591] As with all of these studies, there is much individual variation among bass, however, with one bass moving 713 yards per hour (652 m/h) while another one did not move at all.[1592] Movement rates vary considerably between different bodies of water with the bass in Table Rock Lake moving twice as much as those in a Georgia reservoir in a different study.[1593] Exceptions occur around areas of dense vegetation that attract adequate prey species, so that some bass may simply lurk in the vegetation in these places where prey density is adequate to support their nutritional needs.[1594]

Special Situations:

a. *The Thermocline:*

Gizzard shad and other bait fish tend to stay in areas where the thermocline meets low light structure like humps and ledges during summer months.[1595] Bait and sport fish suspend and "relate to the thermocline during summer" because this is often the deepest depth with adequate oxygenation.[1596] On your electronics, the density

---

[1587] Id.
[1588] Id.
[1589] Jason Harris, *supra* note 1385.
[1590] K.C. Hanson, et al., *Intersexual variation*, *supra* note 1386.
[1591] Jason Harris, *supra* note 1385.
[1592] Id.
[1593] Id.
[1594] Kyle Hanson, et al., *Assessment of largemouth bass behavior*, *supra* note 1402.
[1595] Peter Mathiesen, *Understanding bass forage: shad*, BASSMASTER, December 17, 2019, available at https://www.bassmaster.com/how-to/news/understanding-bass-forage-shad/.
[1596] Todd Driscoll, *supra* note 1396.

changes at the thermocline may make it "show up as a straight line of increased clutter"; you may have to increase some of the sonar sensitivity settings (e.g., the "gain") to see the thermocline on your graphs.[1597] Earlier in this chapter, I included an image showing an early season thermocline on my Garmin Livescope. The thermocline can usually be seen on downscan sonar.[1598] In the image below from my Lowrance 2D downscan sonar, there is a layer of bait fish suspended on the thermocline marked by the yellow arrows at around 27 feet deep:

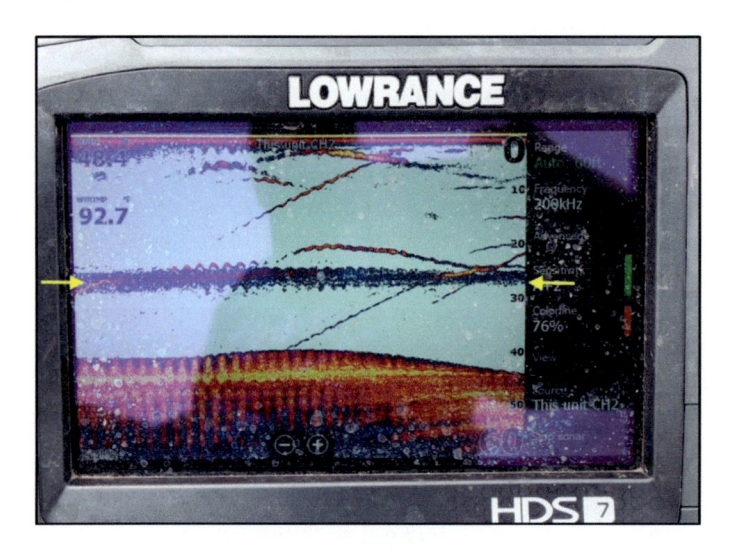

Once I locate the thermocline on a graph like the one above or on my LiveScope, I look for humps and ledges near or slightly above the thermocline depth on a topo map of the lake. Bass will generally "set up on structure [like ledges and humps] that is . . . whatever depth the thermocline is present at."[1599] Below is an image from my 2D downscan sonar unit showing a group of fish moving onto a ledge and feeding:

[1597] Id.
[1598] BassBlog Staff, *supra* note 1562.
[1599] Id.

292

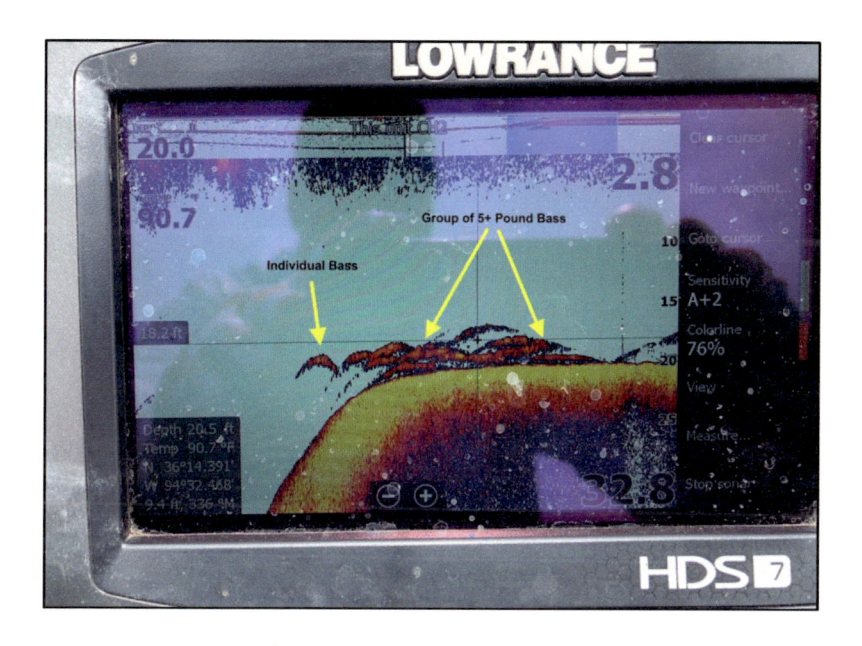

I caught several bass over 5 pounds out of this group of bass on this ledge situated just above the thermocline (which was around 23 feet at that time and visible in other areas of the lake). I found the fish in the images above because I located the thermocline depth in the middle of the lake and then searched ledges and humps that projected up into the thermocline or slightly above with deep water nearby (where the bass will suspend or chase shad in the pelagic areas). One biologist said, "This bass fishing pattern finds the big girls and guys hanging on humps, rock piles and long deep points."[1600]

     In some reservoirs bass and baitfish suspend at the thermocline. In others, like Rayburn and Toledo Bend, oxygen levels "fall to stressful levels below depths of 25 feet," even though the thermocline may be at 40 feet.[1601] Therefore, baitfish and bass "will typically suspend at the lowest depth of adequate oxygen instead of the thermocline (typically 20-30 feet at Sam Rayburn and Toledo Bend)."[1602] So, "finding structure and cover at 20-30 feet will maximize catch rates when fishing deep during summer."[1603]

[1600] BassFishingAndCatching.com, *supra* note 1403.
[1601] Todd Driscoll, *supra* note 1396.
[1602] Id.
[1603] Id.

b. *Open Water:*

During the early summer, bass are scattered and suspended in deep water when they first reach their summer haunts.[1604] Eventually, however, they will "school to chase baitfish."[1605] Largemouth bass "venturing farther from the shore may indicate a shift in prey preference from littoral species (e.g., sunfish) in spring and early summer to pelagic prey (e.g., gizzard shad) during mid-summer."[1606] Gizzard shad prefer quieter areas above the thermocline in open waters (i.e., the pelagic zone).[1607] Depth depends upon the specific lake characteristics like clarity, turbidity, and presence of plankton and algae.[1608] Gizzard shad move deep enough to "stay out of the direct sunlight, yet the water must have enough light to produce algae and plankton."[1609] Remember that threadfin shad prefer water with noticeable current in the upper five feet of the water column with the current often created by wind.[1610]

[1604] BassFishingAndCatching.com, *supra* note 1403.
[1605] Id.
[1606] Jason Harris, *supra* note 1385.
[1607] U.S. Geological Survey, *Fact sheet: Dorosoma cepedianum (Gizzard shad)*, available at https://nas.er.usgs.gov/queries/FactSheet.aspx?speciesID=492.
[1608] Peter Mathiesen, *Understanding bass forage: shad*, *supra* note 1595.
[1609] Id.
[1610] TEXAS PARKS AND WILDLIFE DEPARTMENT, *Threadfin Shad (Dorosoma petenense)*, available at https://tpwd.texas.gov/huntwild/wild/species/threadfinshad/.

In one study, 34% of the bass were suspended in open water during the summer.[1611] These bass are often actively chasing shad in schools and wolf packs and can result in a big bag of bass very quickly if you find the right wolf pack. On a recent trip to Lake O.H. Ivie in Texas, I chased a wolf pack of 4 double digit bass for 20 minutes in water that was 25 feet deep as they chased a group of baitfish throughout the water column, but I could not get any of the 4 to commit to several different lure presentations after one quickly "bumped" my first offering. Remember that unless there is a hump or a ledge or something, you are most likely to find these open water bass still within a few hundred feet of shore. I found these in the middle of the lake over a hump with deeper water nearby.

  c. *Shell beds: See Spring section above in this chapter.*

  d. *Bream beds/Bluegill spawn: See Chapter 10.*

Fall (Water Temperature 75°F to 55°F)

Lunker Statistics: Fall is the season when the least lunker bass were reported in my ShareLunker studies in Chapter 3 with September, October, and November combined accounting for only 11.9% (253/2124) of 8+ pounders and only 8% (7/87) of 13+ pounders. It is possible that fall produces fewer lunkers due to

---

[1611] Ken Smith Fishing YouTube Channel, Part 5, *supra* note 1387.

decreased fishing effort as many fishermen become hunters during the fall.

Lake Stratification: In fall, solar radiation and air temperatures begin to decrease, but the water temperatures take longer to drop because water has great capacity to store the heat energy from the summer, and that energy dissipates slowly.[1612] This means that water temperatures do not begin to fall dramatically until late fall.[1613] In fall, "water temperatures at the surface begin to cool and due to increasing density, the cooler water sinks."[1614] Wave and wind action "assists with distributing the cooler water throughout the upper layer."[1615] When water temperatures in the upper layer (epilimnion) decrease in late fall (increasing the water's density in the upper layer) and approach the temperature of the lower layer, the thermocline breaks down and the two layers intermix.[1616] When the upper and lower layers reach the same temperature, the entire water column mixes, which is called the "fall turnover."[1617] The fall turnover can happen quickly with "an entire reservoir turning over in less than a week during windy conditions."[1618] The fall turnover is usually in October at Rayburn and Toledo Bend, for example.[1619] During this time, debris from the lower layer (hypolimnion) may surface. Fish kills can occur due to the poor water quality in the lower layer mixing with the upper layer causing "pockets of anoxic water."[1620] Fishing is often less productive during the turnover.[1621]

Eventually, lakes become isothermal again in late fall when the temperature and density of the water becomes the same again at all depths.[1622] For example, Possum Kingdom temperatures were 66.5°F at the surface and 65°F at 90 feet deep by one day in November in one study.[1623] The fall turnover is basically a remixing of the epilimnion, thermocline, and hypolimnion layers into a single

---

[1612] *About water temperatures*, *supra* note 1397.
[1613] Id.
[1614] Todd Driscoll, *supra* note 1396.
[1615] Id.
[1616] *About water temperatures*, *supra* note 1397.
[1617] Todd Driscoll, *supra* note 1396.
[1618] Id.
[1619] Id.
[1620] Id.
[1621] Id.
[1622] WaterCenter.org, *supra* note 1395.
[1623] Donald Leifeste and Barney Popkin, *supra* note 1399.

well mixed water column again. This mixing allows oxygen and nutrients from the surface layers to reach the depths and the bottom of the lake.[1624] In addition, this mixing causes plankton and microbes to move between the layers of the lake, which will result in the food chain being better distributed across the entire lake.

Depth and Location: In early fall, as water temperatures begin to drop, bass move more shallow and closer to shore. In one study, tagged bass preferred depths from 9 to 13 feet (3-4 m) within 80 feet of the shore (<25 m) with some structure.[1625] In another study, they preferred depths from 6 to 23 feet within 80 feet (<25 m) of shore.[1626] Writers say that they move shallow to increase their food intake because of their "instinctive urge to 'fill up' reserves needed to help survive the winter months"—however, they have been feeding offshore all summer as well.[1627] When a lake turns over in late fall, it can be harder to locate and catch bass. Once the fishery "turns over," the entire water column becomes more inhabitable, so bass are less confined to the area above the thermocline, and their locations may become less predictable and more spread out.

Activity Level: Bass are active during fall, but overall the "daily activity and swimming performance of largemouth bass decrease with seasonal declines in water temperature."[1628] In one study, "the daily activity of largemouth bass decreased during the fall compared with the summer and further reduction was measured during the winter."[1629] Swimming speeds likewise decreased in fall and in early spring when compared with summer swimming speeds.[1630] Swimming speed and capacity directly correlates with water temperature in ectotherms like largemouth bass "as body temperature influences many physiological processes because of the dependence of enzyme activity on temperature coefficients."[1631]

[1624] Todd Driscoll, *supra* note 1396.
[1625] Jason Harris, *supra* note 1385.
[1626] Id.
[1627] BassFishingAndCatching.com, *supra* note 1403.
[1628] Caleb Hasler, et al., *Effect of water temperature on laboratory swimming performance and natural activity levels of adult largemouth bass*, CAN. J. ZOOL. 87:589-596 (2009), available at http://fishlab.nres.illinois.edu/Reprints/CJZ-Hasler_et_al_2009.pdf.
[1629] Id.
[1630] Id.
[1631] Id.

Heart performance and muscle contraction efficiency are also decreased in bass at lower temperatures in fall compared to summer.[1632]

Special Situations: Backs of Creeks/Pockets/Coves: According to one study, an apparent myth is that bass migrate to the backs of coves during the mid- to late fall. At Toledo Bend, there was no evidence of a fall migration of tracked bass to the backs of coves to chase bait[1633]; instead the researchers found that the bait migrated to the backs of coves and came to the bass that were already there resulting in an improvement in the fishing—but the idea that the fish moved to the backs of the pockets was not true because none of the fish did that in their study.[1634] Instead, the bass stayed put in their home ranges, but the bait came to them making the fishing better in these areas.[1635] More research at other reservoirs is needed to make any broader statements. However, during fall, if you can find areas with increased concentrations of baitfish, generally you can catch more bass around these baitfish, and this is often in the backs of coves and pockets.

[1632] Id.
[1633] Ken Smith Fishing YouTube Channel, Part 5, *supra* note 1387.
[1634] Id.
[1635] Id.

13

Last Cast

"Those fish aren't going to catch themselves!" I've repeated those words with a smile to my wife many times while she looked puzzled as I walked out the door to go fishing with the rain pouring, the snow falling, or the heat radiating. She reflects that line back at me occasionally when my alarm is going off on a morning when I'm a little hesitant to get out of bed to go fishing.

Serious lunker bass fishing is a passion. On nights before fishing trips, I often have trouble sleeping. I wake up thinking about how I'm going to approach the lake that day, what baits I'm going to use, and what order I will try different locations. Fishing for the top 1% of bass in a fishery is a mental challenge that requires execution of a reliable plan based on science and analytics for consistent success.

My favorite moment in fishing is that split second after a good hook set when I think for just a second that my bait is hung up on a stump or a tree or something . . . and then the stump moves! Here is a picture of one such moment with a hook set on a 6-pound bass with my favorite heavy fast action rod:

When the stump moves, I subconsciously utter the words, "The force is strong with this one; a powerful fight this will become," in a voice like Emperor Palpatine when Anakin becomes Vader in Star Wars Revenge of the Sith (my apologizes to any non-Star Wars folks ☺). In that split second, I know that the battle is on, and it will be a memorable one. Those hook sets and the subsequent battle are what I spend countless hours chasing. Some days I don't experience a single such moment, but some days I get several! Every once in a while, I get a battle that I know I will never forget.

    At the beginning of this book, I calculated the value of a cast at Lake Fork using publicly available data. If we assume similar odds for the top 1% of bass at all reservoirs, to catch a bass in the top 1%, the "value of a cast" is approximately a 1/13,000 chance of catching a top 1% bass in any fishery with each cast. This means that if an average angler makes 13,000 average casts at a fishery, that average angler should catch one bass in the top 1% of bass in that fishery on average. At Lake Fork, that is a 7+ pound bass; at your fishery, it may be a much different size bass; at my lakes in Arkansas, I would guess that it is a 5+ pounder. To catch a bass in the top 0.07%, the value of a cast is a 1/215,000 chance for each average cast; so, the average angler needs to make 215,000 casts to catch one bass in that category.

At Lake Fork, that is a 10+ pounder; in the places I fish in Arkansas, I would guess that it is an 8+ pounder.

So, how can you improve those odds and the value of your casts? First, maybe fish somewhere where the bass are not as pressured as Lake Fork. I've seen large groups of big bass ignore countless baits on LiveScope at Lake Fork because the bass are super well educated there due to all the fishing pressure. Unless your fishery is as pressured as Fork, the value of your casts is already likely higher.

Second, learn to *be in the right place at the right time* by understanding the science, analytics, and day-to-day movements of the bass you are chasing. Remember, those cast values are for the average angler—so, *become an above average angler.* The results with my Lake Fork University guide professors prove that knowledge improves your chances. Professional fishing guides have much higher odds because they understand bass behavior, are on the water every day, communicate with each other, and stay on top of the current positions of the bass. I caught two 10+ pound bass on trips with my Lake Fork guide professors. I caught a ten-pound bass for around every 2,700 casts fishing with guides at Lake Fork instead of the 215,000-cast average. For me without a guide to catch a bass over 7 pounds at Lake Fork (top 1%) during the summer when I take my own boat, it currently takes me an average of 2,160 casts, which is much better than the 13,000-cast average even though I only fish Fork a few days each year. Fishing in Arkansas, I catch a top 1% bass (i.e., a 5 pounder) at my home lakes around once every 720 casts (basically every other day on average; with some zero days and dry spells offset by some multi-lunker days and hot spells). I know guys who are better fishermen than me, and I'm sure the value of their casts is much better than mine. My point is that you can increase the value of your own casts with knowledge.

Third, if you are looking for lunkers in a specific category (like 10+ pounders) for the bucket list, then unless you live in Texas or Florida, you will probably need to travel. You can't catch them if they aren't there to be caught, and there aren't many 10+ pounders in most lakes outside the 30th to 32nd parallel if you are fishing in the U.S. east of the Rockies. To plan a trip, look for public databases or tournament information to see where big bass are being caught. States where Florida bass are being stocked are most likely to lead to a bucket list type catch. For example, I would go to Texas'

ShareLunker website, https://texassharelunker.com, and check out the "hot lakes" or go to Florida's Trophy Catch Florida website, https://www.trophycatchflorida.com/search-catches.aspx, and search by lake name to see where the biggest fish are being caught. Hiring a good guide greatly increases your odds of connecting with a giant bass on fisheries with which you are not familiar; so, if it is within your budget, do some research and hire a good guide. Whether you catch a lunker or not while fishing with a good guide, the knowledge gained is usually worth the money and time and may translate to bigger bass when you get back home.

    Looking at all four of my studies of the ShareLunker database and the Sealy Big Bass Splash database together, I made another interesting discovery about these giant fish of a lifetime. Go back and look at the 4 studies in this book and compare the results for 13+ pound bass in the ShareLunker studies and the 10+ pound bass in the Sealy study to the results for 8+ pound bass. *The biggest lunkers (10+ and 13+ pounders) were the most sensitive to all the variables.* The catchability of the biggest lunkers (i.e., the 10-13+ pounders) was *more affected by the month, weather, and time of day* than the smaller lunkers (i.e., the 8+ pounders). The graph below from Chapter 8 shows how barometric pressure was more important for 13+ pound bass than 8+ pound bass:

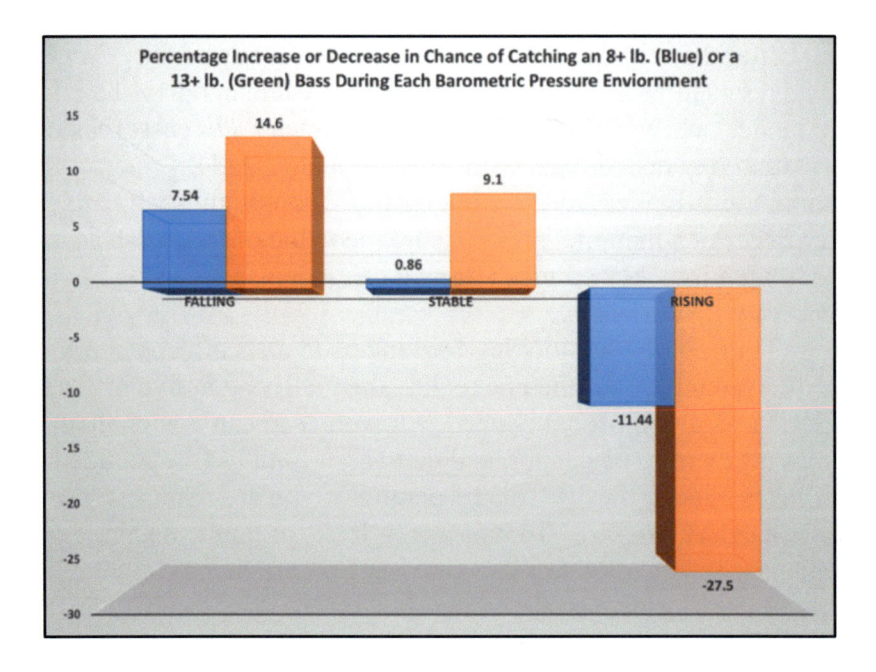

Percentage Increase or Decrease in Chance of Catching an 8+ lb. (Blue) or a 13+ lb. (Green) Bass During Each Barometric Pressure Enviornment

Barometric Pressure	8+ lb. (Blue)	13+ lb. (Green)
FALLING	7.54	14.6
STABLE	0.86	9.1
RISING	-11.44	-27.5

Similarly, the giant bass tended to be more affected by time of day since I found little difference based on time of day for 8+ pounders, but found the graph below for 10+ pounders from Chapter 11:

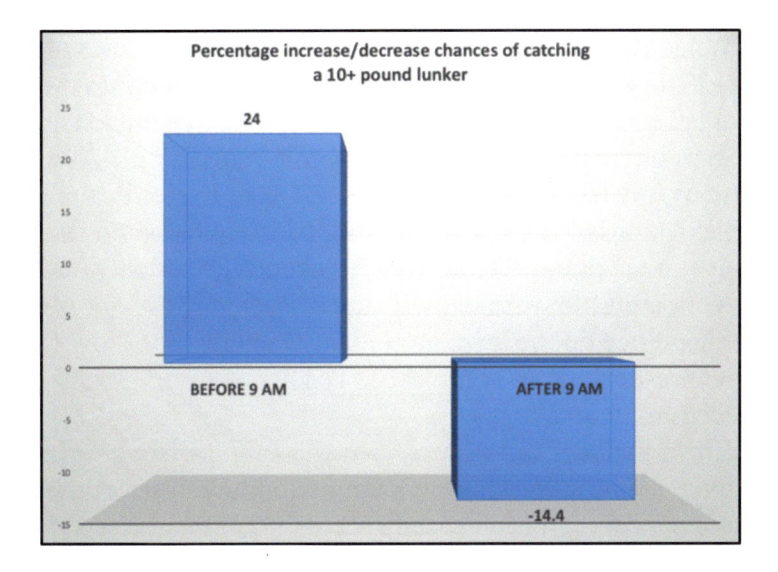

Percentage increase/decrease chances of catching a 10+ pound lunker

- BEFORE 9 AM: 24
- AFTER 9 AM: -14.4

Likewise, the monthly effects were more dramatic in Chapter 3. For example, March increased the odds of an 8+ pounder being reported by 187% over an average month, but for a 13+ pounder the increased chance was much greater at 341% for March versus the average month. In addition, 8+ pound lunkers were more common during a new moon, while 13+ pounders where more common during a full moon in Chapter 5. So, if you are chasing the biggest bass in your home fishery or planning a trip to catch a bass for your bucket list, take these factors into consideration when possible.

Finally, the most important factor in catching lunker bass is effort—especially *well-educated effort*. In other words, *spend more time on the water fishing!* Using the knowledge in this book to keep you in the right place at the right time should increase your chances. Fishing effort is important and shows up in the ShareLunker data from Texas. Guess which days of the week account for the highest percentage of ShareLunkers: Saturdays and Sundays are best because those are the days when most people have time to fish. In my study of the 511 bass over 8 pounds reported to Texas' ShareLunker program in 2022, 145 were caught on Saturday and 94 were caught on Sunday. So, 46.8% (almost half!) were caught over those two days alone. Another researcher also found that lunker bass were reported with greater frequency on Saturdays or Sundays.[1636] And remember, most of the experts, like professional guides, are not fishing on the weekends; so, *effort sometimes trumps expertise*! The old adage is true: "You can't catch fish unless you have a lure in the water." [1637]

When choosing that lure, remember that soft plastics (45%) and jigs (23%) account for the majority of bass entered into the ShareLunker program.[1638] Since lunkers are reactive thinkers, a slow presentation of these baits is most likely to be successful. As a 10-year-old boy, my dad took me to the John Deere tractor dealership in Batesville, Arkansas to meet Bassmaster Classic champion Rayo Breckridge in the mid-1970s, where Breckenridge patiently taught me how to work a plastic worm slowly and deliberately as we casted under a shade tree on the lawn around the tractors. The slow and deliberate presentation of soft plastics has not changed much over the years because it works!

Effort includes the mantra, *"Always keep learning!"* Lunker bass fishing can be a fun lifetime learning journey that requires continuing education for increased success. Important lessons and information can come from fishermen ranging from elite pros to professional fishing guides to an old dude at the tackle shop. Learning to use new tools (when affordable) like forward facing sonar or A-rigs makes bass fishing a continuing challenge to get better and better. If it is within my budget, I like to give new technology and new techniques a try! Here is what "advanced technology" looked like when I started bass fishing:

[1636] Larry Hodge, *March is big bass month*, TEXAS FISH AND GAME MAGAZINE, 2004, available at https://tpwd.texas.gov/fishboat/fish/didyouknow/inland/bassinmarch.phtml.
[1637] Id.
[1638] Id.

I heard old timers back in the day argue that the technology in the picture above was "cheating." For me, it has been more fun to embrace and try new technology (when I can afford it) over time. I am not usually the first one with the newest tech or gear, but I am also not the last. For me, trying new stuff keeps bass fishing exciting and challenging—even though I usually end up using some version of the old tricks that I learned many years ago.

      Effort also means spending a little more time on the water during your trips if you are chasing lunker bass. I spent most of my earlier fishing years going on trips where I spent 2 or 3 hours on the water catching smaller bass. This was still an awesome experience and was about all the time I could afford due to my obligations as an orthopedic surgeon. But when you are able, I think a 6-hour day is far more likely to lead to a lunker bass than two separate 3 hour days because the first hour or two of each fishing day usually involves making some adjustments to strategy based upon what the fish are doing on that particular day. Manns found that he and his buddies had "higher catch rates when fishing for longer periods, perhaps because time on the water led us to spots where bass were concentrated, or we had time to fine-tune presentation."[1639] Sometimes there is an offbeat

---

[1639] Ralph Manns, *Moon Magic Largemouth Bass*, IN-FISHERMAN, June 23, 2023, available at https://www.in-fisherman.com/editorial/moon-magic-largemouth-bass/154779.

bite that you might stumble across by simply being on the water and getting lucky. One such day for me was fishing O.H. Ivie on a hot July afternoon with bluebird skies and 110°F temperatures when a guide and I found the big bass biting topwater baits in shallow water after catching almost nothing for the whole morning. I caught a couple of bass in the 5-to-6-pound range and a few smaller ones, but we also saw two giant double-digit bass patrolling the shallows in the clear water that considered biting the topwater bait before disappearing. Mid-day, hot summer top water bites are not something that I have ever fished before, but at that lake at that time, it was definitely happening. Major bass fishing tournaments have practice days because even the pros have a hard time just showing up and landing on fish within a couple of hours. So, if possible, plan to spend a little longer day on the water to increase lunker success.

Knowledge breeds confidence needed to stick to a plan. Remember that the average fisherman catches one bass every four hours. Lunkers do not come that frequently, so it is easy to give up. Enjoy the chase! The pursuit is much of the fun. It is not just about catching the fish. It is about the process of reaching the point to catch that fish. Preparing your equipment, finding new equipment, and planning your strategy between trips can be a source of enjoyment and fulfillment. For some, it's also about time with friends and family. The constant chance that a giant lunker is about to strike motivates that next cast and means that my announced "last cast" is rarely my actual last cast of each day.

Last Cast (Really this time ☺): Never Give Up!

Pink lemonade nacho for the win! No matter what, keep thinking, paying attention, and fishing! Sometimes you catch a lunker when you least expect it. For two days, Lake O.H. Ivie bashed my ego and confidence in the west Texas 100 degree plus heat on my first solo trip there in 2023. To prep for the trip, I loaded and brought 12 rods and reels of all shapes and sizes and two big tackle boxes full of every type of bait imaginable. I had a plan. All 12 rods had been loaded and re-loaded with baits for two full 8-hour fishing days with only a few small bass to show for my efforts and sweat. My eyes were tired from closely monitoring my electronics. I could find lunker-sized bass on the LiveScope, but none would bite anything that I tried. So, I was feeling tired and discouraged as I pulled into the

Elm Creek boat ramp at around 3 pm at the end of my second day to get out of the sun for a while and was considering canceling my third and final day to head home early. But I had not completely given up.

The prior day I noticed a few smaller bass and some bream hanging around the boat ramp when I came in that afternoon, so I paid particular attention as I pulled my boat up on the ramp. There were only 3 other trucks in the parking lot and no one else around in the humid 103° afternoon heat, so I beached my boat on the ramp and looked around in the nearby water. I started prepping my boat to haul by removing the front seat and stowing it. As I was putting a few things away, I looked around to see if there were any fish nearby like the previous day. There were four ramps, and I was on the farthest ramp to the left with a small floating walkway between me and the next ramp. I immediately noticed a few bream and small bass again on this day. I also noticed a bigger bass lurking a little deeper in maybe 4 feet of water on the 3rd ramp over.

I picked up a swimbait rod and stood up on the back of my boat with the front end still beached on the ramp. The rod had a 7-inch paddle-tail swimbait tied on, and I made a cast past the big bass on the 3rd ramp over. The water was very clear, so I could see exactly how the bass reacted. It seemed to completely ignore the swimbait as it passed right in front of its mouth, but the bass swam a little closer to me and under the walkway next to my boat after my cast. On the second cast, as I brought the swimbait by the walkway, the bass made a lazy, half-hearted pass at the bait about 5 feet from my boat but missed it completely then swam off and disappeared. The bass was much bigger than I had originally thought, so I was sick.

Dejected, I picked up a smaller swimbait rod with a 4.5-inch paddle-tail swimbait called a "nacho" in pink lemonade color (chartreuse with a pink top third) to cast at the smaller bass in the area while I waited to see if the big bass returned. All the smaller bass (probably around 2 pounders) ignored the nacho as it swam past them on a couple casts. This is exactly what I had seen bigger bass do on the LiveScope for the past 2 days. They just would not react to my baits.

I made a long cast to some small bass farther away and noticed the big bass had reappeared near the original spot on the third ramp over. So, I quickly reeled in the nacho. As I reeled it fast, the nacho waked the surface and all the smaller bass suddenly followed it aggressively—after having ignored it for several other casts reeling it underwater near them.

    I made a cast to the big bass. The big bass ignored the nacho as it went past reeling it slowly underwater on the first cast. So, on the next cast, I reeled much faster and waked it near the big bass, and the bass chased it aggressively, but turned away a few feet from my boat. On my final cast, I waked the nacho on the surface and the big bass chased it aggressively waking the water behind it. I killed the nacho about 5 feet from the boat and I watched as the lunker opened its giant mouth and engulfed the falling nacho right in front of me—it was an awesome sight! I set the hook and the picture is below!

Both of my fists would fit in the bass's giant mouth simultaneously. It was 25.5 inches long. My electronic scales were so hot that I could not get a reliable weight. The weather app said it was 103 degrees; my truck thermometer said it was 122 degrees in the parking lot, and my metal boat was so hot that I could barely stand to touch it with my hands.

    Notice that my boat seat is already in the floorboard next to my feet—I was done for the day, but those extra few casts created a memory I will never forget. I'm thankful that I noticed those bass lurking around the boat ramp the day earlier, which made me pay special attention on this day. Needless to say, I stayed and fished the next day. *Never give up! You never know when that next big bite will occur!*

    I love bass fishing—especially lunker bass fishing. Writing this book has helped solidify my knowledge and my confidence. I hope it does the same for you and helps put more bass and some true giants in your hands. While you are out there on the water, take time to look around you and notice the Design and intricacies of the special place surrounding you. Chasing lunker bass on America's beautiful waters is truly an amazing and awesome experience to enjoy throughout a lifetime. So, look up from that sonar monitor and look around because there are a lot of soul-soothing views to take in! *Good luck, tight lines, and happy trails!*

Made in the USA
Columbia, SC
10 September 2024